Balkan holocausts?

Serbian and Croatian victim-centred propaganda and the war in Yugoslavia

DAVID BRUCE MACDONALD

Manchester University Press

MANCHESTER AND NEW YORK

distributed exclusively in the USA by Palgrave

Published by Manchester University Press
Oxford Road, Manchester M13 9NR, UK
and Room 400, 175 Fifth Avenue, New York, NY 10010, USA
http://www.manchesteruniversitypress.co.uk

Distributed exclusively in the USA by
Palgrave, 175 Fifth Avenue, New York, NY 10010, USA

Distributed exclusively in Canada by
UBC Press, University of British Columbia, 2029 West Mall,
Vancouver, BC, Canada V6T 1Z2

British Library Cataloguing-in-Publication Data
A catalogue record for this book is available from the British Library

Library of Congress Cataloging-in-Publication Data applied for

ISBN 0 7190 6466 X *hardback*
      0 7190 6467 8 *paperback*

First published 2002

10 09 08 07 06 05 04 03 02   10 9 8 7 6 5 4 3 2 1

Typeset in Photina
by Action Publishing Technology Ltd, Gloucester
Printed in Great Britain
by Bookcraft (Bath) Ltd, Midsomer Norton

BALKAN HOLOCAUSTS?

MANCHESTER
UNIVERSITY PRESS

New Approaches to
Conflict Analysis

Series editor: Peter Lawler,
Senior Lecturer in International Relations,
Department of Government, University of Manchester

Until recently, the study of conflict and conflict resolution remained compara-
tively immune to broad developments in social and political theory. When the
changing nature and locus of large-scale conflict in the post-Cold War era is also
taken into account, the case for a reconsideration of the fundamentals of
conflict analysis and conflict resolution becomes all the more stark.

New Approaches to Conflict Analysis promotes the development of new theoretical
insights and their application to concrete cases of large-scale conflict, broadly
defined. The series intends not to ignore established approaches to conflict analysis
and conflict resolution, but to contribute to the reconstruction of the field through
a dialogue between orthodoxy and its contemporary critics. Equally, the series
reflects the contemporary porosity of intellectual borderlines rather than simply
perpetuating rigid boundaries around the study of conflict and peace. *New
Approaches to Conflict Analysis* seeks to uphold the normative commitment of the
field's founders yet also recognises that the moral impulse to research is properly
part of its subject matter. To these ends, the series is comprised of the highest
quality work of scholars drawn from throughout the international academic
community, and from a wide range of disciplines within the social sciences.

CONTENTS

Contents

Contents

PREFACE

This book explores, from both a theoretical and a practical basis, how and why Serbian and Croatian nationalist elites used victim-centred propaganda to legitimate new state creation during the collapse of Communist Yugoslavia and the conflict that followed (1986–99). This often involved applying imagery from the Jewish Holocaust, with overt comparisons between Jewish suffering and the perceived genocides of Serbs and Croats. Chapters 1 and 2 discuss why a rhetoric of victimisation and persecution has been an enduring aspect of national identity, from the ancient Hebrews onwards. This theoretical section develops a model for analysing nationalist teleology, comprising a Golden Age, a Fall from grace, and a Redemption. It also provides a critique of nationalism theory, analysing its successes and failures in understanding the importance of victim-centred propaganda and the impact of the Holocaust in nationalist writings.

Chapters 3 to 8 examine how a fear of genocide was used by Serbian and Croatian nationalists to push their people into wars of 'self-defence'. Through a detailed examination of primary source material, these chapters dissect many of the arguments advanced during the conflicts in Kosovo, Croatia, and Bosnia-Hercegovina. Important comparisons can be made about how history was revised and what purposes these revisions served. Serbian and Croatian propaganda is divided into specific time-periods. The time-periods examined include the earliest eras, from the third to the fifteenth centuries AD, followed by the medieval era, and the nineteenth century. The twentieth century is divided into several periods, beginning with the first kingdom of Yugoslavia (1918), the Second World War, Communist Yugoslavia, the breakdown of the Federation, and the rise of nationalism and violence. A chapter on Bosnia-Hercegovina and the Bosnian Moslems demonstrates how effectively Serbian and Croatian propaganda was applied to a third party.

ACKNOWLEDGEMENTS

Many thanks to Ambassador John Fraser, Dejan Guzina, and Professors Teresa Rakowka-Harmstone, the late Carl Jacobsen, Zlatko Isaković, and Mihailo Crnobrnja, for shaping my interest in the Balkans and its people. James Gow's seminar on Yugoslavia at King's College London was also a fount of information, as were the translated documents he kindly provided. Many thanks to the staff at the Matica Hrvatska Iseljenika for their illuminating insight on the people and history of Croatia. I learned much during my research and study trip there in 1994, and during my return in 1999. Thank you to the Hamza family in Sarajevo for their colourful, and at times distressing, stories about the war in Bosnia, and of course, their wonderful hospitality.

A special thanks to the editors of *Slovo* at the School of Slavonic and East European Studies for having published two of my articles. These were based on two conference papers, which were in turn based on several aspects of my doctoral research.[1] I also tested many theories and ideas at the Brave New World II conference at the University of Manchester, and through participation in seminars organised by the Contemporary Research on International Political Theory (CRIPT) work group. Thanks also to Nick Bisley, for his editing skills and suggestions, and to my supervisor Spyros Economides, for ploughing through much of the good, bad, and horribly disfigured, with consummate and tireless skill. George Schöpflin and James Mayall have also provided extremely useful and timely criticisms of this study in their capacity as thesis examiners. My thanks to them. Additional thanks go to the staff at Manchester University Press. I would also like to thank my agent Beverly Friedgood, and the LSE publications department for their invaluable contributions. The staff at the British Library and the British Library of Political and Economic Sciences have also been extremely helpful. A final thank you to Philippe Nemo, for giving me the flexibility to test out many of my theories and ideas in a wide range of courses, during my three years as assistant visiting professor at the École Superieur de Commerce de Paris (ESCP-EAP).

I dedicate this book to my parents, Bruce and Olive, for their love and financial sacrifices, which made it possible for me to live and study in London and create this book, and to my wife, Dana Wensley, for her loving support during this long-drawn-out, but relatively fun-filled, process. The usual caveat of course applies to this book: that all mistakes are entirely my own. However, in any analysis of political propaganda during a major ethnic conflict, the elusive quest for TRUTH can often be fraught with uncertainty and false paths.

David B. MacDonald
Political Studies Department
University of Otago, Dunedin

Introduction

> There is a saying in the Balkans that behind every hero stands a traitor. The difficulty, as often as not, is to determine which is which. Again and again, there is something heroic about the traitor and something treacherous about the hero. (Fitzroy MacLean, *The Heretic*)

IN 1991, THE WORLD watched in amazement as the Socialist Federative Republic of Yugoslavia (SFRY) began what was seemingly a fratricidal civil war. Formerly peaceful republics, joined for almost five decades under the banner of 'Brotherhood and Unity', would soon end their coexistence when the Yugoslav People's Army (JNA) rolled into Slovenia to prevent Slovenian independence by force. In Croatia, Serbian irregulars instigated violent clashes with Croatian paramilitary forces, followed once more by the intervention of the JNA. As the fighting spread from Eastern Slavonia to the Krajina, and then south-east to Bosnia-Hercegovina, it was clear that Europe was witnessing its first major military conflict since the Second World War, and few understood what was going on.

While several constituent nations, such as the Macedonians, Montenegrins, and Slovenians, played a peripheral role in the conflict, the principal actors were to be the Kosovar Albanians, the Bosnian Moslems, the Serbs, and the Croats. The wars that followed the collapse of Yugoslavia would be dominated by an intense Serbian–Croatian rivalry. As extremely bloody wars were being fought on the ground, a war of words took place through magazines, journals, newspapers, and books, as well as on television, the radio, and the internet. All modern means of communication were actively subordinated to the goals of ethnic nationalist leaders in Serbia and Croatia, seeking to promote revised images of their respective histories.

This book explores the rather strange predicament Western observers encountered when trying to understand the collapse of Yugoslavia. Seven distinct national groups, each with their own religious traditions, colonial history, and cultural trappings, had lived in relative peace since 1945. Now

1

four of these sought to advance the same claim – that they were victims of the first genocide on European soil since the Second World War. Serbs, Kosovar Albanians, Croats, and Bosnian Moslems each claimed to be defending themselves from annihilation, arguing that one or more dangerous enemies were trying to destroy their nation, according to an age-old blueprint for hatred and treachery. Images of Serbian, Croatian, Bosnian Moslem, and Kosovar Albanian genocides and 'holocausts' frequently appeared in the popular media, and the reader, listener, or internet surfer was berated with a continuous stream of material, all seemingly arguing the same thing: 'we are the victims first and foremost – our war is legitimate because we are fighting against annihilation'.

The French Slavicist Paul Garde, at a recent gathering in Paris to unveil the second edition of his 1992 classic *Vie et mort de la Yougoslavie*, noted that at the beginning of the war he was severely hampered by a lack of information, not only in terms of factual reporting, but more importantly in terms of viewpoints, as to how each side was justifying its role in the conflict. Nine years later he had exactly the opposite reaction – there was a superfluity of information, and contemporary books on Yugoslavia adorned two entire walls in his large study. In 1991, there was practically nothing to be found on the conflict; but within two years, a war of journals, books, pamphlets, newspapers, and internet sites had begun. Croatian journalist Slavenka Drakulić described this early period in *Balkan Express*: 'Long before the real war, we had a media war, Serbian and Croatian journalists attacking the political leaders from the opposite republic as well as each other as if in some kind of dress rehearsal. So I could see a spiral of hatred descending on us, but until the first bloodshed it seemed to operate on the level of a power struggle that had nothing to do with the common people.'[1]

The former American Ambassador to Yugoslavia, Warren Zimmermann, added this more prescient comment during the escalation of hostilities in 1992: 'What we witnessed was violence-provoking nationalism from the top down ... Many people in the Balkans may be weak or even bigoted, but in Yugoslavia, it is their leaders who have been criminal.' Historian Noel Malcolm described the climate in Serbia before the war as comparable to 'all of television in the USA [being] taken over by the Ku Klux Klan'.[2] And what was true of Serbia was sadly often true of Croatia as well.

This book will address two particular problems: the manipulation of victim imagery, and the powerful war of words that accompanied and often preceded military violence. Of central importance is understanding how and why each side so assiduously chose to portray itself as a victim of genocide, not just in the present, but also in the past. Anyone who followed the conflict from 1991 onwards would have been struck by the constant emphasis on historical victimisation and suffering. This situation paradoxically gave rise to the view that the wars in Yugoslavia were the result of 'ancient ethnic hatreds' between traditionally hostile ethnic groups. Such propaganda would confuse rather than clarify.[3] While it is important to explore the nature of such imagery, it is also important to understand the philosophical and theological underpinnings of a victim-centred strategy in nationalism, while systematically unravelling and comparing Serbian and Croatian propaganda. This involves charting how different periods of history have been revised to make a nation's history one of constant danger, defeat, and martyrdom.

There have been several attempts to understand the nature of Serbian propaganda. Some examples of Serbian propaganda analysis include Branimir Anzulović's *Heavenly Serbia*, Anto Knezević's *Analysis of Serbian Propaganda*, and Philip Cohen's *Serbia's Secret War*. Of these, only Anzulović's analysis does not seem to advance an overtly pro-Croatian viewpoint. Whatever the motivations of these writers, their greatest sin by far has been to study Serbian writing by itself, without adequate reference to what Croats, Kosovar Albanians, or Bosnian Moslems were also arguing at the same time. This has only decontextualised Serbian nationalism, removing it from the environment in which it was written and distributed. Since many Serbian writers were actively debating facts about historical dates, numbers, and key historical personalities with the other parties to these conflicts, studying only one side ignored the motivations and provocations of the Serbs.

Without a clear view of Serbian *and* Croatian arguments, half the debate is missing. Clearly, a comparative study of Serbian and Croatian propaganda is long overdue. While it is obvious that the Serbs were the main aggressors in Bosnia, Croatia, and Kosovo, there is no doubt that Croats, Kosovar Albanians, and Bosnian Moslems were not simply innocent bystanders, waiting to be 'ethnically cleansed'. There were many examples of these other three groups either instigating violence, or responding to it with force of their own.

To many, it might seem obvious why Serbs and Croats would have wished to portray their histories as long periods of suffering and decline, why playing the victim should now, more than ever, seem like a good idea. Since the introduction of the United Nations Conventions on *Genocide* and *Human Rights* in 1948, many people have felt a greater sense of responsibility for human rights abuses around the world. Rather than adopting a policy of non-interference in the internal affairs of other countries, we have become more concerned about what goes on behind closed doors, and more interventionist than ever before. Many feel that the existence of UN conventions gives us the right and the duty to 'care' for the treatment of other people living under despotic regimes. This is a relatively new phenomenon. Geoffrey Robertson has argued that before the Second World War: 'It dawned on no political leader, even after the carnage of the First World War, that international institutions might tell states how to treat their nationals.' 'Human rights', he suggests, mattered little until 'Hitler made them irrelevant.'[4]

Since 1945, many Western academics have assured themselves that the heyday of Nietzschean nihilism is past. Most no longer believe that the weak are extinguished by history, nor do they believe that the 'will to power' is all one needs to control the world. Rather, we tend to sympathise with the victims rather than the aggressors. The human rights sociology favoured by journalists and academics such as Michael Ignatieff demonstrates that the rights of others, or as he terms it 'the needs of strangers' override our more common impulses to stick to our own business and keep our noses out of trouble.[5] Elazar Barkan recently identified a 'victim culture' as becoming increasingly important in international affairs, as evidenced by the plethora of restitution cases that emerged during the 1980s and 1990s. As he explains in *The Guilt of Nations*:

> No longer does the brute and immediate existential need for security form the sole legitimate justification or motive in formulating foreign policy. Instead, opposition to genocide, support for human rights, and the fear of being implicated in crimes against humanity (even by inaction) have become practical, not merely lofty, ideals. These ideals increasingly shape political decisions and the international scene.[6]

In Yugoslavia, an obvious solution for nations struggling to free themselves from decades of Communist rule was to portray themselves as victims – to appeal to a heightened sense of global responsibility and morality. While Serbs and Croats both shared a historic belief in their own victimisation as nations, I will argue that this sense of victimisation was exacerbated during the Tudjman and Milošević eras, and became a central pillar of national identity. The NATO-led bombing of Bosnian Serb positions in 1995, and rump-Yugoslavia in 1999, demonstrated that violence against minorities (at least in Europe) would not be tolerated indefinitely. Once Roy Gutman's lead article in *Newsday* in 1992 – 'The Death Camps of Bosnia' – established the Moslems as victims of seemingly Nazi-esque atrocities, America seriously began to get involved.[7] Sadly, such intervention, even if too late to prevent the horrors of Manjaća, Omarska, and Trnopolje, was not to be found at all in Rwanda, East Timor, or Chechnya.

The rise of Non-Governmental Organisations (NGOs), with tremendous resources and media power, should also alert our attention to the very real benefits to be gained by portraying oneself as the victim of aggression. Human Rights NGOs now dominate the international arena; by 1994, some 67 per cent of the European Union's relief aid was channelled through such organisations. According to the International Red Cross, NGOs collectively disburse more money than the World Bank. One quarter of Oxfam's £98 million budget comes from governmental sources, while in 2000 World Vision US gained

$55 million in aid from the American government.[8] These groups have a direct line to governments around the world, contributing to agenda setting. They help to define who is a victim and how victimised they are. They also wield considerable power in determining the identity of aggressors, even if, as in the case of Rwanda, there is little international will to carry out their recommendations.

Generally, we live in a world where victims are now the subject of pity and financial assistance, not scorn. While these are compelling reasons that explain the practicalities of portraying oneself as a victim, this does not explain why we as outside observers have become more receptive to claims of victimisation. Neither Serbs nor Croats were seeking to curry the favour of NGOs, nor did they invoke international conventions against each other during the conflict itself.[9] Certainly, both sides were seeking international recognition for the new state of affairs in their respective republics. The breakdown of federal authority and legitimacy in Communist Yugoslavia after Josip Broz Tito's death in 1980 changed the nature of the country considerably.

The republics, rather than the federal centre, became the new loci of power, as republic-based elites began building networks of power and influence. Tito's Communism was never able to guarantee the withering away of the state. While he promised that the borders of Yugoslavia's individual republics were nothing more than 'lines on a marble column', it was clear that borders continued to play a pivotal role in Yugoslav politics. After his death in 1980, every aspect of his system was open to dispute, including the administrative divisions of the country, which in some cases were also national.

It is important to understand not only why Serbs and Croats sought to reconstruct their histories as periods of suffering and persecution, but also why Western policy-makers appeared receptive. Chapters 1 and 2 explore how and why victim-centred propaganda has become important in the modern world. Chapter 1 examines how early national entities developed myths, in order to advance a unique view of their place in world history. For the ancient Hebrew nation, a cyclical form of teleology, composed of a Golden Age, a Fall, and a Redemption, constituted what Northrop Frye and others have termed a 'covenantal cycle'. Covenants imply faith in an omnipresent, omnipotent god, able to guide the nation in times of distress and hardship. In return for obedience and faith, the Hebrew god assured his people of their divine election and their 'chosenness' – making them a more spiritual, more special people than any other. Ideas of Covenant, chosenness, Golden Age, Fall, and Redemption have formed the core of several modern nationalisms.

Another important aspect of cyclical teleology has been the constant battle between good and evil throughout history – the 'chosen' nation versus its many enemies. The links between such mythology and Serbian and Croatian nationalism will become obvious. Both subscribed to a cyclical view of history; both groups saw themselves as 'chosen' and unique, while at the same time, they portrayed their own histories as a series of battles against powerful enemies. Both groups consistently held that by proving their own Falls throughout history, they could legitimate the struggles necessary for Redemption.

In Chapter 2, the twentieth-century application of these early Judaeo-Chrisitan concepts will be understood with reference to the Jewish Zionist movement. There was much in Serbian and Croatian nationalism that relied on the Zionist contribution to the history of ideas. For nineteenth-century Zionists, the presence of anti-Semitism confirmed for some that the only way the Jewish people would be free of persecution was through their own Redemption in a territorially bounded nation-state. Zionists modernised cyclical teleology and used it to create their own state, free from the horrors of centuries of discriminatory legislation, pogrom, and massacre. Perhaps the most important aspect of Zionism, however, was something over which they had little control. The Holocaust, which occurred between 1941 and 1945, saw almost 6 million Jews systematically killed by the German Nazi regime – arguably the greatest Fall in the history of Judaism. Some viewed the creation of the State of Israel in 1948 as the greatest recompense and Redemption since the restoration of the Kingdom some 2,000 years before. Thus, the greatest Fall and Redemption of the twentieth century followed one after the other within a three-year period.

An important concept throughout this work will be the idea of performing, or acting out a genocide. On the basis of the legacy of Jewish suffering and the perception (or misperception) that the Holocaust was instrumentalised by Zionist leaders to achieve the State of Israel, historians from marginalised nations, including the Romani, the Armenians, and the Ukrainians, have compared their own historical persecution to that of the Jews. Such historical revisionism has formed the basis of a 'comparative genocide debate', which employs the images and symbols of the Holocaust as a template. This debate has pitted a number of Jewish historians (who argue that the Holocaust is a unique and unprecedented event in modern history) against another group of historians, who claim that their own group's experience of suffering is equal to or in some respects worse than that of the Jews. For many national groups, articulating myths of persecution and victimisation has become an essential part of reconstructing histories and legitimating state-building projects. As I will demonstrate from Chapters 3 to 8, Serbs and Croats entered into this timely and controversial debate. Both groups used claims of victimisation and persecution to legitimate their own state-building or state-expanding projects, with often violent consequences.

Both the Judaeo-Christian covenantal culture and the instrumentalisation of Holocaust imagery have been of central importance in structuring

Serbian and Croatian representations of the past and present. History was reinvented in the 1980s and 1990s, in order to paint each nation as a long-suffering victim of ancient, predatory enemies, bent on their destruction. The following chapters will discuss how Serbs and Croats used such imagery to their advantage. For both groups, portraying history as a series of never-ending 'ancient ethnic antagonisms' or 'centuries of hatred' performed an important function. Events in the 1980s and 1990s were presented as only an extension of past conflicts. By proving that the Other had been an aggressor throughout history, one could prove that history was repeating itself, that the nation was simply defending itself against yet another attempt at annihilation.

As Yugoslavia slowly collapsed, gone was any ambiguity or inner reflection about how one's nation might have committed historic atrocities. A Manichaean morality pervaded both sides, in which the other was unequivocally evil, and the self could do no wrong. Any periods of friendly association or harmonious political projects (such as *Illyrianism* or *Yugoslavism*) were excised from a history that became more and more decontextualised. More 'authentic' national enemies, such as the Ottomans, the Bulgarians, the Austro-Hungarians, and the Italians, were quietly brushed aside as mere backdrops to the more important contest between Serb and Croat. Even Nazi Germany emerged more as a facilitator of Serb and Croat evil, than as the instigator of crimes in the Balkans.

Chapter 3 begins with the rise of nationalism in Serbia, from the death of Josip Broz Tito in 1980 to Slobodan Milošević's historic speech in 1987 to the Kosovo Serbs, pledging to defend their national rights in Kosovo, no matter what the cost. Milošević's genius was to identify the Kierkegaardian 'right moment' in Serbian politics, when he was able to transform himself from a Belgrade banker and communist official into a nationalist phenomenon. Milošević, however forceful a speaker, was never much more than an opportunist. Nevertheless, his own lack of fundamentalism would be mitigated by the presence of dozens of nationalist believers, from author-politicians Dobrica Ćosić and Vuk Drasković, to paramilitary warlords such as Željko Ražnatović Arkan and Vojislav Šešelj.

The invention of 'Serbophobia', often likened to anti-Semitism, was a curious facet of the conflict. Serbs would continually compare themselves to the Jews as fellow victims in world history. This invariably involved a tragedising of history, from the 1389 Battle of Kosovo to the 1974 Yugoslav Constitution – every aspect of Serbian history was seen to be another example of persecution and victimisation at the hands of external negative forces. The Kosovar Albanians, as the first group within part-Tito Yugoslavia to experience a national awakening (in 1981), were the first targets of Serbian nationalism. Kosovo would be important as a template or pattern for the more

7

important propaganda war against the Croats – Serbia's most important competitor during the break-up of Yugoslavia. This chapter will concentrate on the early threats of Croatian nationalism – its strong links to a supposedly xenophobic and expansionist Roman Catholic Church, its genocidal ambitions against Serbia during the nineteenth century, and its hatred of diversity and compromise in the first Yugoslavia.

For Croats, the issue of persecution would be of equal importance. Chapter 4 begins with the rise of Franjo Tudjman and his Croatian Democratic Alliance (HDZ). Tudjman was a true believer in the nationalist cause, and in Croatia there was a thorough process of centralising power and propaganda within the state. Croatian propagandists focused most of their attacks on Serbia, which was in the process of invading and occupying one-quarter of their newly independent country. Croatian reappraisals of history often involved the conjuring up of a 'Greater Serbia' – an evil, expansionary, annihilatory other, seeking first to invade, then to enslave, and then to exterminate the Croatian people. From the time of the Great Schism between Catholic and Orthodox worlds, Croats were supposedly confronted with a Serbian desire to destroy small and peaceful nations. Other key historical periods include the nineteenth century, when the ideals of 'Greater Serbia' were supposedly put into practice, through to the First Yugoslavia after the First World War, when Serbs and Croats entered, along with the Slovenes, into political association for the first time in their history.

Other important myths include the *Antemurale Christianitatis*, the belief that Croatia represented the easternmost outpost of European civilisation. Across the divide were the Serbs, often presented as being on a lower level of civilisation, with an 'Asiatic' mentality, and distinct racial and psychological features, as well as different linguistic and cultural forms of identity. Such forms of differentiation would buttress Croatian arguments that, at all levels, Serbs were more backward, barbarous, and warlike. These innate or primordial characteristics were cited as the cause of Yugoslavia's breakdown and the wars that followed.

Chapters 5 and 6 examine the Second World War, arguably the most important historical period for both sides. Serbs and Croats accused each other of being willing and zealous collaborators with the Nazi occupiers. Each accused the other of being an enthusiastic participant in the Final Solution against Yugoslavian Jews, through membership in the Serbian Četniks or the Croatian Ustaša. Each side also claimed to have suffered a 'Holocaust' at the hands of the other – the Serbs at the Ustaša-run death camp Jasenovac, the Croats, after the war, at the Austrian town of Bleiburg, when Communist Partisans (perhaps Serbian) massacred escaping collaborators. Inflating the number of victims among one's co-religionists, while reducing the numbers killed by one's own side, became a full-time occupation for many academics.

Croatian writers inflated the Bleiburg dead, while reducing Jasenovac to the status of a medium-sized massacre. Serbs, by contrast, touted Jasenovac as the third largest death camp in Europe – often labelling it the 'Serbian Auschwitz'. The purpose of such revisions was clear. Both sides needed a powerful example of the genocidal capabilities of the other, in order to prove that more contemporary atrocities were simply a repetition of the past.

Chapter 7 will be divided into two parts, the first dealing with Serbian and Croatian views of Tito's Communist Yugoslavia, a country that suppressed nationalism, while preaching a form of consensus and harmony. Predictably, both groups would claim to have been the victims of continued persecution by the other, who they claim dominated the federation. Typically, the borders of republics were attacked, as well as the ethnic imbalances in the military, the government, and the civil service. The second and more important part of this chapter details how both Serbs and Croats constructed their pasts, and how they drew parallels between past and contemporary events. Here, Second World War comparisons were the most important, particularly for the Serbs. While the Croats too have used this period of history to their advantage, they also used earlier periods, such as the nineteenth century, and the First Yugoslavia, to argue that the Serbs had followed a continuous pattern of genocide for over a century.

Chapter 8 explores Serbian and Croatian propaganda from a fresh angle – through their reactions to a third party. The war in Bosnia-Hercegovina displayed both sides at their most cynical and opportunistic. Tudjman and Milošević had already divided the republic on paper before a single shot was fired. Both sides committed war crimes, which included 'ethnic cleansing' (using terror to force people from the villages where their families had lived for centuries), the establishment of concentration camps, or 'collection centres' (where victims were beaten, tortured, raped and often killed), the destruction of physical property (including the destruction of approximately 1,400 mosques), and numerous massacres of civilian populations. Bosnian Moslems were presented as little more than an invented artificial nation, with no historic claims to territory. At best, they were members of either the Serbian or the Croatian 'authentic' nation, which meant that their lands and their language could be brought back into the national fold. At worst, the Moslems were the harbingers of a dangerous Islamic conspiracy, poised to take over the Balkans and Western Europe.

While large numbers of Serbs and Croats supported this immense propaganda campaign, there were some notable exceptions. While this work is concerned with distinctly nationalist literature, there have been conscientious writers on both sides, attempting to debunk many of the myths that emerged as a corollary to nationalism. The independent press in both countries was highly critical of their respective regimes, often infusing the debate with strong attacks on extreme nationalism within the government. Editors and journalists often suffered accordingly. Similarly, some writers and academics stood firm against the onslaught of nationalism. In Croatia, Dubravka Ugrešić and Slavenka Drakulić deserve special mention, as does former Croatian diplomat Vane Ivanović. During the war, numerous Croatian academics collaborated in a well-known edited work by Rada Iveković, deploring the rise of nationalism and the escalation of violence in their country.[10]

In Serbia, several attempts were made to combine impartial Serbian scholarship with analysis from Western academics and politicians. One such work, edited by Michael Freeman, Dušan Janjić, and Predrag Veselinović, carefully analysed the importance of liberal theories of justice and their applicability to minority rights in Yugoslavia.[11] Another ambitious work, entitled *Serbia Religion and War*, contained critical lectures and articles published by Serbian academics who had fled Serbia in the 1980s.[12] Such publications entailed certain risks, but demonstrated that not everyone had fallen into the nationalist trap, despite the strong jingoistic mentality that pervaded almost every aspect of life. There were also many politicians who chose not to participate in the violence as such, and openly condemned Tudjman and Milošević for their excesses. The new group of elected officials – the Yugoslav President Vojislav Kostunica, the Croatian Prime Minister Ivica Račan, and the Croatian President Stipe Mesić – are just a few national leaders who did not subscribe to an exclusivist or distinctly violent view of national identity. Such leaders would assume power after Tudjman's death in December 1999 and Milošević's losses in the Serbian elections during the summer of 2000.

As will be clear, many Serbian and Croatian nationalist writers have distorted and given a distinctly nationalist slant to both early and recent history. Of course, the question arises as to whether there are any 'real' or accurate representations of history. Hayden White has taken issue with the idea that there are any 'correct' historical accounts, with only 'certain rhetorical flourishes or poetic effects' to distract readers from the truth of what they are reading.[13] Rather, White argues that all forms of history, be they 'annals', 'chronicles', or 'history proper', are all subject to a process of narrativising, whereby historians try to create a story from the 'real events' of history, often a story with a beginning and a conclusion, and some type of moral lesson that can be learned.

As White argues, the biases, desires, and fantasies of the historian cannot be considered separately from the events he/she is describing. Which events are chosen and how they are presented will depend on a number of personal factors. As White asks:

> What is involved then, in that finding of the 'true story', that discovery of the 'real story' within or behind the events that come to us in the chaotic form of 'histori-

cal records'? What wish is enacted, what desire is gratified by the fantasy that real events are properly represented when they can be shown to display the formal coherency of a story? In the enigma of this wish, this desire, we catch a glimpse of the cultural function of narrativising discourse in general, an intimation of the psychological impulse behind the apparently universal need not only to narrate but to give to events an aspect of narrativity.[14]

While there is perhaps no 'true story' or 'real story' that can emerge from any historical appraisal, both the Serbian and Croatian cases often show deliberate attempts to mislead, by either altering or removing aspects of historical events, so that these alterations cast their nation in a favourable light. In short: they rarely aimed for 'truth' in any sense of the word. For White, the historian's objectives are often an 'enigma', the product of 'psychological impulses'. In these cases, however, the objectives are clearer than in the rather opaque medieval texts White reviews. The process of 'narrativising' was certainly heightened during the wars in Croatia and Bosnia, to the extent that fantasies and desires of nationally oriented writers replaced any semblance of presenting a 'real story' *à la* White. Indeed, the emphasis here was on presenting history from one's own perspective rather than striving for some utopian impartial standard. While this is certainly not a process confined only to Serbs and Croats, this pernicious aspect of identity creation during the 1990s was crucial to legitimating a wide variety of nation-building activities – many of them violent. This book will compare and contrast these nationally biased views of history, highlighting the discrepancies between them.

A note on methodology

The term 'propaganda' has many negative connotations, but is not itself intrinsically negative. Political parties and corporations around the world use propaganda, or spin-doctoring, on a daily basis, to outlaw fox-hunting, promote the Euro, or sell soap. For a definition, I defer to Oliver Thomson, who, in his excellent study of mass persuasion techniques, described propaganda as 'the manipulation of public opinion' and the 'management of collective attitudes' by use of both 'political' and 'significant symbols', those symbols that represent state power and national culture. In terms of how it is spread, Thomson argued that it includes 'any means of projecting or transmitting images, ideas or information which influences behaviour in every active or passive sense. This covers every aspect of art and communication, because nearly all messages have either deliberately or accidentally some persuasive content.'[15]

This is a very general definition of propaganda, which covers almost everything. Within the context of this work, Thomson's definition needs to be narrowed down. I will not be discussing accidental forms of persuasion, but rather deliberate attempts by Serbian and Croatian writers to manipulate public opinion in support of mobilisation for war, and the maintenance of war, both in Croatia and in Bosnia-Hercegovina. Before continuing, please allow me to add the following caveat: this book will also be examining the writings of what we might call 'armchair' nationalists – believers throughout the world who promote their own interpretations of history and current events on the internet, and in the popular press. Such people formed a crucial base of support for Croatian and Serbian nationalist regimes, climbing aboard the nationalist bandwagon even though they were often unaffiliated with either government. I am not arguing that such people had any cynical plans to destroy other nations or promote violence as such, nor that they are guilty by association of 'ethnic cleansing'. Nevertheless, in their own ways, they contributed to the escalation of events by adding more fuel to the fire; and sometimes their arguments were used in ways that they neither intended nor could have foreseen.

Throughout this book, I will be using a form of discourse analysis to explore the themes, ideas and vocabulary present in Serbian and Croatian propaganda. I have used a qualitative method of analysing primary material, isolating their most important themes and images. This is in line with Oliver Thomson's suggestion of paying attention to 'the more obvious pattern frequencies that come from a general view of contents.'[16] This book, however, strives not only to present an analysis of general themes and ideas in Serbian and Croatian historical revisions but also to analyse the vocabulary and structure of their language and how it has been used.

While I have chosen a form of qualitative discourse analysis, the role of quantitative analysis should not be discounted. In a 1993 study commissioned by the Stryelsen for Psykologist Forsvar (Centre for Psychological Research) in Sweden, Marjan Malesić and a team of researchers evaluated 213 newspaper articles from Serbia and Croatia (between August 1991 and January 1992). Using a quantitative approach, they drew up tables charting the frequency of certain topics and terms used by the domestic media in each country.[17] The results of this study were illuminating. In Croatia, the team noted frequent 'homeland-related metaphors', based on 'blood and soil imagery'. The media described the government's actions and those of Croatian forces as 'peace-oriented activities', with an emphasis on countering accusations that Tudjman was a 'proto-fascist'.[18] The team noted similar themes in the Serbian press, with priority given to proving the self-defensive nature of their activities. Tudjman was frequently denounced as a fascist, while the persecution of the Serbs in Croatia was constantly stressed.[19]

The team's findings were in some ways similar to my own, that: 'communications in abnormal and extreme situations are characterised by generalisations combined with the use of stereotypes, labelling and value-weighted, emotionally charged attributes.' They further noted the following:

> Such simplifications can be productive in the short term, especially in abnormal situations, since they ensure the required speed and simple identification. At the same time the effect of categorical patterns of thinking and of labelling is still further enhanced by the use of value-weighted and emotionally negatively charged characterisations, which possess a powerful mobilising force … Mass media completely accomplished the role of political propaganda and war-mongering given them by the politicians.[20]

Even in an analysis of newspaper articles from the early stages of the conflict, it was clear that both sides were mobilising their people for an escalation of hostilities. Thus, either method of discourse analysis should furnish a clear picture of how Serbian and Croatian nationalist elites justified the rise of nationalism and escalation of hostilities to their own people, as well as to the outside world.

Hopefully, this study will be a new contribution to the expanding field of International Relations. Recently, Iver Neumann remarked in his challenging new book, *The Uses of the Other*, that 'The discipline of international relations (IR) is witnessing a surge of interest in identity and identity formation. This development has been permitted and facilitated by the general uncertainty of a discipline which feels itself to have spent the 1980s barking up the wrong trees. A lack of faith in the old has made it easier for the new to break through.'[21] Fresh insight into the links between the Holocaust, nationalism theory, and contemporary warfare is long overdue. My goal throughout is to provide scope for new reflection on these and other issues.

NOTES

1 Quoted in Jonathan Glover, *Humanity: A Moral History of the Twentieth Century* (London: Cape, 1999) p. 130.
2 Both quoted in Richard Holbrooke, *To End a War* (New York: Random House, 1998) p. 24.
3 The matter is raised by Holbrooke, who blamed not only the propaganda campaign, but also Robert Kaplan's travelogue *Balkan Ghosts*, which gave the impression that Balkan conflicts were centuries old and hopelessly inscrutable to the outsider (*ibid.* pp. 22–3).
4 Geoffrey Robertson, *Crimes Against Humanity: The Struggle for Global Justice* (London: Penguin, 2000). Robertson provides a useful outline of human rights legislation in his 'Preface' (see pp. xiii–xiv). For an excellent description of the evolution of Human Rights norms and legislation after the Second World War, see Louis Henkin, 'Human Rights: Ideology and Aspiration, Reality and Prospect', in Samantha Power and Graham Allison (eds), *Realizing Human Rights: Moving from Inspiration to Impact* (New York: St Martin's Press, 2000) pp. 7–18.
5 A general overview of this type of thinking can be found in Michael Ignatieff, *The Warrior's Honour* (London: Chatto and Windus, 1998).
6 Elazar Barkan, *The Guilt of Nations: Restitution and Negotiating Historical Injustices* (New

York: W. W. Norton & Company, 2000) pp. i; xi.

7 See Paul Williams, 'The International Community', in Branka Magaš and Ivo Žanič (eds), *The War in Croatia and Bosnia-Herzegovina 1991–1995* (London: Frank Cass, 2001) p. 277.

8 For an excellent discussion, see Adam Roberts, 'Sins of the Secular Missionaries', *The Economist* (29 January 2000).

9 In 1999, however, during the NATO bombing of Yugoslavia, Croatia did charge Yugoslavia at the Hague Tribunal for genocide, arguing that the FRY had 'committed aggression against Croatia in that it supported, armed, incited and directed the actions of various groups within Croatia to rebel against the democratically elected authorities'. At this stage, Yugoslavia was charged with the deaths of 22,000 people, the injuries of a further 55,000 and the displacement of 600,000. Curiously, even 'the exodus after [the Croatian-led] Operation Storm' was blamed on the Serbs. As Stjepan Mesić has argued, the motivations behind these claims were perhaps the result of 'diplomatic and political speculations', since at least one-third of the 600,000 displaced were Croatian Serbs who had fled the Croatian army in 1995: Stjepan Mesić, 'The Road to War', in Magaš and Žanić (eds), *The War in Croatia and Bosnia-Herzegovina*, p. 8.

10 Rada Iveković (ed.), *La Croatie depuis d'effondrement de la Yougoslavie* (Paris: L'Harmattan, 1994).

11 Michael Freeman, Dragomir Pantić, and Dusan Janjić (eds), *Nationalism and Minorities* (Belgrade: Institute of Social Sciences, 1995).

12 Dušan Janjić, *Serbia Religion and War* (Belgrade: IKV European Movement in Serbia, 1994).

13 Hayden White, *The Content of the Form: Narrative Discourse and Historical Representation* (Baltimore, MD: Johns Hopkins University Press, 1987) pp. x; 24.

14 *Ibid.* p. 4.

15 Oliver Thomson, *Mass Persuasion in History: An Historical Analysis of the Development of Propaganda Techniques* (New York: Crane, Russak & Company, 1977) pp. 3–4.

16 *Ibid.* p. 9.

17 Marjan Malesić, *The Role of the Mass Media in the Serbian–Croatian Conflict* (Stockholm: Stryelsen for Psykologist Forsvar, 1993). Her methodology is explained on pp. 43–6.

18 *Ibid.* pp. 44–8.

19 *Ibid.* pp. 47–51.

20 *Ibid.* pp. 82–3.

21 Iver B. Neumann, *Uses of the Other: 'The East' in European Identity Formation* (Minneapolis, MN: University of Minnesota Press, 1999) p. 1.

1

What is the nation? Towards a teleological model of nationalism

The tradition of the dead generations weighs like a nightmare on the brain of the living. And just when they seem engaged in revolutionising themselves and things, they anxiously conjure up the spirits of the past to their service and borrow from them names, battle cries and costumes in order to present the new scene of world history in this time honoured disguise and borrowed language. (Henry Tudor in *Political Myth*)

FOR SERBIAN AND Croatian nationalists, the manipulation of myths and national history performed an incredibly important role during the collapse of Yugoslavia in the 1980s, and the wars of succession that followed after 1990. Before analysing these national myths, and their specific political objectives, it will be useful to understand what species, or general types, of myths have been used – and why. Reviewing the works of many major nationalism theorists, this chapter introduces a useful analytical model to help understand the nature of Serbian and Croatian myths, the types of imagery they invoke, and how they are structured. This will lay the groundwork for a more detailed study of how national myths have been used instrumentally in Serbia and Croatia to promote self-determination, the shifting of borders and populations, and the installation of despotic and corrupt regimes.

Another goal of this chapter is to examine the legacy of the Biblical tradition on conceptions of nationalist myth and understandings of time in history. This involves applying Northrop Frye's cyclical view of history (Biblical teleology) to explain why certain myths (Covenant, divine election/chosenness, Fall/persecution, and Redemption) were so frequently used in the wars following the collapse of the SFRY. The use of Biblical teleology will also allow us to structure many of the pre-existing theories of nationalism into an analytical framework, with myths of Covenant, Fall, and Redemption acting as hubs in a cyclical view of how nationalists portray mythical time in history.

Central to my analysis is an examination and understanding of Jewish

15

nationalism, and its importance in the development of general species of national myths. Jewish nationalism does not figure as a third case-study here. However, specific aspects of Jewish nationalism have formed a template that Serbian and Croatian authors, politicians, and other leaders, used to legitimate many often violent acts of statecraft. That every Fall leads to a Redemption through a covenantal relationship was a central theme of Jewish nationalism, an idea that was assiduously assimilated by Serbs and Croats.[1] While such a cyclical view of nationalism can be seen in the work of many contemporary theorists, there are some notable detractors. Writers of the Modernist school have generally dismissed the importance of mythology in the formation of nationalism, and many have rejected the concept of negative myths (Fall and persecution) as important aspects of nationalist legitimacy. Equally obvious is Modernism's poverty in dealing with how and why nationalist cohesion is created. While Modernism certainly has its positive aspects, it ignores much that is highly pertinent to the study of nationalism in Yugoslavia.

Myths of the nation: teleology and time

A central tenet of this study is that Biblical history and teleology have contributed greatly to the development of many forms of ethnic national identity. Liah Greenfeld, in her study of nationalism, posited that the return to Old Testament narratives and myths of divine election was of central importance in the development of the first nationalism (which she locates in early modern England), and by extension to all subsequent national movements. Similarly, Michael Walzer has noted the importance of Biblical exodus history, and how it has shaped the 'civic-political aspirations of national liberation movements'.[2]

Certainly the Biblical tradition has played an important role in the development of European history and philosophy, and in the evolution of nationalism. As Conor Cruise O'Brien and Adrian Hastings have both argued, Hebrew collective identity in the Old Testament was one of the first instances of territorial nationalism, functioning as a template for future generations. O'Brien posited that a territorial 'promised land' was always seen to be synonymous with the Jewish 'Heaven', an idea that was rigorously removed from the Christian Bible, when redemption through the suffering of Christ was advocated in its stead.[3] Hastings asserted that 'nations originally "imagined" ... through the mirror of the Bible'.[4] For this reason, he also placed the Hebrew Bible at the centre of early nationalism, with 'the true proto-nation' being responsible for the development of nationalism in Christian countries, inspired, rather than hindered, by religion.[5]

While the Old Testament certainly provided an example of a tribal group

16

seeking, and then gaining, a homeland, one of the main features of Hebrew nationalism was the covenantal culture it created – a special relationship or series of agreements made between a people and their deity. Much of Zionism, and indeed nationalism in general, revolved around the concept of status reversal, or Covenant, the promise of deliverance in the midst of hardship. The Covenant was absolutely central to Jewish identity, in particular the concept of 'chosenness', according to the historian Donald Harman Akenson.[6] The Zionist writer Martin Buber placed the Covenant as central to the transformation of the Jewish people from 'tribe' to 'Israel'.[7]

Following from this idea, Hans Kohn isolated three essential aspects of nationalism introduced by the Jews: 'the idea of the chosen people'; 'the consciousness of national history'; and 'national messianism'.[8] For Kohn, the invention of the Covenant was the defining moment in Jewish nationalism. While other tribes maintained a dialogue between elites and their deities, a Covenant between God and the 'people' made each person an equal member of the nation. Such a distinction gave the Hebrews a 'national ideal and purpose' in history.[9] More importantly, perhaps, a sense of direct Covenant eliminated the need for a specialised caste of priests and other elites functioning as intermediaries with the divine. A form of democratic nationalism was the result. Such a covenantal culture provided a cyclical view of history, a teleology where hardships would be followed by rewards for the faithful, as long as they kept their Covenant with their god.

A reading of philosopher Northrop Frye's critical appraisal of Biblical myth and structure is a useful method by which to understand how Biblical teleology operates. For Frye, a cycle of 'rise, fall and rise again' figured as the primary method by which history progressed in the Bible, what Frye dubbed a 'covenantal cycle'. Here, each negative event was followed by an equally positive reward – or Redemption. Frye posited that biblical myths were in many ways of a common type, 'express[ing] the human bewilderment about why we are here and where we are going, and [they] include myths of creation, of Fall, of exodus, of migration, of destruction of the human race in the present (deluge myths) or the future (apocalyptic myths), and of Redemption'.[10] But while the myths themselves were common, the uniqueness lay in the structure of Biblical narrative, which Frye describes as cyclical, a 'Divine Comedy', with:

> [An] apostasy followed by a descent into disaster and bondage, which in turn is followed by repentance, then by a rise through deliverance to a point more or less on the level from which the descent began. This *U-shaped pattern* recurs in literature as the standard shape of *comedy*, where a series of misfortunes and misunderstandings brings the action to a threateningly low point, after which some fortunate twist in the plot sends the conclusion up to a happy ending. The entire Bible, viewed as a *Divine Comedy*, is contained within a U-shaped story of

this sort, one in which man loses the tree and water of life at the beginning of Genesis and gets them back at the end of Revelation.[11]

Thus Biblical history, and the history of the world for practising Christians, was U-shaped. Within a large U-shaped cycle, which encapsulated the totality of Biblical history, were a series of smaller U-shaped cycles. As Frye summarised these: 'In between, the story of Israel is told as a series of declines into the power of heathen kingdoms: Egypt, Philistia, Babylon, Syria, Rome, each followed by a rise into a brief moment of relative independence.'[12] Some small cycles covered several days, while the largest comprised the entire history of the world – from its creation to its destruction. Of interest to the study of nationalist mythology was the metaphorical linking together of all important Biblical events and symbols, what Frye called a 'sequence of *mythoi*'. In the hands of early myth-makers, the Garden of Eden, the Promised Land, Jerusalem, and Mount Zion became interchangeable symbols for the home of the soul. Similarly, Egypt, Babylon and Rome all became symbols of the Hebrew national Fall.[13]

While such geographic locations thus constituted symbols of Rise and Fall, good and evil, individual characters also came to embody parts of a general agency or force – either positive or negative. Positive actors advanced the Hebrews forward towards a common teleological destiny, while negative actors brought about a series of Falls. Thus, the Pharaoh of the Exodus, Nebuchadnezzar, Antiochus Epiphanes, and Nero were spiritually the same person, personifying negative forces. At the same time, the deliverers of Israel – Abraham, Moses, Joshua, the Judges, David, and Solomon – were all proto-types of the Messiah or final deliverer.[14] Simply put: evil forces caused Falls, good forces engendered Redemptions. For Frye, this constant antagonism propelled Biblical history forward, ultimately allowing for the deliverance of the righteous. In this sense, both positive and negative were essential: the one negated the other. The presence of both created a 'non-self-contradictory' ethical system, where the Hebrews were redeemed, while their enemies were destroyed.

Frye described several main Falls in the Bible, beginning with the physical banishment from the Garden of Eden. This represented humankind's alien-ation from nature, and allegorised humanity's acquisition of sexual knowledge, and the knowledge of good and evil.[15] The myth of the *Tower of Babel* (Genesis 11: 1–9) became significant, as an attempt to build an edifice to overcome the Fall, to bridge the gulf between man and God. Babel's ambitious architects ultimately failed, leading only to the confusion of tongues – and a second great Fall. This not only continued the alienation between man and nature, but heightened the alienation of man from man. The Fall was now complete, with human beings now alienated from God, nature, language, and each other.[16]

It is from this low point that the epic struggle of the Hebrew people began. At this third stage of the cycle, the individual dispersed units joined together. Here, the concept of *kerygma* provided the chosen with a knowledge of the divine plan, imparting to them the idea of destiny and teleology. *Kerygma* figured as a means of 'revelation' – the conveying of information from an objective divine source to a subjective human receptor. This 'kerygmatic' process occurred throughout Biblical history, as the Hebrew people received instructions and laws to govern their interactions and worship.[17] What emerges from a reading of Frye is the importance of a strict teleology in Biblical narratives, the axiomatic link between Fall and Redemption, imparting hope in the midst of hardship. Equally important is the constant battle between positive and negative forces. The Hebrews as the divine elect were constantly delivered when negative forces plotted their destruction. Resulting from such a narrative was the self-perception of a righteous and progressive nation, fighting against negative forces throughout history, in a continuous battle between good and evil.

Historian Norman Cohn has argued that a cyclical teleological view of history stemmed from Jewish experiences of oppression, and their need to create hope for the future. Prophecies were used as a means of rallying members of a group together against the threat of external attack. Cohn notes: 'Precisely because they were so certain of being the chosen people, Jews tended to react to peril, oppression and hardship by fantasies of the total triumph and boundless prosperity which Yahweh, out of his omnipotence, would bestow upon his elect in the fullness of time.'[18] Thus the greater the calamity, the greater the belief in recompense. Fall and Redemption were intimately bound together.

From an instrumentalist perspective, the belief in a covenantal cycle kept Jews loyal to their faith, and to the culture that sustained it. It provided hope for the future, as well as a belief in historical destiny and a sense of predictability in history – perhaps also a passive acceptance of hardship, and a faith in future Redemption. What emerges from a critical reading of Biblical myth and structure are three distinct types of myth, each essential to a belief in the validity of a covenantal culture.

- The first is a belief in the structure itself, a belief that every Fall will automatically lead to a Redemption for the faithful, through the intercession of some benevolent and divine being. Thus the idea of history as a series of turning-points is very important.
- The second concerns the divine or chosen status of the nation, how and why it deserves to be saved. These types of myths deal with the greatness, heroism, faithfulness and overall goodness of the nation, stressing those positive traits which make it a candidate for deliverance.

19

- The third type of myth revolves around the importance of Fall myths – the nation as a victim of evil, ahistorical and eternal negative force, which forces it to suffer before Redemption can come about. In this sense, the third is largely based on the other two types. One has to believe that one's people will be saved, and that one is deserving of being saved, before such an eventuality can realistically be contemplated.

Of these types of myths, the first is usually assumed. If a nation is divine and good, and it can prove its persecution at the hands of evil forces, then it will be delivered. The second needs to be enshrined as part of the founding myth of the nation. As such, these types of myths can remain more or less unchanged, although they require constant reiteration and repetition to retain their influence. Of the three, the third type is the most important, since each Redemption or deliverance depends on proof of continued persecution.

Before proceeding further, it is important to understand how a nationalist teleology or covenantal cycle can be situated within the confines of existing theories of nationalism. This will involve more detail about each stage of the cycle, as well as an examination of the subdivisions within each group. The result will be a workable analytical model, which will prove extremely useful for analysing and describing the nature and character of nationalist movements in Serbia and Croatia. The first group of myths I have termed 'myths of Covenant and renewal'. The second group of myths, focusing on the chosen-ness or divinity of the nation, I have termed 'primary myths of identification', since these, in the created history of nationalism, describe the moment or series of events when the nation was either created or chosen, and imbued with righteous qualities. The third group of myths I have termed 'negative myths of identification', simply because they rely on negative forces or agencies seeking to subvert the nation's destiny, or in more extreme cases, to assimilate or destroy the nation altogether.

Myths of covenant and renewal

In his study of political myth, Henry Tudor argued that most political myths employed a teleological view of history, to give the members of a nation a fixed point of reference, allowing them to express their feelings and explain their experiences of suffering.[19] According to Tudor, the political myth-interpreter orders his experience on the assumption that contemporary events are but an episode in a story, allowing the myth-maker to contextalise the present day within the larger sweep of history, a process similar to that described by White in the case of the 'narrator'. Myths allow individuals to understand their nation's role in history, and the specific stage or time in history in which the nation finds itself. Tudor linked the concepts of political mythology with Biblical mythology, in its teleological similarities. Both are cyclical, and as

Tudor asserted: 'Mythical time is reversible. What was done is not forever lost. It may in the fullness of time repeat itself. Every myth is a story of death and rebirth, of an end or *eschatos* [*sic*; sc. *eschaton*] with simultaneously a new beginning.'[20]

Events in the past or present fit into a complex paradigm by which the world is viewed, thus claiming significance far beyond their present-day reality. As Tudor has argued, this applies not only to historical events, but also to land, where national territory can carry with it certain mythical and emotional connotations:

> Depending on the myth to which he subscribes, he [the myth-interpreter] will see a particular tract of land as part of the territory from which the chosen people were expelled, a particular year as the one in which Christ will establish his kingdom on earth, a particular trade-unionist as an agent of a world-wide communist conspiracy, or a particular industrial dispute as a crucial incident in the class war.[21]

Dušan Kečmanović has similarly discussed what he terms a 'watershed', or the 'theme of the right moment' in the life of a nation or group. Paraphrasing a nationalist view of teleology, he explains: 'We went through a period of national decline, of dissolution, of corruption and anarchy, our national interests were more or less systematically suppressed and ignored to the point where we must do something to radically change our destiny, to take it into our own hands, to make a new order emerge.'[22] Thus a nation that is partially destroyed or suppressed by a Fall may reawaken when the time is right. Of course in most cases the national leader, and not 'History' as such, determines when this period of national renaissance will begin. George Schöpflin has termed such imagery 'myths of rebirth and renewal', which also encapsulates the 'palingenetic' or messianic tradition of Judaism and Biblical teleology. Here, like Kečmanović and Tudor, Schöpflin describes these myths as ones where 'rebirth can create a sense of a clean state, a new start, in which the awfulness of the past can be forgotten'.[23]

What emerges from this view of national history and time is the importance of chosenness and Fall as the keys to Redemption. At a certain point, a nation is given the opportunity to reawaken, and to redeem itself after having suffered a Fall. History is thus composed of Falls and Redemptions, as well as positive and negative forces and individuals – those who help the nation, and those who hinder its progress. While there may be a belief that the nation will always come out ahead, there is still a sense of constant threat from the outside world, forcing co-nationalists to rally together to preserve their customs and traditions.

Primary myths of identification

In this series of mythologies, two distinct types are present. The first deals with the deification of the nation, as holy and chosen, an ideal based on the Jewish example. The second type deals with more secular or 'classical' myths of the nation as heroic and triumphant. These types of myths can exist exclusively, or can underwrite each other. Each claims strong links between the nation and its national territory, from which it draws its strength.

The concept of national chosenness is primarily based on the Jewish example. William Pfaff has described how nationalism elevates the nation to 'a simulacrum of the Deity'.[24] Peter Alter has seen the process of national myth creation as a time when 'the religious is secularised and the national sanctified'.[25] Many theorists of nationalism have attempted to understand exactly how and why nationalism bears many similarities to religious belief. As Kečmanović has understood the process, support for traditional religion declined in the nineteenth century, and people began to abandon their faith in heavenly salvation and eternal life. They began looking for more meaning on earth, and a traditional view of religion was successfully replaced by the 'pseudo-religious qualities of ethnic identification'.[26] The elevation of the nation to something mystical and eternal created a new focus of loyalty, encouraging people to sacrifice everything for their national lands, even if this meant laying down their lives.[27] Thus the adoption of religious imagery by nationalist leaders was an instrumental process, designed to protect a specific territory or legitimate the expansion of the borders of an existing nation-state.

Schöpflin has similarly advanced 'myths of election', where the nation believes it has been specially chosen by God or History to perform some special mission, because of its unique or noble virtues. While such myths are rooted in the Christian tradition, the secularisation of religion in nationalism has forced nationalists to look for other forms of proof that the nation is superior to its rivals. Thus, a nation's capacity for 'civility', 'literacy' or 'Europeanness' would rank it above rival neighbouring groups, legitimating an assumption of moral and cultural uniqueness and pride.[28]

Kečmanović has advanced a similar view, arguing: 'A fixed belief that they are brighter, more courageous, more honest, more righteous, more freedom loving, and the like helps to explain and justify their insufficient regard for the rights and interests of people of other ethnonational groups.'[29] Further, these myths were often applied in times of crisis, such that: '"we"... have better warriors and are more skilled in arms and military dexterity than "our" foe. At the negotiation table the nationalists will claim to be more toler-ant, more fair and more respectful of their given word than their counterparts on the other side of the table.'[30] As Kečmanović and Schöpflin have both argued, secularised religious imagery and a sense of national superiority have grown out of a religious tradition, even if national 'believers' possess only vestiges of religious belief.

Certainly, religion, whether in vestigial form or fully elaborated, can often be an important aspect of national identity. In many cases, nationalists have adopted and manipulated, rather than condemned, religion. In the conflict between Serbian Orthodoxy and Croatian Catholicism or in the cases of the Protestants and Catholics in Northern Ireland, the Palestinians and Israelis in Israel, the Greeks and the Turks in Cyprus, or even the Québecois in Canada, a rise in national awareness and sense of chosenness was often accompanied, or preceded, by a return to religion as a strong focus of identification. While religion may not have been the primary cause of conflict, it did become a justification for the escalation and maintenance of it. Linkages at different levels between nations and their religions can be of central importance in convincing members of nations that their consolidation into national units is somehow part of a divine plan, or the outcome of natural forces.

The golden age of nationalism

Certainly the most complete analysis of Golden Age mythology has been undertaken by Anthony Smith, although his zeal has led to a certain myopia. Arguing for a more secular interpretation of primary identification myths, Smith has taken pains to reduce the importance of religious identification, while similarly marginalising myths of persecution.[31] For Smith, nationalism's most attractive feature is its ability to make members of the nation immortal, 'through the judgement of posterity, rather than through divine judgement in an afterlife'.[32] Nationalism's ability to create secular heroes, saints, and great leaders allows co-nationals to dream of a glorious destiny within their own national history. Smith, perhaps as a result of his own classics and art history background, has seen nationalism as a secular and aesthetic phenomenon, one that relies heavily on myths of the Golden Age. These are further buttressed by 'the foundation charter', and 'ethnic title deeds', derived from a nation's long attachment to the land.[33] Such reasoning is similar to that of Pfaff, Alter, Kečmanović and Schöpflin, but has many notable differences.

For Smith, the Golden Age is the central component of nationalism and national identity. It promises 'a status reversal, where the last shall be first and the world will recognise the chosen people and their sacred values'.[34] Nationalists look to their ancient past for inspiration and self-love. Further, as Smith has argued, a nation's 'immortality' (its eternal or historically significant qualities) has been based on its ability to 'unfold a glorious past, a golden age of saints and heroes, to give meaning to its promise of restoration and dignity'.[35] He has termed this 'the myth of the historical renovation', where one is returned to a basic national 'essence', a 'basic pattern of living and being' – the 'Golden Age' of the nation.[36] Thus, we are presented with descriptions of 'poetic spaces', 'nature', and 'authenticity', as well as 'vivid recreations of the glorious past of the community'.[37] While this bears some similarity to myths of Covenant and renewal, the purely secular bent of Smith's thinking, coupled with his aversion to any negative myths of identification, makes it somewhat different.

Smith's taxonomy of myths is also rooted in this type of national mythology, which he has argued both 'defines the historic culture community', and also endows it with a 'particular energy and power'.[38] His taxonomy includes: myths of origin (ancient and unique origins of nations rooted in folklore); myths of descent (noble lineage and genealogy of nations, myths of founding fathers or tribes); and myths of the heroic age (the Golden Age or high point of the original nation). These types of myths, he has argued, 'set a standard of culture and achievement that has rarely been equalled and can act as a model for subsequent generations and other communities'.[39]

Smith has therefore argued from an instrumentalist perspective. The communal past of a nation forms a 'repository or quarry from which materials may be selected in the construction and invention of nations'.[40] History becomes nothing more than a 'useable past', where nationalists select the myths they need in order to advance certain views of the nation, necessary for rallying people together to reclaim national greatness.[41] Unfortunately, Smith has prioritised these types of myths, to the extent that he sees no other. While he has argued for the importance of warfare as an important 'mobiliser of ethnic sentiments', and as a 'provider of myths and memories for future generations', he has also concluded that 'it would be an exaggeration to deduce the sense of common ethnicity from the fear of the 'outsider' and paired antagonisms'.[42] As will become obvious from the Serbian and Croatian cases, it was indeed the fear of powerful expansionary empires, complete with alien systems of government and religion, that encouraged people to stand together and forge a sense of common identity.

In his discussion of 'anti-colonialism', Smith has also dismissed any sort of fear or loathing of others. Consolidating national identity by means of a hatred of 'conquering outgroups' is denounced as a 'simple and untenable' theory. 'Men', he writes, 'do not seek collective independence and build states simply to react to a "common enemy".'[43] Smith has accused colonised groups of exaggerating the problems they have encountered through colonialism. He has even criticised the use of the labels 'foreigner' and 'alien' to describe colonial leaders, since even foreign masters eventually developed some sort of indigenous characteristics.[44] In his taxonomy of groups (tribe, ethnie, and nation) Smith has included 'In-group sentiment' as an important criterion, but excludes any mention of how fear or loathing of the outgroup could also be important.[45] Curiously, the fear of persecution, Fall, or any aspect of national decline, has not played a role in spurring nations to band together. Rather, Smith describes 'lifting present generations out of their banal reality' as the true motive of national mythology.[46] Such imagery attributed national resurgence to the product of a mundane existence – a theory squarely at odds with reality.

Rather than engaging with those who see persecution as central to national identification, Smith has deflected criticism by the term 'ethnicism', a form of identity for ethnic groups, which exists separately from nationalism. The basis of ethnicism, but not nationalism, is to 'resist . . . perceived threats from outside and corrosion within'. Smith has described 'Ethnicism' as 'fundamentally defensive', only appearing in times of 'military threats', 'socio-economic challenges', and 'culture contact' (when a less developed culture come into prolonged contact with a more developed one).[47] While ethnicism gets closer to other ideas of nationalism, Smith has failed to discuss the relevance of these threats, or how ethnic groups were able to mould external threats into myths for collective action. Additionally, by dividing certain groups into 'ethnies', Smith has been able to deflect challenges to his narrow definition of what constitutes a 'nation'. By dismissing myths of persecution or threat as 'anti-colonial' or 'ethnic' only, he has avoided analysing them as part of the nationalist phenomenon. This artificial separation of nationalism and ethnicism is often at odds with the reality of many nationalist movements around the world.

Problematically, while Smith has described a 'useable past' for nationalism, anything to do with ethnicity is seen as decidedly different. He has derided those who would seek to use 'ethno-history' in the same way as a nation's cultural history. Thus his patronising conclusion: 'Ethno-history is no sweet shop in which nationalists may "pick and mix"; it sets limits to any selective appropriation by providing a distinctive context and pattern of events . . . It furnishes a specific but complete heritage which cannot be dismembered and then served up *à la carte.*'[48]

In one of his more recent works on nationalism theory, Smith purposely excluded discussion of genocide, ethnic cleansing, national minorities and several other current topics, first, in order to save space, and secondly and more importantly, because 'while analyses of these issues are vital and immensely valuable in their own right, it is by no means clear that they can further the task of explaining the origins, development and nature of nations and nationalism'.[49] His limited view of national mythology excludes any discussion of negative elements, which could explain why certain nations have pursued genocidal policies against national minorities within their own borders. Certainly during the pre-modern period in Europe, as well as during Europe's colonial débâcles in the eighteenth and nineteenth centuries, geno-

cide and the forced transfer of populations were integral to creating homogeneous cultures, on which modern nation-states or colonies could be
constructed.

While Smith has overestimated the importance of the Golden Age in his
study of nationalism, his analysis is nevertheless rigorous and well argued.
The Golden Age is certainly an important part of nationalist identity, and
credit needs to be given where it is due. Moreover, his 'myths of origin', 'myths
of descent', and 'myths of the heroic age' provide invaluable sub-species of
myths that are of use in dissecting nationalist historical narratives.
Nevertheless, there is much more to nationalism than Smith's Golden Age.

Other theorists of nationalism, such as Ernest Gellner, have been more
dismissive of the Golden Age, labelling it a 'putative folk culture', drawn from
myths of the 'healthy, pristine, vigorous life of the peasants'.[50] While Gellner
found it laudable that indigenous cultures were able to stand up to oppression
and subjugation by an 'alien high culture', he argued that, in most cases, an
'invented high culture', was introduced after nationalism had been successful, rather than there being a retention of any sort of traditional 'low culture'
on which the aesthetics of the new nationalism were constructed.[51]

Gellner's argument is valid, in that nations rarely attempt to re-create any
form of 'authentic' Golden Age, when an idealised history is far more flatter-
ing. Nevertheless, inauthentic reproductions of past national culture do not
diminish the importance of this type of imagery. Seen first and foremost as an
instrumental construction, 'primary myths of identification' allow the nation
to dream of a glorious and heroic past, positing origins of chosenness or divine
election. This gives national members a feeling of self-worth, while at the same
time forcing them to look to the past for their inspiration. These myths also
reinforce a sense of tragedy: that the nation has somehow fallen from grace,
and must therefore be redeemed. That the nation was once great and then
somehow Fell, owing to internal or external forces, is often a central element
in spurring a nation to reassert itself. Smith's insistence on marginalising Fall
myths is a major failing of his approach, even if his analysis of the Golden Age
is extremely lucid.

Negative myths of identification

Throughout, I will argue that negative myths have formed the nodal point of
Serbian and Croatian nationalism, providing a much-needed stock of
metaphors and imagery. Such myths enabled nationalists to legitimate many
insalubrious and violent acts of statecraft. Myths of persecution and Fall
explain *why* the nation has fallen from its Golden Age. These myths situate the
nation within a teleological framework, where external forces persecuting the
nation will be judged and dealt with as the nation struggles to deliver itself.

Without these types of images, a national revival is simply unnecessary.

For those writing on the Jewish model of nationalism, persecution and Fall were a result of a unified negative force in history. Hugh Trevor-Roper argued that such imagery became normal in European nationalism, and his definition of 'normal nationalism' included a sense of persecution and victimisation. Nationalism, as he saw it, was 'the expression of wounded nationality: the cry of men who have suffered great national defeat, or whose nationality is denied, or who live insecurely on exposed national frontiers, surrounded, and in danger of being swamped by foreigners'.[52] In other words, it was both understandable and commonplace for nations to invoke allegations of persecution or victimisation in order to justify defensive action against external enemies.

Peter Alter, while not including a sense of persecution or oppression in his 'common structural components' of nationalism, has identified 'disrespect for and animosity towards other people' as an important aspect of identity.[53] He has further argued: 'social groups also tend to define their national identity and national consciousness in negative terms ... Encounters with "alien"– other forms of language, religion, customs, political systems – make people aware of close ties, shared values and common ground.'[54] Thus, contrary to Smith's proposition that only positive imagery is important in nationalism, Alter argues that negative encounters with external 'others' are also crucial in creating a cohesive national identity.

Kečmanović has also argued for the centrality of the other in identity formation. 'Counteridentification', as he has explained, reinforces a mandatory respect for 'national standards' and the 'observance of prescribed rituals'. The identification of a 'group enemy', 'smoothes, buffers, or completely neutralises intragroup antagonisms'.[55] Indeed, without a sense of discrimination and aggressiveness against strangers, it is very difficult to maintain strong bonds of friendship or co-operation among co-nationals. Counteridentification is close to Kečmanović's 'pseudospeciation', a term that describes the human tendency to split off into separate groups, creating 'pseudospecies' that behave as if they were separate species – with completely different traditions, cultural habits, and psychologies.[56] This appears to be little more than a modernised definition of racial consciousness, echoing the nineteenth- and early twentieth-century idea that each race had separate unchangeable physical and psychological characteristics that made it behave differently from other races. Again, the main issue here is that of differentiation between one's own group – be it a nation, pseudospecies, or race – and an external negative force trying to destroy it.

Claude Lefort's image of the 'People as one' similarly invokes the importance of an external negative force in the creation of an internally coherent system. For Lefort, membership in the nation is considered the highest form of association, with one's most important duties being loyalty to the nation, and one's pledge to defend it. Lefort's work has very much dealt with the relationship between Communist states and nationalism:

> At the foundation of totalitarianism lies the representation of the People-as-one. In the so-called socialist world, there can be no other division than that between the people and its enemies: a division between inside and outside, no internal division ... the constitution of the People-as-one requires the incessant production of enemies. It is not only necessary to convert, at the level of phantasy [*sic*], real adversaries of the regime or real opponents into the figures of the evil Other, it is also necessary to invent them.[57]

Lefort's conception invoked the centrality of the other to the formation of a stable and homogeneous internal identity.

As Marc Howard Ross has further explained the phenomenon, the isolation of enemies who 'contain unwanted parts of ourselves' can allow the nation to purge itself of many negative attributes, leaving only the good characteristics. Shared images of the world and plans for action are predicated on a shared conception of difference between one's own group and others. As he has described it: 'Outsiders can then serve as objects for externalisation, displacement and projection of intense negative feelings like dissenting perspectives, which are present inside the group but denied.'[58] Thus, a nation that has been traditionally seen as warlike or hostile can portray itself as a victim of aggression. A nation with a reputation for repressing its own national minorities will claim that its own people in far-away lands are being abused, and are in need of protection.

A similar argument was picked up by Michael Ignatieff, who made ample use of Sigmund Freud's 'narcissism of minor differences' to analyse the conflict in Yugoslavia. As he has explained: 'the smaller the real difference between two peoples, the larger it was bound to loom in their imagination ... Without hatred of the other, there would be no clearly defined national self to worship and adore.'[59] It would be hard to imagine a theory more diametrically opposed to that of Smith, although I should add that Ignatieff's rather reductionist analysis seems to negate the idea that national cultures could have any real differences between them or any real elements of their past that might promote national pride.

What these theorists share generally is a view of national identity that needs an other, an external enemy, to consolidate support for an exclusive 'in group'. In many ways, such a view of nationalism appears more plausible than that of Smith. Such imagery is important, as it *creates* a need to belong to the nation for protection and defence against external 'others' seeking to destroy the nation. Of course, national loyalty is also derived from positive aspects as well – national symbols, characteristics, and shared memories worth preserving. Nevertheless, it is only when these positive aspects are threatened that they become truly appreciated. The instrumentality of such national imagery is clear – demonstrating national Falls becomes the key to organising a national movement.

Kenneth Minogue's analysis is particularly useful here. Minogue identifies a three-stage process of nationalist awakening: 'stirrings' – when the nation 'becomes aware of itself as a nation suffering from oppression'; 'struggle' – when the nation is sufficiently organised to fight for its independence; and 'consolidation' – when the nation-state has actually been attained.[60] For Minogue, the central aspect in nationalist 'stirrings' is an organised reaction against oppression. The banding together of co-nationals to rectify the wrongs of history becomes a strong rallying cry. Clearly, the links between fear and hatred of an external enemy and national consolidation appear to be quite strong, according to a wide variety of theorists of nationalism. Most of these theories expand on but also clash with Smith's Golden Age by pointing out that there is more to nationalism than self-love. For many of these writers, negative threats from the outside, rather than great marvels of national history, determine the need for national membership.

A taxonomy of Fall and persecution myths

Both George Schöpflin and Dušan Kečmanović have created useful 'taxonomies' or classifications of Fall myths. Schöpflin has identified two types, and Kečmanović five. Such taxonomies aim further to analyse and deconstruct negative imagery and its role in nationalism theory. Schöpflin's first type of Fall deals with 'myths of redemption and suffering', consisting of 'myths of powerlessness and compensation for the powerless' – both of which stress the importance of status reversal. These, as he argues, turn fatalism and passivity into virtues, while making suffering nations morally superior to their rivals.[61]

The second type, 'myths of unjust treatment', advance the idea that 'history is a malign and unjust actor that has singled out the community for special, negative treatment.'[62] Schöpflin has stressed the purposeful nature of collective suffering, since it endows persecution and victimisation with meaning. Thus, like Biblical teleology, national Redemption follows naturally from a Fall. As he paraphrases the argument: 'The world ... owes those who have suffered a special debt ... the victims of suffering are helpless because they suffered for the wider world and the wider world should recognise this, thereby legitimating the group's special worth.'[63] Schöpflin has placed Holocaust myths here, as well as myths that copy the Holocaust, appropriating its symbolism.[64]

Kečmanović's myths or 'themes' are similar to those of Schöpflin, although each is not mutually exclusive. 'The theme of damage' highlights how frequently the nation has been deprived, economically, legally, religiously, or socially. Competition between rival groups for scarce resources within a state naturally favours one group over another. This leads invariably to a lower level of economic and cultural development for the oppressed group – a common theme, argues Kečmanović, in nationalist writing.[65] The next theme deals with 'threat' – both from internal and external forces. Internally, the nation is threatened by those who refuse to acknowledge the decomposition of the nation, and therefore do nothing to prevent it from crumbling. Externally, 'threat' comes from outside groups who seek to undermine the nation, by destroying its socio-economic potential, while similarly 'deaden[ing] their national self-consciousness'.[66]

Thirdly, Kečmanović has identified the theme of the 'universal culprit', where 'Nationalists perceive the members of another nationality as the source of all evil and as responsible for all the ills that have befallen them.'[67] A fourth theme of 'plot' exists, where nationalists locate enemies around the world, not just among their neighbours. Thus, international organisations, the KGB, the Vatican, Freemasons, or some other pet bogeyman are blamed for all the ills of the nation. Foreign and seemingly omnipotent forces are implicated in sinister plots, creating a paranoia that stresses a sense of national uniqueness in the face of attack from multiple sources.[68] The final theme is that of 'victim and sacrifice', where nationalists become 'victims of envy, of the hegemonic and expansionist tendencies of other people, victims of minority or majority groups that continuously demand greater autonomy or more rights'.[69] In this final case, external forces try to destroy the nation to gain its power for themselves.

Kečmanović and Schöpflin share the view that negative identification is central to the formation of national myths – certainly as important as positive forms of identity. Both writers argue that this type of imagery 'proves' to national members that they either deserve recompense and special status from outside, or the recognition that their own 'self-help' remedies are justified. Both see these types of myths as instrumental, and both advance the importance of negative myths in reinforcing a sense of uniqueness and self-righteousness – that what is good and noble in the nation needs to be preserved, and can only be preserved by national unity and loyalty.

What emerges from an overview of 'myths of negative identification' is their fundamental importance within a teleological and ethical framework. Because a 'chosen', 'noble', and 'golden' nation has fallen, owing to outside influences, it deserves to be given its rightful place in the family of nations. Not only does a nationalist understanding of history teach that a suffering nation deserves Redemption; an understanding of teleology posits that it will eventually be redeemed, should co-nationals band together to accomplish national objectives. In this, Minogue's analysis provides a useful description of how such imagery can be instrumentalised by nationalist leaders. As has been described earlier, a nationalist teleology is largely assumed to be at work in the history of nations. What needs to be proved in order for that teleology to come about are myths of the past greatness of the nation, and myths of its persecution and Fall. The construction and perpetuation of national myths is an instrumental phenomenon, whereby elites order events according to their view of history, creating an ethical system where right and wrong are clearly demarcated.

Modernism and its approach to nationalism

Since the 1960s, Modernism has been an important branch of nationalism theory, accounting for the rise of nations as a concomitant of the industrial revolution and the spread of literacy and the printing press. Modernists have generally had little interest in nationalist mythology, seeing nationalism as a solution for the problems of industrialisation and mass urbanisation, not as an end in itself. While views on the character of nationalism are wide-ranging, they basically share a common theme: that negative imagery (or myth) is an insignificant factor in the development, structuring and articulation of nationalism. For most Modernists, it is generally irrelevant what types of national mythology have been used, what aspects of history have been re-interpreted, or why nationalism has been chosen over some other form of association, such as Communism or Fascism.

Ernest Gellner, for example, begins from the standpoint that there was little intrinsic worth to nationalism, since it is 'not the awakening of nations to self-consciousness; it invents nations where they do not exist'.[70] While he admits that there are some 'pre-existing differentiating marks' that might form part of the basis of nationalism, these are seen as secondary to the larger process of nation-building that occurred in modernity. Such 'marks' are relevant only in so far as every nation seems to have them in its past.[71] The nature or extent of such 'marks' failed to enter into Gellner's discussion, since he argued that 'The cultural shreds and patches used by nationalism are often arbitrary historical inventions. Any old shred and patch would have served as well.'[72] Thus nationalist symbols are seen as instrumental only – they could be anything, so long as they performed a certain social and political function – that of channelling popular support for the nationalist elite.

John Breuilly's observations are similar in many respects. For him, nationalism's usefulness rests almost entirely in its ability to 'exploit the sense of loss modernity creates . . . provid[ing] simple concrete labels for friends and enemies.'[73] It emerges as an institutional instrument for gaining power, useful, Breuilly posits, for opposition groups seeking to wrest control from an established government.[74] There is nothing here to suggest that nationalism has any intrinsic features that make it better than other forms of association, nor that nationalism has any special types of symbolism or imagery at its disposal. I will argue that the opposite is often true, that national leaders often have to choose their 'shreds and patches' very carefully. Often, there is nothing arbitrary about nationalist mythology at all.

Other Modernists, such as the historian Eric Hobsbawm, have a more ambivalent view of the role of negative imagery. Characteristically, Hobsbawm encounters difficulty with the concept of negative identification. For him, ethnic and national identification are divided into separate categories, and while he sees that external attacks on the ethnic group may well help that group bind together, he does not see nationalism suffering from the same process.[75] Hobsbawm is careful not to dismiss racial and ethnic identity outright as an aspect of nationalism. He admits that prejudice based on colour and other physical characteristics has played an important role in politics. Nevertheless, he adds that 'negative ethnicity is virtually always irrelevant to proto-nationalism . . .'.[76]

Hobsbawm later contradicts himself, finding that while racism itself may not be important in developing a proto-nationalism, it becomes crucial as nationalism becomes more widespread, and gains mass appeal. This 'democratisation' of nationalism, as Hobsbawm recalls, often implies an era when 'popular nationalist, or at all events xenophobic sentiments and those of national superiority preached by the new pseudo science of racism, became easier to mobilise.'[77] Reviewing nineteenth-century nationalism, Hobsbawm draws a positive correlation between nationalism and out-group violence, arguing: 'there is no more effective way of bonding together the disparate sections of restless peoples than to unite them against outsiders.'[78] In this approach, modernity creates the conditions for a more xenophobic and racially based nationalism. Further, his analysis prescribes nationalism as a potential cure for the onset of modernity, with its concomitant alienation of various groups in society looking for some form of identity. The fear of losing traditional ways during periods of increased urbanisation made it easier for national elites to gain support by convincing the populace that they were being persecuted because of their national group.[79]

In this way, Hobsbawm blends together some of the Modernist ideas of Gellner and Breuilly concerning industrialisation and the importance of urbanisation in creating a milieu wherein nationalism can come about. While he seemingly rejects racism and negative views of out-groups at the beginning of nationalism, he finds negative forms of nationalism to be crucial later. The question 'Why only later?' is never answered, and this creates several problems. The first is that elite or proto-nationalism is somehow seen as free of racism or negative views of the other, while there is an implication that the masses somehow need someone to hate or fear in order to rally behind a nationalist leader. While ethnic groups and the masses are seen to be xeno-phobic, the national elites are somehow above such attitudes. How and why this is the case is not explained.

If Hobsbawm rejects enemy images in the development of early national-ism, Benedict Anderson has completely dismissed its importance throughout the process of national development and 'democratisation'. He posits that 'nations inspire love, and often profoundly self sacrificing love,' and goes on to argue that while national love inspires 'poetry, prose fiction, music and plastic arts ... how truly rare it is to find analogous nationalist products expressing fear and loathing.'[80] Anderson even posited that colonised people felt little hatred for their former colonial overlords. He was astonished at 'how insignif-icant the element of hatred is in these expressions of national feeling'.[81] However, Anderson's select examples from South-East Asia ignore the reality of those many nations who based at least part of their nationalism on threat and fear. While love of the nation is an important ingredient in activating national sentiments, Anderson's rejection of negative imagery ignores half the picture.

Tom Nairn's view of nationalism differs in many respects from those of others of the Modernist school. Adopting a more populist perspective, he sees the involvement of the masses as the crucial step in nationalism, as well as its source of legitimacy. As such, myths of 'popular revolution' or 'national liber-ation struggle' form the basis of modernist national myths, making nations appear democratic and desirable.[82] Tracing its more recent history, Nairn examines the importance of nationalism for weaker nations as an ideology that was used, particularly in Latin America and 'Indo-China', as a way of rallying people together to fight against 'alien oppression.'[83] His basic goal is to tie modern nationalism to underdevelopment in developing countries. Again, nationalism is a solution to economic backwardness.

Unlike Gellner, Breuilly and Anderson, Nairn sees negative views of foreigners and out-groups as central to emerging national consciousness. In fact, a strong aversion to colonial powers forms the basis of nationalism, as Nairn explains: 'Their rulers ... had to mobilise their societies for this histori-cal short cut. This meant the conscious formation of a militant, inter-class community rendered strongly (if mythically) aware of its own separate iden-tity *vis-à-vis* the outside forces of domination.'[84] This view completely opposes that of Smith and Anderson. Nairn's emphasis on 'mobilisation' stresses the need for emerging twentieth-century nationalism to focus on 'differentiae' as the linchpin of nationalist struggles. However, like Gellner's 'shreds and patches', the specific symbols and images of nationalism are irrelevant, merely a cobbling together of 'inherited *ethnos*, speech, folklore, [and] skin colour', with certain external structures of nationalism, such as a capital city, a currency, a government, a military, and other such trappings.[85] Nairn puts the point more succinctly in a later work, describing nationalism simply as 'the effort by one "backward" culture and people after another to appropriate the powers and benefits of modernity for their own use', largely in reaction to imperialism and colonial domination.[86]

Nairn's view of nationalism as a populist movement, based on a collective will to appropriate the structures of a 'modern' state, is in many ways naive. What he presents is a utopian vision of how such states should have worked, a view that ignores the unfortunate excesses and corruption of many nationalist leaders, who sometimes did more to exploit their own people than did their former colonial masters. Also, the focus on external colonial forces as the object of negative imagery is not easily applied to other cases. In many African and Asian states, for instance, conflict between ethnic groups (or potential nations) was sometimes far more severe and bloody than any struggle against colonialism. The conflict over Jammu and Kashmir between India and Pakistan, and bitter fighting in Angola, Somalia, and Rwanda all indicate the dangers of internal rather than external antagonists.

In conclusion, while Modernism advances several intriguing explanations for the rise of nationalism, it does little to explain why nations evolve as they do, why certain types of myths and ideas are important while others are not, and more importantly, why nationalism is seen to be the best instrumental method of acquiring power within the state. None of the Modernist writers surveyed ascribe any intrinsic worth to nationalism, seeing it merely as a tool in the struggle for power. The appeal of nationalism remains elusive. People either become nationalists because they are confused and dislocated by industrialisation and modernity, or adopt nationalism in order to create an industrialised and modern state. Few conclusions are offered to prove or disprove that such a view of nationalism is historically accurate.

Critics such as Anthony Smith have rightly signalled many emerging nationalisms that disprove the Modernist case. At the same time, he questions how receptive people have actually been to 'official school culture', rightly asking: 'Is the sacrifice for the fatherland really a defence of an educationally sustained high culture?'[87] In most cases, important symbols and traditions, rooted in pre-national culture, seem to be at work. Some of these traditions may be more deeply felt than nationalists realise. Indeed, the drive to use the past to make sense of the present opens a Pandora's box of differing values and interpretations of the past, resulting in struggles to see whose version of reality will prevail. In short, Modernism fails to address the continued importance of nationalist myth and tradition. Explorations into what sort of national myths and traditions are useful in the development of nationalism, and how national time and history are conceived, as well as analyses of the structure of national myths and ideas, are simply not relevant to Modernist studies of nationalism.

Conclusions

A model composed of these three general varieties of myths will allow for a systematic analysis of Serbian and Croatian nationalist myths, including how these myths were selected, and how they were used instrumentally. Of these three types of myths, the first type is largely assumed. Without the promise of a status reversal, there can be no teleology in history, and the nation is deprived of its destiny. Because it has so long been anchored in the Biblical tradition, any group that can prove itself to be chosen, and to have suffered national Falls, can look forward to such a change in status.

'Primary myths of identification' are equally important. They create a utopian vision of what the nation can be, making nationalists proud of their history and traditions. While these myths help a nation understand its own unique character and historical significance, they are less important than 'negative myths of identification'. The reason for this stems from the impor- tance of the Jewish example, and the creation of a post-Holocaust ethic in the Western world, which privileges victims over aggressors. Proving one's Golden Age serves primarily to increase the tragic aspects of the national Fall, thereby demonstrating a greater need for national Redemption.

Throughout this book, priority will be given to an analysis of 'negative myths of identification'. While the other two types of myths will be reviewed, these negative myths have proved the most useful in rallying people together under a common cause, namely – the defence of the nation from external attack. Such myths convince members of a nation that they are in danger, should they choose not to adhere to the national traditions and prescriptions laid forth by their leaders. As will become increasingly obvious, strong propa- ganda campaigns, replete with Fall imagery and the fear of genocide, preceded much of the irredentist behaviour and 'ethnic cleansing' that so traumatised the Yugoslav region. Proving the guilt of the other in trying to destroy the self became a central preoccupation of Serbian and Croatian nationalists seeking to legitimate many of their often violent activities.

NOTES

1 These arguments are elaborated in Chapter 2, which explores the centrality of the Holocaust and a victim-centred mentality in the formation of national myths.
2 Greenfeld and Walzer's arguments are discussed in Conor Cruise O'Brien, *God Land: Reflections on Religion and Nationalism* (Cambridge, MA: Harvard University Press, 1988) p. 141.
3 *Ibid.* pp. 1–4; 7; 26.
4 Adrian Hastings, *The Construction of Nationhood: Ethnicity, Religion and Nationalism* (Cambridge: Cambridge University Press, 1997) p. 187.
5 *Ibid.* pp. 201; 205.
6 See Bruce Cauthen's discussion of 'divine election' in 'The Myth of Divine Election and

Afrikaner Ethnogenesis', in Geoffrey Hosking and George Schöpflin (eds), *Myths and Nationhood* (London: C. Hurst & Company, 1997) p. 113.

7 See Harold Fisch, *The Zionist Revolution* (London: Weidenfeld and Nicolson, 1978) p. 17.

8 Hans Kohn, *The Idea of Nationalism: A Study in Its Origins and Background* (New York: Macmillan, 1945) p. 36.

9 *Ibid.* pp. 37–8.

10 Northrop Frye, *The Great Code: The Bible and Literature* (Toronto: Academic Press Canada, 1982) p. 24.

11 *Ibid.* p. 169. (Italics mine.)

12 *Ibid.* p. 169.

13 *Ibid.* p. 169. (Italics his.)

14 *Ibid.* p. 171.

15 *Ibid.* p. 109.

16 *Ibid.* p. 142.

17 Northrop Frye, *Words With Power: Being a Second Study of 'The Bible and Literature'* (London: Harcourt Brace Jovanovich, 1990) p. 80.

18 Norman Cohn, *The Pursuit of the Millennium* (London: Mercury Books, 1962) pp. 1–2.

19 Henry Tudor, *Political Myth* (London: Pall Mall Press, 1972) pp. 14–15.

20 *Ibid.* pp. 138–9.

21 *Ibid.* p. 36.

22 Dušan Kečmanović, *The Mass Psychology of Ethnonationalism* (New York: Plenum Press, 1996) p. 62.

23 George Schöpflin, 'The Functions of Myth and a Taxonomy of Myth', in Hosking and Schöpflin (eds), *Myths and Nationhood*, pp. 32–3.

24 William Pfaff, *The Wrath of Nations: Civilization and the Furies of Nationalism* (New York: Simon & Schuster, 1993) p. 53.

25 Peter Alter, *Nationalism* (London: Edward Arnold, 1992) p. 10.

26 Kečmanović, *The Mass Psychology of Ethnonationalism*, pp. 68–9.

27 *Ibid.* p. 58.

28 Schöpflin, 'The Functions of Myth and a Taxonomy of Myth', p. 31.

29 Kečmanović, *The Mass Psychology of Ethnonationalism*, p. 65.

30 *Ibid.* p. 66.

31 For example, Smith took great pains to attack any notion that 'millennialism' might be in some way important in nationalism. This he saw as a movement separate from nationalism, for neither 'territory nor ethnicity as such figure much in millennial dreams'. See Anthony D. Smith, *Nationalism in the Twentieth Century* (New York: New York University Press, 1979) p. 26. While he did cite the Jews as an exception to this rule, he denied other national groups the right to engage in a territorial millennialism. If the Jews were an exception to the rule, then his idea that 'only God can actually save; only He can institute the kingdom' (*ibid.* p. 15) was clearly wrong, since millennialist Zionist writers from the very beginning preached a return to the land as a form of self-help, something to prefigure the coming of the Messiah, rather than an act that would signal his return. This also went against assertions by Kohn, Kečmanović and others, who rightly argued for the importance of the Jewish millennial tradition in nationalism. For Smith's discussion of 'millennianism', see *ibid.* pp. 15–26.

32 Anthony D. Smith, *National Identity* (London: Penguin Books, 1990) p. 14.

33 Anthony D. Smith, *The Ethnic Revival* (Cambridge: Cambridge University Press, 1981) p. 13.

34 Smith, *National Identity*, p. 14.

35 Anthony D. Smith, *Theories of Nationalism* (New York: Holmes & Meier, 1983) pp. 153–4.
36 *Ibid.* p. 22.
37 Smith, *National Identity*, pp. 65–6.
38 Smith, *Theories of Nationalism*, p. 152.
39 *Ibid.* p. 153.
40 Anthony D. Smith, 'The "Golden Age" and National Revival', in Hosking and Schöpflin (eds), *Myths and Nationhood*, p. 37.
41 *Ibid.* p. 37.
42 Smith, *National Identity*, p. 27.
43 Smith, *Theories of Nationalism*, pp. 65–8.
44 *Ibid.* p. 66.
45 *Ibid.* p. 189.
46 *Ibid.* p. 154.
47 Anthony D. Smith, *The Ethnic Origins of Nations* (Oxford: Blackwell, 1986) pp. 50; 55–6.
48 Anthony D. Smith, *Nationalism and Modernism* (London: Routledge, 1998) p. 45.
49 *Ibid.* p. xiii.
50 Ernest Gellner, *Nations and Nationalism* (Oxford: Blackwell, 1983) p. 57.
51 *Ibid.* p. 57.
52 Hugh Trevor-Roper, *Jewish and Other Nationalism* (London: Weidenfeld and Nicolson, 1962) p. 12.
53 Alter, *Nationalism*, p. 7
54 *Ibid.* p. 19.
55 Kečmanović, *The Mass Psychology of Ethnonationalism*, p. 36.
56 *Ibid.* p. 41.
57 Quoted in Sandra Bašić-Hrvatin, 'Television and National/Public Memory', in James Gow, Richard Paterson, and Alison Preston (eds), *Bosnia By Television* (London: British Film Institute, 1996) pp. 63–4.
58 Marc Howard Ross, 'Psychocultural Interpretation Theory and Peacemaking in Ethnic Conflicts', *Political Psychology*, 16:3 (1995) p. 533.
59 Michael Ignatieff, *Blood and Belonging: Journeys into the New Nationalism* (Toronto: Viking Books, 1993) p. 14.
60 Kenneth R. Minogue, *Nationalism* (London: B. T. Batsford, 1967) pp. 25–8.
61 Schöpflin, 'The Functions of Myth and a Taxonomy of Myth', p. 29.
62 *Ibid.* pp. 29–30.
63 *Ibid.* pp. 29–30.
64 *Ibid.* pp. 30–1.
65 Kečmanović, *The Mass Psychology of Ethnonationalism*, p. 61.
66 *Ibid.* pp. 62–3.
67 *Ibid.* p. 63.
68 *Ibid.* pp. 63–4.
69 *Ibid.* pp. 66–7.
70 See Ernest Gellner, *Thought and Change* (London: Weidenfeld and Nicolson, 1964) p. 168. A lengthy analysis is offered by Smith, *Nationalism and Modernism*, Chapter 2.
71 *Ibid.* p. 168.
72 Gellner, *Nations and Nationalism*, p. 56.
73 John Breuilly, *Nationalism and the State* (Manchester: Manchester University Press, 1985) p. 30.
74 *Ibid.* p. 381.
75 Eric J. Hobsbawm, *Nations and Nationalism Since 1780: Programme, Myth, Reality* (Cambridge: Cambridge University Press, 1995) pp. 63–4.

76 *Ibid.* p. 66.
77 *Ibid.* p. 91.
78 *Ibid.* p. 91.
79 *Ibid.* p. 109.
80 Benedict Anderson, *Imagined Communities: Reflections on the Origin and Spread of Nationalism* (London: Verso, 1987) p. 141.
81 *Ibid.* pp. 141–2.
82 Tom Nairn, *The Break-up of Britain, New Edition* (London: Verso, 1981) p. 41.
83 *Ibid.* p. 331.
84 *Ibid.* p. 339.
85 *Ibid.* p. 340.
86 Tom Nairn, *Faces of Nationalism: Janus Revisited* (London: Verso, 1997) p. 71.
87 Smith, *Nationalism and Modernism*, pp. 38–9.

2

Instrumentalising the Holocaust: from universalisation to relativism

For the things we have to learn before we can do them, we learn by doing them: e.g. men becoming builders by building and lyre-players by playing the lyre; so too we become just by just acts, temperate by doing temperate acts, brave by doing brave acts. (Aristotle, *Nicomachean Ethics*)[1]

Where once it was said that the life of Jews would be 'a light unto nations' – the bearer of universal lessons – now it is the 'darkness unto nations' of the death of Jews that is said to carry universal lessons ... Individuals from every point on the political compass can find the lessons they wish in the Holocaust; it has become a moral and ideological Rorschach test. (Peter Novick, *The Holocaust and Collective Memory*)[2]

I ARGUE THROUGHOUT this book that negative imagery has been a crucial building-block in Serbian and Croatian national myths. These myths have been used to legitimate the forced shifting of borders, the ethnic cleansing of populations, and various other violent aspects of state formation. Equally important has been the frequent use of the Jewish Holocaust as a template for restructuring nationalist histories. The Holocaust as *the* archetypal national Fall of the twentieth century has arguably left a lasting impression on philosophers and historians, as well as nationalist leaders. In this chapter, three concepts are of importance: firstly, the universalisation (or trivialisation) of the Holocaust as a series of general symbols and metaphors for national suffering; secondly, a debate among historians comparing the Holocaust to other instances of genocide in the twentieth century and before; and thirdly, the concept of 'performativity' – the theory that nations create forms of discourse to advance their own histories of victimisation, even if in some cases an impartial view of history might suggest other interpretations.[3]

During the disintegration of Yugoslavia, 'acting' as a victim formed a central part of Serbian and Croatian propaganda, legitimating the violence necessary to create expanded homelands. Seeking to justify a form of national 'self-help', these two countries produced a legacy of ethnic cleansing, rape,

forced population transfers, and irredentism, as the products of their own feelings of victimisation.

Also important has been the targeting of specific enemies trying to
destroy the nation. As Branimir Anzulović has remarked in his consideration of genocide in Yugoslavia: 'The modern age has added another motive
for genocide: the utopian promise of a perfect society through the elimination of the groups accused of preventing its realization.'[4] Furthermore, 'the
self-defensive "kill so that you may not be killed"', is, again according to
Anzulović, never enough to mobilise one's national group for conflict.
Rather, 'The victim must be seen as a demon, and his killing as a universally
beneficial act.'[5] Certainly the quest for racial purity is not a new one – it goes
back at least as far as the ancient Aryan invaders of the Indian subcontinent,
who introduced a tripartite system of social stratification known as the
system of *varna* (or 'colours'). They adapted this system to the new conditions by adding to it at the bottom end a further fourth and lowest *varna*, the
Shudra, in which the darker-skinned indigenous peoples could be separated
off from the lighter-skinned invaders. What has certainly changed however,
is the wide variety of means available in the modern state to achieve a racial
utopia – means that never existed before the onset of modernity. These
means allow 'demons' to be killed far more easily than at any other time in
history.

An analysis of Serbian and Croatian mythologies, with direct reference to
their instrumental and often violent consequences, demonstrates some of the
practical implications of creating a self-righteous nationalism, based on myths
of Fall and Redemption. Sadly, the case of Yugoslavia provides an example of
how Jewish victimisation and national renewal unwittingly bred a host of
bastard children, seeking to manipulate and abuse the legacy of the Holocaust
to advance a variety of geopolitical agendas.

Biblical and Jewish ethics: nationalism and Zionism

Frye's analysis of biblical structure demarcated a clear ethical system, where
good and evil were at odds with each other, driving history forward. The idea
that there was an axiomatic link between Fall and Redemption provided an
understanding of how Jewish nationalism would structure its own aspirations
for statehood, using the legitimacy of this model to guide it through the nineteenth and twentieth centuries. Indeed, there was little doubt that the Jews
had had a series of metaphorically linked 'Golden Ages' such as Frye has
described, nor was there much doubt as to the persistence of myths of Jews as
chosen, and as the elect of God. What did need to be re-created for Jews to
again situate themselves in the covenantal cycle, to once again dream of
Redemption, was proof of the continued presence of an ahistorical negative

agency, able to bind the Jews together, able to again place them within their historical teleology.

For many nineteenth-century Zionists, the dangers posed by anti-Semitism would prove of crucial importance in rallying co-nationals together to dream of a renewed Israel. While the reality of anti-Semitism arguably stemmed from Roman times, the term was first coined by Wilhelm Marr in 1879, and adopted into his *Antisemiten-Liga*.[6] While anti-Semitism was articulated to denote a fear of 'Jewish Internationalism', implicating Jews in a conspiracy to overthrow nation-states, Hannah Arendt has argued convincingly that some Zionists began to place it at the centre of their emerging nationalism, along with more positive myths of divine election and Covenant. Anti-Semitism provided the necessary means for the Jews to confront their 'otherness' in Europe when they found themselves outsiders in the development of the nation-state and the industrial revolution.[7]

While the Jews had for centuries been the victims of religiously inspired aggression, Arendt argued that anti-Semitism only arose as an instrumental term when it was politically expedient to channel Jewish experiences of victimisation towards a concrete objective, in line with Minogue's three-stage model.[8] At first, this was simply the desire to safeguard existence, while later it was used in promoting collective action. Thus:

> Jews concerned with the survival of their people, would, in a curious and desperate misinterpretation, hit on the consoling idea that antisemitism after all might be an excellent means for keeping the people together, so that the assumption of eternal antisemitism would even imply an eternal guarantee of Jewish existence. This superstition, a secularised travesty of the idea of eternity inherent in a faith in chosenness and a Messianic hope, has been strengthened through the fact that for many centuries the Jews experienced the Christian brand of hostility which was indeed a powerful agent of preservation, spiritually as well as politically.[9]

For some Zionist thinkers, the role of anti-Semitism as a constant foil to Jewish aspirations was to figure as a central component of nineteenth-century Jewish national identity. Zionist writers, seeking justification for the creation of a Jewish state, readily used both persecution myths and the covenantal cycle to argue that such a state was both viable and historically necessary. Theodor Herzl placed the Jewish Fall at the centre of his movement for a national homeland. Positing that the Jews of the Diaspora constituted 'one people', Herzl advocated a mass exodus from Europe, since: 'We have sincerely tried everything to merge with the national communities in which we live, seeking only to preserve the faith of our fathers. It is not permitted us.' Thus did Herzl come to adopt 'the Jewish tragedy' as the 'driving force' of nationalism.[10]

The centrality of persecution myths to Zionism before the Second World War led directly both to efforts to create a coherent Jewish 'nation' and to the

41

channelling of productive energies towards the establishment of a homeland in Palestine. Using anti-Semitism as a rallying call proved useful in establishing a link between the historic victimisation of the Jews as an *apatride* people, and their future Redemption as a *rooted* people on historic soil. Zionist writings often explored deep into the ancient past, exposing a continuous and unending stream of anti-Jewish consciousness, similar to the negative force Frye identified in Old Testament narratives.

The Nazi Holocaust against the Jews of Europe would have devastating effects, destroying Jewish culture and traditions in literally thousands of cities, towns and villages, from Russia to Holland, while resulting in the death of almost six million Jewish victims.[11] For post-Holocaust Zionists, the return to Zion would take on a new and more urgent meaning. For Zionists, the traditional Jewish status in Europe as 'history's orphans' and the 'universal outsider' had relegated them to the margins of humanity, making genocide that much easier to accomplish. As Noam Penkower put it: 'The lack of an independent state doomed those defenceless human beings to the realisation of Adolf Hitler's diabolic final solution.'[12] Anti-Semitism and its ugliest manifestation, the Holocaust, made it clear that Jews were no longer safe in the Diaspora. While pogroms had been a constant feature of Jewish existence since the time of the first crusades, never before had Europe's entire Jewish population been under threat.

For some Zionists, Israel might provide a means of somehow mitigating the horrific effects of the Holocaust, if Jews were willing to work together to create a state. At the very least it would give the Jews a homeland safe from persecution, while ridding Europe's Displaced Persons camps of some of their inhabitants. Thus could triumphalist Zionists like Yehuda Gothelf claim hopefully soon after the war:

> Anti-Semitism ... [can] serve as a force for moral renewal, and for uniting the masses of Jews to make them struggle for their national and individual liberation ... Zionism is not only the outcome of Anti-Semitism; but it puts in *concrete form* the longing for redemption, the national-religious yearning of the past two thousand years.[13]

For some religious Zionists, like Yaakov Herzog, Israel would represent the 'immediate recompense and revival' after the 'greatest crime in history',[14] while for Rabbi Jung, the 'incredible restoration of the homeland' that followed the Holocaust was proof not only of 'the beginning of the emergent redemption', but also of the Jewish people's 'timeless faith in the Divine covenant'.[15] Again, the centrality of covenantal or messianic arguments was clear – Jews had been delivered because of their faith in the teleology of history, and their Covenant with God.

Nevertheless, while Zionist triumphalism was the order of the day for those who believed in the redemptive powers of Israel, other Jewish (non- or a-

Zionist) writers concerned themselves with life outside Israel, as well as the legacy of Hitler's Final Solution and its impact on Western consciousness. Those dealing with the philosophical implications of the Holocaust, that nightmarish outcome of the Western Enlightenment and the development of the modern nation-state, found little solace in the fact that the Jews possessed a narrow strip of earth, threatened on all sides by countries that wanted to drive them into the sea. If 1947 was a year to be celebrated, the 1948 'War of Independence' was a bitter struggle, where, once more, the State of Israel almost ceased to exist.

Universalising the Holocaust

For many, the lessons of the Holocaust were so immense that they could not be applicable simply to the Jewish people. The death of six million in such a systematic and barbaric manner signalled that the fundamental axioms that underpinned Western society were fatally flawed. Philosophers and world leaders entered the twentieth century filled with hope that peace and prosperity would reign, owing to advances in technology, efficiency, and communications. Rationalism and industrialisation were to bring greater prosperity and well-being for everyone. With the Holocaust, such dreams were irretrievably shattered. Some, like philosopher George Steiner, went so far as to describe the Holocaust as a Hell on earth that for ever destroyed our faith in the progress of civilisation. As he wrote of the death-camp system:

> *L'univers concentrationnaire* has no true counterpart in the secular mode. Its analogue is Hell. The camp embodies, often down to the minutiae, the images and chronicles of Hell in European art and thought from the twelfth to the eighteenth centuries. It is these representations which gave to the deranged horrors of Belsen a kind of 'expected logic'. It is in the fantasies of the infernal, as they literally haunt western sensibility, that we find the technology of pain without meaning, of bestiality without end, of gratuitous terror.[16]

The horrors of the camps for Steiner would create a 'post culture', an era characterised by malaise and a lack of utopia, where no one seemed to have faith in Western civilisation's promise of moral and cultural evolution. Steiner described the creation of a 'formidable gap in the co-ordinates of location, of psychological recognition in the western mind'.[17] The world lost its traditional sense of morality, of good and evil. It had abandoned its faith. While some turned to Communism, which Steiner labelled 'the modern totalitarian state', others simply lived in fear, waiting in terror for the re-emergence of a 'Hell above ground'.[18]

As far as Steiner was concerned, Hell had now became immanent. It was an everyday reality – a monster that could re-awaken at any moment. New forms of ethnic, national, or other fratricidal warfare could develop at any time, because our previous ideas of good and evil were destroyed – we were no longer able to distinguish between right and wrong. But what were we to do about this state of affairs? For Steiner, the key to the future lay in creating new ethical poles of good and evil – a new morality. The new Devil, the new Hell, would become associated with Hitler and the Holocaust. Good and evil in the world would therefore be judged in relation to the Nazis. Goodness would be defined in relation to the bad that human beings had done in the twentieth century, not by the fanciful imaginings of theologians or engravers.[19] If evil was represented by the Nazis and their deeds, good would come to be represented by the Jews, who emerged as the archetypal victims of history.

Steiner's second work on the Holocaust, *The Portage to San Cristobal of A. H.*, allegorised the Jewish preoccupation with the Nazis, and how their lives have changed since 1945. In a fictional dialogue between good and evil, Steiner's characters combed the South American jungles in the 1980s, hunting for the still living Hitler, who continued to personify the evils of Nazism. In this novella, the creator of Hell, the secularised Satan, was hunted down and captured by the very people he tried to destroy decades before. Steiner here tapped into what he believed to be the essence of post-war Zionism, and its reliance on negative myths of persecution and Fall. His fictional dialogue demonstrated how the other served to imbue the Jewish nation with an identity separate from mere religious symbology or mythical understanding. But while he echoed this Zionist argument, it was with a great deal of irony. As Hitler was brought to trial at the end of the book, the frail and sickly Führer seemed conscious of his 'world historic role' as the (re)creator of the Jewish nation. As Steiner's Hitler queried:

> [D]id Herzl create Israel or did I? . . . Would Palestine have become Israel, would the Jews have come to that barren patch of the Levant, would the United States and the Soviet Union, Stalin's Soviet Union, have given you recognition and guaranteed your survival had it not been for the Holocaust? It was the Holocaust that gave you the courage of injustice, that made you drive the Arab out of his home, out of his field, because he was in your divinely ordered way . . . Perhaps I *am* the Messiah, the true Messiah, the Sabbatai whose infamous deeds were allowed by God in order to bring his people home . . . *The Holocaust was the necessary mystery before Israel could come into its strength.*[20]

In this sense, negative created positive, just as for early Christians, Satan became central to a belief in the fundamental goodness of God. Strangely, Steiner also paralleled Hitler with a sort of Moses-like figure, who led the Jewish people into the wilderness, so that they could find their promised land. For Steiner, the Jews ironically needed a Hitler-like symbol of evil to live in the modern world, because to kill him, as Friedrich Nietszche 'killed' God, would destroy the cultural and ethical boundaries of the 'post culture'. In this sense, the creation of Hell brought about a sort of Heaven for the Jewish people. Their 'abstract' nature, long a focal point in anti-Semitism, was transformed, and a new dichotomy emerged – with a concretised Heaven and a concretised Hell. Wilsonianism, and the belief in Redemption through the nation-state, became the ultimate godsend for nations, while a national Hell (the Holocaust) threatened rootless or fragmented nations who were unable to defend themselves. Hitler became as essential to the morality of our 'post cultural' world as Satan was to the early Christians. In this work, Hitler emerges as the latest incarnation of evil threatening the Hebrew people, little different (in kind) from the Pharaoh of Exodus, Nebuchadnezzar, and Antiochus Epiphanes, although certainly much worse in degree.

Yet in other respects, Hitler is obviously very different from the others. He is the only modern manifestation of evil, and he is also a Devil that the whole world can hate. He is not just the enemy of the Jews, but also of Russians, Americans, British, French, Yugoslavs and Poles – indeed, the list is endless. Making Hitler the Devil means that, while he is primarily the enemy of the Jews, he is also the enemy of many other people, and they too can potentially claim some sense of victimhood, since he did not simply destroy the Jews – he also destroyed Western civilisation in the process, according to Steiner. In this sense, the lessons of the Holocaust are specifically applicable to the Jews, but universally applicable to everyone else. Because Hitler destroyed Christian morality, Jews have no choice but to share their Devil with the rest of the world, as Harold Kaplan explains: 'all men have become "jews" (with the small "j" in Jean-François Lyotard's usage) and must adopt that suffering at Lodz and Warsaw as the gentiles of old adopted that of Christ. Hitler and his followers were the anti-Christ, because, as vulgar Nietzscheans, they would overthrow a traditional "morality of the weak" for its presumption against nature's law.'[21]

Even postmodernists have joined the fray, as Julia Kristeva and Slavoj Žižek both engage in a species of philosemitism. Through specialised jargon, the Jewish people are transformed into the 'nexus', 'trope', or 'signifiers' for the 'decentered, destabilized, postmodern subject in a theoretical system that persists in defining (or "fetishizing") them from without'. Fetishising Jewish 'otherness', they make it something to be embraced, something useful in understanding the self, in the process, as Elizabeth Bellamy recalls, 'privileg[ing] the very figure of the Diaspora Jew anti-Semitism has traditionally scorned'.[22]

Certainly, there are many well-meaning philosophers and historians who have sought to universalise the lessons of the Holocaust, irrespective of how opaque their vocabulary might appear. Nevertheless, there are inherent dangers in such an exercise, one of the chief dangers being trivialisation. Those who attempt to universalise the Holocaust can forget that its lessons originally applied to the Jewish people, and not the entire human race. Judy

Chicago's work is a typical example of how universalism can be misapplied. For her, the Holocaust has become 'a window into an aspect of the unarticulated but universal human experience of victimization', as well as a 'bridge towards the creation of "a new global community based on human shared values"'.[23] As Lawrence Langer astutely cautions, while it is laudable to try to understand the universal implications of the Holocaust, one must also be wary, lest its original meaning be lost in a sea of meaningless banal optimism. In trying to extract some abstract good from the ashes of the Final Solution, there is the real danger that Chicago and her contemporaries merely belittle the suffering of those who lived and died in the concentration camps by trying to apply the Holocaust's lessons to everyone.[24]

The French intellectual Alain Finkielkraut has taken a position similar to that of Langer and others, raising concerns about the universalisation and metaphorisation of the Jewish tragedy. For him, maintaining the Jewish nature of the Holocaust is of central importance. As part of the post-Holocaust generation, Finkielkraut has often described the tremendous moral value attached to being Jewish after 1945, inheriting the identity of a victim without ever having had to suffer from genocide. It is a moral legacy, passed on, generation after generation. All Jews become heroes in a sense, because they have endured, despite Hitler's evil plans.[25] While this was a positive aspect of his early childhood, this heroising of the victim becomes a worrying aspect of Jewish identity. In coming to terms with the rise of 'negationism' or Holocaust denial in France, Finkielkraut has severely criticised those who, in seeing Israel as a positive outcome of the Holocaust, 'mitigate the genocide by looking for meaning to its absurdity and entertaining the notion that such an affront is reparable'.[26] He criticises Zionists such as Gothelf, Herzog, and Jung, since for these people, 'the existence of Israel gives a minimal justification to the genocide'.[27]

While Steiner raised ontological and philosophical questions about universalising the Holocaust, Finkielkraut has spoken openly against universalisation, arguing that this 'minimal justification' in a philosophical sense has led to concrete problems of Holocaust revisionism. Much of Finkielkraut's writing deals with the lessening importance of the Holocaust as a warning, and as a metaphor. He blames those who reduce the Holocaust to a few symbols and 'these few majestic words, *Auschwitz*, *Holocaust*, the *Six Million*'. Such reductionism, he has argued, leads invariably to a trivialisation of the Holocaust's importance, while contributing to a 'growing lapse of memory'.[28]

The primary problem he sees with this sort of 'lazy' remembrance is that it promotes misuse, creating problems for those who are tasked with keeping Holocaust memories alive. As he laments: 'Used in contexts to which it does not apply, weakened by its metaphorical use, and degraded by needless repetition, the term "genocide" is wearing out and dying. The *exhaustion of meaning* makes it easier for the workers for the negation to do their job.'[29] The more the Holocaust is invoked, Finkielkraut fears, the more it is trivialised and divorced from its original meaning. The Holocaust therefore becomes seen simply for its instrumental uses, to give the Jews special rights because they have suffered more than any other nation.[30]

While Langer is clearly critical of non-Jews who try to universalise the Holocaust without fully grasping its meaning, Finkielkraut attacks Jewish Zionists who have belittled the Holocaust's significance by using Jewish suffering for political purposes. For him, the danger involved in such an exercise is obvious. Not only can Holocaust deniers accuse the Jews of manipulating their own genocide; other non-Jewish groups can follow the Zionist example. Echoing Steiner's view about the creation of a Devil-Hitler, Finkielkraut has also offered his views on this new morality:

> [U]niversal conscience formed itself anew by putting the face of Hitlerism on absolute evil ... Nazism is invoked almost religiously to represent civilization's Other; and to represent Nazism, one invokes its supreme horror, the physical annihilation of peoples or ethnic groups denied human status ... Satan was incarnated in the person of Hitler, who from then on was merely the allegory of the demon. Nazism, the ultimate truth of oppression and the model for all abominations past and future, also became the reference for all accusatory discourse. The event was seized, taken in, and abstracted by the Idea, and the Idea eventually deteriorated into insult: if everyone agrees on a single definition of the enemy, everyone is tempted to apply that image to his own opponent in order to justify the battle he is fighting.[31]

For Finkielkraut, as for Steiner, Hitler has become the world's secularised Devil, and the Holocaust has become the world's worst tragedy – ever. This literally *invites* non-Jewish groups to apply the imagery of the Holocaust to their own situations, since it becomes the ultimate form of national or racial victimhood. Secularising Satan and Hell has spawned a new and dangerous breed of discourse, which, while reducing the importance of Jewish suffering, has allowed other groups to increase their relative power. As Finkielkraut again explains:

> Since Hitler's time, every villain is a fascist, and every victim wears the yellow star. There is no revolution, no revolt, no struggle, no matter how minor its object, that fails to go rummaging through the past only to end up presenting itself in terms of this particular period of history. Every oppressed minority from women to Occitanians saw fit to declare *its* genocide, as if *doing anything short of this* would render that minority uninteresting, incapable of being recognized; as if the revindication of genocide were the cornerstone of the justice of the minority's cause and the validity of its aspirations. By using the word invented in 1944 to designate the *putting to death* of entire peoples, today's minority groups affirm their identity and legitimate their existence ... Antifascism had established the Jews as *value*: as the gold standard of oppression, as the paradigm of the victim.[32]

47

Here clearly is the danger of over-generalisation, a process that appears to be all but inevitable to Finkielkraut, as well as to Steiner. What Finkielkraut is attacking is the extent to which general myths of Fall and Redemption have become specifically intertwined with the Jewish example. If one is to use Fall imagery to promote nationalism, there seems now to be a stronger impulse than every before towards using *Jewish* Fall imagery instead. Rather than being a victim of 'genocide', one is now a victim of a 'Holocaust'. Aggressors become Nazis, victims become Jews. Finkielkraut is certainly not alone in articulating this fear. As more and more non-Jewish groups have seen the moral value of Jewish suffering, its lessons have become universalised and incorporated into a wide variety of movements. Ronnie Landau has described this process as 'hijacking', lamenting: 'It is indeed difficult to conceive of any subject that has been quite so regularly misunderstood, misused and misrepresented.'[33] No doubt because of this, many Jewish historians and philosophers, frustrated by the repetition of 'Holocaust', have dropped the term in favour of the Hebrew term for desolation – 'Shoah'.[34]

What emerges from a philosophical reading of the Holocaust and its aftermath is a confusion among writers on how to address the lessons of the Final Solution. Should they be universalised, or not? For some, like Steiner, universalisation is an inevitable process, one that can no longer be controlled by Jewish intellectuals and historians. Like the suffering of Christ, it becomes part of history and Western thought. Others, like Lyotard, Kristeva, Žižek, Todorov, and Chicago cite the merits of universalisation. Everyone can now live under the same moral rules and obligations, thanks to a new secularised Devil that we can all share. If genocide is a 'crime against humanity', then the human race must collectively come to terms with its consequences. Still others, like Langer, Finkielkraut, and Landau, worry that, just as once the Western world seemed to have forgotten Jesus's Jewish origins as religious anti-Semitism raged through Europe, now those challenging the uniqueness of the Holocaust may well be twisting historical memory in order to imply that the Jewish people themselves are somehow profiting from their own destruction.

For good or ill, the universalisation of the Holocaust, both in a symbolic and historic sense, has become a reality, despite those who rightly caution against it. Throughout this study, the importance of the Holocaust as a series of metaphors and symbols will be stressed. The imagery and vocabulary of the Holocaust has provided a template for many social groups and nations, seeking to articulate (by analogy) their own real or imagined experiences of victimisation and suffering. While specific images of the Holocaust are often stirred up to legitimate social or national projects, even a general view of one's nation as suffering from genocide carries tremendous moral weight.

The comparative genocide debate and the Holocaust

Holocaust universalisation has created a new forum for non-Jewish national and social groups in the modern world. 'Hijacking' the Holocaust has proven to be an effective means of gaining attention, even if the parallels between one group's suffering and that of the Jews are far from obvious. A recent trend of the 1980s and 1990s has been a two-pronged questioning of the Holocaust's importance and relevance. The field of 'comparative genocide studies' has attempted to relativise the Holocaust by comparing it to other tragedies. Proponents of relativism often argue that the attempted genocides of their own groups were equal to or worse than that suffered by the Jews, while opponents, primarily composed of writers of the 'Functionalist' school, have reduced the importance of other genocides (or even denied them), in an attempt to maintain the Holocaust's pre-eminence. As Kaplan has discussed, succeeding generations after the Holocaust have appropriated its ethical components 'as their standard of measure for right and wrong, good and evil in the growth of moral civilization'.[35]

Landau, in discussing the debate among historians, divides the extreme positions between 'Scylla' ('insistence on uniqueness'), and 'Charybdis' ('surrender to banality'). Adopting a pure emotional approach, the 'Scylla' school demonises Nazism, views the lessons of the Holocaust as relevant only for Jews, and finds all non-Jews responsible for 'Planet Auschwitz'. Using a dispassionate and academic approach, the 'Charybdis' school finds the Holocaust 'a mere symbol for the baseness of human nature', rendering it infinitely susceptible to analysis. Further, this school attempts to de-Judaise the subject, submerging it in moral education, philosophy, psychology, and theology – a process that obscures and marginalises the actual events.[36] Landau's dichotomy is unique, as it privileges neither position, while pointing out the dangers of each. While stressing the Holocaust's uniqueness and importance, he also speaks out against the 'grotesque competition in suffering' that has been the inevitable result of such debates, to the extent that: 'Mine [my suffering] is bigger than yours! Only *my* genocide is therefore real genocide.'[37]

The Holocaust as unique in the annals of comparative genocide

As Steiner, Kaplan, Finkielkraut, and others have discussed, the Holocaust *is* unique from many perspectives: technologically, philosophically, numerically, and on many other levels as well. Where scholars such as Steven Katz and Seymour Drescher have differed is in their need to downplay the atrocities inflicted on other groups in order to assert their own theories of uniqueness. In this sense, they become 'comparative genocidalists', initiating an ugly turf war over who is relatively the worst victim.[38] For Katz, asserting the Holocaust's uniqueness has involved downplaying, or even denying, the existence of many other genocides, as if the mere existence of other genocides somehow competes with the Holocaust.

In his discussion of North American indigenous peoples (or First Nations), the Ukrainians, and the Armenians, Katz has denied these peoples the status of having been the victims of genocide. In his example of the First Nations, Katz has used selective statistics to 'prove' that most of the eighteenth- and nineteenth-century indigenous deaths were the result of disease and accident, not deliberate policy.[39] Similarly, in his discussion of famine in Ukraine (1932–34), Katz refuses to use the term genocide, since Stalin was not trying to kill *all* Ukrainians – a highly contentious point, in the light of Robert Conquest's conclusion (in *The Harvest of Sorrow*) that more than 7 million Ukrainians died in the disaster.[40] The Armenian genocide is similarly dismissed, since Armenians were killed for being 'secessionists', 'Russian spies', and 'fifth columnists', not because they were the victims of a 'totalistic' ideology of hate, based on their destruction.[41]

In a similar vein, Seymour Drescher has dismissed any concept of a 'black genocide' deriving from the Atlantic slave trade, since slaves were able to survive, and develop 'religion, family life … leisure and arts, independent economic activities, consumption patterns … complex patterns of human relationships'.[42] Drescher posits that, since Blacks were 'part of a durable system' in which they played a key part as 'actors', their experiences were in no way similar to those of the Jews.[43]

Much of this type of Functionalist thinking stems from a generalised feeling of victimisation, a view that the entire Western world bears some measure of responsibility for the Holocaust. The Nazis are the most violent and obvious exponents of anti-Semitism; but anyone who allowed the Holocaust to happen shares some measure of guilt. Historians such as Daniel Goldhagen and Richard Rubenstein are quick to accuse not only the Germans, but most other Europeans as well, for failing to save the Jews, or at least, for not actively combating Nazism when they had the chance. Rubenstein has argued that 'far more Europeans objected to the methods Hitler employed to eliminate the Jews than to his objectives'.[44] For Goldhagen, the key to understanding the Holocaust is the fact that its perpetrators 'were overwhelmingly and most importantly Germans', and that while 'hundreds of thousands of Germans contributed to the genocide', millions knew about it as well, yet did nothing.[45] For uniqueness theorists, there are few groups unworthy of attack. Other genocides are seen to be competing with Functionalist interpretations, rather than complementing their research by further proving the existence of barbarism and brutality in the world.

An extension of this uniqueness argument concerns the uniqueness of the State of Israel, and its right not have its government or its policies criticised, nor certainly its existence. For some historians and philosophers, there are extremely close links between anti-Zionism and anti-Semitism, as, since 1947, the destiny of Israel and the Jewish people are intimately bound together. Elie Wiesel, for example, has asserted that 'antisemitism and anti-Zionism are one', implying that attacks on the Jewish nation-state constitute attacks on the nation itself.[46] As Irwin Cotler elaborated, at a conference exploring these links:

> The new antisemitism is a denial of the right of Israel, of the Jewish people, to live as an equal member of the family of nations. What is intrinsic to each form of anti-semitism, common to both is the notion of discrimination. It has simply passed from the realm of discrimination against Jews as individuals to discrimination against Jews as a collectivity, against Jewish peoplehood.[47]

Thus the Jewish people, according to Cotler and others, have come to define themselves in relation to their national state, and the State emerges as unique because its founding people, their history, and their sufferings, are unique. However, this type of association has a direct impact on theories of the Holocaust. If Israel is unique and moral because the Holocaust is unique and moral, then logically, if the Holocaust is not unique and unprecedented, then *ipso facto*, the *raison d'être* of the State of Israel comes into question. This is precisely the crux of Finkielkraut's argument – that Israel's legitimacy as a country needs to stand on its own, separate from the actions of the Israeli government. The machinations of Ariel Sharon and others against Palestinian civilians and suicide bombers alike should not open any doors for Holocaust revisionists. The horrors of the Holocaust should not be used for political ends, neither by non-Jewish groups, nor by Zionists, however beneficial such politicisation might appear to be.

Against uniqueness: multiple genocides and holocausts in history

From a more 'Charybdis' perspective, David Stannard has been one of the most ferocious critics of the uniqueness thesis, which he feels has allowed the Israeli government to conceal and condone their own 'on-going genocidal actions' – certainly an extreme position, but one echoed also by some Palestinian nationalists. Engaging in a species of conspiracy theorising, he dismisses the uniqueness theory as 'the hegemonic product of many years of strenuous intellectual labor by a handful of Jewish scholars and writers who have dedicated much if not all of their professional lives to the advancement of this exclusivist idea'.[48] As Stannard laments, anyone questioning the unique-ness of the Holocaust is automatically labelled an anti-Semite. Stannard has thus attacked those, like Katz and Drescher, who have lumped comparative genocide historians with Holocaust deniers and neo-Nazis, denying other national groups the right to articulate their own experiences of victimisa-tion.[49] Moreover, through one's seeing the Jews as 'chosen', other groups become by definition '*un*-chosen'. Their deaths become somehow less important, and therefore less worthy of remembrance, recognition, or compensation.[50]

While his prose is sometimes distasteful, Stannard is no Holocaust denier. Rather, he has been trying to highlight the destruction of North America's First Nations, and has found himself stymied in his efforts. Stannard's *American Holocaust* (1992) advanced that the average rate of depopulation in the Americas since 1492 had been between 90 and 98 per cent, owing to a combination of 'firestorms of microbial pestilence *and* purposeful genocide'.[51] Through a mixture of disease, slave labour, massacre, and forced resettlement, the death toll from continual orgies of violence was fixed at roughly 100 million people, making the destruction of the American Indians 'far and away, the most massive act of genocide in the history of the world'.[52] The lack of recognition for these multiple genocides over five centuries is perhaps responsible for Stannard's acerbic tone, and for his own seeming 'exclusivism'.

A similar motive informs the activities of historians such as Vahakn Dadrian and Ian Hancock, who have been trying to situate the Armenian and Romani genocides within the Holocaust tradition. Dadrian's account of Armenian history, while impeccable researched, does rely on Holocaust comparisons to strengthen its arguments. He has argued, for example, that the Armenian genocide was worse than the Holocaust on an individual level, since the emphasis was not on a quick or technologically advanced form of mass killing. Rather, it focused on 'dying as a prolonged and agonising experience', which involved the use of common farm implements to mutilate bodies horribly. Unlike the Nazi genocide, which was 'streamlined, mechanised and systematic through the use of advanced technology', and which used 'special cadres', the Armenians were brutalised by local Turkish populations, who killed in whatever manner they chose.[53]

Ian Hancock has made a convincing case for the Romani genocide as a primary part of the Holocaust, since the Romani were also singled out for the Final Solution, and had proportionally more of their people killed than did the Jews. Hancock has also claimed that the Romani genocide was worse in some respects, since the Nazis maintained a deliberate policy of killing them from the beginning, unlike their solutions to the 'Jewish Question', which at first focused on deportation and resettlement.[54] Hancock, like Dadrian, has attacked the marginalisation of his people, and specifically the fact that Romani were traditionally dismissed as 'others' in most of the Holocaust literature, and in the Holocaust Museum in Washington DC.[55]

Israel Charny, the executive director of the Institute on the Holocaust and Genocide in Jerusalem, has also raised doubts about the uniqueness thesis, strenuously objecting to what he describes as 'a fetishistic atmosphere in which the masses of bodies that are not to be qualified for the definition of genocide are dumped into a conceptual black hole, where they are forgotten'.[56] This fetishising, he argues, ignores the reality of other peoples' suffering, substituting for sympathy and compassion what has been termed 'moral bookkeeping'.[57] Still others have attacked the uniqueness thesis as 'gerrymandering', and 'an intellectual sleight of hand'. A common argument is that uniqueness theorists have picked specific aspects of the Nazi Holocaust that distinguish it from other genocides, while ignoring important similarities that join many different nations together as fellow sufferers.[58]

Generally, writers on this side of the debate are characterised by their anger and frustration at what they feel is an unfair double standard, and a deliberate attempt on the part of some Holocaust historians to dismiss their sufferings, in the hope of perpetuating the uniqueness of their own experiences. Unfortunately, while these writers do raise important issues about how history should be presented, their attacks on the relative importance of the Holocaust only marginalise them further. Rather than asserting their own experiences as unique, they 'piggy-back' on the Jewish Holocaust, which can at best succeed in making public perceptions of their suffering poor copies of the original 'frame of reference'. While their factual evidence is no doubt correct, there seems to be a certain 'anti-establishment' rhetoric here. Jews as the 'establishment' of victims are somehow obliged to accept criticism; but when they do debate, their own perspectives are condemned.

Reacting against what they perceive as a moral monopoly, Stannard and Buckley are right to criticise the generalised use of the label 'anti-Semite'. At the same time, however, their conspiratorial tone raises questions about their own motivations. The fact that groups need to compare themselves to the Jews tacitly supports the uniqueness thesis, and is in many ways self-defeating. Whether Jews as the archetypal victims of genocide are being challenged or not, there is an acknowledgement that the *status quo* is clearly on the side of uniqueness arguments. Those who attempt to downplay the Holocaust to upgrade their own national groups do themselves no favours. They make recognition of their own nation's victimisation contingent on some sort of 'mild' Holocaust revisionism, which leaves a bitter taste in most mouths.[59]

On the other side, those who deny the importance of other genocides trivialise and downgrade the importance of the Holocaust, demonstrating a lack of sympathy and respect for those who have also suffered tremendous losses. In effect, the uniqueness theorists become genocide deniers themselves – by refusing to accept the reality of Armenian indigenous or Romani genocides, despite a wealth of evidence. Their own denialism may well make them straw men for Holocaust deniers, who can thereby argue that the facts underlying historical atrocities can and should be debated – that there is more than one interpretation, even in proven cases of genocide. However, as Deborah Lipstadt has acutely observed in the case of the Holocaust there are some issues without two 'sides', and the concept of a 'debate' merely introduces the false belief that deniers somehow have a valid case and should be heard. Equally troubling, Functionalists deny themselves the ability to act as mentors to other victimised groups seeking to document their own instances of oppression. Functionalism divides and condemns, alienating potential allies and fellow genocide victims. While there is only one Holocaust, there have been many genocides in the twentieth century, and there is merit in allowing fellow victims to work together to achieve recognition and justice.

'Acting' like a victim: the Holocaust as 'performative'

Contemporary debates over the Holocaust are at an impasse. Those disputing for and against the 'uniqueness' of it remain at loggerheads, each seeming to hit below the belt to advance their own particular theories. While interesting, however, why is this debate important for the study of nationalism in Serbia and Croatia? The importance here lies in understanding the uniqueness of Holocaust in a 'performative' sense, in both the ways it is unique, and the ways that it has been *presented* as unique. As Cynthia Weber has argued, nothing constitutes a 'pre-given subject' or exists as a pre-packaged event or entity. 'Rather than understanding subjects as having natural identities,' she has argued, 'subjects and their various identities might be thought of instead as the effects of citational processes.'[60] On the same subject, Judith Butler has described 'performativity' as the 'reiterative and citational practice by which discourse produces the effect it names'.[61]

While Weber's article concerns itself with the differences between 'sex' and 'gender' and their applicability in unpacking theories of state sovereignty, the implications of 'performativity' are of broader use. The concept of 'performativity' introduces the idea that maintaining the identity of a victim, or anything else for that matter, involves a continuous practice of creating 'discourse'. In other words, the difference between 'being' a victim and portraying oneself (or 'acting') as a victim is sometimes difficult to discern, for the simple reason that most people accept people, nations, and institutions according to how they present themselves.

A similar argument has been raised by David Campbell and William Connolly, who posit that, in the formation of foreign policy, the state invents its own character by 'performing' (generating policy) in a certain way, thereby enacting 'the performative constitution of stable identities'.[62] By adopting certain symbols and invoking certain types of imagery, a state 'becomes' what it wants to be. Its discourse shape its identity. While an activity in and of itself, such as the American-led bombing of Iraq in 1991, might be interpreted as an aggressive act, it might not appear so during and after the fact. If the nation 'acts' as a moral superpower, defending 'innocent' Kuwaitis and punishing a Hitler-like Saddam Hussein, then the reality of a rich and powerful country attacking a relatively weak and poor country can seem to be morally justified, even humanitarian. In describing how states control their own reality, Campbell introduces the term 'narrativizing' – where a policy-maker or nationalist leader writes a 'story', with an 'ordered plot', 'cast of characters', 'attributable motivations', and 'lessons for the future'.[63]

While much of this postmodernist jargon appears confusing, these writers are advancing a relatively straightforward thesis. In order to understand the contemporary significance of historical events, one has to understand how these events have been interpreted and presented. Of course, there is more than one way of presenting events, as we have seen through Hayden White's critique of historical interpretation. In examining the history of the Holocaust, Peter Novick has argued that, while the horrors of the Final Solution and the vast death totals are all too real, the Jewish tragedy, as we now understand it today, was formerly largely submerged under the general war crimes of the Nazis. It was not singled out as a separate tragedy until the 1960s and 1970s. What mattered was the totality of Axis evil, not the specific victimisation of the Jews. As he has written in his book on the Holocaust and collective memory in America:

> The murderous actions of the Nazi regime which killed between five and six million European Jews were all too real. But 'the Holocaust', as we speak of it today, was largely a retrospective construction, something which would not have been recognisable to most people at the time. To speak of 'the Holocaust' as a distinct entity, which Americans responded to (or failed to respond to) in various ways, is to introduce an anachronism that stands in the way of understanding contemporary responses.[64]

Novick's project has been aimed at coming to terms with Western inaction during the Holocaust, and even American Jewish inaction during a time when millions of people were being killed for simply being Jewish. Another goal has been to understand the changes in American responses to the Holocaust, and why the Final Solution began as something that was not discussed in the 1950s and 1960s, and then later evolved into a cornerstone of Jewish identity. Novick has argued that for early American survivors, a key goal after leaving Europe was to suppress the painful memories of the past, submerge themselves in mainstream America, and 'belong'.

I would argue to an extent that the same was true of Israel, where survivors, forging a new country, often looked forward rather than behind, as Flora Lewis recalled in 1961: 'People speak of the present and the future, and only when pressed, do they turn to the past. For Israel now is a self-assured, self-absorbed country, proud and expectant, too busy and eager for growth to feed on the bitter herbs of tragedy.'[65] For Novick, the key change in perception occurred after the Six Day War in 1967, which reinforced Israel's tenuous position in the Middle East. This was a rallying call for Jews to come together in defence of their homeland, and from this time forward, the Holocaust became an important part of American Jewish identity, as did a strong attachment to Israel: '[After 1967] Popular Jewish attitudes underwent a profound "Israelization". The hallmark of the good Jew became the depth of his or her commitment to Israel. Failure to fulfil religious obligations, near-total Jewish illiteracy, even intermarriage were all permissible; lack of enthusiasm for the Israeli cause (not to speak of public criticism of Israel) became unforgivable.'[66]

The war of 1967 was thus a wake-up call, proof that Israelis needed to be constantly vigilant against their hostile Arab neighbours. At the same time, however, the war was a victory, and the successful defence of the country became yet another example of 'Holocaust and Redemption'. If the creation of Israel had been cited as a redemption, so too now would the gaining of Gaza and Sinai from Egypt, the Golan Heights from Syria, and most importantly, Jerusalem and the West Bank from Jordan, herald the completeness of the State, the satisfaction of Israel's geopolitical ambitions. According to Novick, Israel could now afford to remember the Holocaust, because it was operating from a position of strength. In Jacob Neuser's words:

> The extermination of European Jewry could become the Holocaust only on 9 June when, in the aftermath of a remarkable victory, the State of Israel celebrated the return of the people of Israel to the ancient wall of the temple of Jerusalem. On that day the extermination of European Jewry attained the – if not happy, then viable – ending that served to transform events into a myth, and to endow a symbol with a single, ineluctable meaning.[67]

For Novick, 1967 is a pivotal year, both for Israel and for the commemoration of the Holocaust as a crucial nation-building event, once it, as Neuser argued, became part and parcel of Jewish mythology. Yet, even earlier, I would argue that one could see a change in perception, particularly in 1961 during the trial of Adolf Eichmann, who was the first to be charged with 'crimes against the Jewish people', rather than the more general 'crimes against humanity'. Hannah Arendt argued in 1963 that a key objective of the Eichmann trial was to force Israelis to confront their own past, as they were in danger of losing touch with the tragic elements of their history. However, not only would the trial expose the horrors of the Holocaust, it would also reify the Jewish confrontation with a 'hostile world', exemplified by the 'daily incidents on Israel's unhappy borders'.[68]

The key issue here concerns how the Holocaust was commemorated. Many Jewish intellectuals and historians, as well as other survivors, waited for more than twenty years before confronting the horrors of their past. For Novick, coming to terms with the Holocaust – indeed, naming it *The Holocaust* – had much to do with a fear that Israel was in danger of being destroyed, and, even though it had defended itself, was still in constant danger. Thus he, like Finkielkraut, suggests that the emerging importance of the Holocaust from 1967 onwards was in part a political process, to ensure that the struggles and sufferings of those who created the State of Israel would not be in vain – that Redemption would continue to follow the greatest Fall in Jewish history.

It would be remiss not to mention in passing the more extreme extension of Novick's thesis – Norman Finkelstein's *The Holocaust Industry*, which appeared in 2000, parroting many of Novick's themes, while padding them out with fresh polemical assertions. Finkelstein began by taking issue with Novick's conclusion that the use of Holocaust imagery was 'arbitrary'. Rather, he contends that there have been consistent and deliberate attempts to use Jewish suffering to justify human rights atrocities in Israel. As with Novick, for Finkelstein 1967 is the crucial starting-point for the Holocaust becoming a crucial part of modern Jewish identity. While before 1967 the Final Solution was a horrible tragedy that was not often discussed, much less invoked as a defence of Israeli interests, it later became a crucial means of proving that Israelis were victims rather than aggressors who deserved to have their own state in the Middle East.[69]

Crucially, Finkelstein argues that it was not when the Jewish people (whom he takes to be synonymous with Israel) were in a position of weakness, but rather when they were in a position of strength that this so-called Industry became all-important. It was not, he maintains, designed to promote the interests of a marginal, humiliated people, but to legitimate the growing power of a group that was already economically and politically significant: 'Through its [the Holocaust's] deployment, one of the world's most formidable military powers, with a horrendous human rights record, has cast itself as a "victim" state, and the most successful ethnic group in the United States has likewise acquired victim status.'[70] Through Finkelstein's skewed interpretation, the Holocaust Industry is a rhetorical device, a tool for manipulating world public opinion in favour of Israel. In many respects, his theories are little different from those of some Holocaust deniers.

What emerges from Novick's analysis and Finkelstein's rather vitriolic conspiracy theory is the belief (perhaps false) that a nation can recapture the essence of a national tragedy decades after the fact, and then use it instrumentally to achieve geopolitical goals. While I do not share Finkelstein's beliefs about the existence of an 'Industry', both he and Novick nevertheless highlight a certain school of thought – that by proving one's victimhood, one is able to legitimate the creation (and defence) of a national homeland. As I will later argue, the important issue here for my research is not the truth or falsehood of these beliefs, but the fact that they *were* believed by both Serbian and Croatian writers, who assiduously used such imagery in their national writings during the wars in Yugoslavia. The belief, however false, that proving victimhood legitimated past or could legitimate future nation-building activities, was crucial to both national groups. In the Yugoslav case, it became largely irrelevant whether or not this perception is true, because it was often *believed* to be true.

Understanding the importance of the Jewish nationalist experience helps us to see why other nations, (Serbs and Croats for example) have fitted their own experiences into an ethical and teleological framework. For non-Jewish nationalists, creating myths of Covenant, Fall, and Redemption allowed them to situate their nation's history within a cyclical teleological understanding of history, while underwriting this framework with ethical arguments borrowed from the Jewish example. It is certainly for these reasons that many nationalism theorists, such as George Schöpflin and Dušan Kečmanović, have created typologies of negative imagery in their respective studies of new nationalisms, as a means of bringing about 'compensation for the powerless' and 'a special moral superiority for having suffered'.[71]

Conclusions

Elias Canetti in *The Human Province* was perhaps the first to lament the use of post-Holocaust victimisation to form a base of Jewish identity. As he noted in 1945: 'The suffering of the Jews had turned into an institution, but it outlived itself. People don't want to hear about it anymore.'[72] Forty years later, German *Historikerstreit* historian Ernst Nolte would note its continued impact on the lives of Germans, the Nazi era 'seem[ing] to become more alive and powerful, not as a model but as spectre, as a past that is establishing itself as a present, as a sword of judgement hung over the present'.[73] Certainly, Nolte's 'sword of judgement' has continued well past his 1980s movement, which attempted to 'rehabilitate' German history by claiming (misguidedly) that Germans were also the victims of Nazism. The horrors of the Holocaust will continue to serve as a warning to those monitoring violence and conflict around the world.

The central theme of this chapter has been the primary role of Fall imagery in activating Jewish collective identity and nationalism. By placing myths of Fall and Redemption within a Biblical teleological tradition, Zionists argued that a universal negative historic force had been plaguing the Jews since the beginning of recorded history, contributing to a unique Jewish identity. The Holocaust proved to many Jewish writers that their old lives in the Diaspora were no longer possible, while introducing a secular image for Hell that has continued to preoccupy philosophers and nationalists of all stripes.

For many national groups, the belief (however false) that Zionists used the Holocaust instrumentally in order either to create the State of Israel, or to consolidate its borders, has been of particular importance. The apparent success of Jewish nationalists (again, however false a perception this may be) has encouraged other national groups to adopt the symbolism, imagery, and vocabulary of the Holocaust as a means to articulating their own nation's past history of victimisation. In the case of Serbia and Croatia, Holocaust imagery and more general myths of persecution and victimisation were used by nationalist writers to restructure their historical 'discourse'. Such reinterpretations of nationalist history allowed both sides to justify the often violent and illegitimate forms of statecraft they were pursuing.

NOTES

1 Quoted in Jonathan Glover, *Humanity: A Moral History of the Twentieth Century* (London: Cape, 1999) p. 349.
2 Peter Novick, *The Holocaust and Collective Memory: The American Experience* (New York: Bloomsbury, 1999) p. 12.
3 For a definition, see Cynthia Weber, 'Performative States', *Millennium: Journal of International Studies*, 27:1 (1998) pp. 77–8.
4 Branimir Anzulović, *Heavenly Serbia: From Myth to Genocide* (London: C. Hurst & Company, 1999) p. 4.
5 *Ibid.* p. 4.
6 Liah Greenfeld, *Nationalism: Five Roads to Modernity* (Cambridge, MA: Harvard University Press, 1992) p. 551. Traditionally, 'Semite' referred to those speaking a Semitic language, and included such groups as the Arabs, Phoenicians, Ethiopians, Assyrians, and Carthaginians, as well as the Hebrews. Despite its inaccuracy, however, Marr's rather selective use of the term to denote Jewish people only would gain widespread usage from the nineteenth century onward. If older forms of religious anti-Semitism (with its blood libel and 'Christ killer' imagery) had become somewhat shopworn by Marr's time, a racialist discourse based on a 'scientific' taxonomy of races had begun to complement and buttress the more traditional forms long favoured by Protestant, Orthodox, and Catholic alike.
7 Hannah Arendt, *The Origins of Totalitarianism* (London: Harcourt Brace Jovanovich, 1975). See especially pp. 3–4; 13–14; 23.
8 Kenneth R. Minogue, *Nationalism* (London: B. T. Batsford, 1967) p. 15.
9 *Ibid.* pp. 7–8.
10 Quoted in Howard M. Sachar, *A History of Israel: From the Rise of Zionism to Our Time* (Oxford: Basil Blackwell, 1977) p. 40.
11 The literature on the Holocaust is extensive, and I feel no need to offer a summary of what has been an extremely well-researched and well-discussed area. I would, however point the reader's attention to a variety of useful texts that offer a good introduction to the topic. Some general studies include Raul Hilberg's classic work: *The Destruction of the European Jews* (London: Holmes & Meier, 1985); Lucy Dawidowicz's *The War Against the Jews* (London: Pelican, 1975); Ronnie Landau's *The Nazi Holocaust* (London: I. B. Tauris, 1992), his more recent *Studying the Holocaust: Issues, Readings and Documents* (London: Routledge, 1998); and of course Martin Gilbert's impressive *Holocaust* (New York: Holt, Rinehart and Winston, 1985). For perspectives centred on the victims, see Mary Lagerway's *Reading Auschwitz* (London: Sage, 1998), and Allen Adelson and Robert Lapides' fascinating edited work, *Lodz Ghetto* (New York: Viking, 1989). For recent discussions of the perpetrators, see Charles Maier's *The Unmasterable Past* (Cambridge, MA: Harvard University Press, 1995); and Peter Fritsche's *Germans into Nazis*

(Cambridge, MA: Harvard University Press, 1998). For a focus on medical-ethical issues, such as euthanasia, medical experimentation, and forced sterilisation, see Bronwyn McFarland-Icke's *Nurses in Nazi Germany* (Princeton, NJ: Princeton University Press, 1999); Robert Proctor's *Racial Hygiene* (Cambridge, MA: Harvard University Press, 1988); Robert Jay Lifton's *The Nazi Doctors* (New York: Basic Books, 1986); Gotz Aly, Peter Chroust, and Christian Pross's recent classic *Cleansing the Fatherland* (Baltimore, MD: Johns Hopkins University Press, 1994); and of course the works of Michael Burleigh, such as *Death and Deliverance* (Cambridge: Cambridge University Press, 1994) and his later *Ethics and Extermination* (Cambridge: Cambridge University Press, 1997). Personal accounts of life during the war include Samuel Pisar's fascinating memoir *Of Blood and Hope* (New York: Little, Brown & Company, 1979), William Shirer's *The Rise and Fall of the Third Reich* (New York: Fawcett Crest, 1959), Primo Levi's *The Drowned and the Saved* (New York: Simon & Schuster, 1988) and the more recent story of Miklos Hammer, *Sacred Games*, as compiled by Gerald Jacobs of the *Jewish Chronicle* (London: Penguin, 1995).

12 Monty Noam Penkower, *The Holocaust and Israel Reborn: From Catastrophe to Sovereignty* (Urbana, IL: University of Illinois Press, 1994) pp. 248–9.

13 Yehuda Gothelf (ed.), *Zionism: The Permanent Representative of the Jewish People* (Israel: World Labour Zionist Congress, *no date given*) p. 81. (Italics his.)

14 Yaakov Herzog, *A People That Dwells Alone* (London: Weidenfeld and Nicolson, 1975) pp. 140–2.

15 Penkower, *The Holocaust and Israel Reborn*, p. 258.

16 George Steiner, *In Blue Beard's Castle: Some Notes on the Redefinition of Culture* (New Haven, CT: Yale University Press, 1972) pp. 53–4.

17 *Ibid.* pp. 55–6.

18 *Ibid.* pp. 55–6.

19 Curiously, Rudyard Kipling used the same imagery against the Germans in his First World War account of atrocities: 'We – you and I, England and the rest – had begun to doubt the existence of Evil. The Boche is saving us.' For a discussion of First World War era propaganda, see Peter Buittenhuis, *The Great War of Words: British, American and Canadian Propaganda and Fiction, 1914–1933* (Vancouver, BC: University of British Columbia Press, 1987) p. 82.

20 George Steiner, *The Portage to San Cristobal of A. H.* (London: Faber & Faber, 1981) p. 126. (Italics mine.)

21 *Ibid.* p. 40.

22 Elizabeth Bellamy, *Affective Genealogies: Psychoanalysis, Postmodernism, and the 'Jewish Question' After Auschwitz* (Lincoln, NB: University of Nebraska Press, 1997) p. 31.

23 Chicago's work is discussed in Lawrence Langer, *Preempting the Holocaust* (New Haven, CT: Yale University Press, 1998) p. 12.

24 *Ibid.* pp. 16–17.

25 This idea is described in detail in Alain Finkielkraut, *Le juif imaginaire* (Paris: Gallimard, 1982) pp. 13–14.

26 Alain Finkielkraut, *The Future of a Negation: Reflections on the Question of Genocide* translated by Mary Byrd Kelly (Lincoln, NB: University of Nebraska Press, 1998) p. 91.

27 *Ibid.* p. 91.

28 *Ibid.* p. 59. (Italics his.)

29 *Ibid.* p. 95. (Italics his.)

30 *Ibid.* p. 96.

31 *Ibid.* pp. 99–100.

32 *Ibid.* pp. 100–1. (Italics his.)

33 Landau, *Studying the Holocaust*, p. 3.
34 George Schöpflin, 'The Functions of Myth and a Taxonomy of Myth', in Geoffrey Hosking and George Schöpflin (eds), *Myths and Nationhood* (London: C. Hurst & Co., 1997) p. 31.
35 Harold Kaplan, *Conscience And Memory: Meditations in a Museum Of The Holocaust* (Chicago: University of Chicago Press, 1994) p. ix.
36 Landau, *Studying the Holocaust*, pp. 172–4.
37 *Ibid.* p. 5.
38 Steven T. Katz, 'The Uniqueness of the Holocaust: The Historical Dimension', in Alan S. Rosenbaum (ed.), *Is the Holocaust Unique? Perspectives on Comparative Genocide* (Boulder, CO: Westview Press, 1996) pp. 19–38. See pp. 19–20.
39 *Ibid.* pp. 21; 26.
40 Katz also adds, '[Stalin] wanted to exploit them', since children were not singled out for death, allowing future generations to be born. *Ibid.* pp. 30–1.
41 *Ibid.* pp. 32–4.
42 Seymour Drescher, 'The Atlantic Slave Trade and the Holocaust: A Comparative Analysis', in Rosenbaum (ed.) *Is the Holocaust Unique?*, p. 66.
43 *Ibid.* p. 66.
44 Richard L. Rubenstein, 'Religion and the Uniqueness of the Holocaust', in Rosenbaum (ed.) *Is the Holocaust Unique?*, p. 16.
45 Daniel Jonah Goldhagen, *Hitler's Willing Executioners: Ordinary Germans and the Holocaust* (New York: Alfred A. Knopf, 1996) pp. 6; 8.
46 Elie Wiesel, 'Introduction', in Menachem Z. Rosensaft and Yehuda Bauer (eds), *Antisemitism: Threat to Western Civilization: Selected Papers Based on a Conference Held at The New York University School Of Law 27 October 1985* (Jerusalem: Vidal Sassoon Center for the Study of Antisemitism, Hebrew University of Jerusalem, 1989) p. 12.
47 Irwin Colter, 'International Antisemitism', in Rosensaft and Bauer (eds), *Antisemitism*, p. 15.
48 David E. Stannard, 'Uniqueness as Denial: The Politics of Genocide Scholarship', in Rosenbaum (ed.) *Is the Holocaust Unique?*, p. 167.
49 *Ibid.* p. 168.
50 *Ibid.* p. 194.
51 David Stannard, *American Holocaust: Columbus and the Conquest of the New World* (Oxford: Oxford University Press, 1992) p. xii (italics his). Tzvetan Todorov earlier advanced similar themes in his book *The Conquest of America: The Quest for the Other* (New York: Harper & Row, 1984).
52 Stannard, *American Holocaust*, p. x.
53 Vahakn N. Dadrian, 'The Comparative Aspects of the Armenian and Jewish Cases of Genocide: A Sociohistorical Perspective', in Rosenbaum (ed.) *Is the Holocaust Unique?*, p. 105.
54 Ian Hancock, 'Responses to the Porrajmos: The Romani Holocaust', in Rosenbaum (ed.) *Is the Holocaust Unique?*, pp. 42–3. Hancock eventually succeeded in becoming a member of the board of the Holocaust Memorial Museum.
55 *Ibid.* pp. 40–1. A recent addition to comparative genocide issues is Mike Davis's fascinating research on famine and mass death in India, China, and Brazil. As Davis argues, between 12.2 and 20.3 million people died as a result of British corruption, arrogance and misrule during periods of intense drought from 1876 to 1902. The title of his work is a good example of how the term can be used to fit a wide variety of different contexts: Mike Davis, *Late Victorian Holocausts: El Niño Famines and the Making of the Third World* (London: Verso, 2001). See especially pp. 6–16.

56 Stannard, 'Uniqueness as Denial', p. 192. Even though they may be lacking in a specific national agenda, the right-wing American pundit William F. Buckley has also attacked all those who label as anti-Semitic any and all who criticise Israel. This has made Buckley question whether 'the shadow of the Holocaust has been made to stretch too far in contemporary polemics'. Buckley divides Jews who discuss the Holocaust into two groups: 'There are Jews who continue to fear that the fires that lit the Holocaust might one day be rekindled. But there are also Jews who, comfortable with the protocols built up around Auschwitz, are disposed, so to speak, to prolong the period of de-Nazification indefinitely.' See William F. Buckley, *In Search of Anti-Semitism* (New York: Continuum, 1992) p. 4.
57 Stannard, 'Uniqueness as Denial', p. 193.
58 Novick, *The Holocaust and Collective Memory*, p. 9.
59 But lest we believe that all those who criticise the uniqueness thesis are benign, I should add that negationists or deniers have traditionally used the same sort of terminology, making it somewhat complex to decipher individual motivations. The negationist Serge Théon, for example, has publicly spoken out against the 'embalming of memories' by Jewish writers, such that 'Certain people are not far from believing that we are witnessing the birth of a new religion, that of the Holocaust, with its dogmas and priests.' See Finkielkraut, *The Future of a Negation*, p. 57.
60 Weber, 'Performative States', pp. 78–9.
61 *Ibid.* p. 81.
62 David Campbell, *Politics Without Principle: Sovereignty, Ethics and the Narratives of the Gulf War* (Boulder, CO: Lynne Rienner, 1993) pp. 26–7.
63 *Ibid.* p. 7.
64 Novick, *The Holocaust and Collective Memory*, p. 20. Mary Lagerwey's view of the Holocaust is the same: 'Today we think of a historically bounded phenomenon called the "Holocaust." A half-century ago, there was no such understanding: there was murder, even mass murder; there were fragments of experience, perception and information; but there was not coherent story. For as "it" happened, and even for years after, the phenomenon had no name': Mary D. Lagerwey, *Reading Auschwitz* (London: Sage, 1998) p. 47.
65 Flora Lewis, 'Israel on the Eve of Eichmann's Trial', in Bill Adler (ed.), *Israel: A Reader* (Philadelphia, PA: Chilton Books, 1968) p. 80.
66 Novick, *The Holocaust and Collective Memory*, pp. 148–52.
67 Quoted in *Ibid.* p. 150.
68 Hannah Arendt, *Eichmann in Jerusalem: A Report on the Banality of Evil* (London: Faber & Faber, 1963) pp. 7–8.
69 Norman Finkelstein, *The Holocaust Industry: Reflections on the Exploitation of Jewish Suffering* (New York: Verso, 2000) p. 32.
70 *Ibid.* p. 3.
71 Schöpflin, 'The Functions of Myth and a Taxonomy of Myth', pp. 30–1.
72 Quoted in: Robert D. Kaplan, *Balkan Ghosts: A Journey Through History* (New York: St Martin's Press, 1993) pp. 130–1.
73 *Ibid.* p. 151. Eric Hobsbawm similarly described a process of exclusion at work after the Second World War, where German history was marginalised by 'those on the winning side of the Second World War'. He argues: 'Those who were on the losing side or associated with it were not only silent and silenced, but virtually written out of intellectual life except in the role of "the enemy" in the moral world drama of Good versus Evil.' See Eric Hobsbawm, *Age of Extremes: The Short Twentieth Century 1914–1991* (London: Penguin Group, 1994) pp. 4–5.

3

Slobodan Milošević and the construction of Serbophobia

The history of Serbian lands ... is full of instances of genocide against the Serbs and of exoduses to which they were exposed. Processes of annihilation of the Serbs in the most diverse and brutal ways have been continuous. Throughout their history they have faced the fiercest forms of genocide and exoduses that have jeopardised their existence, yet they have always been self-defenders of their own existence, spirituality, culture, and democratic convictions. (SANU, 'Declaration Against the Genocide of the Serbian People')[1]

THIS CHAPTER CHARTS the rise of Serbian nationalism, while examining many of the important myths that evolved as a concomitant to it. The above citation, from a statement by the Serbian Academy of Sciences and Arts, encapsulates what became a dominant view of Serbian history after 1986 – a long-suffering, but heroic nation, struggling for centuries against annihilation. I will begin by exploring elements of the Battle of Kosovo, a battle fought between Serbian and Turkish forces on 28 June 1389, which ultimately resulted in Serbian subjugation to five centuries of Ottoman rule. In legend, the Battle was also a Serbian sacrifice, which elevated them to the status of a heavenly and chosen people. This chapter begins by exploring the legacy of this famous myth, and how it has become a template for many Serbian portrayals of history. It is crucial to understand how this myth was generalised and fused with Jewish imagery, in such a way that Kosovo became the 'Serbian Jerusalem'. Myths highlighting the glorious but tragic aspects of Serbian history were of central importance in legitimating the dismantling of the Yugoslav Federation, and the expansionist ambitions of Milošević and his colleagues.

Kosovo, and more general myths of Golden Age and Fall, were instrumentalised first in the case of the Kosovar Albanians, and secondly, and more importantly, in the case of the Croats. As the conflict progressed, writers came to identify a Serbian version of anti-Semitism – 'Serbophobia' – a genocidal and expansionist strategy, supposedly used throughout history by Serbia's enemies. Using a nationalist teleology, Serbian writers specifically targeted the Croats as the harbingers of Serbophobia, viewing them as a truly Biblical antagonist, which had been operating against the Serbs since the division of the Roman Empire. This chapter reviews the nineteenth- and early twentieth-century manifestations of Croatian 'Serbophobia', laying the basis for an analysis of the Second World War, the SFRY, and the more contemporary conflicts in Croatia and Bosnia-Hercegovina.

Contextualising propaganda: the rise of Serbian nationalism

It is accurate to suggest that for most of the lifetime of the SFRY Serbian nationalism was subordinate to Communism, and did not become an important factor until 1980. The Serbian capital Belgrade became the capital of Yugoslavia, and Josip Broz Tito managed to repress most manifestations of Serbian nationalism during his lifetime. A relatively high percentage of Serbs supported Tito's Communist system, even if they were dissatisfied with particular aspects of it. The crucial break came with Tito's death after nearly four decades at the helm of the country. The lack of any strong, articulate non-nationalistic leader with Tito's charisma, capable of exercising the same level of control, created a power vacuum at the federal centre. This vacuum would soon be filled by aspiring nationalists at the level of the constituent republics. Without a Yugoslav-oriented Tito at the helm, power bases within the individual republics became more important, while power at the Federal centre was greatly weakened.[2]

The rise of Serbian nationalism was largely a reaction to events in the autonomous province of Kosovo, a region that was traditionally seen as the Serbian heartland, but that was also home to an Albanian majority – some 90 per cent of the population. Kosovo was the seat of the early Serbian Orthodox Church, and was the site of some of the most important Orthodox monasteries in Yugoslavia, such as Gračanica – where the remains of the famous Serbian King Milutin (1282–1321) were interred.[3] The Plain of Gazimestan at Kosovo Polje (Field of the Blackbirds) was the scene of the Serbs' battle against the Ottoman Empire, making Kosovo the home of their best-loved religious shrines, and the locus of their most famous defeat.

Albanians, not Serbs, were the first to articulate nationalist demands after 1980. Kosovar Albanian students demonstrated at Pristinë University for Albanian autonomy and republic status, provoking riots that led to a large number of injured Kosovars and security forces, and nine deaths.[4] The Serbian government clamped down the following year with a state of emergency; and over the next eight years almost 600,000 Kosovars, over half the adult population, would face either arrest, interrogation, or police harassment.[5] In reaction to Albanian secessionism, amid fears of 'Greater Albania', the Serbian Academy of Sciences and Arts drew up a *Memorandum* in 1986 – a long list of Serbian grievances against their treatment within the Federation. Much of the document dealt with the 'genocide' of Serbs in Kosovo, and articulated the need for Serbs throughout Yugoslavia to assert themselves collectively. The 1974 Constitution, which decentralised power in Yugoslavia and put an end to Serbia's control over two of its former provinces (Kosovo and Vojvodina), was blamed for the loss of Serbian power and prestige. The *Memorandum*'s architects would eventually play a prominent role in spurring Serbian nationalism and in the dismemberment of the Federation.

Attempts by the President of the Serbian Communist Party, Ivan Stambolić, to deal with Kosovo's civil unrest through constitutional revision and consensus proved to be ineffective, and the friction between Serbs and Albanians escalated.[6] It was into this breach that an unlikely candidate inserted himself. Slobodan Milošević, a former Belgrade banker and protégé of Stambolić, was in all respects a colourless Communist bureaucrat and a most unlikely nationalist. It was he that Stambolić sent to Kosovo on 24 April 1987, to hear the grievances of the Kosovar Serbs, who claimed that they were being discriminated against by the police and local government. While his mission was to pacify the people, Milošević did exactly the opposite after hearing stories of Albanian police assaulting Serbian demonstrators. Milošević's simple phrase *Niko ne sme da bije narod* (No one has the right to beat the People) would make him an instant hero for taking on the Albanian leadership, while making the antagonism between Kosovar Albanian and Serb explicit.[7]

Milošević was one of the first to sense Yugoslavia's changing fortunes, and embraced nationalism with opportunistic fervour, correctly sensing that a 'turning- point' was about to begin. While no nationalist himself, Milošević opened the Pandora's box that for ever changed the nature of Serbian, and by extension Yugoslav, politics. The former American ambassador Warren Zimmermann described Milošević as having made a 'Faustian pact with nationalism', although his 'extraordinary coldness' and inability to care for anyone, even the Serbs, made his choice surprising.[8] Milošević soon ousted his long-time mentor, Stambolić, and, with the support of the media, took power in December 1987. He appealed to an emerging sense of Serbian unity, and claimed to speak for Serbs throughout Yugoslavia – a tacit warning to other republican leaders that their boundaries would provide little protection from Serbian intervention. Promising to end the persecution of Serbs in Croatia, Bosnia-Hercegovina, and Kosovo, he advocated a strengthening of the Orthodox Church and a privileging of Serbian cultural and social institutions, which he argued had long been repressed under Communism.[9]

If we review Kenneth Minogue's three-stage process of nationalism, we can see that Milošević clearly articulated the 'stirrings' stage of Serbian nationalism, through the acknowledgement that Serbs were suffering in Kosovo. The 'struggle' stage was soon to follow.[10] Milošević convinced his people that a great turning-point had arrived in Serbian history. He articulated what Dušan Kečmanović has called the myth of 'the right moment',[11] or what George Schöpflin described as a 'myth of rebirth and renewal'.[12] Both these types of myth basically advanced the same claim – that it was time for Serbia to reassert itself under a powerful nationalist leader who could protect its interests. Milošević was seemingly the man for the job. While alternative readings of Serbian nationalism existed at this time, and continued to hold sway over some segments of the population, the increasing power of the Kosovo myth, the decline of Communism, and the general sense of loss and marginalisation stirred by the SANU and other organisations soon made it increasingly difficult for other voices to be heard.

Another important aspect of this nationalist platform was the re-Serbianisation of Kosovo and Vojvodina, both of which possessed autonomous status under the 1974 Constitution. The effects of this decentralising constitution were soon reversed. By the beginning of 1988, overt discrimination against the Kosovars began, as Milošević stepped up his anti-Albanian rhetoric, to an increasingly fired-up population. Milošević's nationalism was advanced in terms of an 'Anti-Bureaucratic Revolution' and 'The Happening of the People', two rather banal catchphrases that were used to justify the re-emergence of nationalism and Milošević's cementing of political power.

By February 1989 Milošević had pushed through a series of amendments to the Serbian constitution, eliminating the provinces' authority to pass their own legislation. By organising mass rallies, he was able to force the leadership in Vojvodina to resign. By September 1990 a new constitution had fully subordinated Vojvodina and Kosovo to central Serbian control. These two coups quadrupled Serbia's allotted seats in federal institutions, conferring on the republic effective control over the outcome of all votes at the federal level.[13] Serb actions against the Albanians in Kosovo demonstrated definitively the collapse of the federal system. The lesson of Kosovo was obvious – the system was no longer strong enough, or was unwilling, to restrain belligerent republics, and was unable to protect basic human and constitutional rights.[14]

Milošević's intimidation of other republics in the SFRY soon led to secessionist movements around the country. The first overt move was made by the Slovenian leader Milan Kučan, whose overtures for decentralisation were violently rejected by Milošević – who in turn threatened civil unrest and violence. The machinations of the JNA in Slovenia also set the stage for a showdown. Harassed by the JNA and threatened by Serbia, Slovenians pushed for separation from the Federation. In December 1990 Slovenia declared its independence, which later led to a short war between Slovenian and JNA troops that eventually resulted in an independent Slovenia.[15]

While Milošević was often credited with breaking up Yugoslavia and installing nationalism as the ruling ideology in Serbia, he certainly did not act alone. With him were many new nationalists who proved instrumental in the coming years. While Milošević used nationalism as a tool to gain power, he relied on the support of many 'true believers', who formed a crucial spiritual and intellectual base. Among these, the novelist Dobrica Ćosić was perhaps the most famous. Formerly a Communist believer, Ćosić wholeheartedly embraced nationalism with the decline of Yugoslavia, and became an early supporter of Milošević and his government.

While the Western press would later become obsessed with Milošević as a nationalist demagogue, he should be seen more as a supporter of nationalism than its founder. Milošević's regime provided a climate for the unrestrained articulation of nationalist sentiments, and the wholesale revision of Serbian history. Milošević's overt support of the Serbian Orthodox Church was well known. The Church joined with individual journalists, politicians, novelists, academics and military leaders in contributing to the escalation of militant nationalism. However, their role was more important. By acting as the conscience of Serbia, they providing a greatly needed spiritual underpinning for Milošević's movement. But in order to cement political power, Serbia's future strongman also needed to appeal to non-nationalist parts of the population, and promoted a 'multi-pronged ideological strategy', one that was ultimately successful in uniting a great variety of seemingly mutually incompatible forces. As Veljo Vujačić has argued:

> Analyses of the 'Milosevic phenomenon' which insist on only one dimension of his appeal (typically nationalism), are bound to miss the point. On the contrary, it was precisely the combination of simultaneous appeals to different constituencies which helps explain Milosevic's success. Yugoslavia, unity and Titoism for the party orthodox and army officers, Serbia for the nationalists, reform and rehabilitation for the intellectuals, protection for the Kosovo Serbs, social justice for the workers and pensioners – this was the Serbian leader's equivalent of Lenin's 'bread, peace, and land'.[16]

Additionally, the Milošević regime soon became adept at centralising and controlling the media. While the media in the SFRY had operated relatively unfettered, compared with other communist countries new legislation limited the scope of independent reporting. New provisions under the Serbian Penal Code, specifically Article 98, made it an offence to criticise the government or cast doubt on the country's leaders. Government ministries of Information and the Interior now had a mandate to censor, delete, or change any aspect of reporting found to be at odds with official government accounts.[17] The government-controlled Serbian Radio-Television (RTS), soon gained a broad-casting monopoly. The July 1991 Law on Radio and Television transferred parliamentary powers over radio and television directly to the government.[18] The Milošević regime also did its best to limit if not destroy independent print media, by imposing swingeing taxes while cutting supplies of newsprint and fuel. Independent papers such as *Borba, Vreme* and *Republika* were forced to pay four times more for newsprint than loyal government-controlled papers, such as *Vecernje novosti*.[19] Powerful conglomerates, such as the *Politika Group* (which owned twenty publications, a radio station and a television channel) were reduced to government appendages by 1987, giving Milošević full power to implement his nationalistic projects.[20]

While control over the media allowed the regime to determine strictly what people understood about the government and its role in the wars that were to follow, Milošević's key role, once again, was as a catalyst for nation-alism. The role of the media was assessed primarily on its ability to maintain support for Milošević's regime, and not necessarily for Serbian nationalism as such. Indeed, Milošević's role in persecuting nationalist opposition leaders was well known, exemplified by his continuous harassment of the national-ist author and politician Vuk Drasković, which included severe beatings and several attempts on his life. Nevertheless, Milošević's legacy was to create a forum where such men were able to stand for election and dissemi-nate their nationalist views to an increasingly receptive audience. His later support of influential warlords (such as Vojislav Šešelj and Željko Ražnatović Arkan) allowed Milošević to carry out much of the dirty work involved in expanding the Serbian state indirectly, without relying on the official armed forces.

The rise of numerous academic institutions and publishing houses dedi-cated to the promotion of nationalist views proved to be of immense importance. Among the more important promoters of the new Serbian line (although not necessarily linked with the government) were to be found: Velauto International, IDEA, BMG, and SANU (Serbia), the Serbian Unity Congress, and Serbian Heritage Books (USA and Canada). Other publishing houses, such as Minerva Press, The Book Guild, and L'Age D'Homme,[21] appear to have been wittingly or unwittingly pulled into the emerging propa-ganda war. Control over the Serbian Ministry of Information also provided an important outlet for nationalist views. Well- and lesser-known nationalists had access to a government-controlled forum for disseminating their nation-alist opinions. This key ministry was responsible for the co-ordination and consolidation of Serbian propaganda, and its influence in unifying reinterpre-tations of Serbian history and current events should not be underestimated. However, it was clear that, even among opposition leaders, there was surpris-ing consistency in Serbian revisionist views and propaganda, as will become apparent throughout this study. Indeed, other than the non-nationalist opposition media, and curiously, Milošević's wife Mira Marković, there were few dissenting voices within Serbia.[22]

The remainder of this chapter explores how Serbian nationalist novelists, politicians, journalists, and military leaders firmly anchored Serbian nationalism in a cyclical teleological framework, which relied heavily on myths of a Golden Age or 'Heavenly Serbia', with Serbs as a chosen people or a *nebeški narod*. Another central theme woven throughout Serbian writing was the image of the Serbs as a long-suffering, persecuted people, often likened to the Jews.

'Kosovo' and the development of Serbian consciousness

Throughout the conflict, the myth of Kosovo was touted as a key shibboleth of Serbian identity. Kosovo figured as the locus of a historic defeat, but also symbolised the awakening of Serbian values and spirituality. The Kosovo Battle was fought in the year 1389 on St Vitus' Day (28 June). The basic story surrounds Prince Lazar, an elected Serbian prince, who in legend was handed an ultimatum, whereby he was either to pay homage to the Turkish Sultan Murad I, relinquishing control of Serbian lands and taxation, or bring his forces on to Kosovo Polje to face the Sultan's army. Lazar was later approached in a dream by a grey hawk (or falcon) flying from Jerusalem, and was offered a choice: an earthly kingdom (implying victory for his forces against the Sultan), or a heavenly kingdom (where the Serbs would be defeated in battle).[23] As one Serbian source paraphrased Lazar's decision:

> If I decide to choose the earthly kingdom, the earthly kingdom lasts only for a brief time, but the heavenly kingdom always and for ever. Thus the Serbian Tsar chose the heavenly kingdom rather than the kingdom of this world. Thus the holy Tsar Lazar ... wisely led these reason-endowed lambs to lay down their lives courageously in Christ, and obtain the crown of suffering (martyrdom), so that they might all become partakers of the glory on high.[24]

The details of the battle, including the identity of the actual winners and losers, are sketchy at best. While Robert Kaplan and James Marriott both insist that the Serbs lost decisively, Tim Judah advances that the Serbs may have actually won the Battle – based on a variety of contemporary dispatches. Reviewing a wealth of evidence, Noel Malcolm insists that the Battle was a draw – neither side having clinched definitive victory.[25] In the Serbian legend of the Battle, however, there was no ambiguity – the Serbs lost, and were thereafter subjected to five centuries of Ottoman rule. What has emerged most prominently, however, was the heroism of the Serbs, dying so that their nation could be elevated as a spiritual entity. Some Serbian Orthodox Church publications during the conflict would paint the Battle as a moral and spiritual victory for the Serbs, the victory of the divine over the secular, the eternal over the temporal. Like the crucifixion, the martyrdom of Lazar and the Serbian nation raised the Serbian people and made them divine, holy, chosen, special. The following portrayal from North America was in many ways typical:

> [T]he Battle of Kosovo was, in the eyes of the world, a disastrous defeat for the Serbs. But in the eyes of heaven and of those who understand the mystery and meaning of the Battle of Kosovo, it was a glorious victory. It marked the day when the Serbian people ceased to trust in the material things of the kingdom of this world, and began to set their hope on the spiritual values of the heavenly kingdom. It marked the day when the Serbs voluntarily had sacrificed their glorious earthly kingdom and even themselves for Christ their God, so that they might be partakers of the incomparably more glorious heavenly kingdom of Christ. [26]

The Kosovo defeat became nation-defining, allowing the Serbs to transcend mere mortality. As one contemporary historian wrote with disdain, the Kosovo myth seemed like a 'cheat', since its 'merges the contradictory satisfactions of being the winner and the loser'.[27] Nevertheless, Kosovo functioned as a typical covenantal myth. There was a Fall, and a promise of Redemption, embodying the 'covenential culture' described by Akenson.[28] It also fulfilled the three aspects of Hebrew nationalism described by Kohn, as it elevated the Serbs to the status of a 'chosen people', gave them a 'consciousness of national history', and created a form of 'national messianism', while similarly democratising nationalism by means of a Covenant between God and all co-nationals.[29] Like the Jews, the Serbs could regain their promised land, through constant contemplation and 'wholehearted mourning'. This alone would allow 'the seed of that distant defeat ... to bloom into something more wonderful than victory'.[30]

The nineteenth-century development of the myth through the writings of Serbian linguist Vuk Karadzić transformed Lazar into a Christ-like figure – who led the Serbian nation to holy martyrdom so that it would achieve divine status. Furthermore, Lazar's enemies became Judas-like traitors. The Serbian warrior Vuk Branković would be demonised for crossing over to the Turkish side on the eve of the battle, and came to symbolise betrayal from within, the 'Christ killer' who represented Serbian converts to Islam.[31] This would lay the basis for an obvious example of Kečmanović's theory of 'counteridentification' – with the projection of a variety of negative characteristics on to the Moslems.[32]

The fear of traitors would also manifest itself in the Serbian national coat of arms – depicting a cross surrounded by four S's, which were originally fire-lighting flints. As Biljana Vankovska argues, the first interpretation was *Sama Srbija Sebe Spasila* – 'Serbia Alone Delivered Herself', which then changed to *Samo Sloga Srbe Spasava* – 'Only Unity Saves the Serbs', reflecting the fear of internal enemies.[33] Such symbols of counteridentification would be strengthened through the well-known epic poem 'The Mountain Wreath', written by Petar Petrović-Njegoš, a prince-bishop from Montenegro. This nineteenth-century poem glorified the exploits of one Miloš Obilić, a legendary Serbian hero from the Battle of Kosovo, supposedly responsible for the death of the Turkish Sultan Murad I, who was killed during the battle.[34] Obilić exemplified how courage and great deeds could overcome national defeat, epitomising the promise of Redemption for the Serbs, if they held true to their faith in Orthodoxy and Serbdom.

Contemporaneous with Petrović-Njegoš was the geographer Jovan Cvijić, who activated the Kosovo myth as a central component of his 'Dinaric man' – the traditional South Slav inhabitant. As Cvijić explains:

> The Dinaric is consumed with a burning desire to avenge Kosovo, where he lost his independence, and to revive the Serbian empire about which he has never ceased to dream even in the most desperate circumstances in which a man of pure reason would have despaired . . . This tenacity, this absolute faith in the national ideal, is the essential fact of his history, he considers himself chosen by destiny to accomplish the national mission . . . To kill lots of Turks is for him not only a way of avenging his ancestors but of assuaging their pain which he shares.[35]

For Cvijić, as for later interpreters, the Battle contained both positive and negative components – the valiant Serbs against the treacherous Turks. Tens of thousands were rallied for war in the nineteenth and twentieth centuries through the legend of Kosovo. It gave Serbs the will to fight, even in cases of certain defeat.

Milošević's genius in exploiting Kosovo to his advantage was readily apparent by 1989, when a huge rally was planned to commemorate the 600th anniversary of the Battle. As a precursor to the event, the relics of Prince Lazar were paraded around Serbia, with full media coverage, to be finally interred at Ravenica, Lazar's original place of rest.[36] On the plain of Gazimestan, a vast crowd of pilgrims officially estimated at between one and two million gathered for the celebrations. This was to be Milošević's shining moment, as Serbs from around the world gathered to commemorate the renewal of Serbian culture, religion and nationalism. It was at this stage that Milošević was able to transform himself into a nationalist demagogue, as he emerged triumphant from a helicopter amid cheering crowds. Orthodox priests held aloft icons of Milošević and Lazar, while thousands of men and women crowded around the podium.[37] Arguably, this was Milošević's finest hour. Secretly, however, he admitted that most of this was nothing more than 'bullshit'.[38] The spectacle was purely for the benefit of the Serbian people – to cement his growing personal power.

Whatever his personal beliefs, Kosovo secured Milošević's position as both a political and spiritual leader of the Serbian nationalist movement. Such rallies were designed to quell any opposition to Milošević's rule, by co-opting even the most virulent nationalists. By 1989, Milošević's political control over Serbia and Kosovo was unquestioned, as was the emergence of Serbian nationalism. A sharp division between nationalists and Communists appeared, with Serbs as either loyal supporters of the regime, or potential traitors. Vuk Branković, the Serbian Judas, was seemingly lurking behind every corner.[39]

Throughout Serbia, Kosovo fever gripped the population. Serbian bookstores filled their shelves with books on Kosovo, while musical artists dedicated their works to Kosovo. Even a new perfume, 'Miss 1389', evoked images of the Battle.[40] In some respects, Anthony Smith was correct when he noted the aesthetic aspects of Golden Age nationalism. Smith's general description of the use of Golden Age myths easily applied to the Serbs during this time. Serbian leaders were most adept at 'unfold[ing] a glorious past, a golden age of saints and heroes, to give meaning to its promise of restoration and dignity'.[41] Indeed, there was much in Kosovo fever that reflected the 'poetic spaces' described by Smith.

Renewal of the Serbian Orthodox Church

Alongside Kosovo, much of the revision of history involved the glorification of Serbian Orthodoxy as a repository of nationalist expression. Orthodoxy for Serbs had a certain purity, being 'purely spiritual', while 'turned towards Christ and the "Empire of Heaven"'.[42] The rise of Serbian nationalism and the instrumentalisation of Kosovo also brought to the fore a general feeling of Serbian greatness. Serbia as the 'new Byzantium' and the Serbs as a 'heavenly people' were to become increasingly popular motifs.[43] Such imagery stressed the strong Covenant that Serbs supposedly maintained with God, and reinforced the image of the Serbs as a holy, chosen people.

Speaking of his fellow Serbs, Metropolitan Amfilohije Radović of Montenegro preached: 'Our destiny is to carry the cross on this blazing divide between different worlds ... therefore the Serbian people are also divine ... Our people preserves in its bosom, in its collective memory, Jerusalem's holiness.'[44] Nevertheless, he warned that 'an insane wind tries ceaselessly to extinguish this sacred lamp'. These 'insane winds' were to be understood as Catholic and Protestant countries from the West, and Islamic countries from the east. Serbia was seemingly sandwiched in the middle of two expansionist forces, both trying to encroach on its territory.[45] Generally, the Church promoted Kosovo as the spiritual and cultural heartland of the Serbian people.[46] The 600th anniversary of the Battle was to become a year of commemoration for the past 500 years of 'suffering' under which the Orthodox Church claimed the Serbs had suffered.[47]

Coupled with the emergence of this religious-nationalist amalgam were a spate of books and articles, propagating a patriotic view of Serbian superiority. One such book, by Olga Luković-Pejanović, was suggestively titled *The Serbs: The Oldest Nation*, and claimed, among other things, that the Biblical Garden of Eden was located in Serbia, that the Cyrillic script was invented by Serbs, and that numerous ancient writers, such as Ovid, composed their works in Serbian. One curious text entitled 'Serbs – Nations Most Numerous', argued that Serbs were the most numerous (and therefore the most cosmopolitan) nation in history, having inhabited India, Mesopotamia, Siberia, and Africa. The author even claimed Alexander the Great as one of the great Serbian heroes of the past.[48]

Similarly, Serbia's minister of culture, focusing on the Serbs' uniqueness, concluded that the Serbs are one of five imperial peoples: 'It is an ancient people and one of the most Christian ones.' According to another minister of the Serbian government: 'Today, many around the world dream about being Serb ... Be happy you belong to this people. You are eternal.' Likewise, in Bosnia-Hercegovina, Velibor Ostojić, President of the Serbian Democratic Party, proclaimed triumphantly: 'Every nook of Serbian land and the Serbs themselves are a heavenly wonder, and an inspiration and example to all other peoples and countries.'[49]

A tradition of religious tolerance and love was to prove extremely important in demonstrating that the Serbs were religiously and culturally unable to be aggressors in any conflict; they could only be the victims. Kosovo allowed for the creation of a coherent nationalist system, where political and religious leaders worked side by side with opposition politicians, academics, and journalists to promote the cause of Serbian renewal. At this stage, such myths were used to re-awaken the people, and could in some ways be described as Smith's Golden Age of nationalism, with myths of origin, descent, and a heroic age. Certainly, Serbian leaders were taking advantage of their 'useable past' to cement their power as the republic transformed itself.[50]

Generalising Kosovo: Serbian and Jewish connections

We have to persevere or else we are lost. It's similar to the problem the Jews had. Kosovo is our Jerusalem. We'd rather defend it as it is, rather than have just one Wailing Wall. Kosovo is a place of Serbian national identity that we cannot give away, just as Israel can't give away Jerusalem. (Writer and musician Aleksander Pavlović in conversation with Florence Levinsohn)

Certainly a key aspect of Serbian propaganda was the belief that the nation had reached a historic turning-point – that Serbia could now relive its glory, while avenging the wrongs of the past. Nevertheless, while Kosovo resonated strongly with the Serbian people, the government also saw the need to generalise the lessons of Kosovo, to incorporate non-Serbian and contemporary symbolism into the myth, in order to justify the re-emergence of Serbia to the outside world. The lessons had to be universalised, and brought into the late twentieth century. For this reason, a new form of Kosovo interpretation began, bringing Serbia into the comparative genocide debate.

In 1988, a group of eminent Serbian intellectuals formed the Serbian–Jewish Friendship Society, headed by Klara Mandić, in the hope of paralleling the plight of Serbs and Jews. The formation of the Society and its later work proved how important the Serbian notion of 'performing' their own victimisation had become. Its primary goal was to strengthen contacts between Serbia and Israel, relations that had obviously soured with the strong anti-Zionist line advanced by Tito at the behest of his Islamic non-aligned colleagues. Activities such as city twinning were popular, with 22 twinned cities between Serbia and Israel, the most important being between Belgrade and Tel Aviv, where mutual activities, from sporting events to commercial transactions, were encouraged. Mandić brought the mayors of fifteen Serbian cities to Israel during the Gulf War, while ironically, Serbia remained a staunch ally of Iraq. Even the Serbian Crown Prince in exile, Aleksander, visited Israel to stress the commonalities between the two cultures.[51] A new museum was also formed, to show the historic 'Jewishness' of Serbia. North of Belgrade, in Zemun, the supposed ancestral home of Theodor Herzl was restored and turned into a museum.[52]

The purpose of the Society was to equate Serbian suffering with that of the Jews, allowing Serbs to enter into the comparative genocide debate. The Society's role was clearly not to represent Jewish interests, but rather, to court Israeli military support, which Serbia successfully retained until 1999. In reality, the Jewish community in Serbia was relatively small, with only 3,500 Jews in nine local communities affiliated with the Federation of Jewish Communities of Yugoslavia, a non-nationalist representative of Jewish interests.[53] The American journalist Florence Levinsohn was one of the first American Jewish writers to compare the Kosovo Battle to the Jewish legend of Masada, where approximately 1,000 Jewish warriors committed mass suicide, after a losing battle with the attacking Romans some 2,000 years ago.[54] Echoing Jovan Cvijić, Milan Bulajić, Director of the Museum of Victims of Genocide in Belgrade, ascribed a willingness to fight to Serbian 'genes', which made them see themselves as 'victims by destiny'. He also claimed that 'they are the chosen people, like the Jews. They have chosen the heavenly kingdom symbolised by Kosovo.'[55] For nationalists such as Bulajić, what it meant to be a Serb was immutable, and rooted in the ancient past. They seemingly shared much with the Jews, in terms of their willingness to fight heroically in the face of overwhelming odds.

Such views were also evident in clerical circles. As early as 1983, a petition was drawn up by Serbian Orthodox bishops to protest against the persecution of the Serbs in Kosovo. Once again, the links between Serbian and Jewish suffering were stressed:

> The Jewish people, before the menace of their annihilation and by the miracle of the uninterrupted memory, returned to Jerusalem after 2,000 years of suffering, against all logic of history. In a similar manner, the Serbian people have been fighting their battle at Kosovo since 1389, in order to save the memory of its identity, to preserve the meaning of their existence against all odds.[56]

Žarko Korać of Belgrade University also made this link explicit, in his study of the Serbian national revival. Here, he posited that the myth, like a passion play, eventually became primordial, and could not be seen as mere metaphor. The myth became central to the will to fight for a homeland. Thus:

> What [Kosovo] tells the Serbs is 'we are going to make a state again'. Just as 'Jesus is coming back' so is Lazar. It means that because we opted for the kingdom of heaven we cannot lose, and that is what people mean when they talk about Serbs as being a 'heavenly people'. In this way the Serbs identify themselves with the Jews. As victims yes, but also with the idea of 'sacred soil'. The Jews say 'Next year in Jerusalem' and after 2000 years they resurrected their state. The message is 'We are victims, but we are going to survive.'[57]

There can be little doubt that Serbian writers saw the merits of drawing overt comparisons between themselves and the Jews. Serbian claims to Kosovo were no different from Zionist claims to Israel, or so the argument went. Serbs were a persecuted nation, as were the Jews, and both *deserved* to have a national homeland. In this example of Serbian myth-making at its finest, the process of inscription, or narrativising, was obvious.

The first targets: myths of persecution and the Kosovar Albanians

The operationalisation of the Kosovo myth was first used against the Kosovar Albanians, as a means of legitimating the reincorporation of this province into an expanded Serbia. Accusations of genocide levelled against the Albanians acted as a precursor to later accusations of genocide levelled against Croats and Bosnian Moslems. For this reason, it is worth reviewing several aspects of these Serbian claims, and how they constituted the first step in a Serbian merger of Kosovo and Jewish imagery in the service of nationalism. From the very beginning, it was clear that accusing the Albanians of genocide was the key to legitimating Serbian territorial claims. By 1986, 60,000 Serbs had signed a petition, along with Serbian Orthodox bishops from New Zealand, Europe, and North America, detailing a 'fascist genocide' being inflicted on Serbs and Montenegrins.[58]

Echoing the Jewish case, anti-Albanian propaganda focused on a long history of Albanian genocide in Kosovo. Numerous Serbian publications advanced the allegation that Albanians had been killing and forcibly expelling Serbs from the region since the arrival of the Ottoman Turks. Albanians supposedly acted as the 'strong arm of the Ottoman Empire', keeping the weak but proud Serbs in submission from 1389 onward.[59] Even a relatively impartial historian like Bogdan Denitch would describe how, in the 'intervening centuries', Serbs were forced to flee from Kosovo, while the Turks settled the region with Islamicised Albanians, a process 'which today would be called genocide'.[60] Forced expulsions in the nineteenth century were similarly claimed to have been severe, approaching a total of 150,000.[61] For many Serbian writers, the Albanians were a violent and treacherous people. Because they had collaborated with the occupying Ottoman armies, and had set themselves up in Kosovo in order to terrorise the Christian Serbs, they had no claim to be a constituent nation in the region – they were 'morally disqualified'.[62] It was clear that only a chosen nation, like the Serbs, deserved to be in control.

Tito's Yugoslavia would be reinterpreted as a time when Albanian genocide continued with full fury. Dobrica Ćosić was one of the first to reinterpret Kosovar actions during the lifespan of Yugoslavia as an attempt to create 'an ethnically pure Kosovo republic . . . an Albanian state in Yugoslav territory'.[63] Kosovars, not Serbs, were blamed for inventing 'ethnic cleansing'. For others, the long history of 'brutal persecution' included such activities as 'rape and pillage . . . the desecration of Serbian religious institutions and cemeteries, arson and exploitation'.[64] Writers blamed the Albanians for instituting a forty-year policy of ethnic cleansing against the Serbs, in order to create a Republic of Kosovo in the ethnically pure area.[65] Others would describe an 'open and total war', which was leading inexorably to 'the physical, political and cultural genocide of the Serbian population in Kosovo and Metohije'.[66] In a large number of cases, a long and continuous history of genocide was revealed, with the Serbs as the indigenous people of the region constantly under attack from the alien Albanians, brought in either by Ottomans or Communists.

Such a portrayal of Serbian–Albanian relations made Serbian reactions in Kosovo appear as a welcome, though long-delayed, measure, designed to correct centuries of abuse. There was little statistical information to support these Serbian claims of genocide, nor was rape as frequent an occurrence there as the Serbian nationalists alleged it to be. Except for several highly publicised cases, the Kosovo average was far below that of the rest of Serbia before the war, nor were many of the cases of harassment ever proved. What could be proved, however was the large increase in Kosovar Albanian relative to Serbian births (27 per 1,000 for 1981–90 versus the Serb and Croat average of 2.2). This gave rise to another type of genocide accusation, the notion of a demographic conspiracy to out-birth Serbs and therefore to gain control of the province. While this style of paranoid rhetoric was never used for Croats, nor for Bosnian Moslems, it demonstrates both the perseverance and versatility of Serbian writers when faced with the reality that Serbs had not been victims of genocide in any conventional sense.

Ćosić was one of the first to highlight the dangers of a 'demographic explosion' – designed to bring about the separation of Kosovo and its joining with Albania 'by sheer force of numbers'.[67] Some, like the political cartoonist Milenko Mihajlović, blamed Tito's government for encouraging a high birth-rate. His works depicted throngs of Albanian babies with leering grins, swarming out from behind Marshal Tito – the queen bee.[68] Reactions of the academic community were difficult to take seriously. Živorad Igić's monograph on what he described as a 'demographic time bomb' denounced the Albanian birth-rate as 'unique to the world', in that their 'reproductive behaviour is quite unsuited to the time and space in which we live'.[69] A high birth-rate, he reasoned, constituted 'an objective threatening of the rights of the other nationalities'. It became part of a coherent strategy to 'create an *ethnically clean* region', a strategy supposedly pursued by Albanian leaders for national reasons. Poverty and a lack of education were dismissed as irrelevant, while 'tribal leaders' were blamed for forcing women to bear children, in order to take control of Kosovo.[70]

The notion of a gynaecological conspiracy seemed also to be supported by the Serbian Association of Professors and Scientists, who exposed a plot to make Albanian women more fertile, so they could engender a 'demographic explosion never before seen, the most potent in the world'. Claiming that the Albanian population had risen by a factor of 50 (the increase was actually 3.3 times from 1941 to 1981), the Association was clear that a concerted strategy of high Albanian births constituted a form of genocide against the Serbs.[71] This idea was again introduced in a 1995 scientific conference in Pristinë, designed to deal with the 'negative and unacceptable demographic movements' in Kosovo. Their recommendations included the settlement of some 400,000 Serbian refugees from other parts of Yugoslavia, as well as more innocuous provisions, like the 'adoption of a family planning law'.[72]

That ethnic cleansing was eventually pursued should surprise no one. While the conference advocated 'family planning' as a possible method of reducing the Albanian population, the Serbian government appeared to have made no effort to help them with their birth-control concerns.[73] Family planning was advocated solely to reduce the percentage of Albanians relative to Serbs. Had any such coercive measures been implemented, it might potentially have been considered genocide under Article 4 of the United Nations *Genocide Convention* of 1948: 'imposing measures intended to prevent births within the group'. Even if Serbian propaganda were true, Kosovar Albanians out-birthing Serbs would have been neither an instance of genocide nor a crime against humanity under international law, nor, for that matter, under Serbian law.

While the scientific establishment used veiled threats and 'scientific' studies to advance anti-Albanian policies, several writers were more direct. The SANU academic Vešelin Djuretič, for example, rejected such complicated and long-term projects as family planning, proposing instead the 'repatria- tion' of Kosovar Albanians to Albania. The solution was to deport everyone who was not a Serb. Serbs would then be moved into Kosovo to fill the empty houses.[74] Djuretič's plan went to the heart of Serbian political and military objectives in Kosovo. Several convoluted, but by no means universally accepted, definitions of 'genocide' and 'ethnic cleansing' were used to justify the forced removal of Kosovar Albanians from the region, in order to replace them with Serbs.

There was little truth to the claim that a demographic plot was being hatched. An impartial Yugoslav study, conducted in 1988 to assess the situa- tion, revealed that low education levels among females and a high unemployment rate were the crucial contributing factors to a high birth-rate. There was no cynical policy on the part of the Albanian leadership.[75] At the same time, there were only five inter-ethnic murders in Kosovo between 1981 and 1987. This region had the lowest crime rate in Yugoslavia.[76] Nevertheless, the illusion of danger, and the theme of the 'universal culprit', were common during this time.[77] Accusations of persecution soon became self-fulfilling prophecies, as the Kosova Liberation Army – largely funded by expatriate Albanian groups – launched a bitter struggle for independence. This only increased the level of Serbian terror in the province. By 1999, over 850,000 Kosovars had been forced to flee their homes, by a mixture of Serbian paramilitary violence and NATO destruction. Some Serb nationalists took their 'self-defensive' activities quite seriously. Given the Albanians' crime of genocide, the Macedonian economist Vladimir Gligorov remarked ironically, 'the punishment seemed appropriate'.[78]

Contextualising Serbian nationalism in Croatia

For the Serbian government, the lessons of Kosovo were obvious. By activat- ing the Kosovo myth, and by linking it with explicitly Jewish metaphors of 'genocide', the government was able to take over the province and rejoin it to Serbia. Few Serbs openly protested against Milošević's heavy-handed approach to Kosovo, which he ran like a military police state. The fact that Serbs had suffered 'genocide' gave him *carte blanche*. The links between an aesthetic of persecution and state terror were not ignored by outside observers. Shkelsem Maliqi, in his study of Albanian nationalism, drew out the links between Serbs in Kosovo and the Palestinian problem, noting the militaristic capabilities and actions of each:

> Israel used all coercive means to 'liberate' and 'redeem' Palestine as a 'sacred land' which had been 'usurped' by the Palestinians. In the same way the dominant state machinery of the 'unitary' republic of Serbia decided to apply all coercive means to the task of bringing Kosova back into the national possession of the Serbs, on the grounds that Kosovo had been historically 'sacred Serbian soil', which had been 'usurped' by the Albanians a couple of centuries ago.[79]

Maliqi posited that Serbian nationalists and militant Zionists had much in common. As he described it: 'the Serbs as a persecuted and historically tragic people, the notion of the historical right to gather all Serbs within one state, the idea of the crusade against (in this case) the Albanians as an alleged vanguard of Islamic fundamentalism, the right to recolonise "sacred soil", the right to impose demographic control over the "usurpers".'[80] As an Albanian Moslem, Maliqi had clear sympathies with both Kosovars and Palestinians, and his denunciation of both Serbs and Israelis at one stroke is an interesting indication of how far he felt such parallels extended. Clearly, Serbia had entered into the 'comparative genocide debate', and Milošević had success-fully managed the takeover of Kosovo by playing on his people's fear and misunderstanding.

But if Serbian nationalists cut their teeth in Kosovo, their main opponents as Yugoslavia disintegrated were the Croats. While there had been little if any Croatian–Serbian antagonism before 1918, history would be revised to reflect a new reality. By 1990, the Croatian leader Franjo Tudjman, following the example of Slovenia, was trying to pull the Republic of Croatia out of the Yugoslav Federation. Milošević had not opposed Slovenian secession, on the grounds that there was no Serbian minority there in need of his 'protection'. While fighting had broken out between Slovenian secessionist forces and the JNA in June 1991, Milošević had secretly assured Slovenian leaders that he would not try to prevent their secession.[81] What Silber and Little have dubbed 'the phoney war' ended quickly by July, after Milošević vetoed the continued use of force by the JNA.[82] Croatia, however, was different, since its territory contained a sizeable Serbian minority – 13 per cent of Croatia's total popula-tion of 4.7 million people.[83] Moreover, certain regions of Croatia – Eastern Slavonia and the eastern Krajina – were seen to be historically Serbian. Milošević's legitimacy as a national leader was based on uniting Serbian populations and historic lands, and this made a confrontation with Croatia inevitable, even if he had privately assured Tudjman and other Croatian leaders that he had no interest in Croatian land.[84] His attitude was made clear at a secret meeting to Serbian regional leaders in March, 1991. Expressing his conviction that borders were made by the strong at the expense of the weak, he argued:

> We simply consider it as a legitimate right and interest of the Serbian nation to live in one state. This is the beginning and the end ... And if we have to fight, by God we are going to fight. I hope that they [the Croats] will not be so crazy as to fight against us. If we do not know how to work properly or run an economy, at least we know how to fight properly.[85]

As in the Kosovo case, myths proving that parts of Croatia were histori-cally Serbian provided much-needed ammunition against Croatian secession. Territorial claims would simultaneously be backed with moral claims to Croatian territory, again in a fusing of Kosovo and Jewish-style myths. Such myths would advance the claim that the Serbs had been the victims of a long and bloody Croatian expansionist programme, aimed at destroying the Serbian nation. In their analysis of this 'anti-Serbian' or 'Serbophobic' programme, the importance of Catholic expansionism was another important ingredient.

The remainder of this chapter will therefore focus on two different aspects of Serbian propaganda: first of all, on the establishment of territorial claims and the beginnings of Serbian nationalism within Croatia. And secondly, it will be important to review some of the primary Serbian myths of persecution, and how Serbs began to reinterpret their earlier historical associations with the Croats. These sections will lay the basis for a comparison between Serbian and Croatian reappraisals of their historical relationship up to the beginning of the Second World War.

Serbian territorial claims in the Krajina and Eastern Slavonia

Certainly, the Serbs had a number of highly compelling and ancient myths that were operationalised in Kosovo to legitimate control of the province. In the case of Croatia, the two regions claimed by Serbs had a far more ambigu-ous lineage, and while there were arguably towns and villages with a Serbian majority, Krajina and Eastern Slavonia were well inside historic Croatia. The Serbian plan for annexing these two regions was made clear almost from the beginning. Serbia desired to keep these areas within a smaller SFRY, but an amputated 'Croatia' would be free to leave, once Milošević had seized the lion's share of the republic for himself. Had the Serbian plan been successful, Croatia would have been divided in two, somewhat like East and West Pakistan, making Croatia what some ironically called a 'so-called split in half country'.[86]

By 1992, the geographer Jovan Ilić had set forth Serbian territorial ambi-tions. Serbs would participate in a referendum on their separation from

Croatia. The Republika Srpska Krajina would eventually be annexed to Serbia, while those Serbs remaining in Croatia would be traded reciprocally with Croats in Serbia. Remaining Serbs would be obliged to move to Eastern Slavonia (namely Baranja, Vukovar, and Vinkovci) which would also be annexed to Serbia. 'At any rate,' warned Ilić, 'not many Serbs should remain in independent Croatia.'[87] In historic Dubrovnik, at that time being ravaged by JNA shelling, Ilić recognised that the population was predominantly Catholic and Croat. While he accepted that 'according to the ethnic principle this area should belong to Croatia', he proposed the establishment of Dubrovnik and the surrounding area as a separate 'political-territorial, autonomous unit'.[88] Presumably this unit would continue to be a part of the new SFRY, most probably subject to a system of rule similar to that in Kosovo and Vojvodina. While these annexations would unite the Serbians and their supposedly historic territory, the key issue for Ilić was punishing and humiliating the Croats for daring to oppose Serbian nationalism. 'The new borders should primarily be a therapy for the treatment of ethno-psychic disorders', prescribed Ilić, 'primarily among the Croatian population.'[89]

As Ilić maintained, the Krajina, or 'borderland', was historically a Western outpost, controlled by the Austro-Hungarian Empire. It was a border established to keep the Ottoman Empire at bay, and, for this reason, large numbers of Serbs had been settled there as soldiers during the fifteenth and sixteenth centuries.[90] Ilić's claim to the land was based on the fact that Serbs had fought for the 'West' and therefore deserved the region as their reward. He further cited a 1630 charter given to the inhabitants by Ferdinand II of Austria, guaranteeing their autonomy from Croatian control, a reality that persisted until 1881, after which time control was ceded to Croatian administration. Ilić's primary argument was that the Military Frontier as a territorial and political unit had existed outside the boundaries of Croatia for centuries. It was never truly a part of Croatia, and was therefore entitled to exist independently.[91]

Claims on the Krajina included south-eastern Dalmatia, western Srem, Dubrovnik, and eastern Slavonia, even though there were few Serbs there during the conflict, as a result of, 'conversion to Catholicism, Uniating, and Croatisation', as well as 'genocidal destruction'. There were even claims that Serbs formed the majority on some of the Adriatic islands, such as Viš – although writers were forced to concede that these also had been 'Catholicized'.[92] With regard to Eastern Slavonia, there was little historical evidence that the region had been anything but Croatian for many centuries. While there was one claim that Vukovar had been founded by the Serbs, most propaganda directed at this region relied primarily on its proximity to Serbia, and the fact that its people were predominantly Serbian.[93]

Of course, while critically examining such dubious Serbian claims, one should also bear in mind that Croatia was hardly as united as later nationalists would argue. Much of Slavonia had been under direct Viennnese administration for about three centuries (from 1578 onwards), and was only rejoined with Croatia in 1868. Dalmatia was also joined with Croatia in the same year, after centuries of Venetian, Hungarian, and Austrian control. Indeed, one could argue that this region had never been under Croatian control. This in no way legitimates Serbian claims; but, as I will argue later, Croatian nationalists were as adept at reinterpreting history as their Serbian counterparts.[94]

Moral claims: the myth of 'Serbophobia'

While these historical claims were important as a starting-point, it was clear that the Croats had far more claim to these lands than did the Serbs. These had been part of Croatia for many centuries, and while there were Serbian villages and towns, there were also considerable numbers of Croats in these regions as well. Ilić's boast that 'One cannot be the occupying power of one's own country!' was typical of those used throughout the conflict as an important justification for Serbian violence in Croatia.[95] Nevertheless, while territorial arguments were useful, the Serbs in Croatia, as in Kosovo, chose to capitalise on myths of genocide and persecution, asserting a moral, as well as a territorial right to these historic lands. As in Kosovo, Schöpflin's 'myths of powerlessness and compensation for the powerless' were used to justify Serbian autonomy. The Serbs had supposedly fought for centuries against the Ottoman Empire on these lands, and therefore earned the right to be free from Croatian control.[96]

Ilić continually asserted such claims, advancing special moral rights for the Serbian nation, 'because it was exposed to genocidal extermination many times'.[97] His arguments were designed to resemble those of Herzl and other nineteenth-century Zionists, positing that there could be no existence for Serbs outside of Serbia. Of course, the Serbs never truly followed the Zionist approach. Rather than going to their homeland, they preferred to create exclusive ethnic enclaves wherever they lived. A bizarre process developed, of establishing Serbian autonomous pockets throughout the region, which would then be joined by land bridges (or corridors) to Serbia.

An essential precondition and follow-up to Serbian machinations in the Krajina and East Slavonia involved proving the existence of a historic nationalist project aimed against the Serbs. The myth of 'Serbophobia' (a historic fear, hatred, and jealousy of Serbs that Serb nationalists have likened to anti-Semitism) allowed nationalists to trace a continuous legacy of hatred and violence against the Serbs among the Croats. The actions of the JNA and Serbian irregular militias in Croatia could therefore be presented, both at home and to the outside world, as self-defensive and humanitarian – saving the Krajina Serbs from annihilation. Coupled with a project of demonising Croats was the rehabilitation of Serbian history, to prove that Serbs had never harboured any ill feeling towards Croats, and had always behaved nobly in their dealings with them. This propaganda was designed to highlight the irrationality of the Croatian nationalist project, while casting the Serbs as victims throughout history.

The idea that Serbs were forced into the war, and that Croatia had started the violence, were popular themes – found regularly in the media and in scholarly publications. While great moral strength was to be gained from the myth of Kosovo and their parallel suffering with the Jews, an entire history of Croatian duplicity and evil had now to be constructed. Again, this was very much like Kečmanović's theme of the 'universal culprit', or Schöpflin's 'myths of unjust treatment', where Serbs had been singled out for negative treatment throughout history, and therefore had special moral rights to defend themselves from the threat of attack.[98]

Serbophobia became an anti-Semitism for Serbs, making them victims throughout history. Dobrica Ćosić could thus claim: 'We Serbs feel today as the Jews did in Hitler's day. We are a people who are [considered] guilty ... Today, Serbophobia in Europe is a concept and an attitude with the same ideological motivation and fury as anti-Semitism had during the Nazi era.'[99] Ćosić's text also highlighted Serbian and Jewish *Diasporic* conceptions of identity, viewing both nations as having been doomed throughout their history to suffer under persecution, because they lived outside their national borders. Thus Krajina Serbs were likened to Russian and Polish Jews or other *Ashkinazim*.

The nationalist opposition leader and novelist Vuk Drasković also saw the merits of such rhetoric, arguing: 'Israel and the Serbs live in a hellish siege where the sworn goal is to seize and then cover with mosques or Vaticanize the lands of Moses and the people of St. Sava [Serbia's patron saint].'[100] Clearly, many of the most prominent writers and politicians were trying hard to push the connections between Jews and Serbs. Since the Serbian diaspora had suffered in history, the only solution was an expanded state. While Ćosić never operationalised a working definition of 'Serbophobia', its meaning was clearly implied. There were others, however, who did elaborate on the phenomenon. Smilja Avramov (an adviser to Milošević) overtly compared the persecution of Serbs with that of the Jews in history: 'The departure point for the genocide of the Jews was anti-Semitism, and of the Serbs, Serbophobia.'[101] Both movements were morally equal, according to Avramov, and each was to be found in a variety of different countries. By Avramov's definition, Serbophobia was closely tied to the Catholic Church, and was operationalised historically through the Vatican and the Austro-Hungarian Empire. Croatia was in many respects a pawn in a much larger Catholic expansionist plan.

For Serbs, the moment that Croatians became Catholics was the moment they began to hate the Serbian others and their Orthodox faith. The Catholic hatred of Orthodoxy was thus presented in history as a 'continuity of geno- cide' against the Serbs, something 'which has been carried out throughout history and is being implemented today'.[102] Like anti-Semitism, Serbophobia could not be taken seriously if it was not ancient and primordial. Therefore, as Avramov asserted, Catholic aggression and expansionism was part of Croatian nationalism from the outset:

> For [one] thousand years Croats have been in full political dominance by foreign factors, and have tried through them to achieve their own state. Croatian Catholicism, often militant and opposed to the ecumenical spirit, gradually absorbed all other national compounds and subordinated them to the mighty state of Rome. Numerous Popes, in the last thousand years considered the Orthodox Church heretic, schismatic and cursed, so they brought up Croats as its border guardians towards the East. Rome has planted an idea in the Croatian soul, that their land is 'Bulwark of Christianity' which turned them away from the Orthodox brothers, with the aim to exterminate Serbs on the religious basis.[103]

Seen as nothing more than historical slaves to the Vatican and its expan- sionist plans, the Croats were accused of being religious executioners, killing Serbs in order to destroy all vestiges of Orthodoxy in the Balkans. Croatian nationalism and the killing of Serbs were inseparably tied together, with hatred of Serbs forming a crucial part of Croatian national identity. 'Croatian national leaders', Avramov commented, 'had no clear idea of national self- determination, unless it was founded on the genocide over Serbs.' Curiously, however, such views did not apply to the equally Catholic Slovenians.[104] For Serbian writers, the existence of Croatian nationalism and the Catholic Church implied *ipso facto* the existence of Serbophobia. The Croats were to be bearers of a nationalism that had no intrinsic worth – except for its hatred of the Serbian other.

Useful as an ahistorical genocidal project was for Serbian historians, 'Serbophobia' had also to be historicised, to be understood as a political phenomenon. Many traced a general form of Serbophobia from the Great Schism in AD 395, when the Roman Empire split into eastern and western halves. Others traced Serbophobia to much later contact with the Croats, when Serbs were brought in to defend the Krajina against Ottoman attacks. Croatian feudal lords and the Catholic clergy were blamed as the later instiga- tors of it, supposedly frustrated by Serbian autonomy in the Krajina, and by the refusal of the Serbs to convert to Catholicism.

This type of religious-based Serbophobia had seemingly metamorphosed by the nineteenth century into a more organised and systematised concept of hatred. The historian Dušan Bataković wrote profusely on the nineteenth-century development of Croatian and Serbian nationalism during the wars in Croatia and Bosnia. A large number of his works were widely circulated on the internet. Bataković used comparisons of political and social systems in Serbian and Croatia to argue in favour of Serbian tolerance and Croatian xenophobia. He privileged Serbian eastern concepts of nationhood, and his writings contain numerous justifications for what would later be called 'Greater Serbia' – the now famous Serbian strategy of empire-building in the nineteenth century. Bataković noted, and rightly, that Serbs advocated a strong unified state in the nineteenth century as a bulwark against Bulgarian, Russian, and Turkish expansion, and dreamed of uniting South Slavs into a common homeland.

Rather than condemning this process, he argued that 'Greater Serbia' was a positive form of fraternal unity between Serbs and Croats, who were seen to be 'but two branches of the same nation, which had become forcibly divided by the foreign domination'.[105] Thus outside interference and colonialism were blamed for keeping these two groups apart. 'Greater Serbia' would be the solution to their problems. It was, as Batakovič explained, a model for a unitary and democratic state according to the French model.[106] Serbian nation-building was supposedly a constructive, positive phenomenon.

For Bataković, privileging Serbian history as one of tolerance and democracy was of great importance, particularly in the light of the continuous flow of anti-Serbian writings going from Croatia to the West. These often alluded to Serbia's Ottoman roots and eastern practices of despotic rule and violence. Bataković elevated the '*millet* tradition' of self-rule under the Ottoman empire as a great boon for Orthodox nations in the Balkans, as it 'proved itself to be a solid base for transition to the standard European type of national integration – the nation-state model, based on the experience of the French Revolution'.[107] Thus the Serbian evolution to 'democracy' was based on European ideals, and was therefore consonant with Enlightenment values. By contrast, he drew a sharp distinction between the desirable Serbian forms of nationalism, and the supposedly negative and destructive Croatian forms:

> Contrary to the *authentically European model of integration*, in the neighbourhood of the former Ottoman provinces turned into newly established national states . . . within the frontiers of another multinational empire, the Habsburg Monarchy, a Central-European model of national integration arose gradually – a clerical nationalism, mixed with feudal traditions. That model of nationalism was especially apparent in regions where the Roman-Catholic and Orthodox Church coexisted, like Croatia, Dalmatia and Slavonia, and was coloured by an excessive religious intolerance.[108]

Thus could Bataković compare a Serbian 'European' model with its Croatian counterpart, seemingly steeped in religious extremism and intolerance. He called it simply 'a contemporary variant of the Civitas Dei – "God's state"', which continued to rely on anachronistic interpretations of 'feudal "historical rights"' – well into the nineteenth century'.[109] Contrary to Serbian nationalism, this religious-based nationalism was inimical to the 'modern solutions' favoured by the Serbs, from romantic nationalism to liberalism. Thus, one is presented with opposing Serbian and Croatian views of state- and nation-building in the nineteenth century. Serbian nationalism was European, democratic, tolerant, cosmopolitan, and enlightened, while Croats were medieval, hierarchical, xenophobic, and backward. Bataković's theories are an excellent example of Kečmanović's 'counteridentification',[110] in which the enemy's history is seen to be completely opposite to one's own. Now, certainly one could argue that in retaining some archaic features, like speaking Latin in the Diet, the Croats were indeed backward-looking to some extent. Their national identity, faced with Magyar modernising tendencies, often consisted of retaining traditions that had been abandoned elsewhere, leading to the charge of backwardness. However, within the context of a civil war in which Serbia was the primary aggressor (at least at first) Bataković's comments do seem to have overtly political dimensions, particularly when you consider that he avoids discussing any positive aspects of Croatian nationalism in the nineteenth century, while similarly avoiding the many negative aspects of Serbian history from this time. Bataković's selective narrativising of the past was sadly typical.

Within a general analysis of the period was a specific condemnation of Croatian nationalist politicians and activists who were at the vanguard of an anti-Serbian movement. Croatian linguist and nationalist politician Ante Starčević was an obvious target of Serbian writings, as the co-founder of the nationalist 'Croatian Party of Rights' (with Eugen Kvaternik). Starčević and Kvaternik were frequently condemned for inciting Croats to commit genocide against the Serbs, being, as one writer recalled: 'the founders of the idea of genocidal destruction upon Serbs in Croatia'.[111] Starčević's politicking was also linked with the rise of right-wing nationalist Josip Frank, whose Frankovci were later to start 'a systematic anti-Serbian and anti-Orthodox campaign', which resulted in 'pogroms, exiles ... and the first attempt of genocide upon the Serbian people'.[112] It was clear once again that the rise of Croatian nationalism in the nineteenth century equalled genocide.

Historically, Starčević was known as a Croatian linguistic reformer (albeit a Croatian nationalistic one), who standardised the Croatian language as distinct from the Serbian. For contemporary writers, Starčević's project was denounced as inherently racist and xenophobic, on the assumption that his workable common culture was intolerant and destructive of Serbian culture. He was accused of destroying South Slavic unity, of inventing 'an all-together non-existent Croatian language and orthography' – a language constructed only to erect artificial barriers between Serbs and Croats. For some Serbian historians, Starčević's programme consisted exclusively of 'denying and exterminating the Serbian people' as a precondition to Croatian self-determination.[113] Again, the idea of denying South Slavic unity, and denying the existence of cultural, linguistic and historic ties between Serbs and Croats, was presented as the first major step in Serbophobia, a step that led inexorably to genocide.

In Starčević Serbian writers also noted the emergence of racial theories similar to those of the Nazi era. As Serbian politician Vasilije Krestić revealed: 'The "Father of the Homeland" had developed such racial theory about the Serbs, that it can only be compared to Hitler's theory about the Jews.'[114] Krestić's understanding of Croatian motivations was similar to those of his contemporaries. His reading of Croatian history also included violent and xenophobic plans to destroy the Serbs, in accordance with a Machiavellian desire to take over the Krajina. Paraphrasing the Croatian position, he added that 'all means are permitted for the reaching of this aim, including the genocidal extermination of the Serbs'.[115]

For Krestić, a key indicator of Starčević's extremism was the vocabulary used for assimilating non-Croats: 'Alpine Croats' (for Slovenes); 'Orthodox Croats' (for Serbs); 'flower of the Croatian people' (for Moslems); followed by 'Turkish Croatia' (for Bosnia); 'Red Croatia' (for Montenegro); 'White Croatia' (for Dalmatia); and 'Carinthian Croatia' (for Slovenia). Krestič thus explained the rationale behind such identifications: 'These names had been carefully nurtured for hundreds of years and rooted in the consciousness of the Croat with the idea of developing in him a conviction of the greatness of Croatia and of the numerical strength of the Croats.'[116] Such vocabulary also performed an important role in convincing the Croats that other nations were artificial and therefore did not exist. Denying the existence of the Serbs was seen to be crucial to their extermination.

Contrary to Serbian claims, specifically those of Krestić, Starčević was not a genocidal maniac, although his theories might well have been a justification for 'ethnocide'. This, as Israel Charny has argued, aims at the 'intentional destruction of another people', but crucially '[does] not necessarily include destruction of actual lives'.[117] This aside, Starčević's original ideas were assimilationist, not exclusivist. For him everyone was a potential Croat, and the fact that Slovenians were 'mountain Croats', and Serbs 'Orthodox Croats' reflected his assimilatory policies. While he did see 'Serbdom' as an artificial construct, it was not his desire to exterminate Serbs, but rather, to make them into good 'Orthodox Croats'. Starčević was in many ways reacting against the Illyrianism and pro-Serbianism of such Croatian liberal thinkers as Ljudevit Gaj and Juraj Strossmayer, who argued that the great differences between Orthodox and Catholic were artificial and manufactured. Starčević argued that these Croats were giving too much away for the promise of eventual union with the Serbs, even though he still saw a communal state as the best alternative to the 'Balkanisation' of Europe.[118]

Certainly, we can observe many parallels between Starčević and his Serbian contemporary Vuk Karadžić, who preached basically the same philosophy from the Serbian point of view. Nevertheless, Starčević's nationalism does seem to have been particularly obnoxious even if it was not genocidal. C. A. Macartney notes in his *Hungary: A Short History*, how 'gross intolerance' to the Serbs of Salvonia drove them into the arms of the new Ban, Count Khuen-Hédérvary, in 1883, as they 'sought his protection', enabling the Ban to 'maintain what was essentially a dictatorship ... until the end of the century'.[119] The end of Khuen-Hédérvary's rule then culminated, according to Krestić, in a number of anti-Serbian riots, particularly from 1899 to 1902, when Serbian homes and shops were destroyed in downtown Zagreb. This violence, he argued, was stirred up by the Catholic Church in Croatia and the Vatican, who dreamed, along with the 'Party of Rights', of creating a 'Greater Croatia' at the expense of the Serbian populations.[120]

The combination of Serbophobic religious, linguistic and political programmes was to culminate in the butchery of Serbs in the First World War, according to many Serbian sources. This period would be consonant with 'elements of anti-Serb genocide', claimed one writer.[121] Croatian Peasant Party leader Stjepan Radić (later shot by a Montenegrin parliamentary deputy) was specifically accused of whipping up anti-Serb hatred, which led to Croatian massacres of Serbs in the First World War.[122] Other writers described the 'religious warmongering', as well as the 'anti-Serbian demonstrations and pogroms ... plunder and destruction of Serbian property', as proof of the 'holy war' waged against the Serbs during the war.[123]

Such nineteenth- and early twentieth-century imagery was fascinating, because it described an altogether unending period of Serbophobia, when this was in fact a time when many Croatian academics and politicians looked to Serbia and to the idea of Yugoslavism or Illyrianism as a positive phenomenon. Men like Ljudevit Gaj and Bishop Juraj Strossmayer, who created the Yugoslav Academy in Zagreb, were very much pro-Serbian. They argued that a cultural and spiritual union with the Serbs was the best way to secure a strong South Slavic state – wherein some measure of freedom and equality could come about. Similarly, Ivan Meštrović, the world-famous Croatian sculptor and Yugoslav nationalist, pushed for Yugoslav unity, even creating a 'Kosovo Temple' that he exhibited as part of the Serbian, and not the Austro-Hungarian, contribution to the Rome International Exhibition in 1912. These and many more examples demonstrate the counterfactual nature of many Serbian assertions. For many decades, Croatian intellectuals and writers were at the forefront of Illyrianism, even more eager for union than their Serbian counterparts.[124]

Serbian interpretations of the first Yugoslavia

When the first Kingdom of the Serbs, Croats, and Slovenes was created in 1918, it was clear at first that all parties found the union acceptable. The Serbs favoured it, as they saw their state expand dramatically westwards. The Croats also favoured the arrangement, as their lands were now protected against Italian predations after the war. Croatia had been part of the losing side as part of the Austro-Hungarian Empire. However, there were problems, and the Yugoslav state soon became what Bataković had claimed – an extension of the pre-war Serbian kingdom. While it is clear from many accounts that Serbs dominated Yugoslavia, the official Serbian position maintained that the country was decentralised, federal, and equal. As Bataković claimed, it was 'an expression of the modern European spirit, manifesting itself as an integrative idea of the liberal bourgeoisie which advocated the unity of Yugoslav views'.[125] For Bataković and his contemporaries, the Kingdom was as Western as France or Germany, which meant that it conformed to the highest ideals possible.

Further, King Aleksander was credited with favouring the Roman Catholic Church over other religious denominations in Yugoslavia, handing out generous concessions to the Croatian business community, while actively encouraging former Austro-Hungarian army officers to integrate themselves into the Yugoslav army.[126] That such information was often counterfactual did not matter a great deal. Serbian historians wanted to portray Serbian history as one of tolerance and largesse. From its promising beginnings, writers argued that the Serbian policy of 'reconciliation and national tolerance' was soon abused by the Croats, while the generosity of the Serbs 'soon made it possible for all opponents of the Yugoslav common state to work unhindered'.[127]

Moderate writers have described the Croats' drive for increased autonomy as the 'Hungarian complex', implying that they saw the new kingdom as another Austro-Hungarian-style system, with Serbs and Croats in a potential power-sharing arrangement. Others were not so open-minded.[128] Bataković, continuing with his cultural critique of Croatia, blamed the Croats almost entirely for the breakdown of the first Yugoslavia. The Croats, he argued, were backward and narrow-minded, simply unable to adapt to life in a more civilised state: 'The Yugoslav idea could not be implemented in the undeveloped, predominantly agrarian society, impregnated by various feudal traditions, religious intolerance and often a xenophobic mentality.'[129] Dobrica Ćosić would similarly blame the Croatian 'hatred for diversity' as a key reason for the Kingdom's breakdown.[130] Both men were clear that the cultural inadequacies of the Croats made the country unworkable, despite the best efforts of Serbian leaders. Furthermore, it soon became apparent that the

Croats never accepted Yugoslavia as a permanent solution. Rather, union was seen as a 'way-station' on the road to the creation of an 'ethnically pure and independent "greater Croatia"'. Once again, the Serbs found themselves in the way of another nation's expansionist plans, and became victims at a time when 'Serbophobia and hatred for the Serbs' was high.[131]

Such writings were designed to demonstrate the goodness and perhaps naïveté of the Serbs, who in their kind and trusting manner established a state for all South Slavs, only to be stabbed in the back by Croatian ethnic hatred and chauvinism. No matter how good the Serbs were – Serbian historians argued – interethnic harmony was impossible because of the Croatians and their genocidal characteristics. Even the development of King Aleksander's royal dictatorship was justified along these lines. Croatian politicians, instead of recognising that the Yugoslav state provided 'a unique historical opportunity for their own national emancipation', chose instead to 'abuse democratic rights and parliamentary life', exercising an 'extreme primitivism' which led to the dissolution of Parliament and the imposition of a royal dictatorship, 'as in some European countries'.[132]

Royal dictatorship was often defended by the Serbs as the only solution to a full-scale genocide of Serbs by Croats. Croatia was described as nothing less than the locus of 'darkness and insanity', where 'there reigns hatred incomprehensible to the civilised world'.[133] Such hatred, according to Serbian sources, was almost exclusively the product of the Roman Catholic faith, and its general desire to supplant the Orthodox Church. Even in the creation of a dictatorship, in a climate of almost total Serbian control over the population, the Serbs tried to prove that they were in fact the most European and enlightened, while the primitive Croats simply abused democracy and plotted genocide. Serbian writers, owing to their undeniable skill in reinterpreting history, would even make an age of strong Serbian control a time of Serbian victimisation.

Revising Serbian–Croatian antagonisms from the early twentieth century also involved conspiracy theories directed against the Vatican, which was often portrayed as a crucial architect of Balkanisation. By 1989, the well-known Bosnian Serb academic Milorad Ekmečić blamed the Vatican almost exclusively for the destruction of the first Yugoslavia. Ekmečić denounced the 'bureau of archbishops' for destroying all Serbian attempts at Balkan unity, and saw 'Catholic nationalism' as the Serb's worst enemy throughout history.[134] He went so far as to blame the Catholic Church for encouraging the genocide of Serbs throughout much of the twentieth century, through its supposed desire to create a 'Catholic Central Europe' with its frontier on the River Drina.[135]

While he offered a selection of contentious anecdotes, Ekmečić could give little proof of his assertions. Rather than acknowledging that the Serbian centralised monarchy was far from perfect, or that the Croats had legitimate grievances within Yugoslavia, it was much easier for Serbian writers to blame the Croats, or their Catholicism, for Yugoslavia's fragmentation. Further, by implicating the Vatican, a much larger conspiracy could be drawn out. Not only the Serbs, but perhaps other Orthodox countries – Greece, Bulgaria, Romania, or Macedonia – could similarly be threatened by a Catholic expansionist project. Such attacks on the Vatican constituted a tacit call for Balkan unity, or at least Orthodox unity. During the early 1990s, this was a top government priority. If the Ottoman Empire had swept through Serbia in the Middle Ages on its way westward, the Vatican was seen as a Western expansionist power, heading east. Sandwiched between the advancing Turks and Catholics were the seemingly helpless Serbs, with only their legends and their faith to sustain them.[136]

Conclusions

What emerges from an understanding of Serbian conceptions of Kosovar and early Croatian history is the centrality of persecution imagery. This involves the instrumentalisation of Kosovo and Jewish imagery to promote themes of Islamic and Catholic expansionist projects. Creating Serbophobia allowed Serbian writers to employ such metaphors as 'liquidation', 'pogroms', 'purges', 'ethnic cleansing' and 'genocide', in order to prove that they were merely resisting expansionist plans that were centuries old. By casting Albanian and later Croatian nationalism in an exclusivist, xenophobic, and destructive light, certain historical patterns emerged, with clear and distinct themes. Serbs were, like the Jews, the victims of ahistorical, dangerous forces, seeking to enslave and destroy them.

Further, through the use of territorial arguments, Serbian writers claimed that, like the Jews, they were being denied their right to a homeland for all of their people. Their lands and their liberty were being taken away from them, and the roots of this were to be found well before the current conflict. The early history of Serbian–Croatian relations proved crucial to the thesis that Serbs were merely protecting themselves from a well-established pattern of Croatian behaviour. Many of the ideas used against the Kosovar Albanians were later instrumentalised against the Croats as well – the concepts of ethnic intolerance, and the use of violence and genocide historically as a means of ridding Serbian regions of their own people. Many of these themes either anticipated, or were in reaction to Croatian propaganda, which obviously advanced opposing contentions. Croats argued that the Serbs were in fact the most genocidal and bloodthirsty nation in the region. This will be the subject of the next chapter, which will allow for some useful comparisons.

NOTES

1 Branimir Anzulović, *Heavenly Serbia: From Myth to Genocide* (London: C. Hurst & Company, 1999) pp. 123–4.
2 Ivo Banac (ed.), *Eastern Europe in Revolution* (Ithaca, NY: Cornell University Press, 1992) pp. 173–5.
3 A concise summary of Kosovo and its early history can be found in: Tim Judah, *The Serbs: History, Myth and the Destruction of Yugoslavia* (New Haven, CT: Yale University Press, 1997). See pp. 21–2.
4 Aleksander Pavković, *The Fragmentation of Yugoslavia: Nationalism in a Multi-Ethnic State* (Basingstoke: Macmillan, 1996) p. 78.
5 See Jim Seroka and Vukasin Pavlović, *The Tragedy of Yugoslavia* (London: M. E. Sharpe, 1992) p. 77; and Mark Thompson, *Forging War: The Media in Serbia, Croatia and Bosnia-Hercegovina* (London: Article 19/International Center Against Censorship, 1994) p. 128.
6 Bogdan Denitch, *Ethnic Nationalism: The Tragic Death of Yugoslavia* (Minneapolis, MN: University of Minnesota Press, 1994) pp. 119–20.
7 Marcus Tanner, *Croatia: A Nation Forged in War* (New Haven, CT: Yale University Press, 1997) p. 214.
8 The issue is discussed in: Jonathan Glover, *Humanity: A Moral History of the Twentieth Century* (London: Cape, 1999) p. 129.
9 Branka Magaš, *The Destruction of Yugoslavia: Tracing the Breakup 1980–92* (London: Verso, 1993) p. 110; and Christopher Cviić, 'Who's to Blame for the War in Ex-Yugoslavia?', *World Affairs*, (Fall 1993) p. 73.
10 Kenneth R. Minogue, *Nationalism* (London: B. T. Batsford, 1967) pp. 25–8.
11 Dušan Kečmanović, *The Mass Psychology of Ethnonationalism* (New York: Plenum Press, 1996) p. 62.
12 George Schöpflin, 'The Functions of Myth and a Taxonomy of Myth' in Geoffrey Hosking and George Schöpflin (eds), *Myths and Nationhood* (London; C. Hurst & Company, 1997) pp. 32–3.
13 For a discussion of the emerging state of affairs, see Magaš, *The Destruction of Yugoslavia*, p. 161; Sabrina Petra Ramet, *Nationalism and Federalism in Yugoslavia: 1962–1991* (Boulder, CO: Westview Press, 1992) p. 78; Tanner, *Croatia*, pp. 215–16; and Anton Bebler, 'Yugoslavia's Variety of Communism and Her Demise', *Communist and Post Communist Studies* (March 1993) pp. 75–6.
14 Laura Silber and Alan Little, *The Death of Yugoslavia* (London: BBC Books, 1995) p. 66.
15 Mihailo Crnobrnja, *The Yugoslav Drama* (Toronto: McGill-Queens University Press, 1993) p. 154.
16 Quoted in Biljana Vankovska, 'Civil–Military Relations in the Third Yugoslavia', *COPRI Working Papers* (Copenhagen: Copenhagen Peace Research Institute, 2000) p. 27.
17 Thompson, *Forging War*, pp. 59–60.
18 *Ibid.* pp. viii–xi.
19 *Ibid.* pp. x; 65.
20 *Ibid.* p. 73.
21 L'Age D'Homme was seemingly so infamous as a propaganda source that Yves Laplace devoted an entire book to denigrating this Swiss publishing house, and its owner Vladimir Dimitrijević, accused by Laplace of being the biggest publishers of Serbian propaganda in Europe. See Yves Laplace, *L'âge d'homme en Bosnie: petit guide d'une nausée suisse* (Lausanne: En bas, 1997).

22 See Mira Marković, *Night and Day: A Diary* (London: Minerva Press, 1996) pp. 78–9; and *Answer* (London: Minerva Press, 1996) pp. 58; 60; 82; 109–11. Marković claimed to be a Marxist historian and rigorously condemned both nationalism and nationalists, issuing not only denunciations of opposition leaders but veiled attacks against her husband as well. While her motives were unclear, her largely autobiographical texts presented a rather bizarre schizophrenic view of her own social and political position.

23 Brian Hall, *The Impossible Country: A Journey Through the Last Days of Yugoslavia* (Boston, MA: David R. Godine, 1994). See his chapter on Kosovo pp. 235–90.

24 Nikolai Velimirovich and Justin Popovich, 'The Mystery and Meaning of the Battle of Kosovo' (Grayslake, IL: The Serbian Orthodox New Gracanica Metropolitanate Diocese of America and Canada, 1996) http://members.aol.com/gracanica/index.html (accessed 18 June, 1998).

25 See Robert D. Kaplan, *Balkan Ghosts: A Journey Through History* (New York: St Martin's Press, 1993) pp. 35–6; J. A. R. Marriott, *The Eastern Question: An Historical Study in European Diplomacy* (Oxford: Clarendon Press, 1925) p. 65; Judah, *The Serbs*, p. 31; and Noel Malcolm, *Kosovo: A Short History* (London: MacMillan, 1998) pp. 75–9.

26 Velimirovich and Popovich, 'The Mystery and Meaning of the Battle of Kosovo'.

27 Thompson, *Forging War*, p. 144

28 As discussed in Bruce Cauthen, 'The Myth of Divine Election and Afrikaner Ethnogenesis', in Hosking and Schöpflin (eds), *Myths and Nationhood*, p. 113.

29 Hans Kohn, *The Idea of Nationalism: A study in its Origins and Background* (New York: The Macmillan Company, 1945) p. 36.

30 Paul Pavlovich adds: 'King Lazar died a martyr's death and to create such a lasting impression of despair upon those who survived the fall, that they would mend their ways, be inspired by the Kosovo sacrifice to regain and then preserve the will to fight for the time when revenge was to be possible.' See Paul Pavlovich, *The Serbians* (Toronto: Serbian Heritage Books, 1988) p. 56.

31 See Michael A. Sells, 'Religion, History and Genocide in Bosnia-Hercegovina', in G. Scott Davis (ed.), *Religion and Justice in the War Over Bosnia* (London: Routledge, 1996) p. 31; and Judah, *The Serbs*, p. 36.

32 Kečmanović, *The Mass Psychology of Ethnonationalism*, p. 36.

33 Vankovska, 'Civil–Military Relations in the Third Yugoslavia', pp. 6–7.

34 Judah, *The Serbs*, pp. 62–3.

35 Quoted in *ibid.* pp. 65–6.

36 Carl Jacobsen, *The New World Order's Defining Crises: The Clash of Promise and Essence* (Aldershot: Dartmouth Publishing, 1996) p. 48.

37 Ed Vulliamy, *Seasons in Hell: Understanding Bosnia's War* (London: St Martin's Press, 1994) pp. 51–2; also see Misha Glenny's amused and horrified description of the event in his *The Fall of Yugoslavia* (London: Penguin, 1993) pp. 33–6.

38 Milošević's highly ambivalent relationship with Serbian nationalism is very well discussed in Dusko Doder and Louise Branson, *Milosevic: Portrait of a Tyrant* (New York: Simon & Schuster, 1999). See p. 9.

39 Michael A. Sells, *The Bridge Betrayed: Religion And Genocide In Bosnia* (London: University of California Press, 1996) p. 127.

40 Sabrina Petra Ramet, *Balkan Babel* (Boulder, CO: Westview Press, 1996) p. 28.

41 Anthony Smith, *National Identity* (London: Penguin Books, 1990) pp. 65–6.

42 Božidar Zečević (ed.), *The Uprooting: A Dossier of the Croatian Genocide Policy Against the Serbs* (Belgrade: Velauto International, 1992) p. 10.

43 Norman Cigar, *Genocide in Bosnia: The Policy of 'Ethnic Cleansing'* (College Station, TX: Texas A & M University Press, 1995) p. 73.

44 Quoted *ibid*. p. 74.

45 Quoted in Nebojša Popov, 'La populisme serbe' (suite), *Les Temps Modernes*, (May 1994) pp. 35–6. (My translation.)

46 Anne Yelen, *Kossovo 1389–1989: bataille pour les droits de l'âme* (Lausanne: Editions L'Age D'Homme, 1989) p. 133.

47 Denitch, *Ethnic Nationalism*, p. 113.

48 Both of these works are discussed in Cigar, *Genocide in Bosnia*, p. 73.

49 Quoted in *ibid*. p. 74.

50 Anthony Smith, *Theories of Nationalism* (New York: Holmes & Meier, 1983) p. 153.

51 Philip J. Cohen, *Serbia's Secret War: Propaganda and the Deceit of History* (College Station, TX: Texas A & M University Press, 1996) p. 117.

52 *Ibid*. p. 199.

53 Laslo Sekelj, 'Antisemitism and Jewish Identity in Serbia After the 1991 Collapse of the Yugoslav State', in *Analysis of Current Trends in Antisemitism, 1997 acta no. 12* (Jerusalem: The Vidal Sassoon International Center for the Study of Antisemitism/ Hebrew University of Jerusalem, 1997) p. 1.

54 Florence Hamish Levinsohn, *Belgrade: Among the Serbs* (Chicago: Ivan R. Dee, 1994) p. 16.

55 *Ibid*. p. 251.

56 Quoted in Yelen, *Kossovo 1389–1989*, pp. 132–3. (My translation.)

57 Quoted in Judah, *The Serbs*, p. 37.

58 Sells, *The Bridge Betrayed*, p. 58.

59 See Michel Roux, *Les Albanais en Yougoslavie: minorité nationale, territoire et développement* (Paris: Editions de la maison des sciences de l'homme, 1992) p. 427.

60 Denitch, *Ethnic Nationalism*, p. 162.

61 Bojana Adamović, 'Expulsion of Serbs and Montenegrins From Kosovo and Metohija – The Most Sweeping Ethnic Cleansing in Europe', in Nebojša Jerković (ed.), *Kosovo and Metohija, An Integral Part of the Republic of Serbia and FR of Yugoslavia: Documents and Facts* (Belgrade: Review of International Affairs, 1995) pp. 77–80.

62 Yelen, *Kossovo 1389–1989*, p. 52.

63 Dobrica Ćosić, *L'éffondrement de la Yougoslavie: positions d'un résistant* (Paris: L'Age D'Homme, 1994) p. 45. In their 'unjust struggle' Čović further asserts that the Albanians have manipulated the Western powers, in order to promote Greater Albania at the Serbs' expense: 'In the name of protecting human rights, the Albanians are strongly supported in their fight by the American Congress and Senate, the European Parliament, the Islamic centers of power, and the Albanian lobbies, financed by drug dealers and gun runners' (p. 31). (My translation.)

64 Denitch, *Ethnic Nationalism*, pp. 163–4.

65 Dušan T. Bataković, 'Serbia in the 21st Century: the Problem of Kosovo-Metohija' (Belgrade: Serbian Unity Congress Sixth Annual Convention, 1996) www. yugoslavia.com/Society_and_Law/Kosovo/ GLAVA13.HTM (accessed 18 June 1998).

66 SANU (A group of members of the Serbian Academy of Science and Arts on current questions in the Yugoslav society), 'Memorandum', reprinted in Bože Ćosić (ed.), *Roots of Serbian Aggression: Debates/Documents/Cartographic Reviews* (Zagreb: Centar za Strane Jezike/AGM, 1993) pp. 323–4. (Italics mine.)

67 Ćosić, *L'éffondrement de la Yougoslavie*, p. 43.

68 Michael A. Sells, 'Religion, History and Genocide in Bosnia-Hercegovina', in G. Scott Davis (ed.), *Religion and Justice in the War Over Bosnia* (London: Routledge, 1996) p. 63.

69 Zivorad Igić, 'Kosovo-Metohija – A Demographic Time Bomb in Southern Serbia' in

Jerković (ed.), *Kosovo and Metohija*, pp. 99–100.

70 *Ibid.* pp. 101–3.

71 Discussed in Nouvel Observateur et Reporteurs Sans Frontières, *Le Livre Noir de L'ex-Yougoslavie: Purification Ethnique et Crimes de Guèrre* (Paris: Publications Arléa, 1993) pp. 286–7.

72 Serbian Ministry of Information, 'Declaration of Scientific Conference Working Group' (Belgrade: Serbian Ministry of Information, June, 1997) www.yugoslavia.com/Society_and_Law/Kosovo/GLAVA4.HTM (accessed 18 June 1998).

73 Igić, 'Kosovo – Metohija', p. 101.

74 This theory is discussed in Mirko Grmek, Marc Gjidara, and Neven Simac, *Le nettoyage ethnique: Documents historiques sur une idéologie serbe* (Paris: Fayard, 1993) p. 290.

75 Horvat's study is reviewed in Christopher Bennett, *Yugoslavia's Bloody Collapse: Causes, Course and Consequence* (London: C. Hurst & Company, 1995) pp. 92–3.

76 See Doder and Branson, *Milosevic: Portrait of a Tyrant*, p. 39.

77 *Ibid.* p. 63.

78 Vladimir Gligorov, *Why Do Countries Break Up? The Case of Yugoslavia* (Uppsala, Sweden: Uppsala University Press, 1994) p. 69.

79 Shkelzen Maliqi, 'The Albanian Movement in Kosova', in David A. Dyker and Ivan Vejdoda (eds), *Yugoslavia and After: A Study in Fragmentation, Despair and Rebirth* (London: Longman, 1996) p. 142. For an Israeli commentary, see Igor Primoratz, 'Israel and the War in the Balkans', www.hr/darko/etf/isr2.html (accessed 23 November 2000). Primoratz argues that the pro-Serbian bias of the Israeli government had much to do with their own policies of expelling the Palestinians in 1948–9. However, he draws the line at saying that Serbian actions and Israeli actions can be compared equally, since: 'The crucial difference, of course, is the fact that "ethnic cleansing" was carried out in part by means of genocide.'

80 Maliqi, 'The Albanian Movement in Kosova', p. 142.

81 Silber and Little, *The Death of Yugoslavia*, p. 169.

82 *Ibid.* p. 186.

83 *Ibid.* p. 92.

84 The issue of Milošević and Borislav Jović's broken promises to Tudjman are discussed in Stjepan Mesić, 'The Road to War', in Branka Magaš and Ivo Žanić (eds), *The War in Croatia and Bosnia – Hercegovina 1991–1995* (London: Frank Cass, 2001) p. 8.

85 Quoted in Doder and Branson, *Milosevic: Portrait of a Tyrant*, p. 81.

86 Jovan Ilić,'The Serbs in the Former SR of Croatia', in Dušanka Hadži-Jovančić (ed.), *The Serbian Question in the Balkans: Geographical and Historical Aspects* (Belgrade: University of Belgrade Faculty of Geography, 1995) pp. 308–9.

87 Jovan Ilić, 'Possible Borders of New Yugoslavia' in Stanoje Ivanović (ed.), *The Creation and Changes of the Internal Borders of Yugoslavia* (pp. 95–101) (Belgrade: Ministry of Information of the Republic of Serbia, 1992) p. 98.

88 *Ibid.* pp. 100–1.

89 *Ibid.* p. 98.

90 Ilić, 'The Serbs in the Former SR of Croatia', p. 319.

91 *Ibid.* pp. 320–1. Others claimed an even longer lineage for the Serbs, having come only 30 years after the Croats (in 822 AD). See Svetozar Đurđević, *The Continuity of a Crime: The Final Settlement of the Serbian Question in Croatia* (Belgrade: IDEA Publishing House, 1995) p. 9.

92 Ilić, 'The Balkan Geopolitical Knot and the Serbian Question', pp. 316–18. See also Djordje Janković, 'The Serbs in the Balkans in the Light of Archeological Findings', in Hadži-Jovančić (ed.) *The Serbian Question in the Balkans*, p. 127. Typical works by L'Age

D'Homme also supported the independence of the Serbian Krajina. Two French writers discussed the 'martyrdom of this heroic little nation'. The authors are clear – Krajina was not 'occupied', 'annexed' or 'conquered', but was rather the land of the Serbs since the ninth century. See Patrick Barriot and Eve Crépin, *On assassine un peuple: Les serbes de Krajina* (Lausanne: L'Age D'Homme, 1995) pp. 9–11.

93 See Mile Dakić, *The Serbian Krajina: Historical Roots and Its Rebirth* (Knin: Information Agency of the Republic of Serbian Krajina, 1994). He proclaims the Serbian origins of Vukovar on pp. 11–12.

94 See C. A. Macartney: *Hungary: A Short History* (Edinburgh: Edinburgh University Press, 1961) pp. 74–5. I am grateful to David Phelps for this point.

95 *Ibid.* p. 322.

96 *Ibid.* pp. 29–30.

97 *Ibid.* p. 31.

98 *Ibid.* pp. 29–30.

99 Ćosić, *L'éffondrement de la Yougoslavie*, p. 44. Ironically, the idea of claiming national territory based on past occupation or conquest was originally a Croatian one. Pavao Ritter Vitezović (1652–1713) would introduce the concept of 'historical appropriation' to the Balkans, and then use it to expand the geographical size of Croatia. He similarly claimed a wide variety of other nationalities as Croats, a name he adopted as a generic term for the Slavic populations of Europe. See Ivo Banac, *The National Question in Yugoslavia: Origins, History, Politics* (Ithiaca, NY: Cornell University Press, 1992) pp. 73–4.

100 Cigar, *Genocide in Bosnia*, p. 236.

101 Smilja Avramov (ed.), *Genocide Against the Serbs* (Belgrade: Museum of Modern Art, 1992) p. 18.

102 Božidar Zečević (ed.), *The Uprooting: A Dossier of the Croatian Genocide Policy Against the Serbs* (Belgrade: Velauto International, 1992) p. 10.

103 *Ibid.* pp. 10–11.

104 *Ibid.* p. 11. While targeting the Croats for their Catholic evil nature, Zečević is curiously supportive of the Slovenes, in line with official policy: 'the above mentioned does not apply to the Catholic Slovenia; it [left] Yugoslavia on uncertain grounds and used the right moment to become independent; no one has anything against it and let it be'(*ibid.* p. 11). Curiously, Slovenia and Croatia declared independence on the same day, and were recognised on the same day by the Vatican and the following day by Germany.

105 Dušan T. Bataković, 'Frustrated Nationalism in Yugoslavia: From Liberal to Communist Solution', *Serbian Studies*, 11:2 (1997) pp. 67–85. www.bglink.com/personal/batakovic/boston.html (accessed 18 June 1998).

106 *Ibid.*

107 Dušan T. Bataković, 'The National Integration of the Serbs and Croats: A Comparative Analysis', *Dialogue*, 7–8 (September–December, 1994) pp. 5–13. www.bglink.com/personal/batakovic/national.html (accessed 18 June 1998).

108 *Ibid.* (Italics mine.)

109 *Ibid.*

110 Kečmanović, *The Mass Psychology of Ethnonationalism*, p. 36.

111 Momčilo Zečević, 'Second Phase: 1918–1941', in Božidar Zečević (ed.), *The Uprooting*, p. 39.

112 *Ibid.* p. 36.

113 *Ibid.* p. 36.

114 Vasilije Krestić, 'First Phase: Until 1918', in Zečević (ed.), *The Uprooting*, p. 39.

115 Vasilije Krestić, 'Genocide in the Service of the Idea of a Greater Croatia Through

Genocide to a Greater Croatia' (Belgrade: Bigz – Izdavacko preduzece d.o.o./Serbian Unity Congress, 1997) http://suc.suc.org/culture/library/genocide/k7.htm (accessed 5 February 2000).
116 *Ibid.*
117 See Israel Charny, 'Toward a Generic Definition of Genocide', in George Andreopoulos (ed.), *Genocide: Conceptual and Historical Dimensions* (Philadelphia, PA: University of Pennsylvania Press, 1994) p. 85.
118 A good description of these different views and the rivalry between these men can be found in Tanner, *Croatia*, pp. 94–6.
119 Macartney, *Hungary: A Short History*, pp. 188–9.
120 Krestić, 'First Phase', p. 40. Ilić similarly writes of the continuous 'purges', and 'large scale physical attacks' which were supposedly a feature for much of the nineteenth and early twentieth centuries. See Ilić, 'The Serbs in the Former SR of Croatia', p. 327.
121 *Ibid.* p. 327.
122 *Ibid.* p. 45.
123 Zečević, 'Second Phase', p. 54.
124 Judah, *The Serbs*, pp. 57–8.
125 Bataković, 'Frustrated Nationalism in Yugoslavia'.
126 Zečević, 'Second Phase', pp. 52–66.
127 *Ibid.* p. 53.
128 *Ibid.* p. 54.
129 Bataković, 'Frustrated Nationalism in Yugoslavia'.
130 Quoted in Lenard J. Cohen, *Broken Bonds: Yugoslavia's Disintegration and Balkan Politics in Transition* (Boulder, CO: Westview Press, 1993) p. 282.
131 Dušan Vilić and Boško Todorović, *Breaking of Yugoslavia and Armed Secession* of Croatia (Beli Manastir: Cultura Centre 'Vuk Karadzic', 1996) pp. 3–4.
132 Zečević, 'Second Phase', p. 58.
133 *Ibid.* p. 42.
134 Quoted in Popov, 'La populisme serbe', pp. 33–4. Ekmečić was one of many academics who 'went national' following the collapse of Yugoslavia. His views had changed substantially from his early days as a 'Yugoslav' intellectual. See for example Vladimir Dedijer, Ivan Božić, Sima Ćirković, and Milorad Ekmečić, *History of Yugoslavia* (New York: McGraw-Hill, 1974). Ekmečić's 'Part Three' (pp. 249–412) is largely devoted to a study of Yugoslav history and identity from a non-nationalist point of view.
135 Milorad Ekmečić, (Untitled Commentary) in Avramov (ed.), *Genocide Against the Serbs*, p. 75.
136 For several examples of this idea see Avramov, *Genocide Against the Serbs*, p. 18; Radovan Kovačević, 'How Could the Serbs Forgive Vatican', *Serbia: News, Comments, Documents, Facts, Analysis*, 41 (February 1995) p. 46; and Cigar, *Genocide in Bosnia*, p. 77.

4

Croatia, 'Greater Serbianism', and the conflict between East and West

Christ's remarkable principle: 'Love your enemies, bless them that curse you, do good to them that hate you, and pray for them that use and persecute you.' That selfless sentiment has remained throughout history a cry of the weak, or an expression of those who have accepted their doom ... No matter how many examples can be found in life and history to support such renunciation, it has never overcome the passions of hatred and the desire to dominate or to take revenge. (Franjo Tudjman, *Horrors of War*)

SERBIA WAS CERTAINLY not alone in its revision of history, nor in its use of national mythology. The Croatian government also saw the merits of reinterpreting history to buttress their own political objectives. Many of Croatia's most interesting national myths were created well before the collapse of Yugoslavia. Franjo Tudjman's rise to power in 1990, and the eventual independence of Croatia, after almost five decades of Communist federalism, engendered a fertile climate for national myth creation.

Croatia's national propaganda evolved within an authoritarian context, and many of the central themes favoured by Croatian writers were similar to those advanced by their Serbian counterparts. The spectre of 'Greater Serbia' – which became likened to an anti-Semitism for Croats – was remarkably similar to Serbophobia. Many other myths appeared to be a reaction to a fear and strong distrust of the Serbs. Several, like the 'state right' tradition, the *Antemurale Christianitatis*, and Medjugorje, proved the existence of a civilised, peace-loving and enlightened Croatia. Other myths advanced the claim that the Serbs were religiously, culturally, and racially part of an Eastern and therefore inferior civilisation, while the Croats were more Western, more enlightened, better educated, and more democratic.

The beginnings of Croatian nationalism

In contrast to the rise of nationalism in Serbia, Croatian nationalism was not a reactive phenomenon to internal events. There were no Albanians harassing Croats in the 'provinces', and no minority within Croatia agitating for statehood before the 1990s. Nevertheless, Croatian nationalism, like its Serbian counterpart, was born of a sense of cultural submergence and political domination within Yugoslavia, and a perceived threat to Croatian language, culture, and religion. Nationalism came to the forefront in Yugoslavia during a period of decentralisation and liberalisation in the 1960s, when Tito was forced to tone down his hard-line policies on nationalism in return for Western loans. This opened a window of opportunity for a new generation of Croatian Communists, who began pushing for increased autonomy from the federal centre. In what became known as *Maspok*, activists demanded increased national rights within the federation. They cited the fact that Croats were under-represented in their own republic, since Serbs, who constituted roughly 13 per cent of the population, held 40 per cent of the Party posts, and a higher percentage of posts in the police, the secret police, and the JNA. Other contentious issues included the official figures for the number of Serbian war dead during the Second World War, the alleged economic exploitation of Croatia, and the status of Croatians in Bosnia-Hercegovina. The main focus of Croatian grievances, however, was the subordinate status of the Croatian language. A 1967 petition by the *Croatian Writer's Club* called for the designation of Croatian as a distinct language – both for educational and publishing purposes.[1]

Afraid of having '1941 all over again', Tito purged nationalist-oriented Communists, removing reformers from the ranks between 1971 and 1972. Some 1,600 Croatian Communists were subject to 'political measures', including ejection from the party – even arrest.[2] While these purges momentarily suppressed domestic nationalism, nationalism continued in the Diaspora, among Croatian expatriate groups in South America, Australia, New Zealand, the United States, Canada, and Europe. Often well-financed and closely co-ordinated, these groups were solidly anti-Communist, since they had left Yugoslavia as a result of their dislike or fear of the Titoist regime. Most of these people dreamed of one day returning home, and recreating an independent Croatia, freed of Communist control. With Tito's death in 1980, new opportunities opened up for such people, and their contacts with Croatia grew stronger.

The Croatian nationalist movement was eventually led by the former Communist general and historian Franjo Tudjman. Tudjman, born in 1922, was the youngest general in Yugoslav history, and also served as Tito's Head Political Commissar. Tudjman was an extremely successful, high-ranking

Communist, and a true believer, before his conversion to nationalism in the 1960s. It was only in 1967 when he began to challenge the official accounts of Croatian history during the Second World War that Tudjman was sacked for his nationalist writings. He was jailed after the Croatian Spring in 1971 and later in the 1980s. Tudjman exploited his prison time, casting himself as a martyr for the Croatian cause, and wrote extensively on his experiences and his vision for Croatia. His most important works included *An Endless Multitude of Historical Truth* (1977), *Croatia on Trial* (1981), and his most famous work, *Wastelands of Historical Reality* (1987), which was substantially re-edited for the 1996 English edition, *Horrors of War*. Tudjman's writings laid the basis for a movement to discover the truth about Croatia's history. With his typical egocentricity, which at times could assume messianic proportions,[3] he even conferred his own name on the movement that he claimed to have founded. 'Tudjmanism', as he defined it, was to be both a non-Communist nationalism and a 're-examination of Croatian history'.[4] Tudjman's revisions dealt primarily with the Second World War, and will be extensively discussed in the next two chapters dealing with that period of history.

On a practical level, Tudjman's denunciation of Communism and his embrace of Croatian nationalism made him highly popular among Diaspora communities, and allowed him to raise millions of dollars for the re-emergence of nationalism. This impressive war chest would be essential during his rise to power in 1990. So too was the support of the émigrés themselves, such as the former Canadian business-owner Gojko Šušak, who later became Defence Minister in the HDZ government. On 28 February 1989, the HDZ held its first public meeting, bringing together *Maspok* intellectuals and nationalists, both of whom advocated the increasing autonomy and liberalisation of Croatia.[5] By 1990, large numbers of émigrés had been brought in for the February HDZ Congress, mixing with Croatian and Hercegovenian nationalists.[6]

Tudjman's party, with its American-designed posters and slogans, appeared Western and progressive. He alluded to a referendum on Croatian independence, and promised to recreate the Croatian state in all its former glory. While the re-annexation of Kosovo and Vojvodina formed a central part of Milošević's election strategy it, Tudjman focused on the annexation of Bosnia-Hercegovina, referring to the unnatural shape of Croatia as 'an apple with a bite taken out of it'. All this would change – he promised – once the HDZ was in power.[7] While viewed with suspicion outside Croatia, within it, Tudjman enjoyed the same initial support as did Milošević in Serbia. His party gained victory in April 1990, ousting the weak reformed Communists, who were largely taken by surprise.[8] Tudjman's electoral triumph was typical of what Tom Nairn has termed an elite-manufactured 'popular revolution' or 'national liberation struggle'.[9] Whether it was Tudjman's 'Tudjmanism' or Milošević's 'Antibureaucratic Revolution', the myth of popular mobilisation against colonial (or in this case Communist) oppression was integral to the success of nationalism. Nairn also rightly identified the issue of underdevelopment as a key argument in many nationalisms. Tudjman echoed the widely held belief that, since the 1970s, most of Croatia's tourist earnings were being siphoned off by Belgrade. A vote for the HDZ was seemingly a vote for the end of Communist mismanagement and economic plundering.[10]

Unlike Milošević, who was very much an opportunist, Tudjman was a true believer in nationalism, and contributed to many of the nationalist myths used before and during the wars. As a result, control over the spread of nationalist propaganda was centralised within the HDZ apparatus. While there were several nationalist opposition groups, these were not co-opted into government, and remained marginal players. The Communists had been largely discredited by Vladimir Bakarić's slavish adherence to Tito during and after the *Maspok* period, when nationalistic Croatian Communist Party officials, journalists, and academics, were purged, arrested, and sometimes imprisoned. With Communist leaders discredited by Bakarić's legacy, many Croats felt that they had little choice but to seek independence through Tudjman's party. Other nationalist, non-Communist parties simply did not have the HDZ's level of funding, or its long-cultivated level of diaspora support.

Tudjman shared much with Milošević in terms of his hunger for power and his desire to create a national state that he alone could effectively control. As in Serbia, one of the first acts of government was to gain strict control of the media. Article 17 of the 1990 Croatian Constitution granted Tudjman sweeping presidential prerogatives to restrict constitutional rights 'during a state of war or an immediate danger to the independence and unity of the republic', while Article 101 allowed Tudjman to pass decrees without parliamentary approval.[11] These articles allowed for the replacement of media editors and managers in wartime, for the punishment of journalists, and for the banning of media for violating very strict conditions on the reporting of military affairs. Within two months of the 1990 elections, the Croatian Radio-Television Act was rushed through Parliament, changing the name of Radio-Televizija Zagreb to Hrvatska Radio-Televizija (HRT), while completely submitting it to government control.[12] Thereafter, it became a 24–hour mouthpiece for the HDZ regime.

Print media was another favoured target. HDZ faithful replaced journalists and editorial staff at HINA, (formerly TanJug) the state news agency.[13] Journalists of 'mixed origin, one Croat parent, one Serb' were denounced as enemies of Croatia, and were summarily dismissed from their posts. Independent papers, such as the Vjesnik Group, formerly 80 per cent privately owned, were slowly taken over by the government.[14] Vjesnik was one of the largest media groups in Croatia, and through it the government came to dominate the distribution and printing of newspaper and magazines.

Magazines owned by this group were often scuttled if they ran stories contrary to government interests; *Danas*, for example, had its circulation cut by 70 per cent.[15] The satirical weekly *Feral Tribune* was also harshly treated, with a 50 per cent sales tax in 1994, constant defamation in the government press, public paper burnings in the streets of Zagreb, as well as the theft of thousands of copies from newspaper kiosks. Its editors were also drafted into the army after criticising Tudjman.[16]

Centralisation of the media, as in Serbia, allowed HDZ leaders to control communication within the republic. At the same time, distinctly nationalist views could now be co-ordinated and spread throughout the country. As in Serbia, almost every aspect of life seemed to have become co-opted by Tudjman's nationalism, from the Art History Department at the University of Zagreb to the *Croatian Medical Journal*. As in Serbia, the media was seen as a means of supporting the HDZ regime while disseminating a nationalist viewpoint favourable to the government. Organisations such as the Croatian Heritage Foundation/Matica Hrvatska Iseljenika and the Croatian Information Center proved of central importance in reinterpreting Croatian history in line with government priorities. Publishing houses, such as OKC, VIGRAM i VIDEM (Croatia), Dorrance and Company, Northern Tribune, Roy Publishers (USA & Canada), and Fayard (France and Switzerland) also seemed to be affiliated with Croatian nationalists or disseminated their works.

State-controlled institutions would soon perform the same role as did their Serbian counterparts. They would become 'professional producers of subjective visions of the social world', as described by Valery Tishkov. Their responsibility would be enormous. Croatian history would be revised and rein-terpreted to highlight themes of Croatian goodness, chosenness, and victimisation – while the Serbs would be thoroughly demonised.[17] The editor-in-chief of HRT during the war clearly understood his place. HRT was to be the 'Cathedral of the Croatian spirit', with a duty, not to report events accurately as they happened, but rather, 'to frankly support the defence of Croat ethnic and historical space'.[18] For a supposedly democratic, post-Communist country, these were not auspicious beginnings.

While Milošević preferred designer suits, Tudjman revelled in his love of decorative Titoesque uniforms, replete with gold braid and large multi-coloured sashes. He even invented the garish costumes worn by members of his newly established presidential guard. Tudjman's own role in history was the subject of a Croatian-funded documentary film entitled 'Tudjman – Croatian George Washington', featuring highlights from his life, interviews, and the narration of the actor Martin Sheen.[19] This documentary, aired in Croatia in August 1997, portrayed Tudjman as a champion of democracy and a martyr for the Croatian nation.[20] Newspaper articles also praised him as the Croatian 'Moses' – leading his nation away from the 'golden calf' of Titoism that they had falsely worshipped before. Like the Serbs, Croats saw their country as the promised land, for which they had to struggle, since: 'Every day is an exodus from Egypt.'[21] By controlling the media and almost every aspect of communication within Croatia, the HDZ government under Tudjman was able to cement nationalist power virtually unopposed.

Contextualising the war in Croatia

While Serbian nationalism was seen first as a reaction to Kosovar Albanian demands for autonomy, Croatian nationalism was very much reliant on the threat posed by Milošević's own expansionist strategies. While Tudjman consistently argued that the Croatian Serbs were unjustified in their actions against the Croatian state, it often seemed that he was deliberately trying to provoke Serbian anger and resentment. His 1990 Constitution, for example, conspicuously omitted Serbs as a constituent nation within the new country. While it was stated that 'the members of other nations and national minorities, who are her citizens, will be guaranteed equal status with citizens of Croatian nationality', the Serbs were not mentioned by name – an oversight that soon played into the hands of Serbian nationalists. On a practical level, it became obvious that jobs, property rights, and even residence status depended on having Croatian citizenship, which was not an automatic right for non-Croats. A series of exams was required to obtain citizenship, requiring knowledge, but also approval, of a highly nationalistic interpretation of Croatian culture and history.[22]

This situation deteriorated further, as the police, universities, and most government bureaucracies began purging Serbs from their ranks. The resurrection of the *Šahovica*, the chequer-board coat of arms from medieval Croatia, and the Kuna as the new currency also exacerbated tensions – these symbols were starkly similar to those used during the Second World War. Tudjman's habit of renaming Croatian streets in honour of great nationalist heroes of the past, many of whom possessed dubious credentials, cast doubt on his own political views. And another problem was the influx of many former Ustaša collaborators and their families from the diaspora. The rise of extreme nationalism became a worrying phenomenon.

These aspects of the new regime led to the development of two Serbian nationalist parties within Croatia. Dobrica Ćosić encouraged Jovan Rasković and Jovan Opašić to found the Serbian Democratic Party in 1990, as a means of promoting Serbian national rights.[23] A more militant nationalist party, the Democratic Union of Knin, was also founded in 1990, by the dentist Milan Babić. Both groups soon merged at the behest of Ćosić and Milošević; but the differences between the two groups soon became obvious. The more moderate Rasković supported Croatian sovereignty, but advocated negotiating for autonomy and national rights within an independent Croatia. By contrast, Babić demanded complete autonomy for the Serbs in Croatia, and was prepared to back up his demands through armed conflict. Rasković's negotiations with Tudjman only gave Babić the time he needed to increase his stockpile of weapons, while allowing him to create the 'Association of Serb Municipalities' – a nascent Serbian assembly that formed the nucleus of the eventual Republic of Serpska Krajina.[24]

By 1990, with Serbia's backing, the Krajina Serbs became increasingly militant. Babić's list of demands included an autonomous police force and the right not to fly the Croatian flag in the Krajina. When these were rejected by the Croats, a 'state of war' was soon declared over Radio Knin. Open fighting broke out in April, and a referendum on Serbian independence was called for 17 April. The so-called 'log revolution' was one of the most memorable events at the start of the conflict. Armed Croatian Serbs blocked roads to prevent the Croatian police from intervening in the vote – a vote that of course resulted in a call for Serbian secession.[25]

Between February and June 1991 the rebellion escalated, as Croatian Serbs battled Croatian security forces with home-made weapons. Militia units from Serbia were soon brought in at the behest of Milošević, such as Arkan's 'Tigers' and Šešelj's 'White Eagles', both of which were trained and funded by the Serbian Ministry of the Interior. The situation became more dramatic as JNA tanks intervened, under the pretext of protecting Serbian minority rights – they claimed to be acting as 'peacekeepers'.[26] In the midst of this conflict, the Serbian government formally recognised the 'Serbian Autonomous Province of Krajina', a move that was to have lasting political and military consequences.[27]

Croatian leaders also contributed to the volatility of the situation. Defence Minister Gojko Šušak and a handful of paramilitaries fired several rockets into Borovo Selo, a Serbian suburb of Vukovar – seemingly to provoke conflict. Hostilities escalated, as Croatian policemen were killed by local Serbs in retaliation for the rocket bombings.[28] This rocket attack further justified the JNA's 'peacekeeping' initiatives, and by September 1991, Serbian and JNA forces controlled almost one-third of the Croatian territory. The role of the JNA had by this point switched from defence of the Yugoslav constitution to supporting the remaining republics in Yugoslavia, namely Serbia and Montenegro. Their shelling of Vukovar (the last Croatian stronghold in eastern Slavonia) in October 1991 was dramatic proof of this. The JNA also began its wanton attack on Dubrovnik in the same month.[29]

It was very much within this climate of fear and mistrust that militant Croatian propaganda entered the mainstream. While Tudjman, like his counterpart in Serbia, had assumed almost complete control over political and media power within the state, he had yet to operationalise it fully. While the

Serbs were the first to engage in full-scale attack, Tudjman was instrumental in provoking conflict. His narrow-minded exclusive interpretations of Croatian history denied Serbs the cultural and political rights (and privileges) they had enjoyed in the SFRY. Further, by rejecting many of Rasković's pacifist and arguably reasonable demands, he legitimated the rise of Babić and his more violent nationalist cohorts.[30]

It was clear that Šušak and his colleagues had deliberately provoked Serbian military aggression in Vukovar. Tudjman would also be blamed, first for ordering the shelling, and then for refusing to send military aid to relieve the beleaguered Croatian defenders, who were being heavily bombarded. Tudjman used the siege of Vukovar to gain maximum political credibility. He was able to claim that Croats were the victims of Serbian terror – what Gow and Tisley have rightly termed a 'victim strategy'. It is clear that Tudjman's government, rather than sending arms and troops to end the 86-day siege, preferred to use the political capital to be gained by Vukovar's destruction, which led to the charge that 'Tudjman manipulated its position, rather than defending it'.[31] It was clear that nationalists were promoting a form of 'counteridentification' – creating a sense of national cohesion and support for Tudjman though a fear of external attack.[32] Certainly, Tudjman was able to capitalise on Vukovar, ensuring Croatia's perceived position as victim rather than aggressor during the conflict. This view would continue, even during Tudjman's forays into Bosnia-Hercegovina, when he chose to attack another republic rather than take back Croatian territory held by the Serbs.[33]

It was in this context of war that a wholesale reappraisal of Croatian history came about – one that would involve many diverse sectors of the community. Like the Serbs, the Croats argued that they had been the victims of expansionist powers throughout their history. Further, a long and horrific history of Serbian imperialism and danger was created, so that the contemporary crop of Serbian nationalists would not be seen as a cabal of power-hungry opportunists, but rather as representatives of a typical, age-old Serbian strategy of expansion and repression. Croatian–Serbian relations had to be uprooted and decontextualised, and then recontextualised, in the light of new evidence and new historical revisionist arguments. This process was identical to that used by the Serbs, and was similar to Northrop Frye's understanding of positive and negative agencies within Biblical teleology. With some careful manipulation, Milošević could represent, to the Croats, what the Pharaoh of Exodus or Nebuchadnezzar represented to the ancient Hebrews – a symbol of evil and Fall.

By clearly presenting themselves to the outside world as victims of Serbian genocide, Croatians hoped to court Western recognition and aid, both of which would prove vital for their self-defence. Such imagery would also play into their hands during Croatian machinations in Bosnia. Myths of persecution and victimisation laid the basis for other forms of mythology – myths proving that Croatia had every right to exist as a separate state, and then myths dealing with the separateness of almost every aspect of national identity, from culture, religion and language, to racial, linguistic and psychological traits. Once the evils of Greater Serbia had been proved, the great differences between Croats and Serbs were repeatedly stressed.

Croatia confronts 'Greater Serbia'

Croatian nationalism was often less triumphalist or self-exalting than the Serbian variety. The proliferation of books, articles, documentaries, and conference papers dealt mainly with the fear of Serbian aggression – portraying Croatia as the helpless victim of Serbian expansionism. It is therefore appropriate to begin a discussion of Croatian myths with the concept of 'Greater Serbia', a Serbian nationalist project from the nineteenth century aimed primarily at empire-building in the Balkans. Without understanding Croatian perceptions of Greater Serbia, it is difficult to contextualise other forms of Croatian writing, which have largely justified the existence of the Croatian nation in its present borders. It is also difficult to understand how and why Croatian writers have devoted so much effort to myths of differentiation between Croats and Serbs, at cultural, sociological, geographical, psychological, racial and linguistic levels. Greater Serbia for Croats was tantamount to genocide – Serbian expansion implied *ipso facto* a reduction of Croatian territory, ethnic cleansing, and the death of Croatian civilians.

As in the Serbian case, historical amnesia was important to many Croatian writers. The differences between Serbs and Croats were not only to have proved irreconcilable, but more importantly, to have always existed. History was reinterpreted to prove that under no circumstances had Serbs and Croats ever chosen to co-operate. Serbs would figure as Kečmanović's 'universal culprit', or perhaps more accurately as a pseudospecies, completely different from the Croats in absolutely every respect.[34] Their sole ambition throughout history, as understood by Croatian historians, was to expand their state, while destroying any nations that stood in their path.

The origins of Greater Serbia stemmed from before the Ottoman conquest of the Balkans, and were specifically tied to the 'Great Medieval Serbian State' under Tsar Dušan in the fourteenth century. This state was one of the largest in the Balkans, and its dismantling after 1389, some Croatian writers contended, established a template for later Serbian territorial aspirations.[35] The recreation of Dušan's state was linked directly to the efforts of the Serbian Orthodox Church. Serbian writers were always quick to denounce Catholicism, and the Croats were little different in their portrayals of

Orthodoxy. For many, the Church was 'religiously exclusivist', with objectives said to include 'destruction of all members of other nations and faiths, the stealing of possessions and conquering of territories all resulting in religious, national, and political exclusivism and intolerance'.[36]

While Serbian writers accused nineteenth-century Croats of trying to expand their state under the Vatican's wing, Croats portrayed this century as the culmination of the 'Greater Serbian' ideal, as the Serbs engaged in wars of conquest to recreate Dušan's state. As one writer put it:

> The syndrome of Serbian warped notions of heroism, all-Serbian unity, racial domination and megalomaniacal claims of ownership of other people's territories is so powerful that Serbians themselves believe in this lie, let alone the insufficiently informed world public. This gave them sufficient time to commit a great number of crimes from their bloody palette in order to paint the picture of the conquering invasion of South-eastern Europe.[37]

Serbs, from the beginning of the nineteenth century, would stand accused of bloodshed and hatred, based on their need to recreate their former kingdom. Croatian writers compiled anthologies of Serbian writings from the nineteenth century, citing a variety of documents to prove that Serbia had a long history of antagonising its neighbours. 'Of all the parties in the war today', three pro-Croatian French writers concluded during the conflict in Bosnia, 'Serbia is the one that has provided the oldest doctrinal arsenal, and hence the most elaborate and moral and intellectual justifications.'[38] Every stratum of Serbian society, it seemed, was actively engaged in this national project. As they wrote of the history of Serbian ideas:

> [S]ince the beginning of the 19th century, Serbian writers, clergy, military men and politicians have talked of a Greater Serbia, a 'homogenous and pure Serbia' while exalting violence, as well as introducing the term 'ethnic cleansing' (*ciscenje*). There more than anywhere, the origins of patriotism can be found in the fight against Ottoman occupation, which was twisted by nationalism; the unnatural 'Yugoslav' idea was steeped in an imperialism tainted with racism.[39]

Largely a presentation and 'analysis' of Serbian national writings, this anthology began with documents from 1807, positing that the Serbian love of genocide had ancient roots, with Serbian writings being little more than 'reference texts for a school of hate'. In many respects, their approach differed very little from that of Serbian historians, who constantly linked Croatian nationalism with genocide. Echoing these types of Serbian argument, the authors stressed that 'the conceptualisation and application of "ethnic cleansing" is an indispensable means of realising the Greater Serbian project' – thus again linking Serbian nationalism and genocide together.[40]

Such anecdotal writings accompanied reviews of pivotal events in Serbian history, reviews designed to prove the genocidal nature of the Serbs. The first concerned a rebellion against Ottoman rule in 1807, when the Serbs supposedly 'cleansed Belgrade', 'slaughtering Turks', raping children, and banishing the Jews. This was to be the first instance of what the authors termed 'ethnocide and culturocide', a concerted attempt to erase Turkish and Islamic influence in Serbia.[41] Less biased historians have more accurately seen this as a period of rebellion against Ottoman rule, a rebellion that was not always successful owing to the great power politics between the Ottomans, Russians, French and Austrians.[42] Later periods of history were similarly derided. Serbs were accused of using ethnic cleansing as part of a wartime strategy throughout the nineteenth and twentieth centuries, during the 1878 struggle for independence, and the 1912 and 1913 Balkan Wars.[43] Again, it was stressed that Serbian nationalism equalled genocide, and that Serbian state-building was consonant with atrocities of the worst description.

As an ideology, Greater Serbia came into its own in the middle of the nineteenth century, when a series of Greater Serbia political plans were hatched. The first and most famous of these was the 'Načertanije' or 'Outline', written in 1844 by the Serbian government minister Ilija Garašanin. The 'Outline' was a basic plan for expanding the Serbian empire to include most of Dušan's former kingdom. Very much the work of a utopian dreamer, it included claims to Bosnia-Hercegovina, Montenegro, Macedonia, Albania, parts of Bulgaria, and Croatia. Equally famous was Vuk Karadzić's 'Serbs All and Everywhere' (1849), which used a linguistic definition of nationalism (similar to that of Starčević), to posit that Croats and Slovenians were in fact Serbs, who all spoke the same Serbian language. This, as well, was seen to be a justification for the assimilation of non-Serbian nations – particularly the Croats.[44] One historian went to far as to suggest that Karadzić's policies were little different from those of the Nazis, fifty years before Hitler's birth: 'This is quite similar to what the Hitlerites did in Nazi Germany. To deny the actual existence of a certain race is a subliminal way of dehumanizing it – the first step in a planned and systematic genocide. This type of rhetoric was also evident with anti-Semitism, which is the paragon of a planned and systematic genocide.'[45] This is an obvious example of the Manichaean morality that pervaded Croatian and Serbian nationalism. Both sides ignored the real similarities of Starčević's and Karadzić's national programmes, which were both bent on uniting the South Slavs against colonial oppression.

The mid-nineteenth century is consistently presented as the time when the Croats first became a primary target of Serbian aggression. The first anti-Croatian demonstration took place in Belgrade in 1892, followed by riots in Knin and in other regions. Supposedly, there was a concerted Serbian attempt to assimilate the Croats into some form of Serbian nationalism, laying the basis for the eventual annexation of Croatia itself.[46] Other historians would advance the 'Pasić Plan', created by the former Prime Minister Nikola

Pasić, as another example of Serbian expansionist goals. According to Branko Miletić, this plan became the most important political document in Serbia, 'nothing short of a blueprint for a Serb-dominated empire stretching from Thessaloniki to Trieste'.[47] It was also to be a tool by which 'genocide in the Balkans has been honed, fashioned, and recently perfected'.[48]

The beginning of Peter Karađorđević's Serbian kingdom in 1903 was often portrayed as another era of Greater Serbian assertiveness. Politicians such as Nikola Stojanović were also accused of whipping up genocidal hysteria among the Serbs. His 1902 article 'To Extermination: Ours or Yours' has long been cited as a blueprint for ethnic cleansing and genocide, applying a Social Darwinist model of the world (survival of the fittest race) to understanding how Serbs should best approach various non-Serbian groups, including Moslems and Croats.[49] Soon after the publication of Stojanović's article, Serbian nationalists, supposedly inspired by his document, began 'an organised extermination of Croatians and other non-Serbian nations in 1903,' the result being that 'Croatians were victims on their own land from 1903 to 1941.'[50] The beginning of the twentieth century was presented as a time when the Serbs profited by the weakness of the Austro-Hungarian Empire to persecute Croats in their own land:

> From 1906 to 1909, Croatians were forced to endure fear in all villages [*in*] which they resided together with Serbians. Their houses were burned and crops destroyed. There were numerous cases of beatings along with wounding [of] both Croatians and Serbians who did not accept the aggressive Greater-Serbian politics. There were a number of Croatian political leaders who were murdered.[51]

Serbs were also blamed for genocidal acts against the Albanians, the Bosnians and the Macedonians during the First Balkan War in 1912. Supposedly inspired by the 'Načertanije', Serbs 'set entire villages on fire, killing civilians in the most barbaric fashion using knives, axes and dull wooden mallets'.[52] A coherent picture of the Serbs emerges from a reading of Croatian historical descriptions, as bloody, treacherous, cold, calculating, ruthless, greedy, and expansionist. Not all Serbian methods, however, were so public and brutal. For Croatian writers, the rise of Serbian secret societies was also a crucial part of their plan to control the Balkans. Groups like the 'Četniks', the 'Black Hand', the 'Slovenian South', 'Serbian Defence' and 'National Defence' were all accused of undermining Croatian sovereignty, while continuing the genocidal policies of 'Greater Serbia'. King Peter, through the 'Black Hand', was blamed for the assassination of Archduke Ferdinand in 1914, and by extension, for provoking the First World War.[53]

Summarising what lessons could be learned from a review of Serbian history, the director of the Croatian Information Center, Ante Beljo, in the introduction to one of many anthologies of Serbian nationalist documents, would note the following: 'Trying to hide their true motives from the eyes of the world with a series of historic and demographic falsifications, today's proponents of Greater Serbian ambitions are only continuing the promotion of an idea that has been smouldering with various degrees of intensity for over a century.'[54] Such an attitude removed any sense of individual responsibility from the equation during the 1990s. The Serbs were merely acting according to an age-old predetermined plan, as if they somehow had no choice, as if history had been leading up to that moment for over a century. Milošević was therefore not operating from opportunism or self-interest, but was simply continuing a traditional Serbian pattern of behaviour.

Documents from this era of Serbian history were extremely popular with Croatian academics. Without much difficulty, various jingoistic writings from a wide variety of sources could be collated together according to their dates of publication. A noted Croatian glossator would then offer contemporary comments about what each document 'meant' about the war in Croatia, well over a century after it was written. The whole purpose of such an exercise was to demonstrate that, very much like a form of Biblical evil, Serbian expansionism and bloodlust was timeless and had no sell-by date.

The key to understanding the Serbian 'genocidal' mind lay in reading edited volumes such as Beljo's *Greater Serbia: From Ideology to Aggression*, Separović's *Documenta Croatica*, or Grmek, Gjidara, and Simac's influential, *Le nettoyage ethnique: Documents historiques sur une idéologie serbe*, all of which were meant to tell the 'truth' about Serbian contemporary events from a selective reading of history. Such anthologies were meant to inform the reader about what the Croats were about to get themselves into in 1918, when they committed the tragic error of entering into political association with the Serbs for the first time in history. Like some sort of Shakespearean tragedy, the outside world was meant to understand the Croats' fatal flaw (that they did not know how evil the Serbs were), and then wince with pain every time something went wrong.

Unfortunately, most of these nineteenth-century documents did not actually describe a blueprint for genocide at all. For example, Stojanović's 'To Extermination: Ours or Yours' said little about exterminating anyone. The glossating aside, a review of the selected passages of Stojanović's work, even when reprinted in a Croatian anthology, offered little to indicate that all Croats were at risk of being annihilated. He certainly and worryingly argued that 'Croats have neither a separate language, nor unified customs, nor a fully unified lifestyle', making it clear that 'this cannot be a distinct or separate nation'.[55] However, while his writings were extremely patronising, Stojanović advocated Croatia's union with Serbia, to allow Croatia to secure 'economic, political and cultural independence, and freedom from German encroachment'.[56] Stojanović, it seems, was trying to rally his perceived co-nationals together against an external threat, rather than advocating Croatian physical annihilation.

Croatian perceptions of the first Yugoslavia

For Croatian writers, the general public were supposed to view the situation in Yugoslavia during the early 1990s as a tragedy – the Serbs having no choice but to be genocidal tyrants, the Croats with no choice but to play the victim and try to defend themselves against attack. However, by most accounts, the first year of the new Kingdom was relatively positive, and there was a reasonably high level of support for the state. It was, after all, a preferable situation to annexation by Italy or continued colonial domination by Austria-Hungary.[57]

Nevertheless, as history was revised, the reality of Croatian motivations and reactions at that time was left by the wayside. Royalist Yugoslavia became the first time that Serbs and Croats were united politically and economically in a joint state. But it was also seen by Croats as the first real instance of Serbian dominance over Croats, the first time when Croats were truly confronted with Greater Serbia.[58] In practice, this would mean a time when 'Serbian chauvinism transformed itself into virulent anti-Croatianism, culminating in acts of terror and violence.' This period was described as one of 'symbiosis', when 'the theories and ideas of nineteenth-century pro-Greater Serbianism were welded with twentieth-century fascist imperialism and Chetnik terrorism'. Yugoslavia therefore gave 'Greater Serbia' not only a framework, but 'limbs as well', 'limbs with which it struck at the hearts of all non-Serbs in royalist Yugoslavia'.[59] Such imagery, consciously or not, evoked images of some sort of B-movie monster, a black and white Serbia festooned with claws and rubber arms, attacking Croatia – an innocent young maid who could do nothing except valiantly fight back against her aggressor.

Miroslav Krleža also promoted the view that the state was cruel, racist, and despotic. In *Ten Bloody Years*, Krleža argued that the state was founded on 'blood and violence', and provoked instant rebellion by the Croats against the regime, resulting in brutal massacres in Zagreb. Police open fired on crowds demanding an independent Croatia, killing 100 people – these subsequently became immortalised as the 'December victims'.[60] Further, we hear that the Serbian army treated Croatia as 'if it were enemy territory', and actively suppressed Croatian nationalism, imprisoning political leaders while using the Ministry of Internal Affairs to quell opposition.[61] Such ideas clearly refuted Serbian claims that the Kingdom had been an egalitarian, peaceful and democratic country, constructed according to a European model.

However, the horrors of the Serbian kingdom were evident not only in Croatia – according to Croatian accounts. The first genocide in Bosnia, some

111

argued, was not in 1992–93, but back in 1918 and 1919, when Serbian-controlled Yugoslavia instigated a series of agricultural reforms in Bosnia. One academic described these reforms as 'genocide against Bosniacs', when some 1.2 million hectares of land were confiscated from wealthy Bosnian families, without adequate compensation. In this account, 'homelessness' and 'genocide' amounted to the same thing.[62] This 'genocide' (or land redistribution) was designed to allow some 200,000 Serbian families to 'colonise' Bosnia, thereby destroying the demographic balance of the region. The Serbs were further accused of implementing a 'death march' in 1919, where 50,000 Bosnian peasants were forced to leave their homes, over 1,000 of whom were killed by 'Serbian terrorists'. During this time, the author reveals: 'a long colony of victims walked to numerous camps in Kosovo and Sandzak, where they were transported to Turkey and settled in Anatolia'.[63] The imagery created here bears a stark resemblance to the genocide of the Armenians by the Turks, when the Armenians were also forced to abandon their homes on a long 'death march'.

Certainly there was land reform during this time, which led to the confiscation of Bosnian property. However, such policies were designed to help the general population, not to commit genocide against the Moslems. While feudalism had been abandoned by the Austro-Hungarian Empire in 1848, the vestiges of the Ottoman sharecropping tradition nevertheless continued in Bosnia, Macedonia, Kosovo, and Vojvodina. Some 7,000 Bosnian landlords, representing 0.5 per cent of the population, controlled some 85,000 families of feudal serfs, both Moslem and Christian. These serfs were tied to the land, and in addition to labour service, were forced to pay excessive proportions of their produce, often one-eighth of the total. As Phyllis Auty describes, agricultural modernisation and the improvement of peasant life would have been impossible without land reform.[64] While it is certainly true that Serbs received land in Bosnia-Hercegovina, John Lampe argues that the majority of these feudal farmers were in fact Serbs, who had been working the land for a very long time. He also fixes their number at 113,000, not 200,000, and states that while Serbs received the bulk of the appropriated land in Bosnia, they did represent 42 per cent of the population at that time. Jozo Tomasevich, the leading authority on the 1919 land reforms, is clear that this redistribution was 'a political and socio-economic necessity'.[65] There is nothing to suggest in any of these accounts that a policy of genocide was pursued.

In general, Croatian writers conveyed the impression that Yugoslavia was nothing more than Serbian-dominated anarchy, where every non-Serbian group was stripped of its rights and lived in terror. According to one account, Serbian Četniks ran wild throughout the kingdom, and, inspired by their desire to create a Greater Serbia 'killed people, beat them, threatened them, and burned their houses'. At the same time, the assassination of

Croatian Peasant Party leader Stjepan Radić and four other deputies was a further indication of Serbian malevolence and Croatian weakness. But if this situation was not bad enough, King Aleksander's royal dictatorship (1929) was seen as significantly worse, as a time when 'the lives of non-Serbian people had no value'.[66] The disbanding of political parties and the re-division of the country into Banovina would coincide with further political intrigue, mass arrests and bloodshed. This era is generally portrayed as one of torture, police repression, and the liquidation of non-Serbian opposition leaders – the Communists in particular.[67] In short, the Croatian decision to join Yugoslavia was a complete disaster, resulting in Serbian domination and persecution.

The republication of Henri Pozzi's *Black Hand Over Europe* by the Croatian Information Center provided a link between this period and the more contemporary crisis. Ante Beljo was clear about the book's purpose in the introduction: 'The contemporeneity of Pozzi's work derives from the concord of present and past historical manifestations and circumstances … a grave warning to all those who still, like their predecessors underestimate the Balkan precedent.'[68] He would further claim: 'The methods and philosophy of the Black Hand [secret society] can be recognised in many of the present actions of Serbian politicians and generals.'[69] Again, Beljo referred to the timeless, even ahistorical, nature of Serbian nationalism. Serbs were the same, no matter who they were, or which century they lived in. A Serb, it appeared, could be nothing more than a bloodthirsty expansionist nationalist. This is why an understanding of the past was supposedly crucial in understanding later developments. As in the Bible, nothing changed.

Because of the timeless quality of Serbian nationalism, 'Greater Serbia' seemingly meant the same thing to Vuk Drasković as it would have meant to Jovan Cvijić, or Vuk Karadzić. Former Tudjman adviser Slaven Letica, expanding upon the timeless qualities of 'Greater Serbia', would describe it as a 'transhistorical phenomenon', 'frozen and suppressed into the subconscious' – an evil waiting to reappear at an opportune moment.[70] As Letica describes the phenomenon in rather heavy-handed jargon:

> The moment these SUBSTITUTES (Yugoslavism etc.) begin to wear out, become routine or fail, the Greater-Serbian and All-Serbian assertions re-emerge. They experience renaissance, new political and intellectual articulations; again they draw large-scale political attention; they become the basis for new-old All-Serbian populist ideologies and movements … this represents a dull easily predictable and unavoidable historical repetition … its goal is to conquer and its means are to dominate and to exercise force.[71]

Letica's statement was consonant with the general view of the Serbs as genocidal empire-builders, bent not only on enslaving other nations, but on liquidating them as well. The fear of Greater Serbia would thus become the most important Croatian myth of persecution, a myth of Serbia as an ahistorical negative force with a national project based solely on hatred of other nations. If the Hebrews needed the Philistines, the Egyptians, and the Romans to rally their people together, the Croats needed only one negative agency – the Serbs, and only the Serbs, would suffice. After such portrayals of Serbian–Croatian relationships throughout history, there could be no doubt in the 1990s that Serbs were simply following their familiar pattern of genocide, while the Croats were following their familiar pattern of playing the victim. Such an appraisal of Serbian history allowed Croatian nationalists to obfuscate the many embarrassing decades of philoserbianism in Croatia. Early attempts at Yugoslavism and Illyrianism were excised from the history books, while any arguments that Starčević had advanced more or less the same view as Karadzić were summarily ignored.

That Serbs and Croats basically saw each other's history as a mirror image of their own should come as no surprise. A great deal of debate occurred between these two nations during the war, in newspapers, magazines, and most importantly, on the internet. The use of the world wide web as a medium of communication opened many new avenues for propagandists. While it is both expensive and difficult to print and circulate propaganda in large quantities, it was relatively cheap and easy to scan and paste Serbian and Croatian propaganda on a variety of websites. Those who agreed with the government position benefited from links on official sites. This allowed for a continuous stream of new information and publications, designed to rebut arguments advanced by the other side. This new medium of expression allowed for the spread of a great deal of information within a very short time.

Croatian state right and the *Antemurale Christianitatis*

In reaction to the idea of 'Greater Serbia' and its expansionist and seemingly genocidal political project, the Croats were keen to stress their own myths of nationhood and uniqueness, myths that ran counter to the 'genocidal' ambitions of the Serbs. One of the primary myths of identification was that of the 'state right' tradition, the myth of continuous Croatian statehood for the past thousand years. This was designed to prove that Croats had a historic right to exist as an autonomous nation within their current borders. That the 1990 Constitution described the new state as the realisation of 'the thousand year dream of the Croatian People' certainly attested to the centrality of this millennial myth.[72]

The myth of continuous Croatian statehood stemmed from two very early Croatian institutions: the *Banus* (the chief executive), and the *Sabor* (or people's assembly), both of which emerged from the seventh-century ruling traditions of the Croats. These institutions were ratified by a *Pacta Conventa* with Hungary in 1102, when Croats accepted the indirect rule of the

Hungarian king. An elected *Ban*, or Duke, was to be the representative of the Hungarian empire – a man portrayed as a positive symbol of 'heroism, faithfulness, protection for the common people and love of country'.[73] This tradition of 'State Right' was coupled with the advent of Western European feudalism and the rise of an aristocratic hierarchy, both of which intimated that Croatian legislative traditions were heavily influenced by the West.

Numerous writers thus argued for such a continuous state, even during the Austro-Hungarian period, when Croatia was ruled directly from Vienna and Budapest. Even then, Croatian historians argued that the country had 'preserved the characteristics of its constitutional statehood'.[74] Many Croatian historians posited that the *Pacta*, coupled with the later guarantee of free elections from the Habsburgs in 1527, gave clear proof of the continuation of Croatian sovereignty.[75] Such myths proved of central importance after 1990, as Croatia justified its right to existence as an independent nation on historical grounds.

This glorious millennium-long period of Croatian history, the continuous state, was said to have been destroyed precisely with the rise of the Kingdom of the Serbs, Croats and Slovenes, in 1918. As one early historian wrote: 'The "Yugoslav" period of Croat history is definitely the darkest and most humiliating ... for the first time in 13 centuries the institutions of the BANUS and SABOR were completely abolished.'[76] Thus this lengthy period of Croatian 'state right' was effectively ended in the twentieth century, as the Serbs and their genocidal Greater Serbian project swept through the Balkans and destroyed indigenous cultures. Once again, the image of a peaceful, democratic, and Western state destroyed by the genocidal Serbs was presented as proof of the dramatic reversal of fortune the Croats had suffered after their contact with the Serbs.

This thousand-year myth very much resembled Anthony Smith's view of the Golden Age. It was indeed designed to 'unfold a glorious past', while demonstrating to Croats that their traditions were ancient and noble.[77] Nevertheless, it had more in common with George Schöpflin's 'myths of election', where the Croatian nation had somehow been 'chosen' by God or history because of its great and heroic qualities. While this was not a myth of Covenant in any sense, the fact that the Croatian nation still existed after a thousand years and still retained a form of autonomy implied that it was superior to its neighbours, and had withstood the test of time.[78] There is no doubt that the myth of 'state right' gave Croats a sense of moral and cultural superiority, since their nation had outlasted most others in history – supposedly without being conquered.

At the same time, the fact that the millennial dream died in 1918 contained the seeds of tragedy. Like the myth of Kosovo, the loss of Croatian statehood plunged the Croats into a terrible Fall. Unlike what happened in the myth of Kosovo, however, the nation had not been elevated to holy or chosen status. It thus fell to Tudjman and his colleagues to resurrect the Croatian nation and bring about its independence. Such myths were therefore a reflection of a Smithian Golden Age in one respect; but this Golden Age was set up in order to present a historical tragedy, in order to introduce the Fall myth that was its inevitable concomitant. As such, we are confronted once more with the tragic nature of Croatian nationalism. Their proud state tradition was for ever destroyed by the Serbs in the first Yugoslavia.

In many ways, such myths disguised much of the reality of that time. True, Croatia had some autonomy in Austria-Hungary, in that the *Nagodba* allowed the Croats to retain the *Ban* as President. They also had their Sabor, their Supreme Court, and their Domobrani or Home Guard, and Croatian was kept as the language of government, administration, and education. However, autonomy ended there. The Hungarian Prime Minister had the power to appoint and remove *Bans* at will without consulting the Croats, and 55 per cent of Croatian revenues were allocated to the joint treasury of the Hungarian lands, leaving just 45 per cent for domestic use. Furthermore, during the nineteenth century both the Medjimurje region and Rijeka were annexed by Hungary.[79]

Additionally, while some Croatian writers portrayed the Serbs as the worst villains during the First World War, Austria-Hungary was certainly not an innocent bystander in the region. They stood accused of operating concentration camps in Bosnia-Hercegovina during this time, and, as Louis Adamović describes, imprisoned over 40,000 South Slavs, including 'a great many Orthodox priests and teachers and students and intellectuals, Catholic as well as Orthodox'. Of these, he claims that 10,000 died of diseases contracted in these prisons, while another 5,000 were shot.[80] After the War, the Croats could have taken advantage of Wilsonianism and gone it alone. Of course, there was a serious risk that Italy would invade and occupy the country, particularly the Istrian Peninsula, which it had always claimed. Caught between Italian invasion and South Slavic unity, most Croats chose to see where decades of Illyrianism and Yugoslavism could take them.

The civilisational divide between East and West

Like the Serbs with their Kosovo myth, the Croats advanced their own myths of historical courage and power. Another aspect of 'state right' was the myth of the *Antemurale Christianitatis*, the notion that Croatia was the easternmost rampart of Christian Europe, and was the sole defender of the West against the East. While the Serbs had also used similar imagery, suggesting that Orthodoxy was the West's defence against Islam, the Croatian interpretation saw *all* former Ottoman colonies as eastern, with Orthodoxy itself as an eastern religion. Clearly, this moved the eastern border to the Krajina region, within Croatian territory. Writers were quick to cite Croatia's 1,200-year history of suffering, humiliation and sacrifice in defence of Western Christendom.

Very much like the Serbs, the Croats saw themselves as a peace-loving and spiritual people, who had never attacked others outside their borders.[81] Croats were to be a noble and benevolent nation because of their Roman Catholic faith. As legend has it, the Pope sent priests to baptise the Croats in the third century. After this time, the Croats supposedly made a 'covenant' with the Pope, and seemingly with God as well, that in return for living at peace with their neighbours, and never making wars with foreign countries, they would receive both God and 'Peter the disciple of Christ's' protection against attack.[82] This was very much a myth of Covenant and divine election. Croats had supposedly chosen to become a peace-loving nation, and because of this choice, they were protected from on high.

Croatian historians drew a sharp line between the Catholic world, and the Orthodox world further to the east, tracing Serbian–Croatian antagonism to the effective division of the Roman empire into Eastern and Western Empires in the fourth century AD.[83] For contemporary historians, the division of the Roman Empire created an unfathomable gulf between the two nations – who stood on opposite sides of the great divide between East and West. They also traced the same fundamental line of division in later periods of history, and in particular, to the Great Schism of 1054 that divided the Christian Church between adherents of Greek Orthodoxy and of Roman Catholicism. According to Croatian historians, this would further create a civilisational split between 'two different civilizations and cultures, that is eastern and western spheres'. The River Drina was often portrayed as the real dividing line between these two groups, 'figuratively called the border of the two worlds'.[84]

Such imagery would later be expanded to include the period of Ottoman rule, seen also as the beginnings of 'Greater Serbia' and the rise of the Serbian Church. Within these five centuries of Ottoman rule, Serbs supposedly learnt their cruelty and despotism, while becoming further separated culturally from the Croats. That Serbs and Croats had been culturally distinct for centuries made Croatia's decision to seek independence all the more reasonable. That the Serbs were eastern and therefore somehow civilisationally inferior to the Croats made it seem natural that the latter would gravitate towards Western Europe. Themes such as this were rife during the war in Croatia. Most academics referred to such a division, and Tudjman truly believed that a dividing line existed. As he claimed in one speech: 'Croats belong to a different culture, a different civilisation from Serbs. Croats are part of western Europe, part of the Mediterranean tradition. Long before Shakespeare and Molière, our writers were translated into European languages. The Serbs belong to the east. They are eastern peoples, like the Turks and the Albanians. They belong to the Byzantine culture.'[85]

If Tudjman was not Serbophobic, then he was most certainly 'Balkanophobic'. For him, as for many Croats, the idea of Croatia as part of the Balkans was inimical to all their past traditions and values. As he commented in one interview: 'Based on its geopolitical position, its fourteen-centuries-long history, civilization and culture, Croatia belongs to the central European and Mediterranean circle in Europe. Our political links with the Balkans between 1918 and 1990 were just a short episode in the Croatian history and we are determined not to repeat that episode ever again!'[86] He later argued that, geographically, Croatia had always been a part of central Europe, and was culturally a part of this region, except for the 'recent past' when 'balkanism has constantly subordinated the Croatian State territory to an *Asiatic form of government*'.[87] In other words, Croatia's history placed it within the Western world, while Serbia was part of the Eastern or 'Asiatic' world. Any association between these two cultures was purely a historical anomaly.

Croatia's reinterpretation of history also implied rejecting the Balkans itself, a project that found expression in a conference entitled 'South-eastern Europe in the 20th Century', whose organisers stressed categorically that Croatia was not a Balkan country, but rather, a part of 'South-eastern Europe'. For the conference organisers: 'being a part of the Balkans means being a part of the backward part of Europe'.[88] Croats, despite the ravages of war, still had hope for the future: that once their independence was assured, they would somehow be able to become symbolically part of a different world. Certainly, no Croatians wanted to be associated with the Serbs, who were seen as nothing better than 'Vandals' and 'Asian hordes.'[89] The use of such Orientalism with reference to the Serbs shows clearly that culturally, or 'civilisationally', Serbs did not belong in Croatia, as members of a different 'civilisation'. Further, their place was across the Drina, in Serbia. Through their religious and cultural separation after the Great Schism, Serbs seemingly became a pseudospecies. They came to represent all that was opposite to Croatian identity.

This idea of East versus West proved to be of fundamental importance in defining Croatian self-identity. So too was the geography of the region, the liminal quality of Croatia's landmass, the last rampart of the West in the East. The Croatian geographer Zalijka Corak expanded upon the *Antemurale* myth, using a social geographer's eye to understand Croatia's history:

> The very shape of Croatia, the way it looks now is a dramatic sign that its existence has been endangered. It represents a kind of visual unrest which should also be removed as an error . . . A country the shape of which is not the product of a long and authentic historical process cannot assess the paradigm of historical space that Croatia represents. But Croatia's shape is at the same time a shape of

resistance. By standing for centuries on the military border of the western world, Croatia is now fighting for a world which can only survive if this historical space survives.[90]

Here, Corak conveyed the image of a Croatia protecting the West from a barbarous East, with the Serbs trying to invade Europe, in a manner reminiscent of the Ottoman invasion, against which the *Antemurale* was first established. As she further depicted the scenario: 'This is an attack by the last of the barbarians coming from their darkness to the lights of Mediterranean, to Rome. Those barbarians who would like to think of themselves as being the successors of Byzantium or what is more, as Byzantines themselves ... Their conduct is Eastern and different in the sense of different ethics.'[91] Again, the picture of Croatia standing on the border between East and West was a powerful image. It portrayed a sense of heroic struggle, as well as an image of vulnerability, both of which would prove to be positive in Croatia's bid for Western support.

Such imagery reflected more traditional Western views of the Ottoman Empire, reminiscent perhaps of James Marriot's 1918 description of the Ottoman provinces as 'an alien substance, embedded in the living flesh of Europe, akin to the European family neither in creed, race, language, in social customs, nor in political aptitudes and traditions'.[92] It may also have reflected more recent views, such as Samuel Huntington's *Clash of Civilisations* argument (1993), where 'Civilisations' (his term for a religious-cultural amalgam) became the repository for an individual's primary identification, and the nodal point of conflict.[93]

Huntington's conclusion that '[p]olitical boundaries increasingly are redrawn to coincide with cultural ones; ethnic, religious and civilisational' certainly worked to the advantage of Croatian writers, who argued that Yugoslavia was an artificial joining of different civilisations, a project surely doomed to failure. In fact, the Croatian argument that the collapse of Yugoslavia was 'natural' became less controversial as the conflict evolved. Yugoslavia, described as a 'cleft country' by Huntington, contained 'major groups from two or more civilisations', who posited: "We are different peoples and belong in different places."' This alone was sufficient cause for break-up, according to Huntington: 'The force of repulsion drives them apart and they gravitate towards civilisational magnets in other societies.'[94] Theories, both old and new, of the naturalness of a civilisational divide played well into the hands of Croatian secessionists, attempting to justify pulling Croatia out of a union with the Serbs that had been more or less peaceful since 1945. The instrumentalisation of such theories allowed nationalists to paint the conflict as an age-old primordial battle between good and evil – yet another aspect in a multifaceted arsenal of myths and legends.

The myth of Medjugorje

Another aspect of Croatian writing was to stress the chosen or holy elements of the Croatian nation. Catholicism had to be relevant not only historically; it now had to be used to demonstrate the inherent cultural superiority of the nation. While the Serbs had Kosovo, the Croats had no great symbolic defeats that could elevate them to divine status. While there was much currency to be gained from the 'state right' and Antemurale myths, Croatian writers added a religious aspect to their nationalism. They needed a myth able to compete with the Battle of Kosovo, a Battle that had so fired the imagination of Croatian artists and politicians such as Ivan Meštrović, Juraj Stross mayer, and Ljudevit Gaj.

It was precisely for this reason that the myth of Medjugorje was operationalised as part of the Croatian rhetorical arsenal. Describing the apparition of the Virgin Mary to a group of small children in Medjugorje, Hercegovina, in 1981, the myth could not have been better timed. Medjugorje soon became an enduring symbol of the cultural divide between East and West, while creating a tourist haven and pilgrimage site for European Catholics, a new competitor for Assisi and Lourdes.[95] Tudjman was perhaps the first to instrumentalise Medjugorje, at a peace conference there in May 1993, when he invoked the miracle in support of the Bosnian Croats. 'The Madonna's appearance', he maintained, heralded 'the re-awakening of the Croatian nation', a statement that demonstrated his belief that the Croats had been granted the Virgin Mary's favour.[96] This statement was extremely controversial, considering that Tudjman was speaking not in Croatia, but in Bosnia, a new country with internationally recognised borders.

Medjugorje would later become the subject of sociological reflection. Stjepan Meštrović, Slaven Letica, and Miroslav Goreta successfully operationalised it in the service of the Croatian cause. For these authors, it was no accident that 'the dividing line between East and west runs roughly along the present day border between Croatia and Serbia, which is known as the Krajina region'.[97] The mythical aspect of it, at least for Meštrović, lay in the fact that 'Medjugorje itself symbolises a growing rupture between Eastern and Western culture.'[98] In other words, the region itself, situated on a border between East and West, began to carry its own special significance. Firstly, it offered Croats their own divinity, since Mary appeared to them, and not the Serbs. And secondly it also gave them a form of chosenness or divine status preferable to that of the Kosovo myth. As its chroniclers mused aloud: 'it is intriguing that the central message at Medjugorje was "peace", whereas Kosovo was revived by the Serbs as a shrine to their military glory'.[99]

Of course, comparisons between shrines to 'peace' and 'war' were no coincidence. For the authors, the Virgin Mary's appearance constituted lasting proof that right was on the side of the Croatians. Medjugorje became 'the Fatima of our times', symbolising 'the yearnings of Slovenia and Croatia in the west for greater pluralism and democracy versus the Serbian leanings in the East for fascist-like nationalism and monolithic political systems'.[100] This analogy was further drawn out. The Croats now became part of a 'mother-centred culture',[101] with a passive character orientation, a caring, nurturing identity, in contrast to the 'father-dominated' Serbs, who were generally more warlike and destructive.[102] The central aspect of the myth was the goodness of Catholicism, which rendered the Croats more civilised, more peace-loving, and more enlightened. As the authors explained:

> [T]he moral message given by the Madonna from Medjugorje to Poland, seems to be softer: peace, compromise, pluralism. One has to explain Eastern European and former Soviet machismo, totalitarianism and terror in the context of a virgin based cultural system. Mary seems to represent the other side of the authoritarian, father dominated [Serbian] Slavic mindset uncovered by [sociologist Dinko] Tomasević. The female side [Croatian] represents the 'higher' softer, more civilised aspects of Slavic culture.[103]

Thus Medjugorje would become a symbol for the geography, religion and cultural traditions of Croatia, while Catholicism would promote a 'universalist cultural base' which was 'recognisably Western'.[104] Such theories were directly opposed to those of Bataković and his Serbian colleagues. Medjugorje became a useful way of creating a modern myth of chosenness, perhaps to counterbalance the strong influence of Kosovo on the Serbs. At the same time, the linkages were clear – Serbs had to stay on their side of the civilisational divide – they did not belong in Croatia. Some writers went so far as to suggest that the Serbs were in league with Satan in their desire to destroy Medjugorje.[105]

Medjugorje performed several crucial functions in Croatian nationalism. Firstly, it elevated Croatian Catholicism to a chosen and superior religion, and Croatians themselves to the rank of superior nation. While it was not Kosovo, it proved to Croats that they too could be part of the divine elect, as evidenced by the Virgin's appearance. It also demonstrated that a Covenant existed between the Croats and the divine. We see here the use of Schöpflin's 'myth of election': the Croats received this revelation because of their unique qualities as an ancient and peace-loving people, and because they were the innocent victims of Serbian aggression.

Secondly, the myth became a symbol of Westernness, proving that the Croats belonged in Western or (at least) Central Europe, and maintained traditions and ideals that differed significantly from those of the Serbs. Because they had suffered for so long in Yugoslavia under Serbian domination, the Virgin Mary appeared to give them hope in the midst of hardship. Thirdly, Medjugorje endorsed Tudjman's nationalist regime. The Virgin's appearance demonstrated that right was on the side of the Croats, while Serbia was clearly the satanic aggressor. Certainly, Medjugorje was useful in an instrumental sense. It gave the Croats a sense of religious pride, and restored to them a great deal of hope, first of all in 1981, when the Virgin Mary supposedly first appeared, and then throughout the remainder of the crisis.

The different racial origins of the Serbs

Even these aspects of differentiation were not enough to stress the opposing psychological, sociological, and civilisational differences between Serbs and Croats. Yet another theme was to be introduced – that of different racial origins. That both groups were descended from South Slavic tribes was regarded as well established by most impartial historians. However, a number of Croatian writers attempted to debunk the myth of South Slavic unity, arguing that Serbs and Croats were racially distinct, and should never have entered into any political or social institutions together.

Ivo Banac reflected a typical Croatian view at this time, charting the origin of the Croats (and their name as well) to an 'Iranian group' that was somehow assimilated by Slavic populations, sometime before their settlement in the western portions of the Balkan Peninsula.[106] By contrast, Banac posited that the origins of the Serbs were more dubious. He claimed that most of these were 'Orthodox Balkan Vlachs', who moved to Croatia and Bosnia during the Ottoman era.[107] Banac, while an eminent historian and no friend of Tudjman's national regime, nevertheless reflected a typical Croatian theme – that Serbs were racially or ethnically different from Croats. However, few scholars agreed on where Croats and Serbs actually came from, even if there was a consensus that they did not share similar origins.

In 1995, a team of Croatian scholars also tried to prove that Croatia's ancestors were Aryans who came from Persia. Ethnographers, positing that the word *Hrvat* derived from the ancient Persian word *Hu-Urvat*, undertook the largest archaeological project in Croatian history in search of the Croats' ancient Iranian origins. The project received warm support from Tudjman.[108] Another Tudjman-sponsored project, featuring Nedjeljko Kujundzić, president of the Croatian Academy of Educational Sciences at Zagreb University, traced the Croats to early Celtic tribes, while describing the Serbs as descendants of the nomadic Sarmatians.[109]

By contrast, another theory held that the Croats were the only true Slavs, having been in the Balkan region at least four hundred years before the Serbs. This formed the central thesis of the Zagreb University historian Trpimir Macan's summary of Croatian history. Macan cited as proof two Greek tablets from the second century AD containing the words, *Horathos* and *Horuathos*, from whence derived the name *Hrvat* (Croat). Claiming that

Serbs were descendants of a different set of tribes altogether, Macan posited that the Serbs were not Slavic, but Vlach and Gypsy Romanised shepherds.[110] For right-wing radicals on the streets of Zagreb, however, there was no doubt that Serbs were Arabs, as was evidenced by their square fingers. The Croats, meanwhile, were of another race, since their fingers were more rounded.[111]

Another aspect of this racial differentiation concerned Croatian territorial rights. While, generally, Croats and Serbs were presented as having different racial origins, Serbs within Croatia's borders were further differentiated. The Krajina Serbs were to be separated ethnically from the rest of the Serbian population. In line with Macan's theories, Pavličević claimed that Krajina Serbs were 'non-Slavic Vlachs of Greek-orthodox religion', who supposedly settled as farmers in Croatia in the sixteenth century.[112] The theory held that these Vlachs were converted to Serbian Orthodoxy and thus 'became' Serbs in the nineteenth century, owing to the machinations of the Orthodox Church, who 'transform[ed] the non-Slav, Orthodox Vlachs into aggressive, national, conscious Serbs', a group that later formed 'Little Vlaska' in Pakrac in 1876, and began a conspiracy to 'liquidate all Croatian Catholics'.[113] The fact that the Vlachs could be converted supposedly encouraged Serbian leaders to try a form of ethnic cleansing in the nineteenth century, by Serbianising non-Serbian lands near Serbia, and then joining these lands with the expanded Serbian state. If such theories were to be believed, then most Krajina and Slavonian Serbs would have been inauthentic national members whose families were Serbianised only a century ago.

What emerges from a review of these attempts at racial differentiation are two key arguments. The first advanced that the Croats were racially distinct from and somehow ethnically superior to the Serbs, owing to their Iranian, Slavic, or Celtic origin, depending on which scholarly work you chose to believe. This acted to dismiss any Serbian claims that Serbs and Croats belonged together at any time in their history. At the same time, the fact that 'Krajina' Serbs and 'Serbian' Serbs were of different racial origins proved, at least to Croats, that the first group could not even claim the national rights that 'real' Serbs might have possessed. Thus a double onus was created for the Krajina Serbs. Not only did they have to prove that their land was in fact Serbian; they also had to prove that they were actually Serbs.

In other cases, the medical profession concluded their own studies in support of the Croatian cause. In 1995, Ivica Kostović, dean of the medical school in Zagreb, released the findings of the Croatian Institute for Brain Research, which stated conclusively that, while 'it can not seriously be claimed that there are differences between brains of Serbs and Croats . . . differences in outward forms, skulls can be established'. As he further wrote: 'These anthropological differences are evident especially at the racial level . . . but hardly any conclusions about differences at the level of brain functioning can be drawn from them.'[114]

The re-emergence of the pseudo-science of phrenology was one of the more unusual aspects of Croatian propaganda. Kostović's theories, as well as those of Croatian archaeologists, historians, and sociologists, were highly suspect and unrealistic. The notion that Serbs and Croats were somehow different races who had, by some miracle, lived side by side and avoided inter-marrying during their many centuries of association defied all logic. The large number of so-called 'mixed marriages' and births at the present day invali-dates any such arguments.

Much of this rhetoric about East and West was wishful thinking on the part of Croatian politicians. Perhaps they could not give their people democ-racy, imported consumer goods, or a decent standard of living. Perhaps they could not even give their people an entire country with stable borders. However, they did have the ability to make their people feel 'Western', that they had somehow symbolically left Yugoslavia, Communism, and the East behind, simply by 'otherising' it, as people in 'real' Western countries had done. In a sense, Croatian leaders were encouraging their people to 'perform' in a difference sense. They promised their people that if they began 'acting' Western, then sooner or later they would 'become' Western. The best way to be Western, of course, was cut off all associations with the 'Eastern' Serbs.

It was a comforting thought that, when Croatia did become part of the West, all their troubles with Serbia would recede into the ancient past. However, Tudjman and his colleagues were never able to give the Croats more than the *illusion* of 'Westernness', and they were not terribly successful at this either. Slavenka Drakulić rightly observed in *Cafe Europa* that 'Europe is not a mother who owes something to her long-neglected children; neither is she a princess one has to court. She is not a knight sent to free us, nor an apple or a cake to be enjoyed; she is not a silk dress, nor the magic word "democ-racy".'[115] Croatians could continue to worship Europe – but this did not mean that Croatia would ever actually be European in the ways they would have desired simply by distancing themselves from the Serbs.

Conclusions

In reinterpreting their history, the Croatian side shared much with the Serbs. Each was obsessed with self-perception. Each side wanted to see themselves as lovable and heroic victims of history. Each tried to elevate the nation to divine and chosen status, through a series of covenantal myths, myths of election, and myths of Redemption and suffering. Historical claims to the land, myths of Croatian Westernness, and myths of cultural and linguistic uniqueness were used to advance the thesis that Croats were more enlightened, peace-loving, and generally more civilised than the Serbs. Many of these themes mirrored similar ones in Serbian writings, particularly those of Bataković.

Both Croats and Serbs tried to portray the other side as more intolerant, racist, xenophobic, greedy, bloodthirsty, expansionist, and genocidal. The Croats projected every possible negative trait on to their Serbian pseudospecies. Serbs were seen to represent the worst aspects of Eastern civilisation, in a racial, psychological, and sociological sense – making it clear that the Serbs were responsible for the war in which Croatian found herself after 1991. The contrast between the warlike Kosovo myth and the peaceful Medjugorje myth provided just one example of the phenomenon. While there were fewer comparisons between Croats and Jews than between Serbs and Jews, it was clear that Croatian writers had prepared a coherent interpretation of history that ignored decades of co-operation between Serbs and Croats, and chose instead to highlight the negative aspects of their association.

Another characteristic shared by both Serbs and Croats was the frequent use of the internet to disseminate nationalist propaganda. Vast networks connected literally thousands of different sites together, many with complete online books, journals, and magazines, which could be downloaded free of charge. Most nationalist publications available as hard copies could similarly be found floating in 'cyberspace'. Many books and journals that were available only as hard copies in the first two years of the conflict were duly scanned and uploaded into various government websites, with all the scanning mistakes intact. The use of this new medium made many of the historical debates between these two sides extremely vibrant and dynamic.

An interesting aspect of Croatian propaganda was how the focus of attack shifted after 1991. Before Serbia became a threat to Croatian autonomy, Croatian nationalists had little interest in Serbian leaders or Serbian history. Their only true enemies were the Communists, who were solidly in control of the SFRY. It was only after Serbian machinations in eastern Slavonia and the Krajina that any coherent study of Serbian history seems to have taken place. It was only at this time that a Serbian history of evil was truly brought to the forefront.

A long tradition of attacking Communism and Tito as the worst possible enemies of Croatia changed after 1991, when the Serbs, not the Communists generally, became the new source of evil. This issue of propaganda shifting will be explored in the next three chapters. What emerges from a detailed overview of myths of Croatian history before the Second World War is the historical evolution of Serbian hatred against the Croats. What begins as a general condemnation of eastern barbarity, due to the Great Schism, becomes more politicised in the nineteenth century, with the creation of a coherent Serbian nationalist project. While this project is initially aimed at destroying various nations, among whom the Croats are only one of the victims, their association with the Serbs in the first Yugoslavia transforms them into the prime target of Serbian aggression.

In each historical period, Croatia's relationship with Serbia grows more intimate, and therefore more threatening. The concept of evolving hatred is extremely important in both the Serbian and Croatian cases, and will certainly become more obvious in the chapters dealing with the Second World War. For both sides, an understanding of early history established a pattern of behaviour for the enemy nation, a pattern of violence that would only escalate during the twentieth century, seemingly culminating in the 1990s in the worst genocide that either side had seen in its history.

NOTES

1 Marcus Tanner, *Croatia: A Nation Forged in War* (New Haven, CT: Yale University Press, 1997) pp. 191–6.
2 *Ibid.* pp. 197; 200–1.
3 That Tudjman was a man of 'great expectations', full of his own self-importance, was evident even by 1981 in his reply to his accusers after his imprisonment. See Franjo Tudjman, *Croatia on Trial: The Case of the Croatian Historian Dr F. Tudjman* (London: United Publishers, 1981). His defence conveys the image that he somehow represents Croatia, and that his work is of central importance to the nation. Similarly, he analogised his treatment at the hands of the Communists to the suffering of Christ in earlier times: 'In the course of history it has long been known that these methods [exclusion of evidence] make it fairly easy to indict the crucified Christ as the Anti-Christ, or alternatively to prove that Satan's torments are in fact – the kingdom of Heaven' (p. 15).
4 *Ibid.* pp. 20; 29.
5 Norman Cigar, *Genocide in Bosnia: The Policy of 'Ethnic Cleansing'* (College Station, TX: Texas A & M Univesity Press, 1995) p. 88.
6 *Ibid.* p. 91.
7 *Ibid.* pp. 98–9.
8 Lenard J. Cohen, *Broken Bonds: Yugoslavia's Disintegration and Balkan Politics in Transition* (Boulder, CO: Westview Press, 1995) p. 95.
9 Tom Nairn, *The Break-up of Britain New Edition* (London: Verso, 1981) p. 41.
10 Tom Nairn, *Faces of Nationalism: Janus Revisited* (London: Verso, 1997) p. 71.
11 Mark Thompson, *Forging War: The Media in Serbia, Croatia and Bosnia-Hercegovina* (London: Article 19/ International Center Against Censorship, 1994) p. 146.
12 *Ibid.* p. 152.
13 Vesna Pusić, 'A Country by Any Other Name: Transition and Stability in Croatia and Yugoslavia', *East European Politics and Society*, 6:3, p. 259.
14 *Ibid.* pp. 138–42.
15 *Ibid.* pp. 176–7.
16 Viktor Ivancić, 'Dossier: Pakracka Poljana, Part I', *Feral Tribune* (21 August 1995) www.cdsp.neu.edu/info/students/marko/feral/feral13.html (accessed 18 June 1998).
17 Valery Tishkov, *Ethnicity, Nationalism and Conflict In and After the Soviet Union: The Mind Aflame* (London: Sage Publications, 1997) p. 12.
18 Quoted in Thompson, *Forging War*, p. 160.
19 Predrag Lucić, 'Dr. Tudjman and Mr. George', *Feral Tribune* (3 August 1997) www.cdsp.neu.edu/info/students/marko/feral/feral49.html (accessed 18 June 1998).

20 Dubravka Ugrešić, *The Culture of Lies* (London: Phoenix House, 1998) pp. 259–60.
21 Maja Freundlich, 'Bull's Eye: Trials on the Way to the Promised Land', *Vjesnik* (20 December 20 1998)http://www.cdsp.neu.edu/info/students/marko/vjesnik/vjesnik29.html (accessed 18 June 1998).
22 Cohen, *Broken Bonds*, p. 18.
23 Laura Silber and Alan Little, *The Death of Yugoslavia* (London: BBC Books, 1993) pp. 100–1.
24 *Ibid.* pp. 102; 104–5.
25 *Ibid.* pp. 107; 109–11.
26 *Ibid.* pp. 146–7.
27 *Ibid.* pp. 148–9.
28 *Ibid.* pp. 153–6.
29 *Ibid.* pp. 195–201.
30 Marcus Tanner argues that Tudjman's adviser, Slaven Letica, leaked to the press some unfavourable tape-recordings of meetings between Rasković and Tudjman, in which Rasković claimed that the Serbs were mad, and would not listen to him. Rasković's leaked remarks sealed his fate, and forced his retirement. In other words, Letica and Tudjman forced the resignation of the only moderate Croatian Serb leader willing to negotiate with them: see Tanner, *Croatia*, p. 233.
31 James Gow and James Tisley, 'The Strategic Imperative for Media Management', in James Gow, Richard Paterson, and Alison Preston (eds), *Bosnia By Television* (London: BFI, 1996) pp. 107–8.
32 Dušan Kečmanović, *The Mass Psychology of Ethnonationalism* (New York: Plenum Press, 1996) p. 36.
33 As the former Croatian chief of staff Anton Tus has argued recently, Croatia could certainly have been liberated much earlier than 1995, had Tudjman wished to devote his forces to the task. However, Tudjman's belief that Bosnian Croats had to be 'protected' before Croatia could be liberated led to a division of forces that kept the conflict in Croatia continuing at least two or three years longer than was necessary. Tus's disagreement with Tudjman over this issue led to his resignation in 1992. See Anton Tus, 'The War up to the Sarajevo Ceasefire', in Branka Magaš and Ivo Žanić (eds), *The War in Croatia and Bosnia-Herzegovina 1991–1995* (London: Frank Cass, 2001) pp. 65–6. Ozren Žunec adds that *both* Serbian and Croatian forces made a conscious decision to move their theatre of operations to Bosnia in 1992–93. Thus he categorises the war in Croatia as '*une drôle de guerre*, a phoney war'. See Ozren Žunec, 'Operations Flash and Storm', in Magaš and Žanić (eds), *The War in Croatia and Bosnia-Herzegovina*, pp. 71–3.
34 Kečmanović, *The Mass Psychology of Ethnonationalism*, p. 63.
35 Dragutin Pavličević, 'South-Eastern Europa and Balkan Peninsula on the Margin of the Worlds: Foreword', in Aleksander Ravlić (ed.), *Southeastern Europe 1918–1995* (Zagreb: Croatian Heritage Foundation/Croatian Information Centre, 1998) www.hic.hr/books/seeurope/index-e.htm#top (accessed 5 February 2000).
36 *Ibid.*
37 Muhamed Zlatan Hrenovica, 'Structural Aspects of Greater Serbian Crimes in Bosnia and Herzegovina from 1991 to 1995', in Ravlić (ed.), *Southeastern Europe 1918–1995*. While this author's name suggests that he may well have been a Bosnian Moslem, his chapter appeared in a Croatian Information Center publication, and was fully consonant with the Croatian national line being advanced at that time.
38 Mirko Grmek, Marc Gjidara, and Neven Simac, *Le nettoyage ethnique: Documents historques sur une idéologie serbe* (Paris: Fayard, 1993), Back cover (my translation). For

another linkage between nineteenth-century writings (Karadzić, Garašanin etc.) and later twentieth-century Serbian actions in Croatia, see Vedrana Spajić-Vrkaš, *Croatia Discovers Janus* (Zagreb: Croatian University Press, 1992). Her conclusions are clear: 'Today, there is no doubt that the new "Greater Serbian" political leadership turned its own people into automatic sticks for punishment and killing of whatever enemy it might be by using lies, banal demagogy and unrealistic promises' (p. 91).

39 Grmek, Gjidara, and Simac, *Le nettoyage ethnique*, back cover.
40 See this notation *ibid.* pp. 12–13.
41 *Ibid.* p. 13.
42 See for example Tim Judah, *The Serbs: History, Myth and the Destruction of Yogoslavia* (New Haven, CT: Yale University Press, 1997), who gives a short but detailed description of the early anti-Ottoman uprisings, complete with a discussion of the ambiguous role of Russia in these conflicts, which sometimes helped the Serbs, and sometimes went against them (pp. 51–3).
43 Pavličević, 'Persecution and Liquidation of Croats on Croatian Territory From 1903 to 1941', in Ravlić (ed.), *Southeastern Europe 1918–1995*.
44 Ante Beljo, 'The Ideology of Greater Serbia', in Ravlić (ed.), *Southeastern Europe 1918–1995*.
45 Branko Miletić, 'History: Causes of Serbian Aggression' (Zagreb: Croatian Information Center Web Page, 1998) www.algonet.se/~bevanda/agression.htm (accessed 18 June 1998).
46 Pavličević, 'Persecution and Liquidation of Croats on Croatian Territory From 1903 to 1941'.
47 Miletič, 'History: Causes of Serbian Aggression'; see also Bože Ćović (ed.) *Roots of Serbian Aggression: Debates, Documents, Cartographic Reviews* (Zagreb: Centarza Strane Jezike/AGM, 1993) p. 21.
48 Miletić, 'History: Causes of Serbian Aggression'.
49 Beljo, 'The Ideology Of Greater Serbia'.
50 Pavličević, 'Persecution and Liquidation of Croats on Croatian Territory From 1903 to 1941'.
51 *Ibid.*
52 Dzenana Efendia Semiz, 'Serbian Land Reform and Colonization in 1918', in Ravlić (ed.), *Southeastern Europe 1918–1995*.
53 Pavličević, 'Persecution and Liquidation of Croats on Croatian Territory From 1903 to 1941'.
54 Ante Beljo (ed.), *Greater Serbia: From Ideology to Aggression* (Zagreb: Croatian Information Center, 1993) p. 7.
55 See Nikola Stojanović, 'To Extermination: Ours or Yours?', in Ante Beljo (ed.), *Greater Serbia: From Ideology to Aggression* (Zagreb: Croatian Information Center, 1993) pp. 25–6.
56 *Ibid.* p. 29.
57 See Tanner, *Croatia*, p. 99; and Louis Adamović, *My Native Land* (New York: Harper & Brothers, 1943) p. 301.
58 See Bože Ćović, *Croatia Between War and Independence* (Zagreb: University of Zagreb/OKC–Zagreb, 1991) pp. 29–31.
59 Miletić, 'History: Causes of Serbian Aggression'.
60 Discussed in: Pavličević, 'Persecution and Liquidation of Croats On Croatian Territory From 1903 to 1941'.
61 *Ibid.*
62 Semiz, 'Serbian Land Reform and Colonization in 1918'.

63 *Ibid.*

64 Phyllis Auty, *Yugoslavia* (London: Thames and Hudson, 1965) p. 52.

65 John R. Lampe, *Yugoslavia as History: Twice There Was a Country* (Cambridge: Cambridge University Press, 1996) pp. 115; 146–7.

66 Pavličević, 'Persecution and Liquidation of Croats On Croatian Territory From 1903 to 1941'.

67 *Ibid.*

68 Henry Pozzi, *Black Hand Over Europe* (Zagreb: Croatian Information Center, [1935] 1994) p. 2.

69 Josip Sentija, 'Croatia from 1941 to 1991' (Zagreb: University of Zagreb/Matica Hrvatska Iseljenika, 1994) p. 10. This article formed part of the standard curriculum for the University of Zagreb Croatian Language and Culture Programme (Summer, 1994). David Marshland's review of Pozzi's book in a pro-Croat British monthly tried to salvage the anti-Serb elements while denying the rest. The result is somewhat amusing, 'Pozzi's case against the Serbs is so solidly grounded in detailed evidence that it is unchallengeable. Unfortunately this case is weakened by his development of parallel arguments against Czech treatment of the Slovaks and Rumanian oppression of the Hungarians ... [These] are altogether more speculative than the Serb case, and might be used by enemies of the truth to sabotage the credibility of his expose of Pan-Serbian chauvinism. This must not be allowed to happen.' See David Marshland, 'Caught Red-Handed: The Black Hand and War in Europe', *Croatian Times*, 2 (February 1996) p. 5. The contention here is that only the Serbs can do wrong, since both the Czechs and the Romanians were neutral in the later conflict.

70 Slaven Letica, 'Introduction', in Zvonimir Separović (ed.), *Documenta Croatica* (Zagreb: VIGRAM-Zagreb i VIDEM Krsko, 1992) p. 5.

71 *Ibid.* p. 9.

72 Cohen, *Broken Bonds*, p. 18.

73 Vatro Myrvar, 'The Croatian Statehood and its Continuity', in Antun F. Bonifačić and Clement S. Mihanovich (eds), *The Croatian Nation in its Struggle for Freedom and Independence: A Symposium by Seventeen Croatian Writers* (Chicago: 'Croatia' Cultural Pub. Center, 1955) pp. 47–9.

74 Ivan Crkvenčić and Mladen Klemenčić, *Aggression Against Croatia: Geopolitical and Demographic Facts* (Zagreb: Republic of Croatia Central Bureau of Statistics, 1993) p. 7.

75 Stjepan Hefer, *Croatian Struggle for Freedom and Statehood* (Argentina: Croatian Information Service/Croatian Liberation Movement, 1979) p. 25.

76 Myrvar, 'The Croatian Statehood and its Continuity', p. 53.

77 Anthony Smith, 'The Golden Age and National Revival' in Geoffrey Hosking and George Schöpflin (eds), *Myths and Nationhood* (London: C. Hurst & Company, 1997) p. 37.

78 George Schöpflin, 'The Functions of Myth and a Taxonomy of Myth', in Hosking and Schöpflin (eds), *Myths and Nationhood*, p. 31.

79 See Tanner, *Croatia*, p. 99.

80 Adamović, *My Native Land*, p. 301.

81 See Gregory Peroche, *Histoire de la Croatie et des nations slaves du Sud 395–1991* (Paris: F.-X. De Guibert, 1992) pp. 9–11. These arguments are reiterated throughout the book.

82 Zeljko Jack Lupić, 'History of Croatia: Povijest Hrvatske (200 BC – 1998 AD)' (Zagreb: Croatian Information Center, 21 February 1999) www.dalmatia.net/croatia/history/index.htm (accessed 18 June 1998).

83 *Ibid.*

84 Pavličević, 'Persecution and Liquidation of Croats on Croatian Territory From 1903 to 1941'.

85 Quoted in Robert M. Hayden and Milica Bakić-Hayden, 'Orientalist Variations on the Theme Balkan: Symbolic Geography in Recent Yugoslav Politics', *Slavic Review* (Spring 1992) p. 9.

86 Quoted in: Boris Buden, 'Mission: Impossible', *ARKzin*, 83 (31 January 1997) www.cdsp.neu.edu/info/students/marko/ARKzin/arkzin5.html (accessed 18 June, 1998).

87 Hayden and Bakić-Hayden, 'Orientalist Variations on the Theme Balkan', pp. 2–4. (Italics theirs.)

88 A. Hauswitschka, 'Croatia Cannot Be A Part of the Balkans', *Vjesnik* (24 May 1996) www.cdsp.neu.edu/info/students/marko/vjesnik/vjesnik7.html (accessed 18 June 1998).

89 Ivo Skrabelo, 'They Shoot Monuments Don't They?', in Separović (ed.), *Documenta Croatica*, pp. 100–1.

90 See Zaljka Corak, 'Croatian Monuments: Wounds Suffered from Other People's Illnesses', in Separović (ed.), *Documenta Croatica*, p. 97.

91 *Ibid.* p. 101.

92 J. A. R. Marriott, *The Eastern Question: An Historical Study in European Diplomacy* (Oxford: Clarendon Press, 1925) p. 3.

93 Samuel P. Huntington, *The Clash of Civilizations and the Remaking of World Order* (New York: Simon & Schuster, 1996) pp. 21; 28.

94 *Ibid.* pp. 125; 137–8.

95 Stjepan Meštrović, Miroslav Goreta, and Slaven Letica, *The Road from Paradise: Prospects for Democracy in Eastern Europe* (Lexington, KY: The University Press of Kentucky, 1993) p. 131.

96 Ed Vulliamy, *Seasons in Hell: Understanding Bosnia's War* (London: St Martin's Press, 1994) pp. 60–1. Against the idea of Medjugorje as a sign of peace, Serbian sources excavated mass graves of executed Serbs from the Second World War. In this way, the so-called region of peace was portrayed as being stained with blood. See Paul Mojzes, *Yugoslavian Inferno: Ethnoreligious Warfare in the Balkans* (New York: Continuum, 1994) p. 47.

97 Mojzes, *Yugoslavian Inferno*, p. 29.

98 Meštrović, Goreta, and Letica, *The Road from Paradise*, p. xiii.

99 Stjepan Meštrović, Slaven Letica, and Miroslav Goreta, *Habits of the Balkan Heart: Social Character and the Fall of Communism* (College Station, TX: Texas A & M University Press, 1993) p. 139.

100 *Ibid.* p. 108.

101 *Ibid.* p. 111.

102 *Ibid.* pp. 66–7.

103 *Ibid.* pp. 115–16.

104 *Ibid.* p. 30.

105 A similar view of the Serbs appeared in the Catholic priest Richard Foley's work *The Drama of Medjugorje* (Dublin: Veritas, 1992) Here, Foley literally demonised the Serbs for their role in the conflict, concluding that 'much of its intensity and inhumanity could only stem from the powers of darkness'. Indeed, as he describes, Medjugorje became the symbol of a conflict between good and evil, with Croats on the side of Good and Serbs on the side of evil. Thus: '... there is a Satanic element in the attack and atrocities against a defenseless Croatian people. In saying which, we automatically find ourselves standing centre-stage in the Medjugorje drama. For its entire scenario is

essentially, from start to finish, built around the confrontation between two spiritual realities, two invisible totalities – the powers of darkness and the powers of light' (p. 6). At the same time, while Kosovo is the 'Serbian Jerusalem', Medjugorje for Foley becomes 'the Croatian Bethlehem', since throngs of believers are brought to Jesus through the apparitions (see pp. 74–5). Foley manages to articulate further anti-Serbian imagery, particularly in the Virgin Mary's supposed revelations about Satan's work on Earth, revealed from 1981 to 1991 (pp. 89–91). That Satan walks the earth, destroying good and bringing misery, is an important part of the Virgin's message; but more important is Foley's conclusion that Satan is primarily 'anti-Medjogorje'. (pp. 99–100). The implication here is clear. The Serbs were actually, from a Catholic perspective, the enemies of God and the servants of Satan.

106 Ivo Banac, 'Preface/Introduction', in Separović (ed.), *Documenta Croatica*, p. 9.

107 *Ibid.* p. 11. In another work, Banac describes the Vlachs as being 'the descendants of hinterland Romans who survived the sixth- and seventh-century Slavic onslaught by retreating to the peninsula's high mountains. Rather like the unlatinized ancestors of the Albanians, they had lost their Illyrian language after the Roman conquest. These hinterland Romans evolved into highland herdsmen, who for centuries led a primitive nomadic life, moving their flocks with the succession of seasons in search of better pasture. The hinterland Romans called themselves Aromuni, but for the Slavs they were the Vlachs (after the Germanic Wlach for Latin and Celtic foreigners). In the early Middle Ages the Vlachs were heavily concentrated in central Greece (Great Wallachia in Thessaly) and the Carpathian ranges.' See Ivo Banac, *The National Question in Yogoslavia: Origins, History, Politics* (Ithaca, NY: Cornell University Press, 1992) p. 42. Malcolm argues that the Vlachs were closely linked to the Romanians, whose language was virtually identical. Malcolm suggests that these Latinised people were driven south with the advance of the Serbs, Croats and Avars, with large numbers of Vlachs eventually settling in Romania. Those remaining were largely Slavicised. See Noel Malcolm, *Kosovo: A Short History* (London: Macmillan, 1998) pp. 25–6.

108 The research objectives were outlined in a statement made by the head of the team Andrija Zelko Lopčić to the correspondent of the Iranian News Agency (IRNA) located in Zagreb: TanJug News Agency (Belgrade: November, 1995) p. 4.

109 'A Review of Antun Bauer, Franjo Sanjek, and Nedjeljko Kujundzić (eds), *Who Are Croats and Where Did They Come From: A Revision of an Ethnogenesis* (Zagreb: Collection of Works, Scientific Society for the Study of the Ethnogenesis of Croats)', *Feral Tribune* (29 December 1997) www.cdsp.neu.edu/info/students/marko/feral/feral53.html (accessed 12 March 1998).

110 Trpimir Macan, 'The History of the Croatian People' (Zagreb: University of Zagreb/Matica Hrvatska Iseljenika, 1994) p. 2.

111 Brian Hall, *The Impossible Country: A Journey Through the Last Days of Yugoslavia* (Boston: David Godine Publishers, 1994) p. 19.

112 Pavličević, 'Persecution and Liquidation of Croats on Croatian Territory From 1903 To 1941'.

113 *Ibid.*

114 Reprinted from *Globus* in Predrag Kaličanin, *Stresses of War* (Belgrade: Institute for Mental Health, 1993) p. 2.

115 Slavenka Drakulič, *Cafe Europa: Life After Communism* (London: Abacus, 1996) pp. 12–13.

5

Masking the past: the Second World War and the Balkan Historikerstreit

A very considerable part of the Croatian political elite, supported by the Catholic hierarchy and Archbishop Alojzije Stepinac himself, supported this national and religious intolerance, and strongly supported policies of clericalism and racism, marked by mass killings, forced conversions and the deportation of the Serbian Orthodox population as well the slaughter of the Jews and Gypsies. (Dušan Bataković, 'The National Integration of the Serbs and Croats')

An intriguing part of the propaganda campaign has been an attempt to equate the supposed victimization of present-day Serbs with that of the Holocaust Jews. In promoting the image of Serbian spiritual kinship with the Jews as fellow victims, Belgrade has concealed Serb willingness to collaborate with the Nazis in the extermination of Serbia's Jews. (Philip Cohen, *Serbia's Secret War*)

THROUGHOUT THE SERBIAN–CROATIAN conflict, the comparative genocide debate was of particular importance. For both countries, the success of nationalist regimes depended on their ability to present national history as one of righteous struggle against persecution. For both Serbs and Croats, the revision of the history of the Second World War provided a wealth of myths of heroism and persecution. Continual portrayals of enemies as either Četniks or Ustaša, as well as constant references to Second World War atrocities as precursors of events in the 1990s, demonstrated the centrality of German and Italian occupation to contemporary conceptions of national identity. The preceding two chapters examined how pre-twentieth-century history was important for nationalists in both countries. Nevertheless, the national expansion and genocide, bloodshed and mayhem of these earlier times would pale in comparison with those of the Second World War. This was to be the apogee of the Serbian–Croatian conflict, four years when each side supposedly unleashed full-scale genocidal terror against the other.

Thus descriptions of perpetrators and victims in the Second World War became incredibly important. Links would be drawn between atrocities during the 1940s and those after 1990. David Campbell's theory of the 'deconstruction of historical teleologies' provides a useful method of understanding how certain narratives, or views of history, have been created. Campbell's 'deconstruction', in the context of Yugoslavia, allows us to analyse how hatred of the other has been the product of current generations of academics and politicians, working to create the illusion of an inevitable conflict, what Campbell terms 'historical fatalism'. For Campbell, a 'deconstructive reading' allows for the proposition that, 'the conflict is constituted *in the present*, and that "history" is a resource in the contemporary struggle'.[1] Peter Novick has also identified this process in his understanding of 'collective memory', arguing that present concerns, and not just the 'past working its will on the present', determine what aspects of history will be used by historians and when.[2] In other words, history responds to present needs – there are no eternal immutable laws that govern how the process operates.

Contrary to Anthony Smith's position, however, *history as a resource* was not used as a means to relive a Golden Age, but rather to revise and exaggerate the horrors of the past (in this case the Second World War). History could then be placed within a teleological framework, similar to that described by Frye, Tudor, and others. Every negative aspect of the War was re-examined, revised and re-presented to the people, and a clear dichotomy was created between the righteous and suffering self, who resisted Nazism and saved Jews, and the genocidal Nazi-like enemy nation. Such a view of the Second World War made Tito's SFRY appear as a historical anomaly, with the 1991 war figuring as the normal state of affairs between Serbs and Croats. Milica Bakić-Hayden, in her analysis of 'nesting orientalisms', took issue with the idea that Serbian and Croatian antagonisms were primordial and deeply rooted in history. As she explained:

> The explanatory slogan 'ancient hatreds' of the South Slavic peoples ... is but a rhetorical screen obscuring the modernity of conflict based on contested notions of state, nation, national identity, and sovereignty ... all Serbs are identified with Chetniks, all Croats with Ustashas and all Muslims with Islamic fundamentalists, or fascist collaborators. By evoking one of the lowest aspects of their historical association and ignoring the significance of their other interactions and integrations (most notably 45 years of post World War II experience), each group perpetuates not only disparaging rhetoric but destructive modes of association.[3]

Such a view was advanced by both sides, who argued that the contemporary conflict was merely the latest instalment in an ongoing story of genocide and terror, of which the Second World War was one of the most violent episodes. Michael Ignatieff's use of Sigmund Freud's 'narcissism of minor differences' is thus an accurate description of how each side magnified the evils of the others in an attempt to whitewash their own crimes. As he put it: 'Nationalist politicians on both sides have used the narcissism of minor differences and turned it into a monstrous fable according to which their own side appears as blameless victims, the other side as genocidal killers. All Croats become Ustashe assassins, all Serbs become Chetnik beasts.'[4]

A short overview of the Second World War

The Second World War was an era of devastation for both Serbs and Croats. The Germans invaded on 5 April 1941, supported by Italian, Hungarian and Bulgarian forces.[5] The Germans and Italians and their allies took control of the country within two weeks, soon establishing puppet states in both Serbia and Croatia. In Serbia, the Germans launched Operation Punishment, which razed Belgrade to the ground and resulted in 17,000 civilian deaths. Soon after the Yugoslav government fled, General Milan Nedić, Yugoslavia's former minister of war, formed a 'Government of National Salvation'.[6] In Croatia, the Independent State of Croatia (NDH) was formed under Ante Pavelić, the leader of an Italian-trained insurgency group, the Ustaša. While Serbs generally remained loyal to King Aleksander and the Yugoslav government in exile, many Croats saw the NDH as their liberation from over two decades of Serbian control. This initial support soon dampened, as Croatia was forced to cede most of Dalmatia to Italy, and northern Slovenia to Germany under the Treaty of Rome. While Bosnia-Hercegovina was joined to the NDH in compensation, many nationalists felt betrayed by a reduction in their territory.[7] As well, many Ustaša officers and soldiers were poorly trained, and Pavelić's distinct lack of charisma and inability to hold mass rallies reduced his exposure among the population. Nevertheless, the lack of credible resistance was also noticeable. Both the Croatian Peasants Party and the Catholic Church remained largely passive.[8]

At the same time, a degree of support for the regime existed, and large numbers of Croats did join the Ustaša and the more popular Domobran. While Croat writers have downplayed Ustaša crimes, the scale of the atrocities was immense. Large numbers of Serbs, Jews, Gypsies, Communists, and Croatians hostile to the regime were interned in concentration camps, while countless others were massacred in towns and villages. In contrast with the German camps in Poland, Czechoslovakia, and Serbia, in Croation camps the Ustaša were directly involved in the administration and in the orchestration of the killings. In addition, some 200,000 Serbs were forcibly converted to Catholicism.[9]

In Serbia, the Nedić regime enjoyed some support. By 1942, Nedić's Serbian State Guard numbered 13,400 men, who worked closely with the 3,600 men in Dimitrije Ljotić's fascist Zbor movement.[10] More famous however were the Četniks – Serbian royalist irregulars who pledged to restore the monarchy. While the Četniks of General Draža Mihailović were committed to ousting the Germans, the smaller Četnik group of Kosta Pečanac broke early with Mihailović, and openly collaborated with the Germans.[11] If the Četniks were officially supported by the Allies at the beginning of the war, their reluctance to engage the Germans, for fear of reprisals, and their violent conflicts with Communist forces eventually lost them Allied favour. Hampered by indiscipline and acts of cruelty, which included rapes and looting, they were eventually reviled by most non-Serbs. Alienating potential support among Croats and Moslems, they committed massacres in Bosnia-Hercegovina and Croatia, making them as hated as the Ustaša.[12] Mihailović's anti-Communism, coupled with massacres carried out in his name, eventually led to his capture, show trial, and execution in 1946.

In short, the wartime records of some groups of Serbs and Croats were dubious, which allowed later historians to cast doubt on the conduct of each nation during the Second World War. Some groups had collaborated with the occupiers, some had committed massacres of civilian populations. At the same time, each side did participate in the Communist Partisan resistance movement, which greatly increased in popularity as German defeat became certain. Nevertheless, there were clear qualitative differences between the Allied-backed Četnik monarchists and their small-scale massacres, and the Nazi-backed Ustaša with their Croatian-run concentration camps. The work of Serbian and Croatian propagandists involved rehabilitating the role of one's own side, while demonising the wartime activities of the other. Thus the other was described as an enthusiastic and active collaborator with the Nazis, an instigator of genocidal aggression against other nations, and a keen supporter of the Holocaust against the Jews. Here, active Nazi collaborators were seen to be as bad as the Nazis themselves, while being a victim of these two groups made one morally equal to the Jews.

Rehabilitating the NDH: conflicting perceptions among the Croats

One of the earliest aspects of Croatian nationalism revolved around rehabilitating the NDH. Croatian Diaspora accounts tended to be pro-Ustaša, while maintaining an ambiguous view of the German occupation. More official accounts in the 1990s, by contrast, downplayed the importance of the NDH and its crimes, and sought to reduce the importance of its support during the war. It was portrayed simply as a reaction against Serbian genocidal ambitions. Earlier writings, such as those of the Croatian Liberation Movement in Argentina, exonerated the Ustaša regime by stressing the resistance nature of the movement. Pavelić became merely the 'founder and representative of the revolutionary Liberation Movement of the Croatian people.'[13] Such writings favourably compared the Ustaša to earlier French and American revolutionary movements, with their main goals consisting of defending Croatia against

Serbian aggression and against international Communism. There was no doubt in the minds of early Croatian writers that the NDH represented the outcome of a long historical process, and was warmly welcomed by Croats, 'with unprecedented enthusiasm, spontaneously and unanimously', as one account had it.[14]

These early accounts also vindicated the persecution of Serbs and the Orthodox Church, claiming that its influence had to be curbed, since it was 'a centre of propaganda and activity of Serbian chauvinism, Serbian imperialism, and hostility against the Croatian people.'[15] Ustaša actions emerged as 'self-defensive', protecting Croats and their property, even if massacres of Serbs were the inevitable result. While this type of thinking was largely confined to earlier accounts, among later writers Vladimir Mrkoci would also proclaim the self-defensive nature of the Ustaša's activities. He rejected the charge that Ustašism could be fascistic, since 'the fundamental requirement for fascism', the state, did not exist during the Ustaša's formation. That Pavelić and his cohorts were sponsored and equipped by Fascist Italy seemed irrelevant to this analysis. As with earlier writers, Mrkoci operated from the perspective that the Ustaša was fundamentally a defensive organisation, 'created as a reaction to Serb terror, to fascism implemented by Serbs through fascist organizations of Chetniks'.[16]

It fell to other émigré writers, such as Ivo Omerčanin, to highlight the differences between the Ustaša and the Nazis – and there were supposedly many of these. Omerčanin maintained that, while Croats approved of their independent state, which gave them more autonomy and freed them from Serbian domination, they still chafed under Nazi rule.[17] Thus the author drew a sharp distinction between support for an independent state, and support for Nazism, two institutions that were fundamentally different. In support of this, Omerčanin traced the origins of a pro-Allied Croatian 'putsch', which was supposed to have begun in early 1943, featuring such notable Ustaša officials as Interior Minister Mladen Lorković, and Ante Vokić, Minister for Home Defence.[18]

The reason it failed, Omerčanin revealed, was because of American politicking, and a reluctance to land Allied troops in Dalmatia to support an indigenous Croatian rebellion. However, he noted that the *putsch* did succeed internally, since civil and military authorities were ready to depose the government and work with the Allies for a democratic independent Croatia.[19] Omerčanin was clearly trying to vindicate the Ustaša position, using anecdotal evidence to prove that the leading lights of the movement were also anti-fascist. For Omerčanin, the former Ustaša *chargé d'affairs* in Berlin, this *putsch* may have been a useful means of legitimating his role in the government. The *putsch* argument was also advanced by Ante Beljo, although it is clear from a reading of his description (although he doesn't specifically claim this) that any *putsch* would have been largely opportunistic, since the Italians had just surrendered, and the Ustaša were expecting 'the landing of Allied troops on the Croatian Adriatic coast'.[20]

Generally, early Diaspora accounts promoted the Ustaša as a genuine nationalist and revolutionary movement, one that was pro-independence and anti-Nazi. Such views became rife after 1990, when many revisionists moved back to Croatia. The existence of émigré magazines such as *NDH*, edited by a former Ustaša official and the son-in-law of Ante Pavelić, was in part a result of Tudjman's reliance on Diaspora Croats and their financial contributions.[21] *NDH* was notable for its continuation of Croatian Liberation Movement themes – the 'truth' about the Second World War, as well as poems and articles eulogising Ante Pavelić and the Ustaša. The Partisans were often the subject of attack, and were denounced as 'Yugoslav criminals' and 'Serb and Croat scum'.[22]

Such magazines accompanied a spate of revisionist books, which sought to clear the Ustaša's bad name, giving a human face to those who were integrally involved in the regime. One troubling manifestation was the publication of the memoirs of Ivo Rojnica, the former Ustaša administrator for Dubrovnik, later decorated by Tudjman. Rojnica's own skewed understanding of history was obvious. He argued that 250,000 Serbs were expelled to Serbia from Ustaša-controlled Croatia, and were therefore not killed, while claiming that only 420 Serbs were forcibly converted to Catholicism.[23] Another troubling memoir, by Eugen Dido Kvaternik, was reprinted in 1995 with financial support from the Croatian Ministry for Science and Technology. Kvaternik, a founder of the Croatian death-camp system, produced a work notable only for its descriptions of 'courtly life' in Pavelić's inner circle, while omitting any reference to the atrocities committed by the regime.[24] The main thrust of these Diaspora accounts was that the NDH was both a revolutionary and a popular nationalist movement that was suppressed by the Communists. The atrocities committed by the regime were rarely discussed, while many of the worst war criminals were whitewashed as heroes who only wanted to create an independent homeland.

The political climate in Croatia clearly provided for the emergence of such militant and revisionist views. Tudjman did little to discourage them, nor could he. Most of his campaign contributions, and the money needed to finance the war, came from Diaspora Croats, among whom such views were not uncommon. Nevertheless, Tudjman also had Western support to consider, and for this reason government propaganda dealing with the NDH was markedly different from that of the CLM or *NDH* magazine. Officially, support for the NDH was seen to be largely a reaction to Serbian atrocities in royalist Yugoslavia, 'the prison-house of nations'. As was indicated in the last chapter, the first Yugoslavia was condemned as an instrument of Serbian domination.

Croatian support for the NDH was therefore anti-Serbian, rather than pro-German or pro-Italian.[25] Such writings supported the self-defensive nature of the NDH, but denied that the Ustaša were either revolutionary or popular. Tudjman's own writings, for example, advance Vladko Maček's Croatian Peasants Party as the prime focus of Croatian loyalty. This 'middle of the road' party, Tudjman maintained, had the advantage of being '[p]olitically equidistant from both Pavelić's Ustašism and Tito's revolutionary movement'.[26]

A similar view was taken by Philip J. Cohen in his controversial pro-Croatian revision of Serbian history, *Serbia's Secret War*. Cohen described a level of support as low as 2 per cent for the Ustaša regime, which he credited to a general dislike of their 'notorious brutality'.[27] He dismissed claims that the Croats supported the regime positing that the 312,000-strong Croatian Home Guard were 'notoriously unreliable as collaborators', possessing 'poor morale' and an unwillingness to fight that eventually led them to defect to the Partisans.[28]

In reviewing Croatian interpretations of the NDH, we find two conflicting forms of propaganda. One is overtly pro-Ustaša, while the other is cautiously against it, but puts more effort into minimising its importance than into condemning it. This paradoxical strategy is best explained by the division of loyalties under which the Tudjman regime laboured. First, it had financial and moral obligations to the Diaspora Croats, and thus a vindication of wartime Croatia and a denial of Ustaša atrocities were integral to external support for the war effort. At the same time, Tudjman faced heavy criticism from the international community for his revisionism. The solution lay in downplaying the Croats' support for the NDH, while making a clear distinction between wanting independence and being pro-Nazi. The NDH as a haven from Serbian genocide was another popular argument. To maintain power, Tudjman pursued a complicated balancing act, trying to please both the Croatian people and also highly critical Western governments.

Serbian views of the Ustaša and Četniks

Serbian historians were also preoccupied with the Second World War. While the demonisation of Croatians and Moslems was essential, so too was the vindication of Četnik history. Any ambiguous alliances with the Germans or Italians were excised from history books, leaving a picture of the Četniks as righteous freedom fighters, engaged in a liberation struggle against the Nazis. Novels were often a favourite means of reinterpreting history. They could be emotive, convincing, and non-threatening at the same time. Momir Krsmanović's *The Blood-Stained Hands of Islam* was designed to promote a Serbian view of The Second World War to an English-speaking audience. The author, an eastern Bosnian, was heralded as one of the new breed of Serbian writers, and his previous work, *The Drina Runs Red with Blood*, was a best-seller. This book promised an insider's account of the Četniks and their national struggle, motivated by 'the desire to save the Serbian nation and wage an honourable struggle for justice, truth and the right of that nation to a place under the sun'.[29] This was set against the 'vengeful and blood-thirsty Turks and Catholics of Croatia and Bosnia'.[30]

Much of this book was set predictably in the Krajina, the scene of countless battles between Ustaša and Četnik forces. Krsmanović arguably aimed to vindicate Serbia's position in the 1990s by demonstrating how the Croatian Serbs had spent most of the twentieth century defending themselves from the threat of genocide. Important also was nostalgia for Royalist Yugoslavia. Books such as this featured graphic descriptions of Ustaša ethnic cleansing operations, as well as torture, rape, and other atrocities. One description of an Ustaša rape of two Serbian women, followed by the cutting off of their breasts and the slitting of their throats, was typical.[31] Curiously, the Ustaša commanders were given names such as Stipe and Franjo, obvious references to contemporary Croatian politicians. Others, presumably Moslem Ustaša, were called Alija and Ibrahim. Novels such as this advanced a series of pro-Serbian myths, similar to Schöpflin's 'myths of redemption and suffering', and 'myths of powerlessness and compensation for the powerless', where the Serbs were primarily the victims of the Second World War, and had thus earned their right to an autonomous republic in Bosnia.[32]

Novelists like Krsmanović inflated the level of Croatian collaboration, describing how 80 per cent of the Croatian and Moslem male population joined the Ustaša against the Serbs – a statistic that is historically untenable.[33] This new generation of novelists also attempted to rehabilitate Milan Nedić, casting him as a martyr for Serbia, who collaborated with the Nazis in order to minimise German atrocities against the Serbs. Thus his collaboration was dismissed as 'efforts to preserve his people during the harsh enemy occupation'.[34]

Similar views were to be found in Slobodan Selenić's 1989 *Timor mortis*, dealing with the Ustaša massacres of Serbs during the Second World War. This author repeated a common pattern in Serbian writing – that Croatian aggression stretched far back into the remote past. Like those of Krsmanović, his descriptions of Croatian atrocities were extremely graphic.[35] Similarly, Marjorie Radulović's *Rage of the Serbs*, historically situated in the Second World War, attempted to vindicate Serbian history. She praised the heroism and righteousness of the Četniks, their love of justice, their universal support amongst the Serbian people, and their single-minded devotion to freeing their country from Nazism. At the same time, Tito's Partisans were condemned as Ustaša collaborators, while the Ustaša were dehumanised as genocidal beasts.[36]

Vuk Drasković's *Noz* also dwelt on similar themes, namely the genocide of

Serbs by Ustaša, which he placed at well over one million people. His work described the legacy of the death-camps in Croatia, how two-thirds of all Serbian families had lost relatives to the Ustaša, and how many more were sentenced to lengthy prison terms under the Communists for trying to keep the memory of their tragedy alive. Second World War massacres become a 'Calvary' for the Serbian people. Drasković also attacked the Croats for their revisionism, arguing generally: 'those who hide a crime have the intention to commit it anew'.[37]

Of course, with this renewed interest in the Četniks came a glorification and 'performance' of their actions as well. Četnik hats, uniforms, and flags became popular fashion accessories, especially among paramilitary units fighting in Croatia and Bosnia. Arkan caused a sensation when he attired himself in full Četnik regalia during his 1995 wedding. His wife, the well-known turbofolk singer Čeča, was dressed as the 'Maid of Kosovo' (*Kosovka djevojka*), the Mary Magdalen-esque figure who nursed Serbian soldiers as they lay dying on the battlefield.[38] As with Kosovo fever, Četnik kitsch was to be found everywhere. Various journals, including *Duga*, *Pogledi*, and *Srpska Reč*, worked actively to rehabilitate the Četniks. Warlords like Vojislav Šešelj encouraged their followers to destroy anything bearing Tito's name, while calling for the re-establishment of the monarchy.[39] As in Croatia, wartime collaborators were rehabilitated. Dimitrije Ljotić was exonerated in a series of articles published in *Pogledi*, while the Partisans and the Četniks were condemned for inciting German wrath against the population.[40] Such writings performed a similar function to those in Croatia – they stressed the self-defensive nature of Serbian actions in the war, even presenting obvious collaborators as protectors of the Serbs against the Germans. The Second World War's participants were glorified as either great heroes, liberators, or defenders.

Croatian views of the Četniks

For Croatian historians, the ambiguous nature of Četnik history had been a worrying phenomenon. Presented equally in historical accounts as heroes and collaborators, the Četniks still enjoyed a better reputation than the Ustaša. An important objective of Croatian propaganda was portraying the Četniks as genocidal aggressors, who were every bit as evil, if not worse, than Croatia's Fascists.[41] The basic argument was as follows: the Četniks had little interest in liberating the country from the Germans and Italians. Rather, the Second World War was merely a backdrop for the continuing expansion of Greater Serbia, which was to include almost 90 per cent of NDH territory. For this reason, Četnik goals were obvious: 'the destruction of the NDH and cleansing of the Croatian and Muslim population from these territories in order to annex them to Greater Serbia'.[42]

Philip Cohen's analysis was little different, seeing 'terror and genocide' as the Četniks' main instruments in their quest for 'the expansion of Serbia and the assimilation or elimination of non-Serb populations'.[43] As he further elaborated: 'Like the Nazis, who believed that all Germans must live within one large, ethnically pure, German state, the Chetniks believed that all Serbs must live in one large, ethnically pure, Serbian state.'[44] That the Četniks might be seeking revenge for atrocities committed in the NDH was simply not discussed. Rather, the Četniks were presented as genocidal fanatics, who were trying to exterminate the Croats in order to build their super-state. For them, the war and the occupation of their country did nothing to change their expansionist strategies, which were timeless, and infinitely flexible, since the Četniks could seemingly side with both the Germans and the Allies at the same time, Nedić 'manoeuvr[ing] politically with Berlin to secure the creation of Greater Serbia under German patronage', while the Četniks were preparing for the day when they would 'seize power after the Germans were ousted . . . by the Allies'.[45]

The Četniks were also accused of formulating a plan for genocide *before* the establishment of the Ustaša death-camp system. The Četnik commander Stevan Moljević's 'Homogeneous Serbia', yet another essay on Greater Serbia, was frequently cited to balance out atrocity accusations levelled at the Croats. Draža Mihailović's 'Instructions' of December 1941 were also advanced as proof that the Četniks were using the war as a means of creating an 'ethnically cleansed' Greater Serbia. For Croatian writers, Mihailović was little more than a genocidal lunatic, and his sole ambition was to drive Croats, Moslems, and other non-Serbians from Bosnia-Hercegovina. The Četnik claim to be staging an uprising against the occupying powers was cited as the 'formal reason' for fighting. Of course, the true reason was bringing about an ethnically cleansed Greater Serbia, through 'Chetnik terror and genocidal crimes'.[46] The descriptions of Četnik crimes were often extremely graphic, mirroring the Serbs' use of such imagery:

> Physical destruction took the form of massacres, hangings, decapitation, burning, throwing victims into pits and killing them with various objects. Victims were in most cases tortured before being killed . . . rape of Muslim and Croatian women and girls so as to nationally and religiously degrade them. There were two especially significant forms of indirect Chetnik crimes. These were robbery and forced conversion of Catholics and Muslims into the Serbian Orthodox faith . . . The forced conversion to the Serbian Orthodox faith aimed at further degrading the victims and destroying that deepest of ties to the Croatian or Muslim nationality.[47]

Croatian writers also stressed the enormous size of the Četnik movement. A large Četnik membership was often contrasted with a small Ustaša membership – the implication being that Serbs were more genocidal than Croats. One

Croatian historian claimed that some 300 Četnik organisations existed in Bosnia, with another 200 in Croatia by 1941. These organisations were supposedly famous for their terror and barbarity, as well as their penchant for murdering large numbers of Croats and Muslims.[48] Croat historians also presented Mihailović as a dangerous manipulator with direct communication with all his units in the field. This was a highly contested assumption, since many Četnik groups operated in isolation, with a great deal of decentralisation of authority, and many were not even in radio communication with each other. However, what was important in the context of war was to prove that the Četniks were a unified cohesive force, all bent on the genocide of the Croats and the Moslems. Loosely co-ordinated bands of mercenaries did not present the same level of threat. At worst, such people could be likened to the Turks slaughtering the Armenians, but not the Nazis and their well-oiled apparatus.

Another popular argument held that the Četniks had openly collaborated with the Italians and Germans, in order to exterminate Croats on NDH territory. Supposedly, Italian and German forces supplied the Četniks with weapons, food, clothing, and even local currency when they agreed to exterminate Croatian and Moslems on behalf of the occupiers.[49] Such claims seem to have been exaggerated by Croatian historians, who paradoxically argued that Četnik unofficial collaboration was somehow worse than the official highly publicised Ustaša variety. Tim Judah has argued that, by 1943, both the Četniks and the Partisans had commenced dialogue with the Germans, each seeking an alliance against the other. As was clear from wartime accounts, the Četniks were willing to side with the Germans if it could mean the destruction of the Partisans. While these negotiations ultimately failed, owing to a lack of German interest, the Četniks were willing to collaborate, to increase their strength against Partisan forces. It is also clear that in Montenegro they did accept help from the Italians during the Italian surrender in 1943. However, it is highly misleading to suggest that Četniks throughout the war collaborated with the Germans and Italians in order to carry out the genocide of Croats and Moslems.[50]

For Croatian writers, the attempted genocide of Croats and Moslems justified their presence in Ustaša and Domobran units. These two groups were forced to defend themselves against 'Četnik-Communist units', which were formed in the forests in Bosnia-Hercegovina. In this way, they were not guilty of collaboration, since they were merely reacting to the Serbs, who, 'following the example of their Vlach ancestors, began to exterminate the Croat and Muslim population of the Bihac region in horrible and merciless [*sic*] massacres'.[51] Further, Pavelić's crimes were excused on the basis that he was merely countering 'Četnik terrorists with terror of their own', which in any case was not as ruthless as that of the Serbs in Serbia, where 'the persecution of Jews was even more thorough'.[52]

In sum, what emerges from a reading of Croatian perceptions of the Second World War is the reactive nature of Croatian activities. For these writers, the Serbian Četniks seemingly had the upper hand throughout Bosnia-Hercegovina, and were busy instigating a genocide of Croats and Moslems. The problem, of course, was that it was the Ustaša who were (officially, at the very least) in control of Bosnia-Hercegovina, not the Četniks. It was the Ustaša who had the power of the state behind them, as well as Italian and German support. Nevertheless, this view of the Četniks as unrestrained genocidal killers seemingly rang true for the Croatian public.

Tudjman himself used the concept of a genocidal Četnik movement to generalise Serbian guilt. He suggested that 'Maček's middle-of-the-road Croatian Peasant party was to remain the chief political force opposed to the revolutionary NOP on Croatian soil, just as Mihailović's Četnik movement was in Serbia.'[53] While these two movements were likened in terms of support, morally they were far apart, according to Tudjman, who placed the Četniks on a par morally and philosophically with the Ustaša, not the CPP. Tudjman's later development of this argument made his position more obvious:

> Both the Ustaša and Četnik movements were equally the expression of mutually opposing ideas concerning nation and state and of the programs for their implementation, both stemming from the judgement that coexistence in a common state was impossible. This means that Dr. A. Pavelić and General D. Mihailović, in the circumstances of the Second World War, found themselves as the forefront of nationally exclusive and irreconcilable movements, which sought equally to exploit those circumstances for the realization of their respective national programs.[54]

Thus Četnik and Ustaša were paralleled, in terms of their level of atrocities, their ideology, their *modus operandi*, and their aims during the war.[55] Croatian writers ignored the fact that one was a Nazi-backed, Italian-trained terrorist group, and the other, a Royalist, Allied-backed, anti-German and anti-Communist resistance movement. Tudjman implied that, because most Serbs supported a genocidal movement with an expansionist political project, all Serbs were tarred with the Četnik legacy, and, by implication, with a legacy of genocide. At the same time, since Croats were mainly CCP supporters, their culpability was significantly reduced.

Anti-Semitism in Croatia: Stepinac and the people

How Jews were treated in Yugoslavia during the Second World War became another subject of heated debate. If each side was legitimately to claim to be the victims of genocide, of the type experienced by the Jews, then their own relationship with the Jews was crucial. For both Serbs and Croats, Jewish history during the war needed to be carefully revised, to highlight only the positive aspects of their historical relationship. Similarly, the other had to be presented as anti-Semitic collaborators who had participated actively in the Final Solution. Both sides eagerly embarked on this exercise, and were not ashamed to manipulate Jewish leaders in the process.

Croatian writers pursued a dual strategy of touting their own love of Jews, while condemning the Serbs for their complicity in the Holocaust. One aspect of Croatian revisionism was the wholesale rehabilitation of Archbishop Alojzije Stepinac, head of the Roman Catholic Church in Croatia during the war. Croats devoted a great deal of energy to proving that Stepinac was a great friend of the Jews, and inspired most Croats to help them during the war. Of course, Stepinac, like most of the cast of characters in the region, had some rather dubious credentials. As Archbishop of Zagreb, Stepinac officiated at the *Te Deum* that gave thanks for the foundation of the Ustaša state.[56] At first, Stepinac appeared to have been no different from the many Croats who had had great expectations of the regime. However, his enthusiasm soured greatly as the war dragged on and the atrocities of the Ustaša came to light. He is generally painted as a naive and idealistic man, who, while hating the horrors of war, saw Pavelić as a hero and saviour of his people.[57]

While he refused to denounce the regime officially, there is evidence that Stepinac did help some Jews – aiding children to escape to Palestine, and donating food and money to Jews in hiding.[58] What emerged was the portrait of a man sitting on the fence, symbolically supporting the NDH, and condemning Ustaša crimes as far as he could without incurring danger to his person, while secretly easing his conscience with private acts of piety and kindness. Nevertheless, while he seemingly helped some of the Jews, he expressed little remorse over the forced conversions of an estimated 200,000 Serbs, often at gunpoint.[59] Accused of collaboration by the Partisans, Stepinac stood trial in September 1946.[60] He was subsequently sentenced to 16 years imprisonment, served five years, and then returned to his native village, where he died in 1960.[61]

Stepinac, despite his wartime record, was completely rehabilitated by Croatian historians. His supposed love of the Jews was cited as proof of Croatian philosemitism during the Second World War. One writer noted how 70 Croats received 'The Certificate of Honour' and 'The Medal of the Righteous' from Yad Vashem in Jerusalem, as proof of Croatian goodwill during the war, similarly noting how, as early as 1936, Stepinac supported Austrian and German Jews by founding 'Action to help refugees' and 'Croatian Caritas' (1938). [62] Stepinac was also credited with saving 60 inmates of the Jewish Old People's Home in Zagreb, preserving the private library of the Zagreb Chief Rabbi Miroslav Shalom Freiberger at his request, and publicly condemning the destruction of Zagreb's main synagogue in 1941.[63]

Stepinac's usefulness as a symbol of Croatian tolerance was not lost on Franjo Tudjman. In one lengthy defence of Stepinac, Tudjman dismissed the accusations against him as having 'even less of a foundation than does the Jasenovac distortion'.[64] He later emphasised that Pope John Paul II's visit to Croatia, and Stepinac's beatification by the Vatican, completely exonerated Croatia of any wrongdoing during the Second World War. Stepinac, it seemed, had become *the* symbol of Croatia's wartime relationship with the Jews. As Tudjman's logic impelled him to explain:

> With the beatification, the Holy Father and the Vatican sided with this Croatia and Croatian people against attempts to accuse the whole Croatian people of genocide and fascism. The Holy Father, the Vatican, and the Catholicism, all said that Stepinac was not a criminal, as was not the Croatian people. That is a contribution to the truth about the Croatian people in WW II and the truth about the contemporary Croatia.[65]

The Vatican's support for Stepinac was extremely important, further proving that he was a friend of the Jews, as well as a Croatian martyr against both Nazism and Communism, and Tudjman cleverly manipulated Stepinac's rehabilitation to clean the Croatian wartime record. However, his portrayal of Stepinac's beatification is not entirely in keeping with the facts, and seems to be more wishful thinking than anything else. Stepinac was appointed Cardinal primarily for his resistance to Communism, and for his condemnation of Partisan attacks on Catholic clergy after the war. By the end of 1945, an estimated 273 priests had been killed by the Partisans, while countless more had been arrested, or had gone 'missing'. Stepinac was targeted by the Communist authorities only after his condemnation, and he stood trial a year later for collaboration with the NDH regime.[66] Tudjman's claim of 'innocence' is thus highly misleading. Generally, Croats described Stepinac as an outspoken critic of the Nazis and a 'friend of the Jews', because of his wartime efforts to save them. The tarring of Stepinac, one writer posited, was done solely to deflect attention from the dishonourable conduct of the Serbian Orthodox Church.[67]

Stepinac became useful as a leader who constantly stood up to the Ustaša, offering passive spiritual resistance. In Croatian writings, such resistance was often contrasted to the role of the Serbian Orthodox Church, which was described as bent on persecuting Jews and promoting Greater Serbia, which was condemned as a 'racist ideology'.[68] So too was Serbian literary culture condemned. Ljubica Stefan's *From Fairy Tale to Holocaust* was a typical example of this type of thinking, tracing the ancient roots of Serbian anti-Semitism. A large section of her work was devoted to reviewing various anti-Semitic folk tales, assembled by Vuk Karadzić in 1853. One featured work was the 'The Yids' (*Civuti*), the story of Hansel and Gretel, notable for the fact that the 'wicked witch' was a Jewish woman. In Stefan's account of them, these folk tales encouraged Serbs to see the Jewish people as those who 'chased after the gentile children with knives and forks to eat them, which presents the Jews as cannibals.'[69] Certainly as interesting as the tales themselves is Stefan's belief that Serbian anti-Semitism could be traced from nineteenth-century fairy tales to the political traditions of Greater Serbia, and then into the twentieth century, where Serbia was 'the most trustworthy ally of the Third Reich'.[70]

While the Serbs were under direct military occupation, with strict curfews and a particularly brutal police force, Stefan argued that the Serbs had an independent, autonomous state, complete with 'a government, organised ministries, independent governments in cities and villages, its own army equipped by the Germans.'[71] The Serbs were able to gain such autonomy, asserted Stefan, because of their long tradition of anti-Semitism, and their eagerness to participate in the Final Solution. She also argued that the Orthodox Church was instrumental in the genocide of the Jews, since they functioned as 'a sort of a political party and even racist', while they 'totally neglected pastoral and spiritual work'.[72]

This form of 'counteridentification' was crucial during the 1990s, as it showed the continuation, once again, of an age-old Serbian hatred of all things non-Serb, and a desire to expand the Serbian state – and destroy everything in its path. Thus, for Stefan, and for many others, the Jews and the Croats were fellow victims of Serbian aggression during the Second World War. More often than not, Croatian claims of Serbian anti-Semitism were exaggerated. While it was clear that the Serbian puppet government and certain Orthodox officials such as Bishop Nikolaj Velimirović maintained anti-Semitic views (in Velimirović's case from the Second World War well into the 1990s),[73] there is little to support the idea that the Serbs actively and enthusiastically aided in the Holocaust. Serbs had little autonomy within Serbia during the war; this was a country occupied by German troops. Even Philip Cohen, after his lengthy attack on the Serbs, was forced to admit that 'it is indisputable that the executioners of Serbia's Jews were German army personnel or regular police. However, the role of the Serbs as active collaborators in the destruction of the Jews has remained under-explored in Holocaust literature.'[74] While their role may perhaps underexplored, Cohen was unable to argue convincingly that anti-Semitism was an important aspect of Serbian nationalism during the Second World War – important enough at least to have inspired an active role in the Holocaust.

That a large number of Serbs joined the Partisans and the Četniks does indicate that there was little support for the Nedić regime. Futhermore, it seems that there was little love lost between Germans and Serbs. Germans considered the Serbs to be treacherous and dangerous, remembering the heavy losses they sustained at Serbian hands during the First World War.[75] Christopher Browning's analysis of the German occupation of Serbia suggests that support for the Nedić regime was much lower than the level alleged by the Croats.[76] While the Serbian Orthodox Church promoted anti-Semitism to some extent, this did not translate into overt support for the genocide of Yugoslavia's Jews.

Serbian views of collaboration and anti-Semitism

For the Serbs, connections between the suffering of Serbs and Jews during the Second World War were extremely important – anti-Semitism and Serbophobia were continually compared, as proof that the Serbs were also the victims of genocide. For many Serbs, the Second World War was a time when Serbia was close to being wiped out, as Germans 'committed wide scale murders, burning of entire villages, raided and bombed cities'.[77] Jews and Serbs would be symbolically linked, as one writer revealed, for espousing the same values: 'The Jewish-Serbian-Capitalist-Democratic front had to disappear forever from the world ... Jews and Serbs were struck with the same dagger.'[78] Dobrica Ćosić went so far as to assert that the genocide of the Serbs was worse than that of the Jews, in terms of its methods and bestiality.[79] Exaggeration aside, the Serbs did indeed suffer heavy losses during the Second World War, although it was never on the level suggested by contemporary historians.

As with the Croats, the myth of philosemitism was extremely important for the Serbs, who saw themselves, along with the Jews, as fellow victims of Nazi aggression. Laza Kostić's *The Serbs and the Jews* (1988) advanced the view that Serbia was one of the few countries that was free of anti-Semitism during the war. Describing himself as 'a fanatical friend of the Jews in general and of the Serbian ones in particular', Kostić claimed that Serbs were always the best friends of the Jews throughout history:

> The Serbs are one of the rare peoples in the world who have lived with the Jews in peace and love throughout the whole history of their settlement in our lands ... The Serbs never persecuted the Jews, never carried out any demonstrations against them. Not one anti-Semitic text has ever appeared in the press, and hatred against them was not spread orally either ... There was no more tolerant country towards the Jews. Considerably later, many other countries copied the so-called 'emancipation of the Jews' from the Serbs.[80]

This general view was important in vindicating the Serbian role in the Second World War. Kostić even made the suggestion that Nedić had in no way collaborated with the Nazis in the Holocaust of the Jews. While the Nedić regime worked under the Nazis, they refused to 'contemplate participation in

[any] aspect of the extermination of the Jews by the Germans' – so Kostić claimed.[81]

Of course, with daily accusations from the Croatian side that the Serbs were the worst anti-Semites the world had ever seen, the Serbs countered with invective of their own. Mirroring Croatian arguments, Serbian writers alleged that Croatia was neck-deep in anti-Semitism. In Serbian eyes, one of the worst offenders was Alojzije Stepinac, who was presented as an active collaborator and figurehead for Catholic complicity in the genocide of the Serbs and the Jews. Certainly the most vocal critic of Stepinac's rehabilitation was Milan Bulajić, who denounced Stepinac as an enthusiastic NDH supporter.[82] His voluntary loyalty oath to Ante Pavelić and his position as Ustaša army chaplain made him 'the spiritual father of the Ustaši Independent State of Croatia' – a crucial moral prop for the regime.[83] His support of the NDH and denouncing of Yugoslavia also proved that he was a 'fanatical opponent' of the 'Masonic-Jewish state' – a rather strange moniker for Serbia.[84]

Many of Bulajić's efforts were directed towards debunking the myth of Stepinac's philosemitism. He argued that while Stepinac saved individual Jews, these were Jews in mixed marriages with Catholics, or those who had converted to Catholicism to escape death. He argued that Stepinac was only against the racialisation of anti-Semitism. Those Jews who converted to Catholicism could be saved, whereas those who did not could still be condemned to death.[85] The claim that Stepinac saved 200 Jewish orphans was rebutted by the fact that as soon as Stepinac petitioned the Vatican to save them, the Ustaša rounded them up and sent them to Jasenovac. 'This', Bulajić argued, was 'the historical truth of this "humanitarian action".'[86] The case of Miroslav Shalom Freiberger's library was also seen as cancelled out by the fact that Freiberger was later captured by the Ustaša secret police and sent to a German death-camp.

At the same time, Bulajić denounced Stepinac for exercising a double standard: if converting Jews were saved, converting Gypsies were not. 'The Catholic Church in Croatia didn't care too much about them', was his conclusion.[87] Bulajić argued generally that while Stepinac made a show of his philosemitism after the war, his wartime actions came to nothing, since most of the people he supposedly tried to save were eventually killed, implying that these demonstrations of philosemitism were merely for show, concealing the ugly truth of his own anti-Semitism.

Alongside Stepinac, the Catholic Church was often portrayed as a genocidal collaborator with the Nazis. Historians such as Dušan Bataković derided the Church for 'their own brand of religious exclusionism, intolerance, and a militant proselytizing', which formed part of a Church-driven policy to bring about a religiously and racially pure Croatia.[88] 'A very considerable part of

148

the Croatian political elite,' Bataković concluded, 'supported by the Catholic hierarchy and Archbishop Alojzije Stepinac himself, supported this national and religious intolerance, and strongly supported policies of clericalism and racism, marked by mass killings, forced conversions and the deportation of the Serbian Orthodox population as well the slaughter of the Jews and Gypsies.'[89] For Bataković, Church leaders were queuing up to commit genocide against the Serbian and Jewish populations in Croatia.

Other historians would use similar imagery, describing how the Ustaša state was 'soundly and joyously received by the majority of the Croatian people', and how the Catholic Church, and Stepinac in particular, were 'the most loyal [of] Hitler's collaborator[s]'.[90] Other writers were in no doubt that the Vatican had been a keen advocate of genocide, with Church officials inciting Croats from their pulpits to wage '"holy" war for the cause of a pure and independent Croatia'.[91] Serbs commonly portrayed Stepinac as the spiritual leader of an enthusiastic gang of genocidal clergy, only too eager to swear allegiance to Pavelić's regime, in order to begin killing Serbs, Jews, and Communists. If Stepinac's goodness allowed Tudjman to portray the Croatian nation as righteous and good, Stepinac's collaboration tarred all Croats as genocidal killers. Nevertheless, while there was evidence that some priests had participated in atrocities, Stepinac's record seems clear, in so far as he never sanctioned violence or racial hatred. Those Catholic priests who actually helped the Serbs were never mentioned, nor were the many Serbian Orthodox priests who lent their support to the Četnik massacres during the Second World War.

Serbian sources maintained that over 80 per cent of Croatia's Jews were killed during the Ustaša period, only a few surviving by 'sheer accident'. The killing of Jews was ascribed to a uniquely Ustaši approach, spearheaded by Andrija Artuković, the NDH Minister of the Interior, who devastated the 14,000-strong Jewish community in Bosnia-Hercegovina, leaving only 2,000 survivors. Artuković's hatred of the Jews was often linked with a fear of International Communism and capitalism, both of which threatened to swamp Croatia, and the Croatian nation.[92] According to other Serbian sources, the Ustaša regime killed 30,000 of Croatia's Jews during the war, as well as a majority of the Gypsy community, estimated before the war to have comprised between 40,000 and 100,000 people.[93] The divergence between these figures is striking. It seems that no one was certain exactly how many Jews there were in Croatia – either before the war, or after.

Throughout the 1990s, the use of graphic, lugubrious imagery was an important prerequisite of Serbian propaganda. The more graphic the details, the more horrific the crimes of the Croats would appear to be, and by extension, the more important it would be to stop another Croatian genocide. Among the favoured themes was the slaughter of innocent children, proof that the Croats were truly depraved. One description from *Never Again* was typical of Serbian fare:

> Infants were shot in their cribs, babies were foisted on bayonettes, slaughtered with knives, razors and axes, burned in their homes, in brickyards and in the Jasenovac crematorium, boiled in soap melting cauldrons, bound together and thrown into rivers and wells, thrown alive into caves and grottoes, asphyxiated in cyanide and poisoned with caustic soda, killed through hunger, thirst and exposure . . . [94]

This typical account conveyed the savagery of the Ustaša, trying to destroy the future of the Serbian nation. 'The foundations of the Ustaši state,' the authors of this work concluded, 'were laid on the slaughter of children.'[95] Graphic portrayals of a war on children highlighted the depravity of the Ustaša, but also demonstrated the extreme suffering of the Serbs, who had been robbed of the future of their nation.

Constantly mentioned in Serbian literature was the famous encounter between the journalist Curzio Malaparte and Ante Pavelić, during which Malaparte was proudly shown a basket containing what he believed to be Dalmatian oysters, only to be told by a triumphant Pavelić that these were forty pounds of Serbian eyeballs – a gift from 'loyal Ustašas'. This account, described in Malaparte's *Kaputt* (1946), was one of the favourite pieces of imagism used by the Serbs to describe the irrationality and brutality of the NDH. The only intrinsic value possessed by a Serb, it seemed, was his eyes.[96]

Such descriptions of Ustaša terror aimed at completely dehumanising the Croats, imparting the idea that they were nothing more than sadistic, bloodthirsty killers. While a certain percentage of Serbs and Croats did run wild during four years of war, these few psychopaths did not reflect the motivations and actions of the vast majority of the population. At the same time, it was curious that the Serbs sought to invent a variety of anti-Vatican, anti-Stepinac, anti-Ustaša stories, when there were many documented facts about the Second World War that were far more damning. Take for example Mark Aarons and John Loftus's *Ratlines*, which factually analysed the role of the Vatican in helping escaping Nazi war criminals. Through the Intermarium, the Vatican controlled the largest Nazi-smuggling organisation of its kind in Europe after the war, run in part by the Croatian priest Krunoslav Stefano Draganović.[97] The Intermarium even helped Pavelić to escape to Italy, where the Vatican allowed him to live in one of the Pope's summer homes, safe from the British and the Yugoslavs.[98] While this in no way validates the Serbian position, it is curious that Serbs chose to invent and distort history, when using well-established facts would have served their cause more effectively.

The myth of Partisan participation

Another important aspect of Second World War revisionism was the myth of Partisan membership. Each side tried to prove that their nation initiated anti-fascist resistance, and was therefore on the winning side. This was of central importance, because it proved that no one actually collaborated with the Nazis and their puppet states. Each side now became an innocent victim of fascism, instead of collaborators with it. Each side could also claim to have created and founded Tito's Yugoslavia, only to be later betrayed for their national sacrifices – becoming martyrs when they were 'discriminated' against in the SFRY.

The Serbs certainly took Partisan membership seriously. The historian Velimir Ivetić's lengthy monograph examined the annual ratio of Serbs and Croats in each Partisan detachment in Croatia, arguing that the Serbs were the most important resistance force in the region. A summary of his findings included the following: 'that the participation of the Serbs from Croatia in the common struggle against the occupier and his lackeys was enormous'; 'that the Serbs had the "role of initiator" of the uprising'; and, 'that the Serbs helped the rising up of the Croatian people against the occupier'.[99] The Croats only constituted a majority, Ivetić claimed, when defeat was certain. While the Croats were represented as cynical opportunists, Serbs were credited with extending a hand of brotherly friendship to their erstwhile enemies at the war's end. Ever able to forgive and forget, the Serbs supposedly helped their killers join the Partisans.[100]

Similar arguments have been raised by other Serbian writers, one arguing that: 'persecuted Serbs swelled the ranks of Draža Mihailović's Četniks but even more so of Tito's Partisans'.[101] Others concluded: 'The Serbian and Montenegrin people are today among those freedom-loving peoples which share the feeling of pride with the world because of their undeniable contribution to the defeat of the greatest evil of this century.'[102] The Ministry of Information similarly claimed that the Serbs were 'freedom loving, democratic and antifascist ... [by their struggles against] the Croatian genocidal government and the Nazi disintegration of Yugoslavia'.[103] Still others described how Tito was forced to move his headquarters to Belgrade from Zagreb, after the 'enthusiasm with which the German occupiers were greeted in Zagreb in 1941'. Here, the 'rebellious energies' of the Serbs in Serbia, Montenegro and in other Serbian areas were not only 'a primary source of the anti-Fascist struggle, but also a condition for CPY survival'.[104]

It was crucially important to present Serbs as the liberators of Yugoslavia, and the greatest opponents of Fascism. While Partisan participation in the Second World War enhanced Serbian claims to be anti-genocidal in the contemporary conflict, a high Partisan membership also tied in with the Serbian theme of sacrifice. Serbs had supposedly given their all to create

Yugoslavia, and had a legitimate claim to be the inheritors of what remained of the country – rump-Yugoslavia. Such claims also countered Tudjman's assertions that every Serb had been a Četnik. While few Serbs were willing to admit that the Četniks had committed any atrocities during the war, it was a much better strategy to focus on membership of the Partisans – a less morally ambiguous movement.

The Croats advanced similar arguments, positing that *they* were both the first and the largest ethnic group in the Partisan resistance. While this ran counter to Tudjman's thesis that most Croats supported the CPP, it accomplished the same objective – proving that Croats were not wholesale collaborators. Croatian writers argued that the majority of the Croatian population both 'supported and actively participated' in Tito's Partisan movement.[105] Others described how the 'the first rebellion in Europe against the [N]azi and fascist occupation' was led by the Croats, who formed the first Partisan unit near Sisak in June 1941. Included in one account was a list of Croatian notables such as the poet Vladimir Nazor and 'the democratically oriented' Communist leader Andrija Hebrang, as well as descriptions of how the Croatian-based Partisans (ZAVNOH) held more liberated territory than Tito's pan-Yugoslav council (AVNOJ).[106]

Others, while admitting that Serbs at some points formed the majority in the Partisans, dismissed their commitment to the cause, since 'the Serbs were primarily escaping from persecution, while the Croats chose the antifascist side because of their personal beliefs and with the idea of preserving the identity of their state through a war of liberation'.[107] Ironically, while some Serbs may have been opportunistic in trying to save their lives, they were certainly morally superior to those Croats who were killing them. Cohen (in an interview with a Croatian newspaper) similarly posited that the Serbs were the main collaborators in the Second World War, claiming that 70 per cent of Croats but only 11 per cent of Serbs were antifascist. Further, any Četniks who converted to the Partisan cause supposedly did so only to transform the Communists into a 'new tool for "Greater Serbia"'.[108]

Relatively unbiased historians have described the predominance of Serbs among the members of the NDH who joined the Partisans, largely in reaction to the Ustaša atrocities; and thus there is some truth to the Serbian claim of numerical dominance.[109] This does not, however, negate the strong participation of Croats in the Partisans, nor does it detract from the massacres committed by Serbian Četniks during this time. For both sides, it became clear that high Partisan numbers were but one more aspect of a growing revisionist conflict, with each side arguing the opposite of the other. Both sides claimed to have been the key to the anti-fascist liberation of the country, allowing both similarly to claim that their people had been against the Četniks and Ustaša all along.

Conclusions

In general, Serb and Croat arguments apropos the Second World War were almost identical. Each argued in favour of their own philosemitism, victimisation, and heroism, while denouncing the others for their treachery, anti-Semitism, collaboration, and genocide. The recent revisions of history from both sides suggest uneasiness about the legacies of the past. They also suggest a need to vindicate one's own history, excising any negative historical patterns that one might find, while at the same time continuing to identify a coherent pattern of genocidal hatred and destruction on the part of one's perceived enemy.

What emerged was a blurring of the lines between acting and being, as well as a blurring of the concepts of self and other. In both cases, each side could rightly claim victims who were killed in the style of the Četniks or Ustaša, but each side was also guilty of having adopted the symbols and trappings of this earlier period. Resurrected Četnik and Ustaša units battled each other once again, proving for many that the war was very much cast as a continuation of an earlier conflict. Why Arkan wore full Četnik regalia to marry his 'maid of Kosovo' was as difficult to understand as why Dobroslav Paraga's renewed Party of Rights and the HOS regiments in Bosnia-Hercegovina sported Ustaša insignia and used the old Nazi salute. In the cities, Serbs in Belgrade could easily purchase Četnik hats and T-shirts, while in Zagreb, the *Poglavnik*'s portrait was prominently displayed over swimming pools and in restaurants.

However, the complexity of events can be broken down fairly simply – each side attempted to revise and excuse the atrocities their side had committed, and part of that process involved donning their former nationalist dress, and adopting old symbols to prove that they were not ashamed of their past history. Demonisation of the other required the inflation of the other side's atrocities, and a denunciation of the enemy side's parallel process of rehabilitating their own past. Thus, the work of neither side should be studied in isolation, as has been done by both Serbs and Croats, but rather, events should be seen as a series of related actions in an escalating crisis.

The concept of 'performativity' is thus extremely important here. What began as groups 'playing' Ustaša and Četnik soon evolved into neo-Ustaša and neo-Četnik units, complete with traditional weaponry, uniforms, salutes, and styles of killing. What began as a vindication of one's own national past became first a blurring, and then a desecration of it. Paradoxically, each side, in the name of historical revisionism, set out to burn, loot, shell, and commit the same barbarous acts, acts that they refused to admit their predecessors had done. By re-enacting the past crimes of which their grandfathers stood accused, they ironically tarnished their own national past. Curiously, while each side blamed the other, there is no doubt that the escalation could not have begun if only one side had chosen to adopt a historic role. Each side advanced almost identical arguments, countering each other fact by fact, point by point. Without the participation of historians, politicians and journalists from both sides, no debate would have been possible.

NOTES

1 David Campbell, *National Deconstruction: Violence, Identity, and Justice In Bosnia* (Minneapolis, MN: University of Minnesota Press, 1998) p. 84. (Italics his.)
2 Peter Novick, *The Holocaust and Collective Memory: The American Experience* (New York: Bloomsbury, 1999) pp. 3–4.
3 Milica Bakić-Hayden, 'Nesting Orientalisms: The Case of Former Yugoslavia', *Slavic Review* (Winter 1995) p. 8.
4 Michael Ignatieff, *Blood and Belonging: Journeys into the New Nationalism* (Toronto: Viking Books, 1993) p. 14.
5 Marcus Tanner, *Croatia: A Nation Forged in War* (New Haven, CT: Yale University Press, 1997) p. 141.
6 Biljana Vankovska, 'Civil–Military Relations in the Third Yugoslavia', *COPRI Working Papers* (Copenhagen: Copenhagen Peace Research Institute, 2000) pp. 20–1.
7 Jasper Ridley, *Tito* (London: Constable, 1994) p. 164.
8 Barbara Jelavich, *History of the Balkans Volume II* (London: Cambridge University Press, 1993) p. 264.
9 Ridley, *Tito*, p. 164.
10 Tim Judah, *The Serbs: History, Myth and the Destruction of Yugoslavia* (New Haven, CT: Yale University Press, 1997) p. 117.
11 Christopher Browning, *Fateful Months: Essays on the Emergence of the Final Solution* (London: Holmes & Meier, 1991) p. 46.
12 Tanner, *Croatia*, p. 160.
13 See Stjepan Hefer, *Croatian Struggle for Freedom and Statehood* (Argentina: Croatian Information Service/Croatian Liberation Movement, 1979), pp. 10; 13–14; 110.
14 Croats against the regime were also to be few and far between, or, as Hefer puts it: 'The Croatian people unanimously chose the way which led to the 're-establishment of national freedom and state ...' (*ibid.* pp. 129–30). Such comparisons between the Ustaša and other liberation movements are also found in more contemporary analysis. Vladimir Mrkoci argues that the Ustaša were little different from other supposed freedom fighters of the world. For him, the 'Ustashe were a national revolutionary organization similar to Young Europe from the past century, as a belated echo of romanticism. They are similar to all other national revolutionary movements such as the Irish IRA, ETA in Spain and others. They are most similar to the Jewish Irgun Zwai Leumi': Vladimir Mrkoci, 'Historical Guilt of Alain Finkelkraut', *Hrvatski Obzor* (17 August 1996 [translated on 5 October 2001]) http://free.freespeech.org/ex-yupress/hrobzor/hrobzor12.html (accessed 10 January 2002). This article is in essence a defence of the Ustaša after Alain Finkielkraut's earlier denunciation of the regime in the French media.
15 Hefer, *Croatian Struggle for Freedom and Statehood*, p. 135.
16 See Mrkoci, 'Historical Guilt of Alain Finkelkraut'.
17 Ivo Omerčanin, *The Pro-Allied Putsch in Croatia in 1944 and the Massacre of Croatians by Tito's Communists in 1945* (Philadelphia, PA: Dorrance & Company, 1975) p. 18.
18 *Ibid.* pp. 19; 31.

19 *Ibid.* p. 36.

20 Ante Beljo also argues that the government tried to negotiate changing sides in 1943, after Italian surrender, and quotes a memorandum sent to Field Marshal Harold Alexander in May 1945. He also states that Lorković and Vokić were executed for their plans after being arrested in August, 1944, and that they had a 'large number of generals and officers' 'planning the disarming of the German army and the shift to the side of the Allies'. The issue of the memorandum is quite interesting for Beljo, as the 'last significant document of the Croatian government during the war'. Beljo seems to impute a conspiracy to the fact that the Allies never acknowledged its receipt, leading to a false impression about the Croats' intentions. One also gets the impression that such a memorandum should have been taken seriously, even though it was issued so late in the game as to be obviously opportunistic. Such a memorandum in 1943, by contrast, might actually have achieved some result: Ante Beljo, *Genocide in Yugoslavia: A Documentary Analysis* (Sudbury, ON: Northern Tribune Publishing, 1985) pp. 83–5.

21 Vlado Vurusić, 'After 35 Years, We Have Moved Our Ustashe Newspaper "Independent State Croatia" from Toronto to Zagreb', *Globus* (1 December 1995) www.cdsp.neu.edu/info/students/marko/globus2.html (accessed 18 June 1998).

22 Velimir Bujanec, 'Reply to Partisan Ivan Fumić', reprinted from *Vjesnik* in *Nezavisna Drzava Hrvatska* (March 1996) www.cdsp.neu.edu/info/students/marko/ndh/ndh1.html (accessed 18 June 1998).

23 'Review of Ivo Rojnica, *Meetings and Experiences* (Zagreb: DoNeHa, 1994)', *Feral Tribune* (29 December 1997). www.cdsp.neu.edu/info/students/marko/feral/feral53.html (accessed 12 March 1998).

24 'Review of Eugen Dido Kvaternik, *Memories and Observations 1925-1945* (Zagreb: Nakladnicko Drustvo Starcevic, 1995)', *Feral Tribune* (29 December 1997). Available at: www.cdsp.neu.edu/info/students/marko/feral/feral53.html (accessed 12 March 1998).

25 Josip Šentija, 'Croatia from 1941 to 1991' (Zagreb: University of Zagreb/Matica Hrvatska Iseljenika, 1994) p. 1.

26 Franjo Tudjman, *Horrors of War: Historical Reality and Philosophy – Revised Edition*, translated by Katarina Mijatović (New York: M. Evans and Company, 1996) p. 349.

27 Philip J. Cohen, *Serbia's Secret War: Propaganda annd the Deceit of History* (College Station TX: Texas A & M University Press, 1996) p. 93.

28 *Ibid.* p. 99.

29 Momir Krsmanović, *The Blood-Stained Hands of Islam* (Belgrade: BIGZ, 1994) p. 8.

30 *Ibid.* p. 16.

31 *Ibid.* pp. 141–2.

32 *Ibid.* pp. 29–30.

33 *Ibid.* p. 35.

34 *Ibid.* p. 125.

35 Andrew Baruch Wachtel, *Making a Nation Breaking a Nation: Literature and Cultural Politics in Yugoslavia* (Stanford, CA: Stanford University Press, 1998) pp. 219; 222.

36 Marjorie Radulović, *Rage of the Serbs* (Lewes, E. Sussex: The Book Guild, 1998) pp. 192–6; 446–7.

37 Vuk Drasković, *Le Couteau* (Paris: J. C Lattes, 1993) pp. 5–6 (my translation).

38 Michael A. Sells, *The Bridge Betrayed: Religion and Genocide in Bosnia* (London: University of California Press, 1996) pp. 51; 82.

39 Nobojša Popov, 'La populisme serbe' (suite), *Les Temps Modernes* (May 1994) pp. 58–9.

40 *Ibid.* pp. 60–1.

41 One historian summarised this theme well: 'The Chetniks not only intended to perform genocide, they carried out several forms of genocidal crimes against Croatians and Muslims in Bosnia and Herzegovina and Croatians in Croatia during World War II'. See Zdravko Dizdar, 'Chetnik Genocidal Crimes Against Croatians and Muslims in Bosnia and Herzegovina and Against Croatians in Croatia During World War II (1941-1945)', in Aleksander Ravlić (ed.), *Southeastern Europe 1918–1995* (Zagreb: Croatian Heritage Foundation/Croatian Information Center, 1998): www.hic.hr/books/seeurope/index-e.htm top (accessed 5 February 2000).

42 *Ibid.*

43 Philip J. Cohen, *The World War II and Contemporary Chetniks: Their historic-political continuity and implications for stability in the Balkans* (Zagreb: CERES, 1997) p. 26.

44 *Ibid.* p. 32.

45 *Ibid.* p. 32.

46 Dizdar, 'Chetnik Genocidal Crimes Against Croatians and Muslims in Bosnia and Herzegovina and Against Croatians in Croatia During World War II'.

47 *Ibid.*

48 *Ibid.*

49 *Ibid.* Beljo made the same argument. He accused the Italians of wanted to 'exterminate' the Croats, but since they 'could not resort to such primitive and beastly crimes, therefore they left it up to the Chetniks'. See Beljo, *Genocide in Yugoslavia*, p. 51.

50 This complicated situation is discussed in Judah, *The Serbs*, pp. 118–19. I consider his account to be factually accurate, and relatively free of bias.

51 Antun Abramović, 'Excerpts from: "Bihac, a Bulwark of Croatian Glory and Suffering", *Hrvatsko Slovo* (9 August 1995) www.cdsp.neu.edu/info/students/marko/hrslovo/hrslovo3.html (accessed 18 June 1998).

52 Mislav Jezić, 'Problems of Understanding XXth Century History of Croatia' (Zagreb: University of Zagreb) www.dalmatia.net/croatia/history/jezic.htm (accessed 18 June 1998).

53 Tudjman, *Horrors of War*, p. 349.

54 *Ibid.* p. 394.

55 Cohen follows a similar argument to that of Tudjman, seeing both the Ustaša and the Četniks as 'quintessentially genocidal'. The Četniks he charges with 'systematic genocide against Muslims', giving a range of Moslem deaths from between 86,000 to 103,000, most of whom, he claims, were killed by Serbs. See Philip J. Cohen, 'Holocaust History Misappropriated', *MIDSTREAM: A Monthly Jewish Review*, 39:8 (November 1992) http://teletubbie.het.net.je/~sjaak/domovina/domovina/archive/1992/english/holocaust.html (accessed 10 June 2000).

56 Ridley, *Tito*, p. 165.

57 Tanner, *Croatia*, pp. 155–6.

58 *Ibid.* p. 156.

59 Brian Hall, *The Impossible Country: A Journey Through the Last Days of Yugoslavia* (Boston: David Godine Publishers, 1994) p. 43.

60 Ridley, *Tito*, pp. 277–8.

61 Hall, *The Impossible Country*, p. 43.

62 Darko Zubrinić, 'Cardinal Alojzije Stepinac and Saving the Jews in Croatia During the WW 2' (Zagreb: Croatian Information Center, 1996) www.hr/darko/etf/jews.html (accessed 18 June 1998).

63 *Ibid.* pp. 4–5.

64 Tudjman, *Horrors of War*, pp. 292–4.

65 Quoted in: Darko Duretak, and Mladenka Saric, 'HDZ Will Regain Support of Voters

with Clear Policies, not Cheap Tricks: Dr. Franjo Tudman's Speech: We Must not Allow Sheep and Geese to Lead Us into Fog!', *Vecernji List* (8 December 1998) http://www.cdsp.neu.edu/info/students/marko/vecernji/vecernji12.html (accessed 18 June 1998).

66 The issue is well discussed in Tanner, *Croatia*, pp. 179–81.

67 Josip Pečarić, 'Serbian Myth about Jasenovac: Author's Summary of his Book *Srpski mit o Jasenovcu* (Zagreb: Dom i svijet, 1998)' www.hr/darko/etf/pec.html (accessed 18 June 1998) p. 7.

68 Jezić, 'Problems of Understanding XXth Century History of Croatia'.

69 Ljubica Stefan, *From Fairy Tale to Holocaust: Serbia: Quisling Collaboration with the Occupier During the Period of the Third Reich with Reference to Genocide Against the Jewish People* (Zagreb: Hrvatska Matica Iseljenika, 1993) p. 23.

70 *Ibid.* p. 15.

71 *Ibid.* p. 21.

72 *Ibid.* pp. 12–13.

73 Cohen, *Serbia's Secret War*, pp. 130–2.

74 *Ibid.* p. 64.

75 Browning, *Fateful Months*, p. 46. Here, Browning quotes a speech by the German commander General Fritz Boehme, who describes the German mission in Serbia as one of mercilessly avenging German deaths in the First World War.

76 *Ibid.* p. 45. The Serbs later became more efficient and began to serve their authorities better.

77 Smilja Avramov, *Genocide Against the Serbs* (Belgrade: Museum of Modern Art, 1992) p. 32.

78 *Ibid.* p. 32.

79 Dobrica Ćosić, *L'éffondrement de la Yougoslavie: positions d'un résistant* (Paris: Age d'Homme, 1994) p. 24. (Italics mine.)

80 Quoted in Cohen, *Serbia's Secret War*, pp. 117–18.

81 *Ibid.* p. 118.

82 Milan Bulajić, *The Role of the Vatican in the Break-up of Yugoslavia* (Belgrade: Serbian Ministry of Information, 1993) p. 23.

83 *Ibid.* p. 84.

84 *Ibid.* p. 67.

85 *Ibid.* pp. 130–1.

86 *Ibid.* pp. 133–4.

87 *Ibid.* pp. 136–7.

88 Dušan T. Bataković, 'Frustrated Nationalism in Yugoslavia: From Liberal to Communist Solution', *Serbian Studies*, 11:2 (1997) www.bglink.com/personal/batakovic/boston.html (accessed 18 June 1998).

89 *Ibid.*

90 Jovan Ilić, 'The Serbs in the Former SR of Croatia', in Dušanka Hadži-Jovančić (ed.), *The Serbian Question in the Balkans: Geographical and Historical Aspects* (Belgrade: University of Belgrade Faculty of Geography, 1995) p. 330.

91 See Avramov, *Genocide Against the Serbs*, p. 197. Petar Makarov also writes of Stepinac, that he 'approved and frequently inspired all the Ustašas' deeds' (p. 1). Makarov draws direct links between Starčević's writings and the NDH persecution of Serbs, 'Starčević's statements that the Serbs were a race of slaves and that, for this reason, they should be axed was put into practice in the Independent State of Croatia from 1941 to 1945.' See Petar Makarov, 'The Embodied Devils: Who Was Who in NDH?', http://cypress.mcsr.olemiss.edu/~eesrdan/ndh/ndh-kojeko.html (accessed 18 June

1998). Makarov equally writes of how Stepinac was made Pavelić's head military chaplain: 'His Grace Stepinac not only showed his warlike attitude when he was with the military Ustaši in the barracks, but also when he was with the intellectuals taking charge of the mobilization of the Croats for the cause of the Fascist Croatian satellite state, where he helped to encourage and boost their drooping morale' (p. 4). He also writes of how nearly half the 22 death camps in the NDH were run by Catholic clergy: Petar Makarov, 'Croatian Cardinal Stepinac Was Pavelić's Head Military Chaplain', http://cypress.mcsr.olemiss.edu/~eesrdan/ndh/ndh-kojeko.html (accessed 18 June 1998). Others would write of the 'aggressive, intolerant, non-democratic and non-Christian' actions of the Catholic Church, as well as the 'total demonization of our people', which led to 'pogroms over the Serbs in the late nineteenth and early twentieth centuries, [culminating] in the brutal Ustaši raids during World War II . . .'. See Ilić, 'The Serbs in the Former SR of Croatia', p. 328.

92 Serbian National Defense Council of America, *Genocide in Croatia 1941–1945* (Chicago, IL: 1993) pp. 28–30. For another account of the Serbian perspective on the Second World War, see Radislav Petrović, *The Extermination of Serbs on the Territory of the Independent State of Croatia* (Belgrade: Serbian Ministry of Information, 1991).

93 Milan Bulajić, Antun Miletić and Dragoje Lukić, *Never Again: Ustashi Genocide in the Independent State of Croatia (NDH) From 1941–1945* (Belgrade: BIGZ, 1991) p. 2.

94 *Ibid.* p. 55.

95 *Ibid.* p. 63.

96 *Ibid.* p. 1; see also Petrović, *The Extermination of Serbs on the Territory of the Independent State of Croatia*, p. 43; Jean François Furnémont in his *Le Vatican et l'ex Yougoslavie* (Paris: L'Harmattan, 1996) also throws this myth in at the beginning for no apparent reason.

97 Mark Aarons and John Loftus, *Ratlines: How the Vatican's Nazi Networks Betrayed Western Intelligence to the Soviets* (London: Heinemann, 1991) pp. 24; 26–8; 37. For a discussion of Draganović and his activities, largely at the behest of the American CIC, see Ladislas de Hoyos, *Klaus Barbie: The Untold Story* (London: W. H. Allen, 1985) pp. 166–7.

98 *Ibid.* pp. 74–6.

99 Velimir Ivetić, 'The Serbs in The Anti-fascist Struggle in The Territory of The Independent State of Croatia' (Belgrade: Serbian Ministry of Information) http://cypress.mcsr.olemiss.edu/~eesrdan/ndh/ndh-sastav_partizana_u_ndh.html (accessed 18 June 1998).

100 *Ibid.*

101 Vera Vratusa-Zunjić, 'The Intrinsic Connection Between Endogenous and Exogenous Factors of Social (Dis)integration: A Sketch of the Yugoslav Case', *Dialogue*, 22–23 (June–September 1997) www.bglink.com/business/dialogue/vratusa.html (accessed 18 June 1998).

102 Radoje Kontić, 'Great Jubilee of World and Our Own History: Victory Over Fascism the Most Important Event of the XX Century', *Review of International Affairs*, 46 (15 May 1995) pp. 1–3.

103 Serbian Ministry of Information, 'Facts About The Republic of Serbia' (Helsinki: Embassy of the Federal Republic of Yugoslavia, February 1996) p. 26.

104 Mirko Mirković, 'Fourth Phase: 1945–1990', in Božidar Zečević (ed.), *The Uprooting: A Dossier of the Croatian Genocide Policy Against the Serbs* (Belgrade: Velauto International, 1992) p. 109.

105 Zeljko Jack Lupić, 'History of Croatia: Povijest Hrv atske (200 B.C. – 1998 A.D.)' (Zagreb: Croatian Information Center, 21 February 1999) http://www.dalmatia.net/croatia/history/index.htm (accessed 18 June 1998).

106 Jezić, 'Problems of Understanding XXth Century History of Croatia'.
107 Bože Ćović, *Roots of Serbian Aggression: Debates, Documents, Cartographic Reviews* (Zagreb: Centar za Strane Jezike/AGM, 1993) p. 34.
108 Marinko Bobanović, 'Interview with Philip J. Cohen: The International Community is Meddling in Croatia's Internal Affairs', *Vjesnik* (27 April 1998) www.cdsp.neu.edu/info/students/marko/vjesnik/vjesnik27.html (accessed 18 June 1999).
109 Hall, *The Impossible Country*, p. 109.

6

Comparing genocides: 'numbers games' and 'holocausts' at Jasenovac and Bleiburg

What will our children say about us when they read about the Balkan Holocaust in their history books? (Stjepan Meštrović *et al.*, *The Road from Paradise*)

Chapter 5 outlined some of the principal myths of victimisation and persecution stemming from the wartime activities of the Serbs and Croats. By invoking images of historic genocide and persecution, both sides portrayed their actions in the 1990s as defensive only – a reaction to either 'Serbophobia' or 'Greater Serbia'. This chapter reviews two of the most important persecution myths emerging from the Second World War. Revising the history of the Ustaša-run death-camp at Jasenovac was a useful means of casting Serbs as the victims of a 'Holocaust' by Croats. On the Croatian side, the massacre at Bleiburg (Austria) by Communist forces (or Serb-led Communists, as the case might be) in 1945 was also likened to the Holocaust. In both cases, the other side was accused of committing genocide, using either the mask of Nazi or Communist domination to justify their atrocities.

Of central importance was a 'game of numbers', or Ronnie Landau's 'grotesque competition in suffering'.[1] Like the works of Stannard, Dadrian, Hancock, and others reviewed in the comparative genocide debate, Serbs and Croats used the Jews as the litmus test for historical suffering, while also trading genocide stories with each other. By inflating their own numbers of dead, and reducing the numbers of enemy dead, they conducted their own comparative genocide debate within Yugoslavia. Both Jasenovac and Bleiburg became emblematic of national suffering and Fall during the Second World War. Following a victim-centred strategy, both sides advanced negative myths of identification, arguing that they alone had suffered a 'Holocaust' during the war, which was repeating itself in the 1990s.

160

The 'numbers game' at Jasenovac

During the Communist era and afterwards, the Ustaša death-camp at Jasenovac became the most potent twentieth-century symbol of the victimisation of Serbs. It figured as the scene of an attempt at their genocide – some would even refer to it as a Serbian Holocaust. Certainly this former brick-factory was the locus of many horrible massacres, and many thousands lost their lives at the hands of the Ustaša. The controversial issue was not the existence of the camp, but rather, how many Serbs actually died there.

The major problem of Jasenovac history lies in fixing the number of dead. This continues to be politically charged. Claiming that 50,000 died puts one on the Croatian side, while claiming a larger number (one million or more) is more in line with Serbian thinking. Sadly, there is little consensus on the total number of dead, or, indeed, what percentage of the victims were Serbs. Historians, using a variety of statistics, often arrived at startling different figures: Denitch less than 100,000; Vulliamy around 600,000; Štitkovac 'hundreds of thousands'; Dragnich: total in NDH 500,000–700,000; Hall 750,000; Glenny 200,000; Ridley 330,000; and the United States Holocaust Memorial Museum (300,000–400,000).[2] This extreme range of estimates may have resulted from a confusion between the number of dead at Jasenovac and the total number of Serbs killed in Yugoslavia as a whole. Dragnich, Hall, and Vulliamy's numbers, for example, could either be interpretations of Serbian-based totals for Jasenovac, or Croatian-based totals for all Serbs killed in the NDH.

Serbian and Croatian writers would later provoke much of this confusion. However, the original statistics were themselves confusing, as they stemmed from the Yugoslav Communists' own manipulation of war-casualty figures. The figure of 1,706,000 was presented at the International Reparations Commission in 1946 without any documentation to prove its veracity. In 1947, a second-year mathematics student named Vledeta Vučković was ordered to 'compute "a significant number" of war victims', and duly arrived at a figure of 1.7 million victims. This included not only war-related deaths, but also projected future demographic losses as a result of the war – including unborn children.[3] The motives behind such a strategy were clear – the Yugoslav Communists wanted to gain the maximum possible value of war reparations from Germany after their long and bloody conflict. While this financial motive was significant, a symbolic motive was also important. Communist Yugoslavia would rely on a series of myths of 'anti-Fascist liberation' to buttress its legitimacy. A high number of deaths allowed the Partisans to cast themselves as martyrs to Fascism, while creating an axiomatic link between nationalism and genocide. Nationalism would be an evil associated with racism, extermination, and death-camps, while the future would lie in a multiethnic, peaceful Communist society.

Early attempts to assess the number of dead impartially after the first postwar census in 1951 yielded new statistical results. The Americans Paul Myers and Arthur Campbell fixed the total numbers of dead in Yugoslavia (for all nations) at 1.067 million people, a number significantly lower than the official estimate.[4] Later analyses in the 1980s by the Montenegrin Serb Bogoljub Kočović, and the Croat Vladimir Žerjavić arrived at similar totals – 1.014 million and 1.027 million respectively. Within this number, Kočović posited a Serbian total of 487,000 deaths, while Žerjavić published a slightly higher number (530,000).[5] With regard to the numbers of Serbs killed at Jasenovac, both Kočović and Žerjavić arrived at a figure of 83,000 deaths – each using different statistical methods.

While Žerjavić seems to have been drawn into the Croatian propaganda war against the Serbs, his numbers appeared to be reasonably impartial, with incredibly detailed descriptions of the number of 'skeletons per square meter' calculated over the total surface area of mass graves.[6] The figure of 83,000 can, of course, never be proved conclusively, and a belief in any estimate requires a great deal of trust in the researcher, and in his or her motives. This explains the huge variance in estimates between impartial historians, who simply do not know whom to believe, and have no means of verifying any conclusions. As the wars in Croatia, and then in Bosnia-Hercegovina, escalated more and more statistical surveys from each side made the Jasenovac total even more difficult to determine.

Jasenovac and the Serbian 'holocaust'

For many Serbs, maintaining a high number of Jasenovac deaths was absolutely central to their national self-identity. A high number proved that they had suffered from a Croat-inspired genocide during the Second World War. Jasenovac attested to the genocidal possibilities of the Croatian nation, proving their willingness to annihilate the Serbs in the past and in the present. A high number also made the Serbs one of the primary victims of the Second World War, rather than an aggressor. The Serbian Unity Congress, for example, claimed Jasenovac as 'the third largest concentration camp of the WW II occupied Europe', a common theme in Serbian writing, which advanced a clear case for a Serbian 'holocaust'.[7] The Serbian Ministry of Information also saw Jasenovac as a Serbian 'holocaust' – a holocaust that acted as a precursor to Croatian and Bosnian Moslem aggression fifty years later.[8]

Predictably, the Serbian Orthodox Church also took a leading role in propagating the Jasenovac myth, denouncing the Croats for their part in the genocide of the Serbs. As Patriarch Paul asserted at the beginning of the war:

> Nothing can be worse than Jasenovac, where during four years of war, 700,000 people were killed ... Jasenovac is the scene of the most important horrors committed against the Serbs, the place of ... their annihilation, their extermination, their execution, their torture, where they suffered under a blood lust, the like of which could not be paralleled by the antichrist himself ... This is the new crucifixion of Christ. This is the sin of sins.[9]

Such imagery of a violent, annihilatory Croatian other proved central in motivating the Serbs to 'defend' the Serbian minorities who were seen to be victims of a renewed Croatian aggression in 1991. It was not only Jasenovac, but also the covering up of the genocide after 1945 that captured the imagination of Serbian writers. Slobodan Kljakić's *Conspiracy of Silence*, for example, traced a Communist conspiracy to lower the number of Serbian dead in the Second World War, a project propelled by the Vatican and the Croats. He blamed Croatian authorities for bulldozing Jasenovac to the ground in the 1950s, supposedly 'on orders from authorities in Zagreb'.[10] Croatian Communist leaders, such as Stevo Krajačić and Andrija Hebrang, received the lion's share of the blame for trying to resurrect Croatian nationalism by suppressing negative aspects of Croatian history.[11]

As well as being an outspoken critic of Stepinac, Milan Bulajić became famous during the 1990s for his Goldhagen-esque theorising on the Jasenovac camps. He blamed everyone in Croatia, from the 'paramilitary formations of the Croat Peasant Party' – the so-called 'Guardians' – to the Catholic Church, which supposedly wanted to establish a Catholic state in the Balkans. For Bulajić, the motivations of the Croats and the Vatican never changed. As in the nineteenth century, these two groups still wanted to destroy the Orthodox Church, in order to expand Roman Catholicism in the Balkans.[12]

On the basis of various reports Bulajić drew up his own estimates of Serbian war-related deaths: 1,467,000 (through direct war losses), and a further 390,000–440,000 deaths (300,000–350,000 in refugee camps; 50,000 quislings; 40,000 Jews). In total, he charted the deaths of 1,850,000 Serbs, a figure surpassing even the Communist estimate, which had referred to all national groups, not just the Serbs.[13] He also famously accused the Croats of shelling the Jasenovac memorial, 'the largest Serbian underground town' – in an effort to erase the legacy of the past. That the shelling was later proven by the Croats to be false was not discussed.[14] Bulajić also attacked Franjo Tudjman's very low estimate of the numbers of dead, as expressed in *Horrors of War*:

> All that this book says leaves no room for surprise because it is a deplorable confirmation that the Ustasha clerico-nationalism has not been fully uprooted and the result of the failure to de-nazify the Independent State of Croatia which committed the crime of genocide against the Orthodox Serbs, Jews and Gypsies, and the pro-Yugoslav Croats.[15]

163

Bulajić was one of Tudjman's greatest critics in the Jasenovac debate.[16] He was quick to condemn 'Tudjmanism' as 'a mixture of radical Croatian chauvinism and clericalism, which is a certain form of clerical Nazism'.[17] His opinion of Tudjman himself was no less virulent. Bulajić often focused on the specifically 'Catholic' nature of Jasenovac, questioning why so many Church officials seemed to be in charge. The camp's commandant, 'Friar Satan', was attacked along with other priests, such as Friar Zvoniko Brekalo, who was simultaneously attached to the Jasenovac camp while being affiliated to the Vatican representative in Croatia. His supposed penchant for torturing and liquidating prisoners while engaging in 'orgies and immoral life' with his fellow priests was graphically described, and likewise the sadism, mass murder, and 'whoring' of Friars Anzelmo Čulina, and Zvonko Lipovac.[18] Bulajić's view that Jasenovac was a specifically 'Catholic' death camp articulated the strong links between Catholicism and genocide. By extension, Jasenovac was not simply the product of Croatian nationalism, or a generalised hatred of Serbs: it was a religiously inspired exercise.

While the issue of genocidal priests was not a common theme in Serbian writing, the numbers of Serbs killed at Jasenovac was a frequent subject of scholarly debate. As with more impartial accounts, no Serbian writer seemed exactly sure how many people died at Jasenovac or in Yugoslavia during the War. Jovan Ilić's total was 700,000, with Serbs 'the most numerous victims by far'.[19] Svetozar Đurđević's number was the same, as were the totals of Patriarch Paul and Dušan Bataković.[20] Božidar Zečević put the numbers killed at over 1,000,000.[21] Radoje Kontić added: 'We are proud to note that with 1,706,000 killed citizens, Yugoslavia ranks third by the number of victims in the Second World War.'[22] Paul Pavlovich also endorsed 1.7 million, describing how 'mostly Serb lives' were brutally ended, 'and by the Croat hand for the most part'. [23] Petar Damjanov also put the number at 1,700,000 victims, claiming that every ninth Yugoslav was killed.[24] Vojislav Stojanović, president of the Serbian Association of University Teachers and Scientists, placed the number of Serbs killed during their 'genocide' at over 2,000,000, which he posited was, 'in terms of suffering', no less important than the fate of Jews in occupied Europe.[25] Similarly, Serbian General Velimir Terzić arrived at a total of 'over one million', while Vuk Drasković advanced a figure of 1,500,000 Serbs for the whole of Croatia during the war.[26] While these Serbian numbers differed by more than one million people, the totals were certainly much higher than those advanced by impartial observers.

Revisionist novels and scholarly works were also designed to maintain or increase the Communist estimate of Serbian deaths. Some of these include Strahinja Kurdulija's *Serbs on Their Own Land* (1993)[27] and Lazo Kostich's *The Holocaust in the Independent State of Croatia* (1981), reprinted by the Serbian government.[28] Such books, as well as shorter surveys by Serbian academics, perpetuated the story of a high number of deaths, continuing the theme that Serbs were victims of are of the worst genocides in the Second World War, with only the Jews and the Russians ahead of them. These high numbers were advanced to prove Ustaša evil during the war. They were also designed to reduce the level of Serbian guilt and complicity. Dušan Bataković gave perhaps the most honest reason why promoting a figure of 700,000 was central to the Serbian cause, writing:

> [T]he number of Serbian victims has, over numerous decades become the object of political manipulation, because in reducing the dimensions of the Serbian Holocaust, it will either be discounted completed or minimised and placed in the ranks of vengeance done to Moslems in Oriental Bosnia and the mass shooting of those Ustasha who were captured at the end of the war.[29]

Bataković was quite right. If Serbs could not maintain the high number of deaths, then they too could be accused of being genocidal killers. His oblique references to the ethnic cleansing of Moslems by the Četniks and the massacre of Ustaša at Bleiburg demonstrated an awareness that each group had a symbolic 'holocaust' of its own. It was therefore the responsibility of the Serbian historian to ensure that his own nation's genocide received top billing. Jovan Ilić, for similar reasons, described the Serbs' 'additional right to self-determination and uniting' because of their exposure to 'genocidal extermination many times'.[30] For both Bataković and Ilić, it was crucial that Serbian historians did their utmost to advance Serbian claims, since historians on the other side would be doing precisely the same thing for their own claims.

Because so much of the conflict was rooted in perceptions of past victimisations and the need for 'self-defence', such writing proved essential in maintaining a high level of morale within Serbia. As the hardest-hit victims of the Second World War, they had an obligation to 'defend' their brothers in the Krajina, in Eastern Slavonia, and in Bosnia-Hercegovina. The myth of Jasenovac was similar to Schöpflin's 'myths of redemption and suffering', where Serbs had a moral right to create an expanded Serbian state after 1990, in order to prevent another genocide from occurring. [31] It was also similar to Kečmanović's myth of the 'universal culprit'.[32] The Croats, and their cynical master, the Vatican, had been continuously trying to push the Serbs out of the Balkans. Jasenovac would be yet another example of this phenomenon.

Jasenovac, the Croatians, and the 'black legend'

Long preoccupied with the high official numbers of Serbian dead in the SFRY, Croatian nationalists had been trying for decades to reduce the significance of Jasenovac. As was pointed out in Chapter 1, Tudjman had been writing on the issue since the mid-1960s, and in his efforts to combat the official statistics with statistics of his own he was consistently denounced and punished for his efforts.[33] A watershed therefore occurred in 1990, when at last, with the creation of an independent Croatian state, the government was now able publicly to open the debate, to ask that long awaited question: 'How many Serbs actually died at Jasenovac?' While few impartial historians would deny that the Communist figures were much too high (and likewise those for the Serbs), Croatian estimates were almost always extremely low.

For the Croatian side, it was vital to downplay the importance of Jasenovac, to prove that the death-camp was insignificant by the standards of the Second World War. This performed several important functions. The first was to minimise the historic guilt of Croatia in the war, by denouncing Serbian accusations as part of an insidious propaganda campaign. This was meant to restore the prestige of the Croatian wartime record, while exonerating the NDH. Secondly, low numbers allowed Croatian writers to counter their Serbian 'victims' with their own 'Holocaust' at Bleiburg, thus balancing or neutralising atrocities in the comparative genocide debate. Thirdly, reducing the numbers of Jasenovac dead made liars and schemers of the Serbs. They were merely trying to cover up their own sinister wartime record by accusing innocents of exaggerated crimes.

Tudjman played a starring role in this debate. He had aroused much controversy over his Second World War revisionist writings and his founding of 'Tudjmanism' as a means of re-examining and interpreting Croatian history. One of his primary aims was to resurrect Croatian national pride, after it had suffered from what he termed the 'black legend of the historical guilt of the entire Croatian nation'.[34] This guilt was clearly attributed to the statistically high number of Jasenovac deaths, which Tudjman interpreted as a Serbian plot to suppress Croatian nationalism. It is worth quoting his explanation in full:

> There is also the systematic creation of the black legend of historical guilt of the entire Croatian nation. For if the dimensions of the Ustasha crime are stretched to hundreds of thousands and even millions of victims, and if, by contrast, there are no commensurate crimes on the opposite side, then the responsibility for the crimes does not fall upon a mere handful of Pavelic's fanatical followers, blinded by vengeful impulses, but on the entire Croatian nation. From this point, it follows logically that . . . Croatianness can be equated with Ustashism which is branded as worse than Fascism or Nazism.[35]

The purpose of this 'black legend' was to maintain Serbian domination in Yugoslavia. For Tudjman, there was a direct correlation between the existence of the 'Jasenovac distortion' and Serbian control. This 'distortion', he claimed, kept 'Croatianness in shackles', while 'instigat[ing] Serbdom against Croatianness'.[36] This contributed to his larger thesis – that the Serbs had been oppressing and persecuting the Croats since 1945. They had manipulated a false sense of Croatian guilt to humble and humiliate them. This was to be a time of 'watershed', as described by Kečmanović: a time had at last arrived when Croatia could break free of its shackles – the TRUTH could now be revealed.

Tudjman's theories were controversial. Using various statistics, he arrived at a total of 50,000 killed overall, not just Serbs, and not just at Jasenovac – but for all of the Ustaša camps in Croatia.[37] He estimated that between 30,000 and 40,000 inmates had died at Jasenovac, and he listed them as 'Gypsies, Jews and Serbs, and even Croatians' – reversing the conventional order of deaths to imply that more Gypsies and Jews were killed than Serbs.[38] Satiated with his own statistics, Tudjman concluded: 'the fabled numbers of hundreds of thousands of slayings at Jasenovac are utter nonsense'.[39] While Bulajić argued that the Jasenovac numbers were too low, and blamed the Vatican, Tudjman lashed out at the Serbian Orthodox Church, accusing them of inflating the numbers in order to divide Serbs and Croats, while rehabilitating the Nedić regime.[40]

While a statistical analysis of Jasenovac deaths was important, 'Tudjmanism' also consisted of more general historical revisionism. Though the account in which they were embessed was somewhat conspiratorial and melodramatic, Tudjman's Jasenovac numbers were not unduly controversial when compared to other revisionist numbers. More problematic was his application of 'Tudjmanism' to other periods of history, as part of a larger project to relativise the Ustaša genocide. A section of his book was devoted to violence, traced back for as long as humanity 'has been aware of its own existence'. Genocide also had an ancient pedigree, having existed 'since the dawn of our primitive prehistory'.[41] History according to Tudjman was a never-ending series of violent conflicts and wars, beginning with Old Testament history, when 'violence, hatred, crime, and revenge are inseparable components in the life of man'.[42]

Almost unbelievably for a head of state, Tudjman launched a series of poorly aimed attacks on the Jews. He argued that the Jews had invented ethnic cleansing, as part of their Covenant with God. 'Israel', he claimed, 'in both aggressive and defensive wars, acted as the executor of the will of God in history, which induced religious fervour and military heroism, but also mercilessness.'[43] The Hebrew God was one who 'demands utter annihilation; that is, complete destruction of the enemy, both of living beings and material goods.'[44] While there may well have been a certain 'mercilessness' in early Hebrew battles, Tudjman covered much more controversial ground when he applied these historical 'lessons' to his understanding of the twentieth century. Of the Holocaust, he famously wrote: 'The estimated loss of up to 6 million dead is founded too much on emotional, biased testimony and on exaggerated data in the post-war reckonings of war crimes and squaring of accounts with the defeated.'[45] He also accused the Jews of committing genocide against the Palestinians in 1947, remarking: 'After everything that it had suffered in history, particularly because of the monstrous suffering in the Second World War, the Jewish people would in a very short time initiate such a brutal and genocidal policy towards the Palestinians people that it has rightly been named as "Judeo-Nazism".'[46]

The 1996 edition of *Horrors of War* was a substantially revised edition from Tudjman's original *Wilderness of Historical Reality*, published in 1987. While his new edition had undergone much editing to make it palatable to a Western market, it nevertheless retained many of its more controversial elements. If these revisionist arguments were not enough to raise questions about Tudjman's motivations, he also sought to reduce the culpability of Ustaša death-camp administrators. He claimed that the inmates' administration at Jasenovac was entirely composed of Jewish *capos*, who were blamed for stealing gold and other valuables from the Gypsies. Theft, he claimed, and not racism, was the reason why the Jews were executed by the Ustaša.[47] What emerged from Tudjman's extreme moral relativism was the intrinsic unimportance of Jasenovac and indeed the Holocaust in world history.

While almost universally condemned for his revisionism, Tudjman pressed ahead with his plans to rehabilitate Croatian history. Because both the Holocaust and Jasenovac were reduced in importance and significance, Tudjman advocated converting Jasenovac into a memorial park, to commemorate 'All Croatian war victims'.[48] This plan was unveiled during his 'State of the Croatian State and Nation Address' in 1995. Tudjman planned to have both the 'victims of Communism' and the 'victims of fascism' buried at Jasenovac side by side. There were even plans to reinter Ante Pavelić at Jasenovac, before Tudjman met with a storm of criticism. He later credited his idea to Spain's former fascist leader General Franco, and his plan for a chapel in Toledo to commemorate both sides who had died in the Spanish Civil War. Worryingly, Tudjman stated glowingly on one occasion: 'In the figure of Franco, Spain found someone who had the courage and wisdom to say that Spanish Communists and Spanish Falangists equally fought for Spain, but under separate flags. The same was happening in Croatia.'[49] Tudjman failed to mention, however, that such magnanimous behaviour only developed after Franco's more partisan view of history had been assured. Franco's Spain proliferated with massive public war memorials which were distinctly anti-Communist. That he should have developed some 'courage and wisdom' later in life provided little solace for those who had suffered at his hands during the 1930s and after.

Tudjman's writings might have been influenced by the *Historikerstreit*, and the debate over the normalisation of German history. Nevertheless, Ernst

Nolte and his colleagues did not minimise Nazi crimes, nor did they endeavour to rehabilitate Adolf Hitler. Tudjman's agenda was qualitatively different. But while his views on Jasenovac were highly publicised, his was neither the first nor the last word on the subject. The literature is extensive, and was devised in part to counter the huge estimates advanced by Belgrade academics and the Orthodox Church. Croatian writers blamed the Serbian Orthodox Church and Tito's government for inflating the number of war dead, the latter in order to promote Serbian interests, and the former in order to subdue the Croats while gaining larger war reparations from Germany.

For some Croatian historians, Žerjavić's statistics formed the basis of analysis, while Kočović's were ignored. Josip Pečarić, for example, supported Žerjavić's arguments, but blamed the Serbs in particular for manipulating the figures. The Orthodox Church and the Serbian intelligentsia, he argued, were guilty of raising the number of dead, in order to obscure Serbian collaboration with the Germans, since they 'believed that it was possible to achieve Great Serbian ambitions within Hitler's system'.[50] He also posited that such high numbers were designed to incite the Serbs of Croatia to revolt against the government.

Other high profile writers proposed other statistics in their stead, following Tudjman's lead. Ante Beljo, in *Genocide in Yugoslavia* (1985), contributed to the revisionist movement, claiming: 'The very fact that the killings which are attributed to the Croats range from one hundred thousand to one million seven hundred thousand are a fabrication.'[51] He also cited Tudjman's belief that the Ustaša state was created primarily as an attempt to quell the 'hegemonic tyranny over the Croatian people in Yugoslavia under the monarchy'.[52] Echoing Tudjman's earlier numbers, Beljo appears to support a total of 50,000 people killed at Jasenovac, quoting Ivan Supek to the effect that the victims were 'leftist Croats, followed by some Serbs, Gypsies and Jews, but mainly Communists'.[53] The figure of 50,000 was also echoed by Grmek, Gjidara, and Simac, in their anti-Serbian anthology. Their numbers included 18,000 Jews, as well as some Gypsies and Croatians, leaving little space for Serbian deaths.[54] Other writers put the total number of dead from concentration camps at 215,000, with only 79,000 Serbian casualties for all camps.[55] Like Tudjman, Croatian academics substantially reduced the number of Serbian deaths, arguing that the Serbs had falsified their own victimisation in order to humble and humiliate Croatia.

Both sides, it appears, manipulated the number of Jasenovac deaths to achieve specific nationalist goals. For the Croats, a low number exonerated the nation from its 'black legend', proving that the Croats were persecuted and mistreated during the Titoist period by the Serbs, who manipulated Jasenovac to portray themselves falsely as martyrs. By reducing the number of dead, Croatian writers debunked the myth of a genocidal Croatian nation.[56] From the obverse perspective, a continued high number of deaths strengthened Serbian claims that they were the victims of a 'holocaust' during the Second World War. While one will never know the true number of deaths at Jasenovac, the politics and manipulations involved in such a cynical 'numbers game' give valuable insight once again into the narcissism of minor differences that so characterised Serbian and Croatian academe. While relatively impartial surveys did exist, both sides chose to ignore these, instead arguing that their unrealistic high or low numbers were accurate. In such a case, the performative aspect of these revisions was clear – each side tried to play the victim, to cast themselves as martyrs, having suffered not only from genocide, but also a concerted effort by the enemy to cover up the TRUTH.

Bleiburg: the Croatian 'holocaust'

For Croats, the massacre of Croatian, Slovenian and Serbian collaborators by Tito's Partisans was rich in imagery. It symbolised Croatian repression in the Second World War, and later during the Communist period. That Croats were forbidden to discuss it, let alone debate the numbers killed during Tito's lifetime, made it a sort of 'underground' secret, which had to be discussed carefully with trusted friends. The facts of the story can be substantiated, although the number of deaths is, again, difficult to establish with certainty. Towards the end of the Second World War, large numbers of Croatian Ustaša officials and soldiers, together with Croatian Domobrani, Slovenian White Guards, and Serbian Zbor, along with their families, retreated north, making their way to the Austrian border, where they hoped to escape Partisan reprisals. On 16 May, they encountered approximately 150 British troops. On condition that they be interned outside Yugoslavia, a large number of soldiers, administrators, and civilians surrendered to the British. Bluffed by the British commander, they were packed into trains and rolled back into Yugoslavia, where they were massacred by Partisan forces.[57] Bleiburg became the scene of British treachery, and the symbol for the mass murder of wartime collaborators (namely: Croats) by the Partisans.

As with Jasenovac, establishing the numbers of dead was central to the debate over whether or not Bleiburg constituted a Croatian 'Holocaust'. By contrast with Jasenovac, however, most impartial historians converged on much lower numbers of dead, suggesting that Bleiburg was by no means as significant as the largest death-camp in Yugoslavia. For example, Judah put the numbers killed at between 20,000 and 40,000,[58] Anzulović at 50,000,[59] Jelavich at between 40,000 and 100,000, 'including civilians',[60] and Tanner, at somewhere between the 200,000 suggested by 'Croatian nationalists' and the 30,000 suggested by 'others'.[61]

Jasper Ridley attempts a more precise figure, although there is no way of knowing for sure. He described how 200,000 members of anti-Partisan forces, Slovenian White Guards, Croatian Ustašas and Domobrani, and Serbian Zbor, succeeded in reaching Austria after the war.[62] Of these, he noted that the Allies agreed to surrender 23,000 to the Partisans between 24 and 29 May – a mixture of Slovenians, Serbians, and Croatians. Reports from the time, according to Ridley, indicate that not all the 23,000 were killed. Supposedly, most of the young boys were saved, since Colonel Penezić, the chief of Tito's political police in Serbia, felt that the youth could still be 'cherished and re-educated to be good and useful Communists'.[63] Ridley gives a range of between 20,000 and 23,000 killed, a high number of deaths that would indicate a horrific massacre. This also squares well with the early references to the massacre in Milovan Djilas's *Wartime* (1977), wherein he confirmed that the British handed over the escaping collaborators to the Partisans, who then subsequently massacred them. Djilas confirmed the numbers killed, mentioning between 20,000 and 30,000 people: 'Chetniks, the Ustashi, [and] the Slovenian Home guards'. There is no denying the severity of the massacre either, which Djilas described as 'senseless acts of wrathful retribution', and 'sheer frenzy'.[64]

Obviously there was little mention of the massacre officially, and Djilas's dissident account was one of the few descriptions of it, although he failed to mention it by name. Of course, it is certainly possible that both Ridley and Djilas are mistaken in their lower totals, but the truth of the matter is that no one will ever know how many died at Bleiburg and other Communist-inspired post-war massacres. Information about Bleiburg was obviously suppressed during the lifetime of the SFRY, in keeping with much of Titoist policy surrounding the Partisans' actions during wartime. The 'underground' nature of this knowledge arguably gave it a certain cachet during the Communist era. Everybody knew about it – but no one could discuss it publicly. Nevertheless, irrespective of its suppression, Bleiburg has fared as well as the history of any other Second World War massacre. The main problem for Croats, however, was not simply that Bleiburg had not been adequately discussed, but that, seen in relation to the horrors of Jasenovac, it was non-existent.

Inflating the numbers of dead at Bleiburg had several layers of significance. Firstly, it gave the Croats their own massacre at the hands of Serbs and/or Communists, which allowed them to counter the Serbs' Jasenovac genocide with one of their own. Secondly, it allowed Croats to distance themselves from the Serbs and the Communist regime that had carried out the massacres. They could portray Croatia as an unwilling participant in the SFRY, more a prisoner than a constituent nation. Thirdly, by suffering such a massacre, the Croats underwent their own 'way of the Cross', as it was frequently dubbed in Croatian writings. The sins of the Ustaša could be cleansed by their martyrdom at Bleiburg, vindicating both the Croatian nation and the NDH.

Croats and the numbers game

There is little convergence among Croatian writers on the actual numbers of dead. Some, like Vladimir Žerjavić, cited a low number of between 54,500–65,000 (45,000–55,000 Croatians and Moslems, 1,500 – 2,000 Serbian and Montenegrin Četniks, and about 8,000 Slovenian Belogardists), one that balanced out his low figure for Jasenovac.[65] Josip Šentija described one massacre of between 30,000 and 40,000 Croats, and then argued that 'several times that number' were killed at Bleiburg, 'and also along the roads in north-west Slovenia'.[66] Another article contended that 'more than 100,000 Croatian civilians and soldiers were executed'.[67] While high, these numbers suggest a conscientious effort to advance realistic numbers.

More radical writers, however, would follow the Serbian example with the Jasenovac statistics, and inflate the numbers of dead. C. Michael McAdams, for example, posited a range from 100,000 to 250,000.[68] Ivo Omerčanin arrived at a figure of '500,000 Catholic and Muslim Croats'.[69] Stjepan Hefer's numbers were roughly the same: 150,000 soldiers and 300,000 civilians.[70] Putting the total killed at 400,000, Mislav Jezić described how soldiers and civilians fled to Austria, 'out of fear of the greater-Serbian and communist terror'.[71] Ante Beljo's theories about what he terms the 'Croatian Holocaust' were equally contentious, in that he reproduced, and seemed to advance, the argument of the Diaspora journal *Nova Hrvatska* that those killed at Bleiburg were slaughtered at a rate of 15,000 per day, a figure that made Bleiburg 'worse than Auschwitz', where only 6,000 were supposedly killed each day.[72] He would also reproduce George Prpić's 1973 research, which described Bleiburg as 'the bloodiest orgy in Balkan history ... result[ing] in the death and exodus of over one million men, women, and children', although he had earlier referred to a more realistic figure of 'tens of thousands of Croatian lives', which he blamed the Communists for taking.[73] Much of his research and the lengthy reproductions of other research in his book stemmed from the belief that 'Throughout history there is probably no nation which has suffered as much, which has had as many victims and which was at the same time labelled criminal as the Croatian nation is.'[74]

The only high-ranking detractor of the Bleiburg myth was Franjo Tudjman, who placed the number of dead at 'some 35,000 to 40,000 people'. He even criticised Beljo's figures, as well as those of other noted revisionists.[75] Tudjman's motives behind this are unclear, particularly since a proportion of Beljo's work was based on Tudjman's earlier writings. Perhaps

Tudjman was trying to distance himself from the whole debate. He seemed anxious during the war to have the number of Jasenovac and Bleiburg deaths be the same – his figure of 50,000 was used for both. Similarly, the fact that he was a former Partisan general (and thus a long-term supporter of the regime) may also have contributed to his reluctance to inflate the numbers any further.

Motives and participants in Bleiburg

In general, the high numbers of dead and the rate of killings ensured that Bleiburg was seen as no ordinary massacre, but one that could be compared numerically with the Holocaust. This was of course only part of the story; equally important were the identities of the participants and their motivations. Some writers, like McAdams, seemed to accuse the British and Americans of initiating the massacres. He described a 'march of death' where Croatian soldiers and government officials were forced out of Zagreb at gunpoint by the Allied Expeditionary Forces. An exodus supposedly began in May 1945, with 200,000 civilians and 200,000 soldiers, all of whom were apparently led to Bleiburg by the Allies, and then handed over to the Communists for execution. As McAdams wrote: 'Some were shot at the border, while others joined the infamous death march which took them deeper into the new People's Republic for liquidation.'[76]

While the Allies were sometimes blamed, other revisionist historians manipulated the story of Bleiburg to transform it into a massacre of Croats by Serbs. One of Philip Cohen's more controversial arguments was that Serbian Communists, not just Communists in general, had carried out the Bleiburg massacres. Beginning with a dismissal of Serbian Partisans as opportunists, former collaborators and fascist killers, he went on to articulate his main argument:

> It was only after the withdrawal of the Germans and the overthrow of the Nedić regime by advancing Soviet forces and their Partisan allies in October, 1944, that the Serbs in Serbia began to join the Partisans in large numbers. These new Partisans included tens of thousands of former Nazi collaborators responding to Tito's promise of amnesty, as well as to the call of the Serbian king-in-exile – reluctantly and under British pressure – for Serbian Chetniks to join British forces.[77]

Here, the Croats were presented as indigenous resisters, while the Serbs joined merely to save themselves. Cohen used this idea of the opportunist Serbs to explain the Bleiburg massacre 'of repatriated Croats and Slovenes, and even a number of Chetniks'.[78] While Cohen noted Tito's strategy of 'instituting state terror to ensure the Communists' post-war monopoly of power', he also cited the more important reason why Bleiburg took place. This was to allow for 'a Serb-driven blood letting' – to help cement Serbia's loyalty to Tito's movement.[79] In Cohen's analysis, the massacres had little to do with Tito's exacting revenge, and much more to do with Serb-driven malice, which even membership in the Partisans could not erase.[80]

One can thus isolate several layers to the Bleiburg story. At one level, the massacre was likened to the Holocaust, in terms of the numbers of people killed, and the rate of killing. This allowed for a general myth of victimisation – that the Croats had suffered, like the Jews, because of Bleiburg. At another level, not only were the Partisans to blame, but rather, the *Serbian-led* Partisans, who were in fact genocidal Četniks, using Communism as a screen for Greater Serbian aggression. Thus the Croats, who suffered a holocaust at the hands of genocidal Serbs, were likened to the Jews. In this way, a conflict between fascist collaborators and vengeful Communists became a battle between victimised Croats and genocidal Serbs.

Cohen was clear that the Bleiburg massacre was Serbian-led. Because of Bleiburg, they succeeded in dominating the SFRY and controlling it until its collapse. Further, Cohen accused Tito of allowing high-ranking Serbian collaborators to continue to oppress Croats and Slovenes in the SFRY. It is worth quoting his conclusion in full:

> These events [the Bleiburg massacre] led to Serb numerical domination of Yugoslavia's Communist Party and provided the window of opportunity for a substantial core of Serbian Nazi collaborators to attain influential positions in the postwar Yugoslav government. Although some of the most prominent Serbian pro-Axis collaborators were condemned and punished after the war, Tito nevertheless allowed a significant degree of historical revisionism by Serbian apologists rather than risk offending this much needed constituency.[81]

Here too the Serbs were seen at the core of a Yugoslavia that figured merely as another instrument of Serbian domination. Needless to say, many of Cohen's conclusions were virtually impossible to prove. In the case of Bleiburg, he is unable to identify the actual soldiers who carried out the massacres, nor is he able to present any real proof that these Partisans were in fact Serbian.

Bleiburg as a Ustaša 'sacrifice'

Croatian arguments supported the belief that the Croats were victims of a Serb-inspired holocaust, one that Serbs used instrumentally to gain control of the second Yugoslavia. But Bleiburg also performed another important role – that of vindication. Terms such as 'holocaust', 'march of death', 'exodus' and 'genocide' were used with the specific intent of rehabilitating the Ustaša. Ustaša war criminals were 'magically' transformed into innocent victims of Serbian aggression. They were not killed as collaborators, but as Croatian patriots who wanted an independent homeland. This rehabilitation proved central to the Bleiburg project, particularly for those, like Beljo, who fundamentally believed that Croatians had never done anything in their history that they should be ashamed of, since: '[t]hroughout history we have never conquered, plundered or exploited other nations', a belief little different from Drasković's contention that 'Serbs cannot hate.'[82]

Academics, such as Josip Šentija, elaborated on this rehabilitation. Using such metaphors as 'march of death' and 'way of the cross', Šentija seems to suggest that the Croats redeemed themselves for the Ustaša period by dying in mass numbers at the hands of the Communists. They may have been misled, but their sacrifice somehow purified the entire Croatian nation of its sins.[83] Such imagery was indeed fascinating, as it reflected many of the themes raised in the Serbian myth of Kosovo, primarily the aestheticisation of the victim, and the ideal of being morally victorious in defeat. Rather than being massacred by the Partisans, these soldiers seemingly gave their lives in defence of Croatia. Bleiburg thus became a 'myth of election' in its own right, in that it transformed Nazi collaborators into patriots, making Croats victims in the Second World War, rather than aggressors.

The official perpetuation of this form of amnesia regarding Ustaša crimes took shape most recently on 15 May 1997, when the Croatian government organised a holy mass at Bleiburg, to commemorate the 52nd anniversary of the tragedy. The mass brought 1,000 pilgrims to Austria, at which time Dubravko Jelčić, the representative of the chair of the Croatian Assembly (Sabor), described Bleiburg as 'one of the greatest tragedies in [the] history of the Croatian people', marking, 'a new kind of slavery await[ing] Croatia' (clearly a reference to a 'Serb-dominated' Yugoslavia). Continuing the process of rehabilitating the Ustašas, he painted them as patriots rather than fascists: '[T]he issue is about Croats who fanatically believed in a Croatian state, not about an ideology – red or black – that was not even apparent.' This type of revisionism glossed over the very real atrocities committed by Croats during the war. It is also a way of discrediting Yugoslavia, for, as Jelčić was keen to add: 'All that is founded on evil collapses, and that is why Yugoslavia is forevermore our past and Croatia our awakened future .'[84]

The chair of the Croatian Assembly, Vlatko Pavletić, took Bleiburg a step further, and universalised the massacre, arguing that it had become nothing less than 'the generic term for the suffering of Croats'. Further, he maintained that the struggle against fascism and Nazism had been supported by the entire Croatian population – another instance of an extreme form of revisionism that ran counter to historical fact. Other controversial theories included the contention that 'Croats were the first antifascists in Europe and the world' and that 'the majority of NDH military units fought against fascism'. These statements were revisionist in the extreme.[85] By this time, a form of collective amnesia had taken hold of many HDZ officials. By acting out or performing their role as martyred victims, Croatian nationalist leaders convinced themselves and their fellow Croats that Croatia had nothing to be ashamed of. The slate had now been wiped clean.

Pavletić's attempt to universalise the lessons of Bleiburg is another fascinating aspect of this particular myth. As with the universalisation of the Holocaust, Bleiburg was supposedly sufficiently significant to become a symbol for Croatia as a whole. Bleiburg made victims of the Croatian fascists, while once again demonising the Serbs for their age-old plans to construct a 'Greater Serbia' in the Balkans. Whether they were Četniks or Communists, the lesson was clear – a Serb was always a Serb, and would continue to hate Croatians, no matter what ideology he or she followed. At the same time Bleiburg encapsulated the antagonism between the Croatian self and the Serbian-dominated Communist others in the SFRY. Because Bleiburg was covered up, and the Serbs supposedly dominated Yugoslavia, the Croatian 'holocaust' continued for another forty-five years after the Second World War. This made Croatian involvement in the SFRY seem unnatural, which again buttressed their decision to leave the Federation.

Ubiquitous throughout the conflict has been nationalist kitsch; Bleiburg has fared no differently. The New Zealand artist Suzanne Brooks-Pinčević recently produced a series of paintings on the 'Bleiburg Tragedy', which she dedicated to 'the Croatian cause'. The paintings and her subsequent book gave an overview of 'Croatia's violent rebirth'. Typically, the book covered the links between the Second World War 'genocide' against the Croats by the Serbs and Communists, and the 'complicity' of Britain in mass murder. It further promised to 'slash open the fabric of silence that has shrouded the truth of Croatia's past'. In the end the reader was confronted with 'a century of genocide' committed by the Serbs against the Croats.[86] While Croatian writers had been obsessed with Bleiburg for many decades, the innovation after 1990 was the targeting of Serbs as the prime culprit in the massacre. Krunoslav Draginović (one of the Croatian founders of the 'Ratlines') wrote an exposé of the massacre in 1955, citing a figure of between 100,000–140,000 soldiers and civilians killed. He even used Biblical imagery such as 'Calvary' and the 'way of the cross' to describe the forced marches and the positioning of mass graves.[87] The difference between old and new lay in Bleiburg's executioners. In Draginović's account, Tito and the Communists were clearly the instigators of the massacres. His own attempts to smuggle Nazi leaders like Klaus Barbie out of Europe certainly attested to his hatred of Communism. Nevertheless, leaving aside Draginović's political motives, the Serbs are not even mentioned. The same holds true for Beljo's *Genocide in Yugoslavia* (1985), which attempted to engage with the Communist regime and its atrocities. Beljo's sixth chapter entitled 'The Bleiburg Tragedy Isn't

Over', accuses the Yugoslav government, in particular the UBDa ('Uprava drzavne bezbednosti', in English 'The Department for State Security'), of a wide variety of atrocious crimes throughout the world against certain members of Diaspora Croatian communities.[88] Generally, until Milošević, there was simply no need to highlight any form of Serbian aggression, even for the future director of the Matica Hrvatska.

There is an obvious problem with the high numbers for Bleiburg – they conflicted with the equally common claims of Croatian historians that few Croats supported the NDH, that defection was high, and that most Croats were part of the Partisan movement. Two clear contradictions emerge here. First of all, if it was indeed so easy for the Četniks to join up with the Partisans during Tito's quest for volunteers, why did the Ustaša and the Domobran not do the same? And also, if the Croats were the vanguard of Partisan resistance, why were they not able to stop the massacres? Indeed, if they claim to have been the majority, it is almost certain that the massacre, no matter how large, must have involved many Croatian Partisans, which makes perfect sense, since they too would have an axe to grind against their fellow nationals who had collaborated. This logical conundrum can be simply explained by the fact that Croatian historians were attempting to cover all bases. They want to be victims of a 'holocaust', the leaders in anti-Fascist resistance, the founders of the SFRY, and conscientious objectors to the NDH regime.

Conclusions

As this chapter indicates, the legacy of the Second World War continued to be of paramount importance during the recent war in Croatia and the later war in Bosnia-Hercegovina. High among Serbian and Croatian concerns was the extent to which they were the victims of the Second World War. By proving their own victimisation at the hands of Croatian enemy, Serbs portrayed their machinations in Croatia as self-defensive, preventing a 'repeated genocide' of Serbs. Similarly, for Croats, the massacre at Bleiburg demonstrated a pattern of Serbian genocidal aggression, followed by scheming, cover-ups and political dominance. Clearly, being a victim of a 'holocaust' carried tremendous moral and political weight, and each side was anxious to use such imagery to its fullest extent. As Finkielkraut, Landau and others have noted, the universalisation of the Holocaust has allowed for the borrowing of its symbols in the service of social and political movements.

The issue of performativity is of central importance in understanding the Jasenovac and Bleiburg revisions. By casting themselves as victims of genocide in in Second World War, both sides were able to play the victim in the 1990s, arguing that contemporary events were a repeat of the past. Kečmanović's negative myths, those of 'damage', 'plot', 'universal culprit', and 'counteridentification', were commonly used by both sides to highlight the strong differences between the two sides and their respective roles in the Second World War. The reinterpretation of Serbian and Croatian history was extremely important. If actions in the 1990s were to be extensions of those in the 1940s it was imperative to prove that these earlier actions were horrific and genocidal. Each side, by proving its own 'holocaust' was able to convince its own people that they needed to defend themselves against the renewed horrors of genocide. At the same time, recalling the Second World War allowed both sides to deny the reality of Serbian–Croatian co-operation during the SFRY, leading to the view that its break-up was both inevitable and natural.

NOTES

1 Ronnie S. Landau, *Studying the Holocaust: Issues, Readings and Documents* (London: Routledge, 1998) p. 54.
2 To appreciate the enormous variance in Jasenovac statistics, see the following: Bogdan Denitch, *Ethnic Nationalism: The Tragic Death of Yugoslavia* (Minneapolis, MN: University of Minnesota Press, 1994) p. 33; Ed Vulliamy, *Seasons in Hell Understanding Bosnia's War* (London: St Martin's Press, 1994) p. 23; Ejub Štitkovac, 'Croatia: The First War', in Jasminka Udovički and James Ridgeway (eds), *Burn This House* (London: Duke University Press, 1997) p. 154; Tim Judah, *The Serbs: History, Myth and the Destruction of Yugoslavia* (New Haven, CT: Yale University Press, 1997), p. 129; Alex Dragnitch, *Serbs and Croats: The Struggle in Yugoslavia* (New York: Harcourt Brace Jovanovich, 1992) p. 103; Brian Hall, *The Impossible Country: A Journey Through the Last Days of Yugoslavia* (Boston: David Godine Publishers, 1994), p. 23; Misha Glenny, *The Fall of Yugoslavia: The Third Balkan War* (London: Penguin Books, 1994) p. 81; Jasper Ridley, *Tito* (London: Constable, 1994), p. 165; United States Holocaust Memorial Museum, *Genocide in Yugoslavia During the Holocaust* (Washington DC: United States Holocaust Memorial Museum, 1995).
3 Branimir Anzulović, *Heavenly Serbia: From Myth to Genocide* (London: C. Hurst and Company, 1999) p. 100.
4 *Ibid.* p. 101.
5 *Ibid.* pp. 101–3.
6 See Vladimir Žerjavić, 'Yugoslavia – Manipulations with the Number of Second World War Victims (Zagreb: Croatian Information Center, 1998) http://hrvati.cronet.com/ cic/manip/sadrzaj.htm (accessed 18 June 1998), see pp. 12–14. An earlier work, 'The Inventions And Lies of Dr. Bulajić on Internet' (Zagreb: Croatian Institute of History, 30 July 1997) http://misp.isp.hr/dokumenti/balajic.htm (accessed 18 June 1998) is more propagandised, but is largely a response to Bulajić's obviously inflated data.
7 Serbian Unity Congress, 'Jasenovac' (21 April 1996). http://suc.Suc.Org/~kosta/tar/jasenovac/intro.html (accessed 18 June 1998).
8 Serbian Ministry of Information, 'Facts About The Republic of Serbia' (Helsinki: Embassy of the Federal Republic of Yugoslavia, February 1996).
9 Quoted in Nouvel Observateur et Raporteurs sans Frontières, *Le Livre Noir de L'Ex-Yougoslavie: Purification Ethnique et Crimes de Guerre* (Paris: Publications Arléa, 1993) p. 277. (My translation.)
10 Slobodan Kljakić, *A Conspiracy of Silence: Genocide in the Independent State of Croatia and*

Concentration Camp Jasenovac (Belgrade: The Ministry of Information of the Federal Republic of Yugoslavia, 1991) p. 23.

11 *Ibid.* pp. 29–33.

12 Milan Bulajić, 'Never Again: Genocide in the NDH: Ustashi Genocide the Independent State of Croatia (NDH) From 1941-1945' (Belgrade: Serbian Ministry of Information) www.yugoslavia.com/Society_and_Law/Jasenovac/ndh.htm (accessed 18 June 1998).

13 *Ibid.*

14 Sandra Bašić-Hrvatin, 'Television and National/Public Memory', in James Gow, Richard Paterson and Alison Preston (eds), *Bosnia by Television* (London: British Film Institute, 1996) p. 164.

15 Milan Bulajić, *Tudjman's 'Jasenovac Myth': Genocide Against, Serbs, Jews and Gypsies* (Belgrade: Strućna Kniga, 1994) pp. 13–14.

16 *Ibid.* p. 5. This book no doubt inspired Anto Knezević's apologist account of Tudjman's writings, which unfortunately only proved much of what he was trying to contest (see Note 45 in this chapter).

17 Milan Bulajić, *The Role of the Vatican in the Break-up of Yugoslavia* (Belgrade: Serbian Ministry of Information, 1993) p. 23.

18 *Ibid.* pp. 153–4.

19 Ilić, 'The Serbs in the Former SR of Croatia', in Dušanka Hadži-Jovančić (ed.), *The Serbian Question in the Balkans: Geograpical and Historical Aspects* (Belgrade: University of Belgrade Faculty of Geography, 1995) p. 333.

20 Svetozar Đurđević, *The Continuity of a Crime* The Final Settlement of the Serbian Question in Croatia (Belgrade: IDEA Publishing House, 1995) p. 15; Nouvel Observateur et Raporteurs sans Frontières, *Le Livre Noir de L'Ex-Yougoslavie*, p. 277; and Dušan T. Bataković, 'Le génocide dans l'état independant croate 1941–1945', *Hérodote*, 67 (1992) http.bglink.com/personal/batakovicustasefr.html (accessed 15 November 1999).

21 Momčilo Zečević, 'Second Phase: 1918–1941', in Božidar Zečević (ed.), *The Uprooting: A Dossier of the Croatian Genocide Policy Against the Serbs* (Belgrade: Velauto International, 1992) p. 7.

22 Radoje Kontić, 'Great Jubilee of World and our own History: Victory Over Fascism the Most Important Event of the XX Century', *Review of International Affairs*, 45: 15 (May 1995) p. 2.

23 Paul Pavlovich, *The Serbians* (Toronto: Serbian Heritage Books, 1988) p. 226. Pavlovich's study was of course written well before the conflict began.

24 Petar Damjanov, 'Yugoslavia in the World War Two', *Review of International Affairs*, 46 (15 May 1995) p. 6.

25 See *Politika*, (9 February, 1990) p. 19. For a long quotation of the article, see Mirko Grmek, Marc Gjidara, and Neven Simac, *Le nettoyage ethnique: Documents historiques une idéologie serbe* (Paris: Fayard, 1993) pp. 285–6. A similar theory is promoted by Smilja Avramov (ed.) *Genocide Against the Serbs* (Belgrade: Museum of Modern Art, 1992), p. 170.

26 Quoted in Anzulović, *Heavenly Serbia*, pp. 103–4.

27 For a synopsis of this see the Serbian Unity Congress Website http://suc.Suc.Org/~kosta/tar/knjige/atlas/index.html (accessed 18 June 1999).

28 Lazo M. Kostich, *The Holocaust in the Independent State of Croatia: An Account Based on German, Italian and the Other Sources* (Chicago: Liberty Press, 1981). A short synopsis and copy of the 'Foreword' is available at http://suc.Suc.Org/~kosta/tar/knjige/book-holocaust-lazoKostic.html (accessed 17 July 1999).

29 Bataković, 'Le génocide dans l'état independant croate 1941–1945' (my translation).

30 Jovan Ilić, 'The Balkan Geopolitical Knot and the Serbian Question', in Hadži-Jovančić (ed.), *The Serbian Question in the Balkans*, p. 31.

31 *Ibid.* pp. 29–30.

32 *Ibid.* p. 63.

33 In his *Hrvatska u Jugoslavija* (Croatia in Yugoslavia), published in 1981, Tudjman would assert that the Jasenovac figures were impossibly inflated. As he argued: 'In order to illustrate the absurdity of the statement that just in the Jasenovac camp from 700,000 – 800,000 people were killed, I pointed out to the government representatives that it would mean that every day 500 people were killed and buried, or 600 if one does not include holidays, or 20 to 25 people every hour, and I indicated the estimates ... [for] all of Yugoslavia during World War II ... do not exceed those figures!' See Ante Beljo, *Genocide in Yugoslavia: A Documentary Analysis* (Sudbury, ON: Northern Tribune Publishing, 1985) p. 40.

34 Franjo Tudjman, *Horrors of War: Historical Reality and Philosophy–Revised Edition*, trans. Katrina Mijatović (New York: M. Evans & Company, 1996) p. 15.

35 *Ibid.* p. 90. George Prpić also used the term in his 1973 work *Tragedies and Migrations in Croatian History*, and perhaps influenced Tudjman's later use of it. See Beljo, *Genocide in Yugoslavia*, p. 299.The actual origins of the term 'black legend' had nothing whatsoever to do with Croatia, but described the four centuries of genocide perpetrated by the Spanish against the South American indigenous people from the fifteenth century to the nineteenth. Tudjman's use of the term is strange, given the fact that the first black legend was certainly true and was used to denote the extermination of between 90 and 98 per cent of Latin America's indigenous inhabitants. For a general discussion, see David E. Stannard, *American Holocaust Columbus and the Conquest of the New World* (Oxford: Oxford University Press, 1992) Chapters 1–3.

36 Tudjman, *Horrors of War*, p. 245.

37 *Ibid.* p. 73.

38 *Ibid.* p. 233.

39 *Ibid.* pp. 231.

40 *Ibid.* pp. 55–6; 58–9.

41 *Ibid.* pp. 129–30.

42 *Ibid.* p. 97.

43 *Ibid.* pp. 98–9.

44 *Ibid.* pp. 130–1.

45 Quoted in Anto Knezević, *An Analysis of Serbian Propaganda: The Misrepresentation of the Writings of Historian Franjo Tudjman in Light of the Serbian Croatian War* (Zagreb: Croatian Information Center/Hrvatska Matica Iseljenika, 1992) p. 28. Tudjman's revisionist writings have been so well known and documented that Knezević, published a book through the Croatian Matica to defend Tudjman against accusations that he was anti-Semitic. Many of the scandalous quotations from Tudjman's original book, published in Croatian, are available in English only through Knezević's account. The irony here is obvious.

46 *Ibid.* pp. 318–19. Knezević quoted this passage from Tudjman's book in order to prove that Tudjman was not anti-Semitic, in response to Robert Kaplan's article in *The New Republic*, where he referred to Tudjman as a fascist. This quotation was part of Knezević's denunciation of Kaplan, in which he observed that 'Tudjman writes "Judeo-Nazi" in quotation marks', in the hope of proving that Tudjman had merely borrowed the term, rather than inventing it outright (see p. 33).

47 *Ibid.* p. 28.

48 Živko Gruden, Toni Gabrić, and Ivica Buljan, 'Black Chronicle of Croatian History:

Methods Used to Rehabilitate Ustashe and Stigmatize Antifascists: Depravity and Now',
Feral Tribune (29 December 1997) http://www.cdsp.neu.edu/info/students/marko/
feral/feral53.html (accessed 5 July 1999).

49 Quoted in Sven Balas, 'The Opposition in Croatia', in Udovički and Ridgeway (eds) *Burn This House*, p. 274. Ante Beljo had earlier advocated the same thing, although it was to be a monument to Yugoslavia's crimes against all peoples, including Serbs and Montenegrins (Beljo, *Genocide in Yugoslavia*, p. 279).

50 Josip Pečarić, 'Author's summary of *Serbian Myth about Jasenovac* (Zagreb: Naklada Stih, 2001)' www.hr/darko/etf/pec.html (accessed 12 December 2001).

51 Beljo, *Genocide in Yugoslavia*, p. 27.

52 *Ibid*. p. 41.

53 *Ibid*. p. 42. One must be careful of drawing any conclusions about Beljo's numbers here, on account of the fact that, though he advanced so many, he does not seem to be inordinately attached to any one in particular.

54 Grmek, Gjidara, and Simac, *Le nettoyage ethnique*, pp. 278–9.

55 Bože Ćović, *Croatia Between War and Independence* (Zagreb: University of Zagreb/OKC-Zagreb, 1991) p. 35.

56 Another strategy was to counterbalance Jasenovac with the Serbian concentration camp Banjica, according to Philip Cohen a concentration camp located in Belgrade, where 'there survive death lists written entirely in Serbian in the Cyrillic alphabet. At least 23,697 victims passed through the Serbian section of this camp. Many were Jews, including at least 798 children, of whom at least 120 were shot by Serbian guards.' See Philip J. Cohen, 'Holocaust History Misappropriated', *MIDSTREAM: A Monthly Jewish Review*, 39: 8 (November 1992) http://teletubbie.pet.net.je/~sjaak/domivina/archive/1992/english/holocaust.html (accessed 10 June 2000).

57 These facts are supported by Marcus Tanner in his description of the incident. See Marcus Tanner, *Croatia: A Nation Forged in War* (New Haven, CT: Yale University Press, 1997) pp. 167–70; also Judah, *The Serbs*, pp. 130–3; and Ridley, *Tito*, pp. 255–8.

58 Judah, *The Serbs*, p. 130.

59 Anzulović, *Heavenly Serbia*, p. 102.

60 Barbara Jelavich, *History of the Balkans Volume II* (London: Cambridge University Press, 1993) p. 272.

61 Tanner, *Croatia*, p. 170.

62 Ridley, *Tito*, p. 255.

63 *Ibid*. pp. 256–7.

64 Milovan Djilas, *Wartime* (London: Harcourt, Brace, Jovanovich, 1977) p. 447.

65 Žerjavić, *Yugoslavia – Manipulations with the Number of Second World War Victims*.

66 Josip Šentija, 'Croatia from 1941 to 1991' (Zagreb: University of Zagreb/Matica Hrvatska Iseljenika, 1994) p. 2.

67 'Commemorating the Bleiburg Tragedy', *Vjesnik* (12 May, 1997) www.cdsp.neu.edu/info/students/marko (accessed 18 June 1998).

68 C. Michael McAdams, *Croatia: Myth & Reality* (New York: Croatian Information Center, 1994) pp. 56–8.

69 Croatian Information Center, 'The Bleiburg Tragedy' (Zagreb: Croatian Information Center) www.hrnet.org/BLEIBURG/The Bleiburg Tragedy (accessed 5 July 1999); see also Ivo Omerčanin, *The Pro-Allied Putsch in Croatia in 1944 and the Massacre of Croatians by Tito's Communists in 1945* (Philadelphia, PA: Dorrance & Company, 1975) p. 41.

70 Stjepan Hefer, *Croatian Struggle for Freedom and Statehood* Argentina: Croatian Information Service/Croatian Liberation Movement, 1979) pp. 216–17.

71 Mislav Jezić, 'Problems of Understanding XXth Century History of Croatia' (Zagreb:

181

University of Zagreb) www.dalmatia.net/croatia/history/jezic.htm (accessed 18 June 1998).

72 Beljo, *Genocide in Yugoslavia*, p. 281. Again the same caveat applies to the *Nova Hrvatska* figures, which appear to me to be Beljo's preferred choice, but are nevertheless located in a sea of other totals.

73 Quoted *ibid.* p. 299. For his ambiguous total, see p. 279.

74 *Ibid.* p. 8.

75 Tudjman, *Horrors of War*, pp. 74–7.

76 McAdams, *Croatia*, pp. 56–8. Jack Lupić adds: 'Serbs suffered great casualties at Jasenovac prison camp while the Croats lost even more people in Bleiburg Death Marches starting in May 1945.' See Zeljko Jack Lupić, 'History of Croatia: Povijest Hrvatske (200 B.C. – 1998 A.D.)' (Zagreb: Croatian Information Center, 21 February 1999) http://www.dalmatia.net/croatia/history/index.htm (accessed 18 June 1998).

77 Philip Cohen, *Serbia's Secret War: Propoganda and the Deceit of History* (College Station, TX: Texas A & M University Press, 1996) pp. 6–7.

78 *Ibid.* p. xxii.

79 *Ibid.* pp. xxii–xxiii.

80 Mislav Jezić advanced the same position. While describing, 'many tens of thousands Jews, Gypsies, Serbs and Croats' executed at Jasenovac, the greater crime, he posited, was at Bleiburg, where the outcome of the massacre indicated that the Serbs would, 'continue in a less obvious manner following their bloody greater-Serbian ideology': Jezić, 'Problems of Understanding XXth Century History of Croatia'.

81 Cohen, *Serbia's Secret War*, p. xxiii.

82 Beljo, *Genocide in Yugoslavia*, p. 43.

83 Šentija, 'Croatia from 1941 to 1991', p. 2.

84 'Marking the 52nd anniversary of Bleiburg and the Croatian Calvary', *Croatia Weekly* (5 March 1998).

85 Živko Gruden, Toni Gabrić, and Ivica Buljan, 'Black Chronicle of Croatian History: Methods Used to Rehabilitate Ustashe and Stigmatize Antifascists: Depravity and Now', *Feral Tribute* (29 December 1997) www.cdsp.neu.edu/info/students/marko/feral53.html (accessed 5 July 1999).

86 'Suzanne Brooks-Pinčević, *Britain And The Bleiburg Tragedy*', *The Zajednicar* (11 November 1998) www.dalmatia.net/croatia/history/bleiburg.htm (accessed 5 July 1999).

87 Krunoslav Draginović, 'The Biological Extermination of the Croats in Tito's Yugoslavia', in Anton Bonifačić and Clement Mihanovich (eds), *The Croatian Nation*: Its Struggle for Freedom and Independence (Chicago, IL: 'Croatia' Cultural Publishing Center, 1955) pp. 296–7.

88 Beljo, *Genocide in Yugoslavia*, pp. 301–51.

7

Tito's Yugoslavia and after: Communism, post-Communism, and the war in Croatia

> Not only is the Yugoslav reality as twisted as the tunnels that held the Minotaur, but the observer keeps coming face to face with himself, seeing his own image spring out from what he thinks are the events of history, unable to separate projection from observation, fact from reflection, self from other. (E. A. Hammel in *The Yugoslav Labyrinth*)

After the Second World War and the devastation caused by German and Italian invasion, the Yugoslav peoples had the task of rebuilding their society after it had been torn apart by occupation and fratricidal warfare. The legends surrounding Tito's Communist Partisans and their war of liberation are well known, immortalised in such works as Milovan Djilas' *Wartime*, Fitzroy Maclean's *The Heretic*, and Frank Lindsay's *Beacons in the Night*. However, as has been seen in the preceding two chapters, contemporary Serbian and Croatian reinterpretations of this period were often negative. The Croatian myth of Bleiburg maintained that the foundations of Tito's Yugoslavia were constructed on the genocide of Croatian soldiers. For the Serbs, Tito was little more than an ethnic Croat with a grudge against Yugoslavia's largest and most powerful nation. Both sides presented the lifetime of the SFRY as an era when national identity was suppressed under a barrage of Communist propaganda. National symbols were replaced with 'Brotherhood and Unity' and Tito's own cult of personality. In Tito's Yugoslavia, ethnic hatreds seemingly smouldered below the surface, manifesting themselves in bizarre and often contradictory ways.

The first part of this chapter explores Serbian and Croatian nationalist interpretations of the Yugoslav period, during its rise, its decline, and finally, its Fall. The second examines how propagandists succeeded in making direct connections between past eras of persecution and the contemporary wars of the 1990s. For both sides, the past was nothing more than a template for the present and the future. Past patterns of behaviour, values, morals, paradigms, and ideologies directly determined national goals and priorities in the 1990s.

183

National leaders were seen as little more than the latest exponents of age-old ideologies and national strategies. The theme of the 'universal culprit' was advanced throughout the conflict.

Milošević became a nineteenth-century Greater Serbian politician, with a bit of Adolf Hitler thrown in for good measure. Tudjman was nothing less than the reincarnation of Ante Pavelić. The Second World War was being re-enacted in Serbia and Croatia, and all decisions would be calculated on an analysis of the past, not on a realistic assessment of contemporary events. Propagandists seemingly lived in the past; but this was a past that was cleverly manufactured. Milošević's huge rallies and religious processions, and Tudjman's elaborate uniforms and ubiquitous memorials, turned parts of Serbia, Croatia, and Bosnia-Hercegovina into giant surreal nationalist theme parks.

Set against a conflict of Biblical proportions, participants in the contemporary conflict were presented as actors in a drama, performing according to well-rehearsed nationalist patterns of behaviour. The originality behind such revisionism lay in the fatalism attached to events as they transpired. Everyone saw their actions as responses, rather than as individual initiatives. Leaders claimed that they were responding to historic injustices, rather than actively creating something new. They also portrayed nationalism as a movement to correct the injustices of the past, rather than advancing a utopian project or a grand vision of the future.

The Communist era: 1945–90

In coming to terms with the Communist period, there was certainly much to criticise. Tito's dictatorial rule relied on a corrupt base of power, and a personality cult of messianic proportions. The country was burdened by overcentralisation, massive foreign debt, and a powerful secret police force that cracked down on any internal dissent. Many saw Communism as an artificially imposed Russian system, forced on the people by Tito and Stalin – an attempt to destroy indigenous nationalisms. One might even add that, in the Partisans' expulsion of Yugoslavia's German minorities after 1945, they were promoting the ideals of ethnic cleansing that would become a key facet of nationalism in Bosnia-Hercegovina five decades later. Banac argues that there were more than 513,000 Germans in the 1921 census, most of whom were descendants of German colonists brought in by the Habsburgs in the eighteenth century. Most of these people were forced out after the Partisans gained control of the country.[1]

Despite these detractions, Yugoslavia was arguably the freest country in Eastern Europe, the most open to the West, and certainly one of the richest and most cosmopolitan in the Balkans. While most of the wealth was concentrated in Slovenia and Croatia, Yugoslavia's economy did come close to rivalling that of Czechoslovakia and the German Democratic Republic. Additionally, Tito was genuinely popular with his people, despite his egomania and corruption (or perhaps in part because of them). In many ways, he held the country together, and was more successful as a leader than his other Balkan counterparts – Nikolai Ceausescu, Todor Zhivkov, and Enver Hoxha.

The positive aspects of Communism in Yugoslavia were obvious – a high standard of living, the freedom to travel and work abroad, and a strong sense of patriotism. Yugoslavia was a founder of the Non-Aligned Movement, and played an important geopolitical role as a symbolic bridge between East and West, Capitalism and Communism. When nationalism rose to the forefront in the 1980s, there was little attempt actually to bring about a post-Communist society, such as was marginally achieved in Hungary, Poland, and the Czech and Slovak Republics. The Yugoslav successor states, like their Balkan neighbours, did not fully dismantle Communism as a system of government – many of the authoritarian structures and values remained. Little attempt was made to criticise the legacy of Communism itself, or to attack the rampant corruption, the rising foreign debts, or any of the other stark realities of the system. Both Tudjman and Milošević appreciated the extent of the power a Communist dictator could enjoy, and they were not about to relinquish the many advantages that leadership afforded in the old system.

When Serbian and Croatian nationalists criticised the Titoist era, the national question loomed large, out of proportion with more important issues. Yugoslavia was condemned because it inhibited nationalism, because it allowed 'enemy' national groups to gain power and control events. Tito was not condemned for being dictatorial or corrupt, but rather, for being controlled by either the Serbs or the Croats – for giving away too much of one's own nation's historic possessions to another national group. Communism was seen as a catalyst enabling the enemy nation to gain power and influence. It was not condemned as a failed system, but as an instrument – infinitely subject to manipulation. Thus there was never any real attempt to purge Communism from the country as such: only to correct the national imbalances of the system.

While Poland, Hungary, and Czechoslovakia saw Communism as a crime committed against all citizens, Serbian and Croatian nationalists painted *federal* Communism as the root of their problems, an evil that was selectively deployed against specific national groups, not against the country as a whole. Milošević's solution was to recentralise the SFRY; Tudjman's was to pull Croatia out of it. By separating Communism and Federalism, Serb and Croat leaders managed to retain most aspects of the Communist system intact. While purged of non-nationals, most of the key ministries remained the same. Rigid control over state enterprises, the media and other aspects of life remained. Both Tudjman and Milošević were keen to carve out their own Tito-esque cults of personality, Milošević as a reincarnation of Prince Lazar, Tudjman with his gold-braided uniforms as a ready-made Tito-for-Croats.

This separation of Communism and Federalism was all-important, as it allowed nationalists to demonise certain aspects of Titoist Yugoslavia, while preserving others. There was no doubt that Tito's Communism had improved the state considerably, and very much brought Yugoslavia, technologically and industrially, into the twentieth century. It was not the generation of wealth or industry that was attacked, but the balance between the different national groups – who got what, and how much. Even when the Communist government was attacked for persecuting the people (the use of police harassment, or imprisonment on the prison island Goli Otok), persecution was not seen as part of the system, but was blamed on nationalists manipulating the system against members of other nations. When Communism was attacked, the variant (not necessarily the structure) was condemned. Serbs were constantly blamed for trying to over-centralise or Stalinise the system. Croats were blamed for wanting decentralisation, while hoarding all the profits of tourism for themselves. Such issues demonstrated the system's failure to restrain nationalism, not the system's failure itself.

Serbian views of Tito's Yugoslavia

Arguably, Serbian writers had generally supported the Communist regime in Yugoslavia. Certainly, the execution of Draža Mihailović, the purges of Četnik sympathisers, the decentralising 1974 constitution, and other anti-Serbian aspects of the regime raised troubling questions about Serbia's place in the SFRY. Nevertheless, while Tito was alive, there seemed to be a high level of support for the regime and its policies. An obvious example of this was the 1969 election, when Serbs were offered the choice between reformers and hard-line candidates. While the rest of the country chose reform-oriented newcomers, Serbs overwhelmingly supported the old guard.[2]

Nevertheless, by 1986 Serbian writers had turned on the system, as Yugoslavia began to fall apart. Danko Popović's celebrated *Knjiga o Milutinu* (*The Book About Milutin*) became an instant best-seller in 1986, promoting the thesis that Serbs had made a 'fatal error' in liberating their Slavic 'brothers' during the Second World War, and then another in once more engaging in political union with them. Milutin's sayings were printed on placards during nationalist demonstrations; even group recitation during public gatherings was not unknown.[3] Dobrica Ćosić's work reflected similar themes: that Tito's Yugoslavia had reduced Serbia to a mere Communist province without history, culture, or national identity. In *The Sinner* and *The Outcast*, Ćosić derided the federal system for suppressing Serbian identity and nationalism.

Moscow and the Comintern, he posited, had installed an 'anti-Serbian' Communist regime in Yugoslavia.[4] He would later add:

> In the course of the four decades of Titoist tyranny, the Serbian people suffered from a veritable de-historification. Serbian identity and historical, spiritual, economic and political integrity were systematically demolished. The symbols and the fruits of the war of liberation belonging to the Serbian people were denigrated and falsified, while confiscating our magnificent Middle Age, shortening our history . . . the entire history of the Serbian people was reduced to the history of the socialist movement, while the history of the communist party itself was reduced to the era of Tito.[5]

Themes of an anti-Serbian Communism would eventually find their way into the 1986 SANU *Memorandum*. Among the Communists' damnable offences was their explicit support of anti-Yugoslav secessionist movements in 1925. The fact that there was no Serbian Communist Party organisation until 1945 was also seen to indicate a consistent anti-Serbian bias.[6] While one cannot deny the veracity of the events in question, it is clear that Tito's early movement was aimed at destroying a repressive, nationalist monarchy, according to his own Communist beliefs. Any Croatian or Slovenian national convictions were most certainly of secondary importance.

Other Serbian views included the theory that the Serbs had been continuously exploited economically. The *Memorandum* claimed that the Communists had reduced the economic potential of Serbia in favour of Slovenia and Croatia. Serbia was forced to support undeveloped regions, while selling its natural resources at subsidised prices to the developed republics. For the *Memorandum*'s authors, this came as no surprise, given that the 'Croat' Tito and the 'Slovene' Kardelj were the key officials behind such economic policies.[7] Thus, Serbia was seen to have been simultaneously exploited, both by the richer republics of Croatia and Slovenia, and by poorer republics, such as Kosovo and Macedonia. Rather than attack the massive foreign debts, the corruption and the wholesale neglect of the economy by Tito and his Partisan clique, known affectionately at the 'Club of 1941', Serbian writers chose to focus on what they perceived to be the deliberate and conscious impoverishment of Serbia. In reality, Serbia's poverty was an indirect result of much larger problems.

Administrative versus natural borders

As has been discussed in earlier chapters, a key issue during the war in Croatia was the legitimacy of borders. Because the borders of all federal republics were put in place by Tito and the Djilas Commission, Serbian writers argued that these borders were purely artificial, the result of Croatian machinations to reduce the size of historic Serbia. For some of the more powerful Serbian institutions, like the Serbian Association of University Teachers, Tito's Croatian background was blamed for the supposed increase in Croatia's size after 1945, and Serbia's shrinking. For such associations, Tito had created nothing less than a 'Greater Croatia' during the lifetime of the SFRY.[8] Others similarly denounced the borders as 'political improvisation', denying that they had any historic basis.[9]

For Serbian writers, the implications were very clear. The Serbs alone were targeted by 'Croat Josip Broz Tito'.[10] While the other nations, such as the Slovenes, Croats, Bosnian Moslems, and Macedonians were granted their own national republics, one-third of Serbs were forced to live outside Serbia. It was Tito's ethnic identity that was all-important for the Serbs. He had purposely weakened them, the largest and most important nation in Yugoslavia, with some 40 per cent of the population. Because of his ethnicity, and the fact that the borders had been created to favour Croatia, Serbian writers argued that there was a serious divergence between the borders of nations and the borders of republics. The result was a clear denial of Croatia's right to leave Yugoslavia with its borders intact. Any secession without negotiations on new borders was considered to be illegal: hence the need for the JNA.

The most common view of the conflict was promoted by various Serbian 'constitutional' and 'federalism' experts, who claimed to be analysing the break-up of Yugoslavia according to the prescriptions of international law. Milošević's contribution to the breakdown of the Federation was always avoided. Rather, a highly legalistic interpretation of developments would conveniently gloss over Serbian politicking. Serbian writers often blamed the war in Croatia on what was termed 'the unilateral and illegal secession' of Slovenia and Croatia from Yugoslavia. They further blamed the international community, primarily Germany and the Vatican, for recognising Slovenia, Croatia and Bosnia-Hercegovina, turning their 'administrative' borders into international borders when minority rights were still hanging in the balance. The problem for such writers was that 'almost 3 million Serbs' lived in these newly independent republics, and were now cut off from their fellow Serbs.[11]

Croatia was therefore accused of several things – of leaving Yugoslavia without consulting the other republics, and of deliberately endangering the lives of Serbian minorities living there. The claim of the supposed 'illegality' of Croatian actions was hypocritical at best, when compared with Milošević's own manipulation of borders and boundaries. Nevertheless, such accusations followed logically from accusations that Tito had deliberately conspired with Croatian and Slovenian Communists to reduce the power of his 'enemy' – Serbia. Because of this situation, the Serbs were now justified, from a purely legalistic viewpoint, in having their own referendum on the independence of the Krajina, 'since their ancestors settled these territories more than 500 years ago'.[12] While the Croats were denounced for not upholding the democratic will of the Serbs, they were also condemned as hypocrites for expecting the Yugoslav government to honour their own referendum on sovereignty.

As Slobodan Samardzić argued, the 'illegal' secession of Croatia and Slovenia destroyed the basic 'constitutional corpus of "acquired rights"' that had been present in the Federation. Within the SFRY, Croatian Serbs had special rights as a constitutive people, a status that disappeared once Croatia became independent. From a purely legalistic and constitutional standpoint, Samardzić justified the war in Croatia. Serbs, he posited, had to protect themselves against the 'ethnic homogenization' of the country, which was making Croatian Serbs 'minorities against their will'.[13] This view that Croatian Serbs were being forced to leave Yugoslavia was a key argument in promoting the Krajina referendum. Using a variety of persuasive technical and legal arguments, Samardzić tried to gloss over the reality of what was happening in Croatia at that time. Paramilitary forces and the JNA, both encouraged by Milošević, were in control of one-third of Croatian territory in 1994 when his article was written. Clearly, there was much more at stake than Serbs worried about a change in their 'constitutional status'.

The difference between the borders of federal units and the borders of states was a theme constantly reiterated by Serbian academics. Serbs were quick to argue that 'only nations can secede from Yugoslavia, and not territories of republics'.[14] One Ministry of Information spokesperson thus described Croatia's manipulation of international law, in order to 'seize another nation and another territory and to lend legal force to such an act' – clearly something the Serbs disputed.[15] The main argument was simple – Tito had never intended to allow individual republics to secede. He saw republican borders as administrative only.

Croatian nationalists obviously had a contrary view of the situation. They commonly argued that Croatia's borders were not administrative, but ethnic and cultural. Serbian arguments were refuted by Croatian geographers, who described their borders as 'among the oldest in Europe'. A survey by the geographers Ivan Crkvenčić and Mladen Klemenčić maintained that there had been only a 10 per cent change in Croatia's borders in the twentieth century – a loss of Croatian territory after 1918, owing to the success of 'Greater Serbia'.[16] Other writers traced the historic origin of Croatia's borders, which were defined during war against the Ottomans in the seventeenth and eighteenth centuries, and had remained more or less unchanged since that time.[17]

Croatian writers also managed to defend the minority issue, since Croatia, with 80 per cent of its people being 'Croat', had the same degree of homogeneity as Spain or Great Britain, allowing these writers to allege that: 'Croatia presents a common European phenomenon.'[18] Still others pointed out that while 24 per cent of Serbs lived outside Serbia, some 22 per cent of Croats lived outside Croatia. Since Croatia 'had never demanded the annexation of those areas of other republics', the Serbs were obliged to accept their minority status.[19] The problem, of course, was that neither Spain nor Great Britain saw themselves as a homeland for one people only, while both have extended provisions for regional minorities. There were no ethnic nationalist dictators in those countries, preaching intolerance against their minority groups. At the time these books were written, Croatia had not yet attacked Bosnia-Hercegovina, but this too would soon change, as Croatia pledged itself to defending its own people in Bosnia. It would then do exactly what it accused the Serbs of doing – demand the annexation of territory in other republics.

The 1974 constitution and genocide

In 1974, an ailing Tito decided to reform the constitution of Yugoslavia. He wanted to ensure that the Federation continued in some form after his death. However, the new constitution was a highly contentious development. It greatly decentralised the SFRY, granting autonomy to Kosovo and Vojvodina, while reducing many of the administrative and financial functions controlled by the federal government. The constitution also established an unwieldy rotating presidency, with a seven-member presidium. One presidium representative from each republic after another would take a turn at running the country. Croatian nationalist writers, in reviewing the constitution, had little to complain about, as it practically gave each republic the status of a separate state, including such attributes as the inviolability of borders. Thus Croats used this decentralising document to argue that their separation from Yugoslavia was perfectly justified and legal.[20]

The Serbs, by contrast, saw the constitution as the root of many of their problems. It reduced their control over Kosovo and Vojvodina, while significantly hampering the power of the federal centre to make decisions for the Federation. It also reduced the power of the federal government to guarantee Serbian minority rights in other republics. Without centralised power, Serbs worried that they would suffer discrimination outside Serbia. Kosovo was a particularly important thorn in Serbia's side. Their loss of control here seemed to reflect the age-old Serbian catastrophist maxim: 'Winners in war, losers in peace'. Journalists blamed the constitution for creating Serbian minorities in Croatia, Bosnia-Hercegovina, and Kosovo. For many Serbs, the creation of minorities in autonomous republics was the first stage in a campaign of genocide.[21] With its many lurid photos and graphic descriptions, *The Uprooting*, by Božidar Žečević, was one of many publications that denounced Tito's manipulation of Kosovo to humiliate the Serbs. Rather than contributing to Serbian greatness, Kosovo was used as an instrument to reduce Serbian power. Žečević attacked the 'treacherous' Yugoslav Communists for working with Kosovar Albanian separatists to create a 'Greater Albania' in Kosovo.[22]

Encouraging Albanian nationalism was presumably a way of weakening the Serbs – supposedly a central goal of the Communist regime.

Tito was also accused of ethnically cleansing Serbs during his four decades of rule. Examples of this line of argumentation were analysed in Chapter 3. What began as a fear of persecution in Kosovo spread to Croatia and Bosnia-Hercegovina. As the Serbian Unity Congress described the process: 'Tito's favourite method of punishing the Serbs, whom he hated personally and discriminated against officially, was to allow the Croats and Muslims to rid their territories of Serbs by depriving them of their political, cultural, religious, and human rights.' Included here was a list of the number of Serbs 'ethnically cleansed' during Tito's rule: 121,376 from Croatia, and 205,542 from Bosnia-Herzegovina, making a grand total of 326,918.[23] The SUC neglected to explain how these numbers were calculated.

The 1974 constitution was thus at the root of Yugoslavia's many ills. Samardzić noted how it weakened the federal state, devolving power to the increasingly authoritarian republics. Decentralisation, and not Milošević's attempts to over-centralise the country, was blamed for the 'internal disintegration' of Yugoslavia in the 1980s. If anything, Milošević was credited with trying to re-establish 'the integrational link between the federal units', to prevent the 'anarchoid form' that it had taken after 1974.[24] Again, blaming Tito's legacy for the breakdown of Yugoslavia deflected criticism away from Milošević's obvious attempts to hijack the federal system.

Genocidal Croats: Croatian nationalism in the SFRY

Structurally, the SFRY seemingly went against Serbian interests. However, Tito was not the only one responsible for Serbia's weakened status. Two Croatian Communist officials were often cited in Serbian literature as enemies of the Serbian nation – Ivan 'Stevo' Krajačić and Andrija Hebrang. Hebrang was often condemned as a Croatian nationalist with influential connections, who tried to manipulate Tito into reducing Serbian power. In reality, Hebrang was one of Tito's most bitter rivals. As one of the most powerful Partisan leaders in Croatia, he tried unsuccessfully to advance Croatian interests at the Federal level, arguing that Croatia's borders had been clipped by the Djilas Commission. He also argued against the unfair exchange rates imposed on Croatia after 1945, while similarly condemning the many show trials set up to punish supposed collaborators. Hebrang was never a serious threat to Serbian interests, since he was demoted several times after 1945, and was eventually placed under house arrest in 1948.[25]

Krajačić was seemingly a more dangerous and shadowy figure. Krajačić was not a typical Croatian Communist; he was also the main resident representative of the Fourth Soviet Intelligence Service, and was cast as a sinister puppet-master, with powerful contacts in Moscow. He was supposedly so powerful that even Tito was afraid of him. For Serbian historians, Krajačić was a useful scapegoat for why the system went wrong, for why the Serbs were victims in Yugoslavia. He, and not Tito, was blamed for persecuting Serbs during the bloody Communist purges after the Second World War. He was even blamed for founding the infamous prison camp at Goli Otok, as a means of punishing Serbs and Montenegrins, who constituted 'the over-whelming majority of those detained and carefully watched over'.[26]

Krajačić was presented as a cynical Croatian nationalist with incredible personal power. He would later be blamed for the fall of the Serbian Communist leader Aleksander Ranković, having supposedly engineered his downfall in order to carry out increased decentralisation, a plan of benefit only to Croatia, since 'the virus of Croatian nationalism kept smouldering in him'.[27] His supposed nickname – 'The Conducator of Separatism' – was derived from his advocacy of Croatian separatism, as well as his dictatorial qualities, which made him similar to Romania's own 'Conducator' – Nikolai Ceausescu. Krajačić was also accused of being a supporter of the Ustaša, and a keen advocate of genocide as a means of dealing with the Serbs. He suppos-edly commented at the opening of the Jasenovac memorial in 1966: 'Here we killed too few of you!', a statement for which he was purportedly forced to resign as President of the Croatian Parliament.[28]

The Krajačić conspiracy had some rather obvious motives. By the mid-1980s, Serbian historians had begun the process of rehabilitating Ranković, who had been stripped of his powers in 1966. Ranković founded Yugoslavia's secret police – the State Security Administration (the *Uprava Državne Bezbednosti*, or UDBa) – and served as Minister of the Interior during Yugoslavia's most oppressive period after the Second World War. He was often portrayed in Croatian writing as a die-hard Serbian nationalist who abused his powers to advance Serbian interests. It was clear that Ranković was a keen advocate of centralisation, and was seen to be the natural succes-sor to Tito once he died or retired. His fall from grace was therefore a serious blow to Serbian prestige, and to those who cherished the idea that a Serb could have ruled Yugoslavia – if it were not for Croatian back-room dealings.[29]

A primary reason why Ranković was stripped of his position was his persecution of the Kosovar Albanian population. Police repression in the province, and several staged show trials of supposed 'Albanian spies' at Prizren in 1956, greatly increased the friction between Serbs and Croats. While Ranković was seen as a man who could keep the Kosovars in their place, he also provoked Kosovar anger and desires for separatism. While some Serbs saw him as a hero, whose demise ushered in Albanian nationalism, the reverse was probably true.[30] It was also certain that Ranković, and not Krajačić, had established Goli Otok, where Tito sent some 7,000 people.

Rumours that he was bugging Tito's telephones did not help matters either, nor did accusations that he was behind assassination attempts on the Slovene Communist leader Edvard Kardelj in 1959.[31] Ultimately, the quest for a suitable scapegoat to take the blame for Ranković's activities was never very successful. For one thing, everyone knew who Ranković was, whereas no one had ever heard of Krajačić. Whether he was as all-powerful as some Serbs suggest, or simply another long forgotten Communist official, is still open to dispute.

Croatian perceptions of the SFRY

Like their Serbian counterparts, the Croats presented Yugoslavia as an era of persecution and repression. Their national spirit was choked under the rigours of Titoist Communism, their nationalist leaders were driven into exile, and Croatia's most acclaimed writers and scholars were imprisoned. While earlier Croatian Diaspora accounts often focused on the horrors of Tito's regime, later accounts during the 1990s blamed the Serbs, and not Tito, for destroying the system. Attacks on Communist tyranny were soon replaced with even more vitriolic attacks on Serbian treachery and greed. In an attempt to justify their separation from the SFRY, Croatian nationalists insisted that Serbian dominance remained the central focus in Tito's political project. They argued that since Belgrade was the political, financial, military, judicial, and administrative capital of the SFRY, the Serbs had naturally been privileged. Any form of centralisation – even the Slovenian ideologue Edvard Kardelj's 'Yugoslav consciousness' – was therefore dismissed as an attempt at greater Serbianisation.

Croatian writers often argued that the federal system in the SFRY was identical to that imposed on the Croats in the first Yugoslavia. Yugoslav Communism was described as a 'disguised Greater Serbia'.[32] More graphically and colourfully, Communist Yugoslavia metamorphosed into 'a resurrected ghost of the expansionist, hegemonistic, unitaristic and centralist state of the old Yugoslavia type, this time in a more horrible form enabled by the centralised, monolithic political power of the Communist Party'.[33] For this writer, as for many others, the SFRY was simply 'a new artificial Greater Serbian nation concealed under the name of Yugoslavia', entrenched 'behind the facade of pretended socialism.'[34] Others argued that the entire government bureaucracy, federal government officials, the army, and the diplomatic corps were completely dominated by Serbs.[35] Thus Yugoslavia never truly existed. It was a pseudo-Communist state controlled by Serbian nationalists, who manipulated Tito into reducing Croatian power. In this process of revision, aspects of Communist life that were present in all Communist countries, such as a one-party state and a powerful police force, were blamed on Serbian domination. Rather than being seen as typically Communist, they were characteristics of Greater Serbia.

For Croatian historians, Serbs were presented as a highly privileged national group in Yugoslav society. Their language, culture, and political customs became the cornerstone of the state, while Serbs similarly maintained numerical dominance in most of the key ministries, the police forces, and the military. Other aspects of control, such as economic exploitation, were often described in terms of a core–periphery relationship. Echoing Nairn's theories, Croatian writers saw nationalism as a solution to their problems of underdevelopment. Kečmanović's 'theme of damage', with its emphasis on economic, cultural, and social decline – due to decades of Serbian domination – was a theme constantly invoked.[36] At every level, Croats argued that the Serbs were in full control of the SFRY. This became a useful justification for why it was time for them to leave, and why the Serbs were clearly the aggressors.

Serbian economic domination

A reason for attacking the federal system was Serbian economic exploitation. While Tito's government had channelled hundreds of millions of dollars into a world-class tourist industry in Croatia, a portion of this tourist revenue had to be paid to the federal centre. While the tourist industry had been established in order to increase Yugoslavia's foreign currency reserves, a strategy aimed to help the entire Federation, not just Croatia, Croatian writers painted this as an example of economic exploitation. A typical argument held that for seventy years 'Croatia was exploited and drained', and had no control over where her money was going, and why. Croats argued that Croatia and Slovenia funded some 50 per cent of the Yugoslav federal budget – the loss of this income having been a crucial reason for Serbia's invasion after 1991.[37] While a sense of economic exploitation was justified to an extent, the oft-quoted figure of 50 per cent was deliberately misleading. Croatia brought in some 50 per cent of foreign exchange earnings during the 1960s and 1970s, but did not fund 50 per cent of the federal budget. While Croatians did contribute considerably to the Yugoslav economy, and certainly paid a disproportionate share of the federal budget relative to their population size, their exploitation was not as high as that alleged during the break-up.[38]

One of the better-known documents alleging various levels of Serbian exploitation – economic and otherwise – was Miroslav Brandt's *Antimemorandum*, written five years after the SANU *Memorandum* was leaked to the press. Brandt's whinging style perfectly mirrored the intent of the SANU original. Brandt echoed several common themes – that the Serbs controlled the military, the political system, and the economy. For too long, Croats had suffered from 'Greater Serbian centralisation'.[39] Independence was the solution to all Croatia's economic difficulties. Brandt reinterpreted many of the ideas found in Milovan Djilas' *New Class*, wherein Djilas had attacked the massive power of the Communist bureaucracy during the 1950s. He argued that Yugoslavia had become more inegalitarian since the Partisan revolution. As he described it, a 'new class' had been formed, which administered and controlled the economy, distributed everything, and consequently enjoyed the fruits of production.[40]

Predictably, Brandt reasoned that Djilas's 'new class' was dominated by the Serbs – who had milked the system for all it was worth. He argued that the great majority of Yugoslav millionaires were Serbian 'rich profiteers', who benefited from other nations in Yugoslavia by supposedly confiscating other people's property, and then exploiting it for their own gain. For Brandt, the Serbs were the only true 'plutocrats'.[41] By contrast, the Croats constituted an exploited class and nation rolled into one. 'Croatia is,' Brandt asserted, 'a thoroughly oppressed country enslaved, plundered, pauperized, brought down to the verge of existence, forced to massive emigration of its population seeking a way to survive, exposed to national liquidation under a military and police regime or occupation.'[42] Serbs were described simultaneously as bourgeois overlords, colonial oppressors, Bolshevik dictators, and Fascists.

For many Croats, Communism had been an utter failure – Tito's 'pretended socialism' had done nothing to eliminate the economic exploitation by the Serbian/Bourgeois Class/Nation over the Croatian/Proletarian/ Peasant Class/Nation. Concocting his own type of Hegelian dialectic, Brandt managed to merge class and nation to demonstrate how Greater Serbia continued to dominate Croatia in every respect during the Communist era. Brandt represented a typical view of Croatia's exploitation within Yugoslavia. The view that the Serbs controlled everything from Belgrade was common, as was the argument that the Serbian occupation of Croatia was an attempt to regain control of Croatia's economy. Perhaps it attests to the 'reasonableness' of certain Croatian economists that they were willing to see only an economic motive for Serbian aggression, while dismissing the 'irrationality' of nationalism.

The Serbian character explained

Perhaps the most thorough, and at the same time the most insidious examination of the conflict between Serbs and Croats in Yugoslavia was the product of three sociologists. As with their analysis of Medjugorje, Meštrović, Letica, and Goreta used a sociological model to come to terms with the 'social character' of the Serbs, something similar to primordial characteristics or acting as a 'substitute for biological instinct'.[43] For the authors, being 'Dinaric' in the Cvijić-ian sense implied being both 'predatory' and 'barbaric' – containing the seeds of 'totalitarianism'.[44] Much of their work seemed to be little more than a rhetorical window-dressing for a fairly simple thesis: Serbs were warlike and aggressive by nature, lazy and Eastern, while Croats were democratic, peace-loving, and Western. As such, their forced union within Yugoslavia led to Serbian dominance and violence, while the Croats were exploited and victimised. Most of their sociological metaphors and historical studies, while interesting, had little or no bearing on the reality of events in Yugoslavia.

One such example was an examination of Alexis de Tocqueville's study of the American Civil War. The United States became an analogy for Communist Yugoslavia, described as 'the sometimes unhappy union of two distinct and opposing cultures', composed of the 'Southern aristocrat' and the Northerner. The Southerner was described as a 'domestic dictator from infancy … a haughty and hasty man, irascible, violent, ardent in his desires, impatient of obstacles … fond of grandeur, luxury and renown, of gaiety, pleasure, and above all, of idleness'.[45] This was in marked contrast to Northerners, who were 'educated, talented, and family-oriented citizens … the best elements of order and morality'.[46] It was not difficult to see where this analogy was going: two opposing cultures, one backwards, lazy and despotic, the other, hard-working, educated, and moral. The combination of these two groups in a single state created a sociological 'clash of civilisations'. For the three authors, the American analogy played out well in Yugoslavia, since the Balkans 'exhibit[s] more extremely the opposition between barbaric and peaceable traits that is found all over the world'.[47] The disintegration of Yugoslavia was clearly blamed on the Serbs, who, living on a lower level of civilisation, could not help but dominate and abuse the helpless Croats. For example:

> [I]t is well known in Yugoslavia that Serbs and Montenegrins adhere to a sort of cult of the warrior. They have continually dominated the police and armed forces. They habitually own guns and engage in hunting as part of a machismo set of values. Within Yugoslavia, they are known for being stubborn, irascible, and emotionally unstable. It is interesting that many of these same traits can still be found ascribed to male residents of the southern United States, in comparison with males in the North.[48]

Meštrović *et al.*'s dubious sociology supported the contention that Serbian actions were a result of a primordial and unchanging social character. The only solution was separation. There was an evident paradox in using this particular study of de Tocqueville. In the case of the American Civil War, the Southerners declared independence and separated, with the support of various outside powers. The North refused to allow the South to leave, waging war rather than having the country split apart. Ironically, the Serbs arguably had more in common with the North than the South, since they too were supposedly fighting a war against separatism, with a federal army to keep their 'union' intact. While these authors' attempts at analogy were somewhat confused and inaccurate, the suggestion that the Serbs were somehow more warlike, lazy, exploitative and generally inferior, struck a chord with many readers.[49] Such theories maintained that Communist Yugoslavia was an untenable construction, completely controlled by Serbs, who dominated every aspect of life. Both the break-up of the federation and the war that followed were natural outcomes of a Serbian psychology, which was seemingly fundamentally different to that of the Croats.

Linguistic repression in Yugoslavia

The status of the Croatian language during the lifetime of the SFRY was an extremely important consideration.[50] Since the time of Ljudevit Gaj and Ante Starčević, a separate Croatian language was one of the key hallmarks of national identity. Tito was roundly condemned for outlawing the use of the 'Croatian' language, imposing instead the Serbo-Croatian language, with Occidental (Croatian) and Oriental (Serbian) variants. A joint language was seen as an important aspect of Tito's 'Brotherhood and Unity', and was central to repressing manifestations of Croatian nationalism. Linguistic reform was a key demand of nationalist politicians during the Maspok movement in the 1970s. The demand for a separate Croatian language was largely responsible for the 1971 'Croat Spring', during which the famed Croatian novelist Miroslav Krleža led a group of 130 leading Croatian academics on a crusade to designate 'Croatian' as a separate language for education and literature. The Serbian Communist Party followed suit with a demand for reciprocal rights to a Serbian language for their people living within Croatia.[51]

For Croats, the Serbo-Croatian language was little more than a 'political tool' that had been used throughout the history of Yugoslavia to homogenise different peoples into a single nation. Even when Tito was alive, Croats had rejected the *Novi Sad Agreement* and pushed for their own language. With Tito's death, and the rise of nationalism, the Croatian language once more became a crucial issue in Croatian identity. Moreover, the Serbo-Croatian language became symbolic of Serbian cultural dominance and Croatian weakness. As one historian argued: 'The only reason that "Serbo-Croatian" existed and the only reason it has been forced upon unwilling populations were the politics of an artificial Yugoslavia united by force against the will of the majority of its population.'[52]

After independence, Croatian writers and linguists were able to reclaim 'Croatian' as their own distinct and unique national language. This was an extremely important 'turning-point', or 'watershed', in Croatian history, when Croats at last had the freedom to re-create a national language. For many Croats, there had once been a linguistic Golden Age in need of rediscovery. At some stage, there was a pure, authentic and unadulterated Croatian language waiting to be dusted off, polished, and shined, after decades of being covered with Serbian and Communist dirt and tarnish. The well-known Croatian writer Slobodan Novak commented on the new 'purity' of Croatia by proclaiming triumphantly:

> Croatia is cleansing itself of Yugo-unitarist and Great-Serb rubbish which had been spread all over it for a whole century. Croatia is simply restored to its original form and returning to its true self. If today it has to make painful incisions in its language, history, scholarship and even the names of its towns and streets, that only shows the extent to which it was contaminated and how polluted were all facets of its life and all segments of its corpus.[53]

For Novak, as for many others, one of the most painful legacies of Communism was the loss of the national language. Once they had their language back, the Croatian soul could once more be found. But what exactly was the language to look like? Various dictionaries soon appeared on the scene. Stjepan Brodnjak's *Razlkovni Rjecnik* (Separate Dictionary) featured 35,000 entries, composed mainly of technical terms and archaisms.

The zeal to 'de-Serbianise' the language led to revisions of distinctly 'Croatian' texts. Jasna Baresić's 1994 Croatian language reader *Dobro Dosli* had to be cleansed of 'Serbianisms' by other Croatian linguists on a daily basis, since new 'impurities' were constantly being identified. Even Miroslav Krleža, the 'martyr' for the Croatian language, had his works translated from 'Serbo-Croat' for new school textbooks. Eager advocates of a pure 'Croatian' introduced a bill before the Croatian *Sabor*, proposing fines and prison terms for those who used words of 'foreign' origin.[54]

In many cases, an entirely new language was being created. While some sort of linguistic Golden Age was the aim of the policy, most of the new words had no historical origin. What seemed to matter more was differentiating 'Croatian' from 'Serbian'. More extreme voices, such as the writers at *NDH* magazine, proposed going even further than Starčević to create a completely different national language. Advocating the 'Croatian "korienski" orthography', one journalist argued that the adoption of a new dialect would be the only way to create an authentic Croatian language. Nevertheless, it was clear that such a language would be neither historically 'pure' nor accurate. This, apparently, was not particularly important. As the author explained: 'Only the renewal and rebirth of the unique character of the Croatian language and "korienski" orthography (because that way Croatian and Serb languages would become mutually unintelligible) can destroy Serb appetite for Croatian lands and free us from fear of violent "unification" of parts of Croatia with Serbia.'[55] Creating their own Babel would allow Croats to be safe from Serbian attacks:

> [T]he loss of mutual intelligibility of Croatian and Serb languages is the best guar-
> antee that Croatia will never again join some Yugo-associations which could lead
> to the renewal of the common state with the Serbs, because our languages,
> cultures, and religions would be different. Since [Serbs and Croats belong to] two
> different civilizations there can be no coexistence for us. Let us work hard, with
> love, and learn the Croatian language cleansed of all non-Croatian traces which
> had been imposed by force on it, and renew its Croatian character.[56]

That the 'Croatian character' to which the author referred would be unintelligible to the vast majority of Croats themselves seemed to matter little.
What mattered was not how useful the new language might be as a tool for
communication, but its separate status. In general, the differences between
'Serbian', 'Croatian', and 'Bosnian' were dialectical, and were matters of
regionalism, not nationality. Within Croatia itself, Istrians, Dalmatians, and
those living around Zagreb all spoke with different dialects, which could, with
little effort, be transformed into other 'national' languages. The linguist Celia
Hawksworth, in her language training guide to the now defunct 'Serbo-
Croat', taught both the Serbian and Croatian variants of what she certainly
saw as a common language. As she wrote somewhat ironically:

> This book introduces the version of the language known to its speakers as
> 'Croatian', but if you learn this version you will be understood by all the other
> peoples listed above, who call their version of the language 'Bosnian' or 'Serbian'
> respectively. One way of looking at this complex situation is that it is extraordi-
> narily cost-effective: if you learn one language you will find that you
> automatically know three or four![57]

While this process of linguistic revisionism appeared to be revolutionary
during the early 1990s, it was clear by 1995 how farcical it truly was. During
the Dayton Accord negotiations between the Serbs, the Croats, and the
Bosnian Moslems, participants had the choice of simultaneous translation
into 'Serbian', 'Croatian', and 'Bosnian'. However, while there were three
separate channels from which to select, there was only one translator for all
three. In short, the language was identical, and none of the three parties
seemed to care. For them it was the principle, not the language, that
mattered.[58]

Now certainly many nations have produced their own standardised
language, based on one specific variant, and of course not everyone can speak
it. In France, on the eve of its Revolution, 50 per cent of the population did not
speak French at all, and only 12–13 per cent spoke the Parisian variant that
would eventually become the standard form. When Italy began its unification
process in 1861, scarcely 2.5 per cent of the population used standard Italian
for everyday communication.[59] Thus, even the *korienski* orthography might
be historically defensible. What needs to be addressed in the Croatian case is
not simply a nation's right to re-create its language, but the motivations

behind it. Linguistic re-creation in Croatia was a means of creating artificial divisions between Serbs and Croats in the state. It was specifically designed to exclude non-Croats from the national ethos during a time of warfare and violence. Like all examples of linguistic standardisation, the reformulation of Croatian was of necessity exclusivist, a process designed to suppress regional variations and deny people the right to communicate on their own terms with one another.

The rise of Serbian and Croatian nationalism: interpretations

The demonisation of the Communist period was extremely important for both sides, as both were seeking to justify why Yugoslavia had to be abandoned in its former shape and structure. Serbs and Croats used history as a resource, as a tool for explaining events during and after the war in Croatia, while inscripting narratives of victimisation and persecution. While benign theories of economic exploitation and Tito's border machinations were cited by academics, the great bulk of the wartime propaganda focused on the fear of genocide. Ronnie Landau's 'grotesque competition in suffering' had begun. Historical patterns of hatred and genocidal aggression had been identified for almost every historical period. All that remained was to apply the horrors of the past to understanding war in the 1990s.

For Serbian writers, the fear of a renewed genocide, comparable to the Ustaša genocide in the Second World War was a central feature of their propaganda. This became the key justification for the rise of Serbian nationalism in Croatia and the JNA's later invasion of what was recognised as a sovereign country. From the first day of Tudjman's presidency, Croatian Serbs argued that the HDZ was trying to remove all Serbian power in the republic. The HDZ government was purging Serbs from almost every aspect of Croatian life, using what was described as an 'ethnical broom', to remove Serbs from the government bureaucracies, the police, the judiciary, the mass media, and the school system. Even blue-collar workers were supposedly purged.[60] Serbian historians presented Tudjman's regime as nothing more than the rehabilitation and restoration of the NDH.[61] The first Croatian constitution was often cited as proof that the HDZ was trying to assimilate Croatian Serbs, by denying them their national rights. This seemingly indicated that a new genocide was beginning.[62]

A common theme among Serbian historians and politicians was that the Serbs had merely reacted to the Croatian threat – they had only defended themselves. The assassination in July 1991 of Osijek's moderate police chief, Josip Reichl-Kir, by Croatian extremists was constantly cited as the first act of aggression in the Croatian conflict. Reichl-Kir had been negotiating with Serbian irregulars at the time, and was seemingly killed for trying to promote peace instead of war.[63] The death of Reichl-Kir certainly demonstrated the duplicity of the Croatian government; but it was not the first act of violence, since by this point the 'log revolution' was well under way. Croatian Serbs had already begun blocking off roads and assaulting Croatian police forces. Nevertheless, Reichl-Kir came to symbolise how the HDZ regime was willing to kill off its own people, should they try to negotiate with Serbs. The Serbian Krajina politician Mile Dakić soon denounced the HDZ for their 'fascist state policy and kalashnikov democracy'.[64] The view that an independent Croatia was forced on the Serbs at gunpoint was widespread.

A constant level of Croatian aggression against Serbs was a necessary theme in the latter's self-representation as victims of genocide. Dismissing claims that the HDZ administration was democratically elected, Serbian sources argued that a multi-party system did not guarantee democracy. 'Hitler,' according to one historian, was a good example of another populist who manipulated democracy, since he 'came to power in Germany within the framework of a multi-party mechanism but subsequently became a great dictator, aggressor and criminal.'[65] While the writer was clearly referring to Tudjman, the irony was, of course, that Milošević had risen to power in an identical fashion, and was little different from his Croatian counterpart. Nevertheless, Serbian writers worked tirelessly to debunk the myth of Croatian democracy, and specifically the Western belief at that time that Croatia had become an open, Westernised, post-Communist country.

By the time JNA tanks rolled into Eastern Slavonia in July 1991, it was clear that the Army no longer represented the interests of Yugoslavia, but had become an instrument of Serbian power.[66] While the JNA was simply trying to enlarge the Serbian state, the Serbs claimed that they were coming as 'peace-keepers', to prevent a genocide of Serbs. Humanitarian arguments would be used throughout the conflict to legitimize the invasion and occupation of Croatia. In justifying military intervention, Serbs often compared Croatian leaders to Nazis and fascist aggressors, re-hoisting Second World War flags while instigating continuous 'pogroms' of the Serbian population.[67]

The Serbian Ministry of Information also portrayed the Tudjman regime as neo-fascistic, making vague allusions to Aaron and Loftus's book *Ratlines*, with its description of the Vatican smuggling networks for Nazi war criminals. This time, however, the 'rat channels' were reversed, and instead of smuggling war criminals out of Europe, war criminals were now being smuggled back in – to Croatia. The strategy of welcoming back these former Ustaša was to be the precursor to a renewed Serbian genocide – a genocide that was to be identical to that of some fifty years before.[68] Dobrica Ćosić also saw Tudjman's regime as an emerging Nazi dictatorship. He had this to say in a published collection of his wartime essays:

We see in Croatia, many aspects of a Nazi resurrection. This state is governed by a totalitarian and chauvinistic regime, which has abolished the elementary civil and national rights of the Serbs by simply erasing them from its Constitution. This provoked a Serbian insurrection in Croatia, those who justly fear a new program of extermination, the same as the one during the Second World War to which they fell victim.[69]

Because of their historical victimisation, Ćosić had no difficulty in believing that a second genocide was on the way, necessitating a 'defensive war' against Croatian attacks.[70] Other Serbian writers urged Croatian Serbs not to surrender any weapons to the Croatian police, since politics there had blossomed into 'mass chauvinist hysteria'.[71] In justifying the 'log revolution', and other memorable moments in Krajina Serb history, links were drawn between the surprise night inspections for weapons carried out by the Ustaša in 1941 and a similar strategy of disarming mixed Serbian and Croatian units, supposedly instigated by the new Ministry of the Interior in 1991. This time, however, the Serbs had learned from their mistakes. Since the Ustaša had slaughtered large numbers of unarmed Serbs after disarming them, Serbs had learned this lesson of the past, and had refused to surrender their weapons.[72]

These Serbian warnings were sometimes supported by graphic evidence. Always interested in theatrics, the Krajina Serbs organised the exhumation of a Serbian mass grave from the Second World War. Serbian journalists were invited to photograph the bones of those who had been massacred by the Ustaša, providing a strong imagistic appeal to the Serbian nation to defend their 'brothers' against the threat of repeated genocide.[73] Dragutin Brčin's glossy and disturbing book of bodies supposedly mutilated at the hands of the Croats in 1991 was another example of a picture saying a thousand words. Brčin's views of the Croats echoed Kečmanović's theory of pseudospeciation. Because the Serbs were seen as a 'lower species', they were being targeted with biological and physical extermination 'for the third time this century – for the second time from the Ustashas in the last 50 years'. Brčin also spread the story of one 'Ustashi war criminal' who wore a necklace made of the fingers of Serbian children.[74] While this was originally an ancient Hindu myth, it seemed to have travelled far by the 1990s.

There is little doubt that many Serbs thought the threat of annihilation was real. Serbs in Croatia by 1991 began to complain of an 'ethnic tax' that they alone had to pay to the government.[75] Croatian Serb authorities complained of a 'formal brand' devised by the Croatian government to separate the Serbs from the rest of the population. As one writer reported, each Serb in Croatia was given the number 3 as the eighth figure of his personal identity number. This, as the Serbian Krajina President Goran Hadžić remarked, 'is nothing else for us than the David's star, our race label'.[76] Included in the general theme of Croatian genocide of Serbs were testimonials of those who had suffered in Croatian 'concentration camps' during the early part of the war. The journalist Nikola Marinović, searching for the Croatian version of the 1942 Wannsee Conference, traced the Croatian 'Final Solution' to a small cabal of HDZ leaders and representatives from Slavonia. These men supposedly met in early 1991 to form an organisation bent on 'the extermination of Serbs from western Srem and Eastern Slavonija'. According to Marinović, this group of HDZ officials 'started "everything" in all Croatia'. They deliberately planned and executed the genocide of Serbs, through a three-pronged strategy – replacing prominent Serbs, harassing the entire Serbian population, and then liquidating them.[77]

Marinović included a number of quotations from the initial meeting, unfortunately without indicating how he managed to get them. Either this was some form of dramatic licence, or Marinović was perched below the window through which the end of Serbdom was being contemplated. How he could have acquired such information is not explained; but, for some readers, detailed explanations would not have been necessary. Whatever the book's original purpose , it soon became part of a justification for the Serbian military actions that followed. Therefore it came as no surprise that the primary objects of Serbian attacks were the places where the Serbs were supposedly tortured and murdered by the Croats as a result of this key meeting. Thus, Poljane and Marino, villages near Pakrac, were noted as sites of mass atrocities, as were Kip, near Daruvar, and Moscenica and Cesko, near Sisak.[78] Similar atrocities were recounted for Vukovar, one of the first cities that fell to the Serbs. Here, Marinović described the 'hair-raising savagery' of the manager of the Vukovar Hospital, Vesna Bosanac, who earned the title of the 'Vukovar Mengele' after supposedly threatening one Serbian patient by putting a gun to his head, and then threatening to slit his throat, and then placing a bomb in his bed. Another patient was described as being beaten and then urinated on at a hospital near Pakrac. Other horrors, such as torture, euthanasia, the general denial of medical treatment to Serbian soldiers, and even murder of the wounded were also described here.[79]

Each region was seen as the venue for terrible atrocities committed by the Croatian National Guard, proving that the Serbs had had no choice but to shell the towns where these atrocities were supposedly taking place. Such descriptions instilled the notion that the new Croatian institutions, such as the police and even the medical services, were Serbophobic, and therefore part of a genocidal conspiracy. Certainly some of the testimonials were true. Serbs were beaten and mistreated. But what was significant for this book was why certain regions were selected, and what they signified. According to the Serbs' own accounts, a form of defensive ethnic cleansing had to take place to avoid a repetition of the Second World War.

The Orthodox Church also contributed to the increasing paranoia.

Spiritual Genocide (1994) outlined a continuous desecration of Serbian churches, claiming that more than 400 had been destroyed since 1941, leading the author to describe a 'total spiritual genocide', which continued from the time of the NDH, through the Communist era, to the conflict in the 1990s.[80] This work featured detailed descriptions of large numbers of bombed out churches, as well as photographs, drawing a link between the Second World War destruction of churches and their destruction in the 1990s. To stress the similarities between events in 1994 and 1941, Second World War photographs were mixed with more recent ones, all in grainy black and white – blurring the distinction between historic and contemporary atrocities.

The purpose behind this onslaught of subjective and emotive propaganda was clear – it buttressed Serbian arguments that the war was forced on the Serbian people. The Serbian Orthodox Church and its parishioners had been brought to the 'verge of annihilation'.[81] That this work appeared in 1994, after countless attacks on the Serbs in the international press for their destruction of Catholic churches and mosques, was no coincidence. Obviously Serbian churches were destroyed; but such one-sided portrayals were mirror images of Croatian publications. This even extended to a contest on a city-by-city basis between Serbian and Croatian propagandists, to see which national group had been the most victimised. Thus Croats published photographs and descriptions of the destruction of Catholic churches in Vukovar and Mostar, and the Serbs responded in kind with Orthodox ruins in the same cities.[82]

'Operation storm'

One of the most tragic aspects of the war in Croatia was Milošević's cynical handling of the Croatian Serbs after they were no longer useful to him. Seemingly abandoning his dream of creating a Greater Serbia, Milošević repackaged himself as a peacemaker in 1995, bringing the Bosnian Serbs to the negotiating table to sign the Dayton Accords. It was also the year that he abandoned the Croatian Serbs in Eastern Slavonia and Knin, and left the playing-field open for a Croatian offensive. With the way clear, the American negotiator Richard Holbrooke encouraged Tudjman to take control of the Serbian Krajina and Serbian-controlled north-western Bosnia.[83] In late April 1995, the Croats launched an attack on western Slavonia, and within 36 hours managed to take back the region, which had been violently taken by Serbian forces at the beginning of the conflict.[84] By the summer, much of the Serbian population in the former Srpska Krajina had fled, leaving towns and villages deserted.

By July, Tudjman had amassed an army of over 200,000 troops, ready to sweep into the Krajina. After calling for the surrender of the Serbian Krajina government and the handover of weapons, Tudjman launched 'Operation

Storm' on 4 August. While the Serbs had 40,000 troops and 400 tanks, they were no match for Croatian forces, who managed to seize Knin after only two days of fighting. The whole region fell in just 84 hours, as Serbs fled for their lives.[85] While it was clear that Milošević had left the Croatian Serbs to their fate, Serbian propagandists continued to advance the dangers of a Croatian genocide of Serbs. At this stage, the same arguments as before were used to highlight the consequences of Tudjman's conquest. While Milošević had little interest in reoccupying Croatia, the propaganda machine continued to advance the same arguments.

The Serbian Academy of Sciences and Arts soon reacted to the Croatian offensive, issuing a *Memorandum* to alert the public to the renewed dangers of genocide that lay ahead. SANU urged the Serbian government to mobilise without delay, since the Serbs were facing 'extinction and the obliteration of all traces of their existence in these lands'.[86] Once again, the spectre of Croatian fascist terror was reiterated, but SANU was at this stage trying to push the Serbian government to act. They claimed that some 300,000 Serbs had already been 'forcibly expelled' from Croatia, even before 'Operation Storm' had begun, and they urged the Serbian government to act against a 'repeated genocide'.[87] Svetozar Đurđević cited the 'speed at which the inhuman and uncivilized method of Croatization of the Krajina has been carried out' as proof of the 'vandal destruction and annihilation of all the traces and symbols of Serbian life, culture and spirituality in the region'. Franjo Tudjman, he argued, was only pursuing the same fascist policies that the NDH regime had followed some fifty years earlier. Serbs had to be killed, since they continued to be the main obstacle to Croatian expansionism in the Balkans.[88]

The Serbian Ministry of Information joined the fray, describing the offensive as 'the final solution to the Serbian question', while stressing the links between Croatian actions in 1941 and 1995. They too condemned Tudjman for wanting to create 'a pure Croatian state', through 'pure Croatism' in the Balkans. The Americans were also drawn into this 'Blitzkreig'. Having perfected their killing skills in Desert Storm they were looking for a small 'Balkan Storm'.[89] The Serbian Unity Congress also played their part, noting:

> The current civil and religious war in the former Yugoslavia is but the resumption of the 1941–1945 civil war in which the Croatian Fascists, collaborators of the Nazi regime, and Muslim religious extremists murdered between 600,000 and 1,200,000 Serbs. The issues are the same, the battlefields are the same, even the flags and army insignia are the same.[90]

By 1995–96, this type of imagery was increasingly common. It was almost impossible to find descriptions of the war in Croatia that did not refer explicitly to the links between the 1940s and the 1990s. Serbs were once again fighting against annihilation. It occurred to few of the participants that this was not a repeat of the past. Rather, it was as if they had actually gone back in time, and were reliving the struggles of their parents and grandparents. The motto 'Never Again' was constantly invoked by the Krajina Serbs, as proof that they were like the Jews during the Holocaust, ready to defend themselves against annihilation.[91] Sadly, however, it was not Tudjman, but Milošević who had sold them out. This time, the Croats were only taking advantage of an opportunity that had been given to them by the Serbian president.

Contemporary fears of the Catholic Church

Accusations of Vatican and Croatian Catholic complicity in genocide were popular in Serbian historical revisions. Their involvement in genocide was traced from the nineteenth century through to the first Yugoslavia, the Second World War, and into the Communist era. Such a pattern of Catholic 'Serbophobia' was also applied to an understanding of the war in Croatia during the 1990s. A popular fear among propagandists was that Serbs were being forcibly converted to Catholicism, as they had been during the 1940s. In 1995, the Serbian Ministry of Information claimed that the Croats had converted 11,000 Serbian children to Catholicism in just two and a half years. Another 14,000 Serbian children, some 90 per cent of the total in Croatia, were supposedly forced to enrol in Catholic schools – by implication they too were in the initial stages of assimilation. This 'plot' was revealed by Orthodox Church sources, who posited that the true intent behind this policy was not simply educational. Rather: 'Once they convert to Catholicism, the former Orthodox people will *automatically* become members of the Croatian nation, because Catholicism and Croatian nationality are equated in Croatia.'[92]

The overall Croatian plan, as a government official from Novi Sad maintained, aimed at converting 700,000 Serbs in Croatia to Catholicism, making them first 'Croatian Serbs', then 'Orthodox Croats', and then finally 'pure Croats', after their language, alphabet, Church and other symbols of their 'authentic and centuries old Serbian identity' had been destroyed.[93] Such writing demonstrated how fragile many officials thought Serbian identity truly was, and how easy it would be for the Catholic Church to destroy the Serbian nation, now that Croatia was independent. Needless to say, such theories were not backed up with the names of any of the schools actually involved, nor was there any type of documentation cited to support such accusations.

There were of course other more direct attacks on the Vatican itself, dealing with specific aspects of the war in Croatia and later in Bosnia. During the 1995 NATO air-strikes on Bosnian Serb military positions, the Vatican, and not the Germans or the Americans, was accused of genocide. One University of Belgrade professor was clear that the prime culprits behind the attack were the Pope and his followers, as during earlier times:

> [E]ncouragement came from Vatican clericalists pursuing the centuries-old goal of establishing the world Catholic multinational empire ... Pope John Paul II developed the doctrines of 'limited sovereignty', of 'humanitarian military intervention' and of 'disarming the aggressor'. The head of the Catholic Christian Church supported the idea of 'bombs for peace'. The peace that can be brought by bombs is the peace of extermination of Serbs in Croatia and B&H. For those who survive there is conversion to Catholicism or expulsion to the 'Belgrade Pashaluk', the territory that will remain to Serbia after Kosovo-Metohija and Vojvodina are again taken out of its jurisdiction.[94]

The imagery was curious. The Pope himself was charged with trying to exterminate the Bosnian Serbs, as part of an imperial project that could only be compared to the machinations of the old Holy Roman Empire during the sixteenth and seventeenth centuries. The idea that Serbs would be left with a small territory around Belgrade ('Pashaluk' referring to the old Ottoman regional divisions of Serbia) certainly exaggerated the extent of the bombing campaign, a campaign that never entered Serbia proper. Accusing the Pope of genocide was not overly controversial in Serbian circles, where Vatican plots to destroy the nation had seemingly existed since the Great Schism.

In general, Serbian propaganda disguised the reality of Serbian aggression in Croatia and Bosnia-Hercegovina. While the Serbs claimed only to be defending Serbs against annihilation, the Croatian government never advanced any deliberate policies to kill its Serbian population systematically. While the Serbian community was clearly demarcated and singled out in the new state, and while there was discrimination, xenophobia did not lead to genocide.

Croatian views of the war in Croatia

In many ways, Croatian propaganda mirrored that of the Serbs. The war in Croatia was traced to the age-old project of Greater Serbia, and numerous links between past and present were joined together. In understanding Serbian aggression, Croatian writers divided up their understanding of events into three separate categories. The first dealt with the Serbs as Nazis, seeking territorial expansion, or *Lebensraum*. Like the Czechs or the Poles, Croatia was doomed to be colonised, then enslaved. A second argument compared Greater Serbian style empire-building to the Holocaust. In the second argument, the Serbs had no real economic motivations for invading Croatia. Rather, their general hatred of the Croats drove them to round up and kill as many people as possible. The third argument relied on the work of Croatian psychiatrists. Serbs were analysed as a group, and their pathology was blamed for the war in Croatia. Both mentally and civilisationally inferior to the Croats, Serbian hatred, envy, and resentment towards them for having abandoned Yugoslavia were responsible for the Serb decision to invade.

Such a line of reasoning evolved into predictions of what would happen if the Serbs managed successfully to invade and occupy Croatia. Miroslav Brandt was perhaps the most vocal on what a reassertion of Serbian control would mean. 'Non-Serbian peoples,' he predicted, 'would be slaves, a subjugated mob, expected and doomed to extinction as separate national entities in the future, their land, area for colonisation and a target to exploit, brought to the level of provinces working for the benefit of a new giant, super-wealthy and carefree state centre of Belgrade.'[95] Brandt was particularly clear on what the Croats were fighting against by defending the Krajina and Eastern Slavonia from Serbian predations:

> These regions are simply resisting the annihilation of their particular national cultures, the persistent proven widely organised and continuous decades-long activities of the Greater-Serbian plutocratic oligarchy to primarily deprive the Croatian people of their own language, to impose upon them the Serbian language, to suppress Croatian literature and other forms of Croatian culture, to wipe out the Croatian national awareness, to destroy and prevent Croats from learning their own history and to crush their dignity, to annihilate their faith, to impoverish them, and by a discriminatory economic policy to drive the Croats away from their own millennium-long ethnic homeland and then systematically colonise these regions with Serbian nationals.[96]

Brandt's theme of economic exploitation was common. Bože Ćović also blamed Serbia's economic motives for the conflict. The Serbs were trying to compensate for their underdevelopment by exploiting the riches of Croatia. Since the Serbian economy was inefficient, burdened by losses and debts, and thus unable to 'stimulate its own creative potential', it needed Croatia as a colony to dominate and exploit.[97] Like Brandt, Ćović similarly argued that both Serbia and Montenegro, starved of resources, were keen to exploit Croatia, to enable the flow of riches from the periphery to the core.[98] Ćović was evidently no dependency theorist, and this aspect of his analysis soon gave way to analogies between Serbian economic exploitation and Nazi expansionist plans during the 1930s:

> Serbia needs new *lebensraum* and new economic resources (on the ethnically cleansed i.e. completely Serbian, territory) given that 'Greater Serbia' with only Bosnia-Herzegovina, Montenegro, Macedonia and the amputated parts of Croatia would find itself in the company of complete undeveloped areas ... It is a question of *lebensraum* and the concept of 'blood and soil' which ensure the new nation-building ambitions of 'Greater Serbia'. The problem of ethnic cleansing should be

stressed here, i.e. firstly forcing Croats and all other ethnic groups to flee, so that only the Serbs remain, and secondly settling Serbian colonists in the emptied areas.[99]

There was little evidence to support the claim that Serbs were trying to colonise all of Croatia, and, as I have argued earlier, they could have pushed further had they so desired, had not both leaders been committed to the annexation of Bosnia-Hercegovina. Nevertheless, the fears of economic exploitation were justifiable, given the fact that when these documents were written Serbian irregulars had been continually looting Croatian and Bosnian homes. At the same time, the use of the term *Lebensraum* served as a rebuttal to Serbian accusations that Tudjman and his government were composed of neo-Ustaša criminals. Accusing the Serbs of trying to exploit and dominate Croatia also covered up the very real machinations of the Croats in Bosnia-Hercegovina. While they accused the Serbs of expanding their territory and colonising a region that was not theirs, the Croats were doing the same thing. These themes were extremely common.

The long-awaited evil – Greater Serbia

The second key argument delved much deeper into the past, exposing many long-term Serbian plans for the invasion of Croatia – plans that were purportedly hatched well before Hitler and the Third Reich. In Ćović's view, the war in Croatia was 'the bloody finale of the long-prepared Greater Serbian plan of conquest', supposedly the culmination of two hundred years of planning.[100] Hitler's speech to the Reichstag in 1939 was often invoked – one that famously justified the invasion of Poland as a defensive measure to protect Poland's German minority.[101] The Serbian conspiracy, according to Ćović, consisted of claiming victimhood as a means of justifying territorial expansion:

> The notion of victim and victimization is extended to the evaluation of conditions in which the Serbs live in non-Serbian regions and [are] used for political action whenever a privilege is at stake. In recent years this myth has served to justify and promulgate the political thesis that all Serbs must live in one state. It is a screen for military aggression against Croatia and the realization of the Greater Serbia scheme.[102]

Ironically, Ćović did exactly what he accused the Serbs of doing themselves – invoking myths of persecution and holocaust in order to legitimate 'self-defensive' measures against the 'enemy'. Ćović seems to have been in no doubt that his own side was completely innocent and trustworthy, while the Serbs were evil and expansionist. While the regimes in Serbia and Croatia were surprisingly similar, writers like Ćović continued to argue that Serbian violence in the 1990s far surpassed anything that had happened during the Second World War, a statement that was to an extent correct, but served to masked the reality of this many-sided conflict.[103]

For many Croatian historians, the myth of Greater Serbia was all-consuming. The basis of Serbian national identity was territorial expansionism. Like some form of plague, the bloodlust to create a Greater Serbia could lie dormant for decades, before being unleashed on unsuspecting neighbours. Branko Miletić therefore asked somewhat conspiratorially: 'What drives the docile Serb peasant to rape, butcher and incinerate his peaceful Muslim or Croat neighbor?' The answer was of course: 'The double-edged theory of Greater Serbianism.' Greater Serbianism was supposedly 'double-edged' because it was worse than either fascism or Communism, since it made co-nationals feel 'politically and culturally threatened', and 'emboldened' at the same time.[104] Like Ćović, Miletić saw how Serbian leaders had used the rhetoric of victimisation to mobilise their people for war. In his tally of the costs of this ideology, Miletić concluded:

> Greater Serbianism has cost the lives of some 600,000 Croatians, 400,000 Muslims, 100,000 Albanians, and countless others this century, not to mention non-conformist Serbs, and even people not from the Balkans. It has ethnically cleansed some five million inhabitants since 1900, wounded, maimed and imprisoned over two million, and caused hundreds of billions of dollars worth of material damage.[105]

What Miletić offered was a complete picture of Serbian violence in the twentieth century. Each period of history was seen to be tragically the same; Serbs promoting Greater Serbia while killing hundreds of thousands of people. How exactly the author tallied these figures is not explained, nor would this have been particularly important. What was curious about these analyses of Serbian nationalism was how their assumption of the role of the victim was discussed. This was seen to be a purely Serbian strategy, not something that the Croats would ever have thought to employ.

Serbian Nazis and collective psychosis

It was certainly clear that Croatia was under serious threat by the beginning of 1991. As has been pointed out earlier, one-third of Croatia was occupied by this time, and the future of the country remained uncertain. It was in this climate of fear that mountains of seemingly spontaneous anti-Serbian propaganda began pouring out of Croatia. Certainly much of this was genuine, and there is no reason to doubt that most of these people truly believed, for good reason, that their country was in serious trouble. However, while Croatia was seemingly unable to defend herself against the Serbs, Tudjman and Milošević were already making plans together to carve up Bosnia-Hercegovina. That Croatia had enough soldiers, equipment and weapons to maintain a defensive war *and* an offensive war indicates that they were doing much better than they publicly admitted. As I pointed out earlier, Tudjman could well have liberated his country, had he not had wanted to push into Bosnia-Hercegovina.

As the war progressed, it became clear that Croatia's position was far stronger than people realised. While a climate of fear was created and certainly existed, it is doubtful that the Serbs could ever have taken all of Croatia. It is also doubtful that they wanted to. Nevertheless, the emphasis during this time was on rallying the people together, to project to the outside world an image of unity in the face of hardship. For this reason, much of what emerged from Croatia used images of the Second World War to make sense of the tragedy. Rather than appearing as the victims of one aggressive war, while simultaneously waging another in Bosnia, Croatian writers, architects, historians, and other academics strove to portray themselves as victims of genocide.

It seems that almost all facets of academic life in Croatia became subordinated to the war effort. Even such seemingly apolitical departments as Art History at Zagreb University contributed to the advancement of a victim position. In a picture book on the destruction of Croatia's ancient buildings and monuments, the editor described the 'culturocide' of the Croatian people, where Serbs were deliberately destroying ancient symbols of the past in order to 'annihilate ... the consciousness of our existence in time and space'.[106] Much of this project aimed to demonstrate that Croatia was part of Europe. This 'European' identity was crucial throughout the war. Croats used it to court Western aid, but also, more importantly, to give some form of hope to the people who were suffering through the war. What was important was that a 'European' country was being destroyed by an Eastern power.

Croatian scientists at the prestigious Ruder Bošković Institute also became embroiled in the conflict, after they realised that 'total destruction' was immanent. Most of this work involved contacting outside scientific agencies through a variety of connections in order to sway world opinion in favour of Croatia. These scientists sent more than 9,000 letters and petitions abroad, and many met with favourable responses.[107] Many scientists expressed a typical Croatian view of the war as a conflict between, 'two different types of people', concluding that, 'Western catholics and Byzantine orthodoxes simply do not belong together'. Everything was reduced to an 'ethnic clash' between the, 'democratically oriented West ... and the bolshevik East'.[108]

This was coupled with accusations of Serbian genocidal ambition. American institutions from the Fulbright Commission to the White House were subjected to intense public relations efforts. A vigorous e-mail campaign was also launched, to counter the 'Goebbelsian campaign of lies', which had 'enslaved the Albanians in Kosovo'. One of the stock e-mails also contained numerous references to 'Great Serbian totalitarianism' and Serb attempts to impose themselves as a 'master race' over other nations in the Balkans.[109] That much of the scientific community was involved in this massive public relations effort demonstrated the extent to which Croats were convinced of the genocidal threat of the Serbs. The whole nation, it seemed, was mobilised for war.

Other groups, such as the Association of Architects of Mostar, contributed their photographs of the 'urban genocide against Mostar'.[110] For the authors, Mostar constituted a bridge between East and West, one that was destroyed by the Serbs, for ever sealing the fate of their relations with the Croats. Serbs here were accused of trying to 'exterminate the Croat and Moslem being' by laying waste to a town that figured as a religious and cultural crossroads.[111] There is no doubt that the Serbs destroyed at least half the major buildings in the town. Certainly there was much barbarity in the attack on Mostar – the Serbs shelled nine out of ten of Mostar's bridges. Nevertheless, the Croats (not the Serbs) destroyed the famous Stari Most, or Old Bridge, which still lies in pieces. Still others combined a variety of formats to develop an image of Serbian aggression. Đorđe Obradović's *Suffering of Dubrovnik* was a strange mixture of historical novel (set during the siege), glossy before-and-after pictures, and children's drawings of the war.[112]

A still more interesting aspect of the war was the co-option of the psychiatric profession. Several psychiatrists quickly abandoned their professionalism, along with many of the well-established rules of psychiatry, to defend their country against Serbian genocide. Wartime writing was intended to prove that Serbs had actually internalised their civilisational differences in many psychologically nuanced ways. Trained medical professionals were encouraged to buttress the work of Croatian propagandists with psychiatric jargon. That such theories were published in the prestigious *Croatian Medical Journal* ensured maximum credibility. Breaking perhaps the first and most important rule of psychiatry, trying to understand the individual before making a diagnosis, Eduard Klain, in his article, 'Yugoslavia as a Group', isolated certain Serbian group traits in order come to terms with the war in Croatia. Through the use of psychiatric language, he concluded:

> The Serbs are burdened with an inferiority complex compared to the peoples of the western part of Yugoslavia, for they are conscious that they are on a lower level of civilisation. They try to get rid of that feeling by means of various defence mechanisms, such as negation, projections, denial and destruction. The Serbs are inclined to regress to a schizoparanoid position and exhibit an archaic type of aggression which can explain the torturing of the wounded and massacring dead bodies.[113]

How all Serbs could exhibit the same traits was not explained, nor was it clear why and how the Serbs were civilisationally inferior. While Klain's theories may well have been useful for analysing many of the more sadistic Serbian war criminals, he proposed his analysis for all Serbs, not a select group. The psychiatrist Viktor Gruden similarly used the vocabulary of his profession. The Serbs were identified as being in a 'vicious circle of frustration aggression' compounded with a 'collective paranoia'. The Serbian 'disintegrated self' was blamed for their 'their tendency to massacre the Croats', over which they seemingly had no choice. Much of this aggression had to do with the Easternness, and therefore the inferiority, of the Serbs. There was no doubt in Gruden's mind that:

> [T]he Serbs envy them [the Croats] and because they [the Serbs] are inferior ...
> The Croats are not only a biological being (like the Serbs) but a psychological one
> as well. The Serbs also feel guilty, therefore their only reaction is a tendency to
> destroy the source of frustration, hence the source of destruction and the impulse
> to demolish everything that is related to the Croats.'[114]

In other words, the Croats were more Western, more enlightened, more open, and more democratic – the Serbs were merely trying to destroy what they could never hope to be.

The Serbs were similarly diagnosed (collectively) as suffering from a 'paranoiac collective unconsciousness', and a 'malignant ethnocentrism'. The war in Croatia was thus broken down into a conflict between a 'paranoic political culture' and a 'narcissistic political culture', the former (Serbian) seemingly the result of a demented political mind. The latter (Croatian) was denoted as peaceful and 'on a higher level of civilisation'. Further conclusions that 'Serbs are militant and primitive, a nation of death and necrophilia, wild barbarians, the greatest vultures of political victories, descendants of Turkish bastardism [and] disturbing factors in Croatia', were rounded off with the lamentation: 'unhappy is the nation that has Serbs as its neighbours'.[115]

Generally, the first rule of psychiatry is to approach each subject as an individual, not as part of a collective. Under standard medical definitions, it is simply impossible to diagnose a 'group' as one would an individual. Only individuals can be defined as having psychiatric disorders under the DSM-III classification system – the standard system for understanding and classifying mental illnesses. While individuals may be influenced by membership in a collective, no two individuals possess an identical psychology. One is only able to comprehend the psychology of an individual after many hours of patient study and interview sessions. To lump a group of diverse individuals into a racial category, treat them as a individual and study them accordingly was truly an entirely pointless endeavour. From a psychiatric perspective it was sloppy and unprofessional. From a political standpoint, however, it made perfect sense. Psychiatrists, like artists, academics, and politicians, were all

213

seemingly under attack from genocidal Serbs, and therefore had to use all means at their disposal to counter the threat.

Conclusions

Representations of the past proved to be absolutely crucial to understanding and justifying Serbian and Croatian nationalism during the war in Croatia. Each side claimed to be a victim of the other, both during the Communist period, and after, as the Federation disintegrated. While references to earlier periods of history were important, the Second World War provided the most important stock of metaphors and ideas. Of central importance throughout the conflict was the idea that actions during the war were merely a continuation of the past. Both sides were accused of acting or performing as their parents and grandparents had earlier in the twentieth century. Serbian actions were merely a continuation of a desire to create a Greater Serbia, while Croats were simply trying to resurrect the NDH. In both cases, genocide was presented as the inevitable result.

In reviewing the main arguments of both sides, a strong performative aspect was evident. Each side portrayed themselves as victims, and eventually, by manipulating public opinion within their own countries, succeeded in creating an aura of victimhood by constantly reiterating this perceived reality, a process identified by both Weber and Butler.[116] Campbell's definition of 'narrativizing' could also be found here. Serbian and Croatian writers both tried to create the types of 'stories' Campbell identified, with an 'ordered plot', a 'cast of characters', 'attributable motivations', and 'lessons for the future'.[117] In both cases, a past history of victimisation and genocide was purposefully manufactured and presented to a receptive audience. In both cases, these 'stories' proved to be absolutely essential in creating and supporting war.

NOTES

1 Ivo Banac, *The National Question in Yugoslavia: Origins, History, Politics* (Ithaca, NY: Cornell University Press, 1992) p. 55.
2 Branimir Anzulović, *Heavenly Serbia: From Myth to Genocide* (London: C. Hurst & Company, 1999) pp. 96–7.
3 See Rusmir Mahmutćehanjić, 'The Road to War', in Branka Magaš and Ivo Žanić (eds), *The War in Croatia and Bosnia-Herzegovina 1991–1995* (London: Frank Cass, 2001) pp. 136–7.
4 As discussed in Veljko Vujačić, 'Serbian Nationalism, Slobodan Milosevic and the Origins of the Yugoslav War', *The Harriman Review*, 8:4 (December 1995) www.suc.org/politics/papers/history/vujacic.html (accessed 5 July 1999).
5 Dobrica Čosić, *L'éffondrement de la Yougoslavie: positions d'un resistant* (Paris: L'Age D'Homme, 1994) p. 40. (My translation.)

6 Vujačić, 'Serbian Nationalism, Slobodan Milosevic and the Origins of the Yugoslav War'.

7 *Ibid.*

8 Association of University Teachers and Scholars of Serbia, *Information on the New Crime of Genocide Against the Serbian People Within the Administrative Borders of Croatia* (Belgrade: The Association of University Teachers and Scholars of Serbia, 1991) p. 6.

9 Ratko Marković, 'What are Yugoslavia's Internal Borders?', in Stanoje Ivanović (ed.), *The Creation and Changes of the Internal Borders of Yugoslavia* (Belgrade: Ministry of Information of the Republic of Yugoslavia, 1992) pp. 9–12. This point is also raised by Kosta Čavoški, 'The Formation of Borders and the Serbian Question', also in Ivanović (ed.), *The Creation and Changes of the Internal Borders of Yugoslavia*, pp. 33–41.

10 Serbian Unity Congress, 'Yugoslav Crisis – One Hundred Irrefutable Facts' (Serbian Unity Congress, 1996) www.suc.org/politics/100facts/index.html (accessed 16 February 2000).

11 *Ibid.*

12 *Ibid.*

13 Slobodan Samardzić, 'Yugoslav Federalism – Unsuccessful Model of a Multinational Community' (Belgrade: Institute of European Studies, Belgrade, 1994) www.suc.org/politics/papers/history/samard.html (accessed 5 July 1999).

14 Marko Pavlović, 'Yugoslavia and Serbian Lands' in Ivanović (ed.), *The Creation and Changes of the Internal Borders of Yugoslavia*, pp. 15–16.

15 *Ibid.* p. 16.

16 Ivan Crkvenčić and Mladen Klemenčić, *Aggression Against Croatia: Geopolitical and Demographic Facts* (Zagreb: Republic of Croatia Central Bureau of Statistics, 1993) p. 9.

17 Discussed in Bože Ćović (ed.), *Croatia Between War and Independence* (Zagreb: University of Zagreb/OKC-Zagreb, 1991) pp. 31–3.

18 Crkvenčić and Klemenčić, *Aggression Against Croatia*, p. 12.

19 Ćosić, *Croatia Between War and Independence*, p. 34.

20 *Ibid.* p. 33.

21 Michel Roux, *Les Albanais en Yougoslavie minorité nationale, territoire et développement* (Paris: Editions de la Maison des sciences de l'homme, 1992) p. 443.

22 Momčilo Zečević, 'Second Phase 1918–1941', in Božidar Zevčević (ed.), *The Uprooting: A Dossier of the Croatian Genocide Policy Against the Serbs* (Belgrade: Velanto International, 1992) p. 122.

23 Serbian Unity Congress, 'Yugoslav Crisis'.

24 Samardzić, 'Yugoslav Federalism'.

25 See Marcus Tanner, *Croatia: A Nation Forged in War* (New Haven, CT: Yale University Press, 1997) pp. 181–2.

26 Mirko Mirković, 'Fourth Phase: 1945–1990', in Zevčević (ed.), *The Uprooting*, pp. 117–18.

27 *Ibid.*

28 *Ibid.* p. 38.

29 Anzulović, *Heavenly Serbia*, pp. 95–6.

30 For a discussion, see Sabrina Petra Ramet, *Nationalism and Federalism in Yugoslavia 1962–1991* (Bloomington, IN: Indiana University Press, 1992) pp. 188–9.

31 *Ibid.* pp. 90–1.

32 Josip Jurčević, 'The Serbian Armed Aggression Against Croatia From 1990 to 1995', in Aleksander Ravlić (ed.), *Southeastern Europe 1918–1995* (Zagreb: Croatian Heritage Foundation & Croatian Information Centre, 1998), http://www.hic.hr/books/seeurope/index-e.htm#top (accessed 5 July 1999); see also Josip Šentija, 'Croatia from

215

1941 to 1991' (Zagreb: University of Zagreb/Matica Hrvatska Iseljenika, 1994) p. 7.

33 Radovan Pavić, 'Greater Serbia from 1844 to 1990/91', in Bože Čović (ed.), *Roots of Serbian Aggression Debates, Documents, Cartographic Reviews* (Zagreb: Centar za Strane Jezike/AGM, 1993) p. 238.

34 *Ibid.* p. 273.

35 Dragutin Pavličević, 'Persecution and Liquidation of Croats on Croatian Territory From 1903 To 1941', in Ravlić (ed.), *Southeastern Europe 1918–1995*.

36 Dušan Kečmanović, *The Mass Psychology of Ethnonationalism* (New York: Plenum Press, 1996) p. 61.

37 Čović, *Croatia Between War and Independence*, pp. 123–5.

38 Ramet, *Nationalism and Federalism in Yugoslavia*, pp. 98–9.

39 Miroslav Brandt, 'The Antimemorandum', in Čović (ed.), *Roots of Serbian Aggression*, p. 232.

40 Milovan Djilas, *The New Class: An Analysis of the Communist System* (New York: Praeger Publishing, 1957). For a good overview of this theory, see pp. 25–31.

41 Brandt, 'The Antimemorandum', p. 269.

42 *Ibid.* p. 251.

43 Stjepan Meštrović, Miroslav Goreta, and Slaven Letica: *The Road from Paradise: Prospects for Democracy in Eastern Europe* (Lexington, KY: The University Press of Kentucky, 1993) p. x.

44 *Ibid.* p. xii.

45 *Ibid.* p. 33.

46 *Ibid.* p. 34.

47 *Ibid.* p. 59.

48 *Ibid.* p. 36.

49 Other Croatian writers made similar parallels. One psychiatrist, for example, tried to understand how the Serbs had managed to 'dominate' the Communist system so successfully. His conclusions were similar to those of Meštrović and his colleagues: '[the] Communist ideology based on the political mechanism of splitting, paranoid projection, dual thinking and double standards . . . has struck the deepest roots among the Serbs'. He further concluded that the Serbian culture is inimical to democracy, when he states that, 'Democratic elections in Croatia . . . markedly increased the frustrations and anxiety of the Serbian paranoiac political mind. The fear of something new and of the arrival of democracy, the likelihood of losing unjustly obtained privileges . . . result in aggressive impulses (displacement of frustration by aggression)'. See M. Jakoljević, 'Psychiatric Perspectives of the War in Croatia During 1990–1991: Sociopolitical Perspectives', *Croatian Medical Journal*, War Supplement 2:33 (1991) p. 10.

50 Parts of this section first appeared as an article I published in 2001. See 'La Croatie : un exemple d'« épuration langagière »?', *Raisons Politiques*, 2 (May 2001).

51 Nouvel Observateur et Raporteurs sans Frontières, *Le Livre Noir de L'ex-Yougoslavie: Purification Ethnique et Crimes de Guerre* (Paris: Publications Arléa, 1993) p. 125. See also Barbara Jelavich, *History of the Balkans Volume II* (London: Cambridge University Press, 1993) p. 396.

52 C. Michael McAdams, 'The Demise of "Serbo-Croatian"' (Zagreb: Croatian Information Center Web Page, 1998) www.algonet.se/~bevanda/mceng.htm (accessed 18 June 1998).

53 Quoted in Dubravka Ugrešić, *The Culture of Lies* (London: Phoenix House, 1998) pp. 64–5.

54 For an excellent discussion of linguistic changes in the new Croatia, see Chris Hedges, 'Words Replacing Bullets in Latest Balkan Battle', *The Globe and Mail* (16 May 1996).

55 Marijan Krmpotić, 'Why is Croatian Language Still Suppressed in Croatia?', *NDH* (December 1997) www.cdsp.neu.edu/info/students/marko/ndh/ndh2.html (accessed 18 June 1998).

56 *Ibid.*

57 Celia Hawksworth, *Colloquial Serbo-Croat* (London: Routledge, 1993) p. xv.

58 Richard Holbrooke, *To End a War* (New York: Random House, 1998) p. 232.

59 Umut Ozkirimli, *Theories of Nationalism: A Critical Introduction* (London: Macmillan, 2000) p. 220.

60 Milan Lučić, *Terror Nad Srbima '91/The Extermination of Serbs '91* (Novi Sad: Pokrajinski sekretarijat za informacije AP Vojvodine, 1991) p. 2.

61 Vera Vratusa-Zunjić, 'The Intrinsic Connection Between Endogenous and Exogenous Factors of Social (Dis)integration: A Sketch of the Yugoslav Case', *Dialogue*, 22–23 (June/September 1997) www.bglink.com/business/dialogue/vratusa.html (accessed 18 June 1998).

62 *Ibid.*

63 *Ibid.*

64 Mile Dakić, *The Serbian Krayina: Historical Roots and Its Rebirth* (Knin: Information Agency of the Republic of Serbian Krayina, 1994) p. 48.

65 Jovan Ilić, 'Characteristics and Importance of Some Ethno-National and Political-Geographic Factors Relevant for the Possible Political-Legal Disintegration of Yugoslavia' in Ivanović (ed.), *The Creation and Changes of the Internal Borders of Yugoslavia*, p. 93.

66 This unfortunate shift in loyalties is discussed in Laura Silber and Alan Little, *The Death of Yugoslavia* (London: BBC Books, 1993) pp. 186–8.

67 Svetozar Đurđević's views were typical of this type of thinking: 'The unprecedented national-chauvinist euphoria in Croatia has resulted in the renewed hoisting of the chequered banner under which the *Ustashe* in World War II *exterminated* innocent Serbian civilians, the aged, women and children. The political scene of Croatia has been filled again with ideologists of the Ustashe ideology and their progeny.' See Đurđević, *The Continuity of a Crime: The Final Settlement of the Serbian Question in Croatia* (Belgrade: IDEA Publishing House, November 1995).

68 The Ministry wrote, 'By opening doors to the escaped and long hidden Ustashi criminals, Tudjman has sufficiently clearly announced a new banishment, extermination or assimilation of the Serbs who remained within his reach.' See: Serbian Ministry of Information, '"Blitz-Krieg" Aggression as a Method of "Ethnic Cleansing" of the Serbs: The Road of Crime "Final Solution to the Serbian Question in Croatia"' (Belgrade: Serbian Ministry of Information, 1995) www.yugoslavia.com/Bulletin/95/9509/950901.htm (accessed 18 June 1998).

69 Ćosić, *L'éffondrement de la Yougoslavie*, pp. 58–9. (My translation.)

70 *Ibid.* p. 78.

71 Dušan Vilić and Boško Todorović, *Breaking of Yugoslavia and Armed Secession of Croatia* (Beli Manastir: Cultura Centre 'Vuk Karadzić', 1996) pp. 14–15.

72 *Ibid.* p. 16.

73 Glenn Bowman, 'Xenophobia, Phantasy and the Nation: The Logic of Ethnic Violence in Former Yugoslavia', in Michael Freeman, Dragomir Pantić, and Dušan Janjić (eds), *Nationalism and Minorities* (Belgrade: Institute of Social Sciences, 1995) pp. 56–7.

74 Dragutin Brčin (ed.), *Genocide Once Again: The Ustasha Terror Over Serbs in 1991* (Belgrade: Serbian Ministry of Information, 1991) pp. 3–5.

75 Radmila Nakrada, *The Disintegration of Yugoslavia and the New World Order* (Belgrade: Institute for European Studies, 1994–5) p. 378.

76 Quoted in Zečević, *The Uprooting*, pp. 8; 126.
77 Nikola Marinović, *Stories from Hell: Confessions of Serbs, Tortured in the Concentration Camps in Croatia and Bosnia and Herzegovina in 1991 and 1992* (Belgrade: Serbian Ministry of Information, 1993) pp. 12–13.
78 *Ibid.* p. 14.
79 *Ibid.* pp. 21–2.
80 Slobodan Mileusnić, *Spiritual Genocide 1991–1993* (Belgrade: Belgrade Museum of the Serbian Orthodox Church, 1995) p. 7.
81 *Ibid* p. 8.
82 Brčin, *Genocide Once Again*, pp. 13–16.
83 Holbrooke, *To End a War*, pp. 160–2.
84 Tanner, *Croatia*, p. 294.
85 Tim Judah, *The Serbs: History, Myth and the Destruction of Yugoslavia* (New Haven, CT: Yale University Press, 1997) pp. 195–8.
86 Serbian Academy of Arts and Science, 'Memorandum on the Ethnic Cleansing of and Genocide Against the Serb People of Croatia and Krajina', *Review of International Affairs*, 46 (15 November, 1995) p. 13.
87 *Ibid.* p. 13.
88 Đurđević, *The Continuity of a Crime*, p. 7 (italics mine.) This perhaps reflected Slobodan Kljakić's earlier argument that Tudjman's regime was a resurrection of the NDH, and that hence 'The resistence of Serbs in Croatia against such terror, genocidal threats and against actions of Croatian authorities was logical and necessary': see Slobodan Kljakić, *A Conspiracy of Silence: Genocide in the Independent State of Croatia and Concentration Camp Jasenovac* (Belgrade: The Ministry of Information of the Republic of Serbia, 1991) p. 46.
89 Serbian Ministry of Information, '"Blitz-Krieg" Aggression as a Method of "Ethnic Cleansing" of the Serbs.'
90 Serbian Unity Congress, 'Yugoslav Crisis – One Hundred Irrefutable Facts'.
91 *Ibid.*
92 Jovan Pokrajac, 'Religious Instruction for New Croats', *Serbia: News, Comments, Documents, Facts, Analysis*, 41 (February 1995) pp. 22–3. (Italics mine.)
93 Lučić *Terror Nad Srbima '91* p. 1.
94 Vratusa-Zunjić, 'The Intrinsic Connection Between Endogenous and Exogenous Factors of Social (Dis)integration'.
95 Brandt, 'The Antimemorandum', p. 245.
96 *Ibid.* pp. 247–8. (Italics mine.)
97 Ćosić, *L'éffondrement de la Yougoslavie*, p. 46.
98 *Ibid.* p. 68.
99 *Ibid.* p. 71. Dusko Topalović, a self-styled 'geopolitician', similarly analyses the 'battle for Serbian Lebensraum' and 'blood and soil', describing the similarities between Serbs and Nazis. See his 'The Territorialization of the "Greater Serbian" Idea', in Ante Beljo and Bozica Erčegovac-Jambrović (eds), *Genocide: Ethnic Cleansing in Northwestern Bosnia* (Zagreb: Croatian Information Center, 1993) p. 11–12. Another contribution in the same book by Vladimir Tonković also described Serbian activities in the light of the Holocaust. See 'In Memoriam to Innocent Victims', p. 101.
100 At the same time, Serbian aggression would also be compared with Nazism. Playing the victim, Ćović argued, 'what we are faced with is an aggressive and expansionist strategy, identical to the plans and policies pursued by Hitler, Mussolini and Stalin in their time …': Ćović (ed.), *Roots of Serbian Aggression: Debates, Documents, Cartographic Reviews*, p. 89.

101 *Ibid.* pp. 89–90.

102 *Ibid.* p. 63.

103 *Ibid.* p. 90.

104 Branko Miletić, 'History: Causes of Serbian Aggression' (Zagreb: Croatian Information Center Web Page, 1998) www.algonet.se/~bevanda/aggression.htm (accessed 18 June 1998).

105 *Ibid.*

106 Radovan Ivančević (ed.), *Cultural Heritage of Croatia in the War 1991–1992* (Zagreb: Hrvatska Sveučilišna Naklada, 1993), p. 1. For another pictorial account of the war, see Ivo Lajtman (ed.) *War Crimes Against Croatia* (Zagreb: Verčenji list, 1991).

107 Greta Pifat-Mrzljak (ed.), *Scientists Against the War in Croatia: World Responses to the Ruđer Bošković Institute's Endeavour for Peace in Croatia* (Zagreb: Hrvatska Sveučilišna Naklada, 1992) p. 5.

108 See Nikola Cindro's letter, *ibid.* p. 13.

109 *Ibid.* pp. 465–6.

110 Association of Architects of Mostar, *Mostar 92 Urbicide* (Mostar: Croatian Defence Council, 1992) p. 6.

111 *Ibid.* p. 24.

112 See Đorđe Obradović, *Suffering of Dubrovnik* (Dubrovnik: Dubrovački Vjesnik, 1993).

113 Eduard Klain, 'Yugoslavia as a Group', *Croatian Medical Journal*, 33 (1992) (War Supplement 1) pp. 3–14. I first found this article discussed in Predrag Kaličanin, *Stresses of War* (Belgrade: Institute for Mental Health, 1993), and later verified the quotations for myself against the original.

114 *Ibid.* p. 9.

115 M. Jakovljević, 'Psychiatric Perspectives of the War against Croatia ', *Croatian Medical Journal*, 33 (1992) (War Supplement 2), pp. 10–18. As with Klain's article, I first found this discussed in Kaličanin, *Stresses of War*, and later verified the quotations for myself against the original.

116 Cynthia Weber, 'Performative States,' *Millennium: Journal of International Studies*, 27: 1 (1998).

117 David Campbell, *Politics Without Principle: Sovereignty, Ethics and the Narratives of the Gulf War* (Boulder, CO: Lynne Rienner, 1993).

8

'Greater Serbia' and 'Greater Croatia': the Moslem question in Bosnia-Hercegovina

We live in the borderland between two worlds, on the border between nations, within everybody's reach, always someone's scapegoat. Against us the waves of history break, as if against a cliff. (Meša Selimoviš: Dervish and Death)[1]

I can see that the situation is far more complicated and more difficult than other problems I have seen, even Cambodia. It is the peculiar three-sided nature of the struggle here that makes it so difficult. Everyone says that most people do not want this to happen. Yet it does. Everybody says it must stop. Yet it doesn't. (Richard Holbrooke: To End a War)[2]

WHILE THIS STUDY has focused on the continuous and vitriolic debate over history and current events pursued by Serbian and Croatian politicians, historians, and journalists, another aspect of the war of words and images deserves special consideration. The debate over Bosnia-Hercegovina was of immense importance throughout the crisis. Both Milošević and Tudjman, together with their nationalist supporters, dreamed of creating their respective 'Greater Serbias' and 'Greater Croatias'. In the Bosnian crisis, Serbs and Croats often worked together, and, as early as 1991, Milošević and Tudjman had carved up Bosnia on paper. At a diplomatic cocktail party with Western leaders in London, Tudjman was the first to boast of his geopolitical ambitions, famously drawing a detailed map on a napkin.[3] In Bosnia, the Moslems were seen as the primary threat to the creating of larger national states. Serbian and Croatian machinations, including the production of propaganda, thus followed very similar strategies.

Incorporating chunks of Bosnia-Hercegovina into Croatia and Serbia became central to the legitimacy of both governments, who had pledged to unite Diaspora nationals throughout the region. In line with a cyclical view of history, Serbian and Croatian leaders argued that many of the Falls suffered by their peoples could be rectified once the size and power of the nation-state had been expanded. Then, and only then, could all co-nationals be safe from the threat of genocide. Such political ends were buttressed by distinctly military objectives. For Croatia, the addition of Bosnian and Hercegovinian lands would have substantially reduced its eastern border with Serbia, creating an important buffer zone between Dalmatia and Serbia proper. The Serbs likewise saw the merits of incorporating this geo-strategic region into their smaller rump-Yugoslavia, giving them a much larger common border with Croatia. Each regime thus had political and military objectives in mind, which made the annexation of Bosnian territory paramount.

However, both nations had had historic claims to Bosnia-Hercegovina – Milošević and Tudjman were hardly original. In 1908, Jovan Cvijić produced 'The Annexation of Bosnia-Herzegovina and the Serb Issue', claiming this territory as the 'central region and core' of an imagined expanded Serbian state. Similarly, Stjepan Radić, a short time after, published his own study: 'The Live Croatian Rights to Bosnia-Herzegovina', arguing that Bosnia had only flourished when Austria-Hungary had been in control. Thus, logically, Croatia could and should claim the region for itself, as the only agent capable of insuring 'peace, legal order and progress'. The fact that Bosnia-Hercegovina was surrounded on three sides by Croatia, and thus formed (echoing Cvijić) 'the core of the old Croatian state', only sweetened the argument.[4] However, while some contemporary claims reflected the older musings of Cvijić and Radić, much of the discourse would be entirely new.

Primordial and constructed nations: the case of the Bosnian Moslems

Myths of victimisation and persecution were of central importance in legitimating the war in Bosnia-Hercegovina, a war that today evokes images of mass rape, torture, indiscriminate killing, and 'collection centres' – purportedly the first functional concentration camps in Europe since the Second World War. In delineating the use of such propaganda, it will be useful to focus on several specific themes:

1   Firstly, the idea of Moslems as either ethnic Croats or Serbs; and Moslem nationalism as invented or constructed;
2   Secondly, the notion that Bosnia-Herzegovina had historically been either Serbian or Croatian;
3   Thirdly, that claims to Moslem national identity and autonomy concealed an Islamic conspiracy to take over Europe.

While the third theme will be discussed later, it is useful to understand the first one clearly. To summarise this argument: while the Moslems of Bosnia had been forced to convert to Islam, certain linguistic and cultural attributes still marked them as either Serb or Croat. Bosnian Moslems were seen to be members of one religious community, while at the same time belonging to an altogether different ethnic group. Because of these highly contested ethnic and historical 'facts', Serbian and Croatian leaders both argued that Moslems were Fallen members of their own nation, who had been forced to abandon their true identity after Ottoman invasion. Military leaders argued that they were simply 'liberating' parts of their ethnic homeland that had long been submerged under foreign rule, while 'freeing' Moslems from their artificial attachments.

Such arguments were possible only because Moslem identity was not taken seriously by either side. While both Serbs and Croats shared a view of their nations as having precise racial and national origins, complete with national myths and legends, Bosnian Moslem nationalism de-emphasised ethnicity, preferring to focus on shared cultural practices, social traditions, common experiences, and religious faith. Such forms of collective identity were condemned as weaker and therefore illegitimate when compared with more 'concrete' nationalist assertions. While Serbs and Croats saw themselves as primordial nations, the Moslem nation was denounced as constructed, an artificial creation fabricated by the Moslems and Josip Broz Tito.

One major debate over the status of the Moslems, carried out in the summer of 1990 in the Sarajevo daily *Oslobodenje*, concluded that while the Serbs and Croats were 'natural' nations, based on 'unambiguous and common ethnic origin', Moslem identity was based on 'psychological identification', subject to self-observation. They were therefore seen as an 'invented nation' – not to be considered relevant in the more important dispute between 'natural' Serbs and Croats.[5] Thus the Croatian writer Vladimir Mrkoci could argue a year after the Dayton Accords that the division of Bosnia was perfectly understandable, 'a process that appeared with the absence of external force, a natural, although belated process, of national enlightenment and unification, because Bosnia-Hercegovina is one of the last national knots of Europe that will sooner or later have to be untied to the end'. Multicultural Bosnia, at least for this author, was nothing more than a 'meaningless phrase'.[6] For Serbian and Croatian policy-makers, invented nations had no real histories, and could not claim to have ever been chosen, divine, or even to have suffered a Fall. Fortunately, outside powers did not see the importance of such distinctions.[7]

The 'naturalness' of Serbian and Croatian claims to territory was privileged over the artificial and constructed nature of Moslem identity. Gone was the narcissism of minor differences, and the myths of 'counteridentification', as Serbs and Croats worked towards a common goal. Since the Moslems were not an ethnic nation, they logically belonged to another ethnic group. Serbs would thus claim the Moslems as their own, and Croats would do the same. The idealised presentation of a multicultural, tolerant Bosnia-Hercegovina, long favoured in Titoist Yugoslavia, was summarily rejected. While Serbs constituted some 31.1 per cent of the population and the Croats some 17.3 per cent, the Moslems (43.7 per cent) could now be operationalised as a group of ethnic 'undecideds'. Their population would provide an ethnic 'swing vote' – badly needed by both sides in their attempts to expand national boundaries.[8] The key problem of course, was that Serbs, Croats and Moslems were found throughout the republic – there were few homogeneous enclaves. According to the 1991 census, Serbs could be found in 94.5 per cent of the republic's territory, Moslems in 94 per cent, and Croats in 70 per cent. Clearly, any carve-up would be messy and dangerous.[9]

Serbian and Croatian reactions to the Bosnian Moslems presented clear examples of how a cyclical view of time was represented. Moslems had abandoned their 'true' identity; they represented the historic Fall of both the Serb and Croat nations. Now, with the disintegration of Yugoslavia, both groups had a golden opportunity to right the wrongs of history, to join former national lands and people to an enlarged national state. Kečmanović's themes of 'watershed' and 'turning-point' are useful here.[10] Both of these types of myth suggest a change in the historical destiny of the nation, when the nation is at last able to correct the injustices of the past. In this case, the historic injustice was the conversion of Serbs, or Croats, to Islam, and the loss of these people and their lands.

Denouncing constructed nationalism and Islam

While their nationalism was publicly denounced, Bosnian Moslems did consider themselves to be a defined national group. While they were willing to share power with Serbs and Croats within the country, they had no intention of being incorporated into an expanded Serbian or Croatian state. When Alija Izetbegović formed his Party of Democratic Action (SDA) in May 1990, it became clear to Serbian and Croatian leaders that the Moslems would not be so easily assimilated, or relinquish their desire to preserve a multinational, multiconfessional republic. While appealing to Moslems with its green banners and crescents, the official policy of the SDA was the preservation of a tolerant and unitary Bosnia, with national and religious rights for all.[11] Most of the SDA's actions, as well as the uncontroversial Bosnian flag (with its Kotromanić fleur-de-lis from the medieval period) seemed to support this claim.[12]

Nevertheless, the presence of a Moslem ruling party, even one committed to multiculturalism, was anathema to Serbian and Croatian interests, who in turn, formed their own nationalist parties. The Serbian Democratic Party (SDS) was founded two months after the SDA. Radovan Karadzić, long a favourite of Dobrica Ćosić, was seen as the best man to represent the Serbian cause. Similarly, a Bosnian branch of the Croatian HDZ was formed under Stjepan Kljuić. This party would initially support the Bosnian government, but then later seek to undermine it.[13] Events in 1991 were to prove crucial to later developments. By April, Serbs had established a regional Bosanska Krajina parliament at Banja Luka. By July, the SDS had announced their boycott of the Bosnian Parliament, amid denunciations of Izetbegović's rule. They reacted particularly harshly to Izetbegović's call for a referendum on the future status of Bosnia-Hercegovina. Soon after the Bosnian referendum in August, four autonomous Serbian units had sprung up in the republic. Walking out of the Bosnian Parliament in October, the Bosnian Serbs held their own referendum in November, which resulted in near-unanimous support for separation from Bosnia-Hercegovina and union with the SFRY.[14]

At the same time, the Croatian side were also working towards their autonomy. Only one day after the results of the Bosnian Serb referendum, the Croats established a *Posavina* community of eight units, forming an autonomous area in northern Bosnia. This was followed scarcely a week later by the formation of Herceg-Bosna (with 18 units) in western Hercegovina. In retaliation, the SDS in December announced the creation of the Serbian Republic of Bosnia-Hercegovina. In the same month, the Croats founded the Republic of Herceg-Bosna.[15] It was clear that both Serbs and Croats were preparing for the eventual dismemberment of the Bosnian republic. Nationalist myths were operationalised within this context of ethnic polarisation – myths that spoke of ancient national territory and peoples legitimated the creation of ethnic enclaves. Myths were also necessary to justify the presence of the JNA and a wide range of paramilitary groups, such as the Tigers and White Eagles (Serbian), and Autumn Rain and the Croatian Defence Forces-HOS (Croatian). The violent seizing of territory necessitated a barrage of propaganda, to prove that the Bosnian Moslems had somehow brought the horrors of ethnic cleansing on themselves.

The Moslems as 'fallen' Serbs: ethnic and territorial dimensions

Of extreme importance in the war in Bosnia-Hercegovina was the legitimisation of land-grabbing activities, as well as some of the more insalubrious acts of Serbian statecraft: rape, ethnic cleansing, looting, and physical destruction. Serbian propagandists advanced two key arguments during this time: that Bosnian Moslems were ethnically Serbian, and that Bosnian territory was part of ancient Serbia.

Serbian geographer Jovan Ilić's geopolitical plans for Bosnia-Hercegovina had, by 1992, taken into account the agreements reached between Milošević and Tudjman. His strategy for the dismemberment of the republic thus exuded a tinge of 'impartiality', whereby both nationalist regimes would receive their proper reward. Western Hercegovina and part of Posavina were to be annexed to Croatia, with Eastern Hercegovina joined with Montenegro. Serbia would then take all of Bosnia, as well as the Neretva Valley and Mostar, which would be joined with it. In this early stage of the conflict, Ilić remained convinced that the Moslems would be quite happy under Serbian rule, since 'As regards psychic construction, Muslims and Serbs are much closer to each other than Muslims and Croats.' This tune may well have changed when Izetbegović decided to take Bosnia-Hercegovina in its entirety out of the Federation.[16]

Often, official Serbian propaganda focused on Serbia's historic claim to the republic in its entirety, deriving much of its support from the supposed ethnic identity of the people. Owing to either persecution or opportunism, Serbs held that their own people had converted to Islam in mass numbers during the Ottoman occupation. The Serbian Ministry of Information, for example, concluded that 'most of today's Bosnian Moslems are descended from Serbs', declaring Bosnian Moslems to be 'Serbs of Moslem faith'.[17] The Serbian government blamed Communism for the spread of an 'artificial' Moslem identity. Further, since Communism was itself a major suppresser of authentic forms of nationalism, it was clear that Moslem 'nationality' was simply a political tool, nothing more.[18]

One could also trace the rule of historic Serbian kings to prove the case, and for some, Bosnia-Hercegovina had always been a part of Serbia, from the rule of Serbian king Chaslav in 927 until 1918.[19] Most Serbian historians pointed to the long history of a Serbian majority in the region, positing that Serbian values and culture had influenced the region's character and traditions. In reviewing the history of Bosnia-Hercegovina, Dušan Bataković described how large portions of the republic were populated by Serbs. As he explained: 'Bosnian and Herzegovinian rulers, themselves of Serbian origin, were naturally drawn to Serbian civilization and culture as it unfolded in neighbouring Serbia, irrespective of whether they professed the Roman Catholic, the Orthodox or the Dualist faith.'[20] Part of Bataković's claim, as it was for many others, was that Serbian nationality could be ascertained by a variety of features, including linguistic criteria, which betrayed an unconscious or primordial Serbian identity. Such views were common. One historian concluded: 'The Moslem power brokers and the oppressed common people spoke the same Serbian language', while another writer claimed hopefully: '[One could find] Serbs as polytheists as Serbian Orthodox, as Bogomils, therefore they remained Serbs even as Moslems, their ethnic character is also their language.'[21] Serbian archaeologists employed other forms of historical evidence. The use of the Cyrillic script on tombstones, rather than the 'Croatian' Glagolitic script, also proved that Bosnia's ancient inhabitants had been Serbs.[22]

Moslems were denied the luxury of a separate ethnic, national, and religious identity. Further, Serbian writers advanced dubious linguistic and historical 'proof' that the Serbs had a right to most of the land in Bosnia-

Hercegovina. In practice, Bosnian Serb General Ratko Mladić used such ideas to legitimate his army's conduct, explaining in one interview, 'I have not conquered anything in this war. I only liberated that which was always Serbian, although I am far from liberating all that really is Serbian.'[23] Militia leaders, such as the warlord Vojislav Šešelj, advanced similar theories, claiming that Bosnian Moslems were 'Islamicized Serbs', while many 'so-called Croats' were in fact 'Catholic Serbs'.[24] Again, the theme of the 'watershed' was important here. While, for centuries, Moslem 'Serbs' had been submerged under a variety of despotic empires and false identities, the Serbs were now coming back to free their own ethnic brothers from centuries of misguided loyalty. This was seen to be a great era in Serbian history.

Converting ethnic Serbs from Islam to Orthodoxy became a top priority for the Bosnian Serb political leadership. Moslems would also have the 'opportunity' to abandon their constructed identity, embracing their 'natural' ethnicity – that of Serbdom. In one domestic radio broadcast, Radovan Karadzić urged Bosnian Moslems to abandon Islam, claiming hopefully that 'many Moslems who are well educated and sensible are being baptized and are becoming Christian in Europe as a way of reacting against fundamentalism and the introduction of militant Islam into Bosnia ... it is clear that we must cross the Rubicon since we are dealing with exceptional people in whom the memory of their Serbian origin is alive'.[25] On another occasion, he had argued: 'the Croats and Moslems, in falsifying history, in using our literature and our culture have created the bases for their future states, on lands which are ethnically and historically Serb'.[26] The implications were clear. The Serbs were going to liberate the Moslems whether they liked it or not.

Of central importance was the argument that Serbs were improving the lives of the Bosnian Moslems. Their nationalism was somehow positive, because it was freeing Moslem 'Serbs' from a false identity and religion, while allowing them to become more Western and more civilised. Images of a return to historic soil and national liberation justified the irredentist ambitions of Serbs in Bosnia and Serbia. The need to convert the Moslems was based on the dangerous assumption that Moslem national identity was irrelevant in a blood-based ethnic conflict. While a fraternal discourse was promoted officially, Serbian forces were busy shelling villages and committing ethnic cleansing against their former 'brothers'.

Bosnian Moslems and their Croatian heritage

Many of the primordial themes found in Serbian writings were, not surprisingly, echoed in the Croatian media. Croats also had historic claims to Bosnia-Hercegovina, and, like the Serbs, saw the Moslems as part of their nation. In some respects, the Croatian claim seemed to be stronger, as evidenced by the willingness of Moslems and Croats to enter into coalitions and military alliances. Nevertheless, while alliances existed, demographic balance was often the primary consideration. After all, there were more than twice as many Serbs as there were Croats in the region. This explains why the Croats were so keen to forge strategic alliances with the Moslems. During key periods, demographics also informed Moslem decisions.

The idea that Croats and Bosnian Moslems were of the same ethnic stock was certainly not new, nor was the portrayal of Moslems as fallen Croats. Such ideas were common during the nineteenth century, and were exploited during the Second World War, when Ustaša propaganda described Catholicism and Islam as the two founding religions of the NDH. Such imagery allowed Croatian forces to justify the takeover of Bosnian Moslem lands in the 1900s. Like the Serbs, Croatian propagandists held that one could not commit 'ethnic cleansing' against one's own nation. The first stirring of this idea after the Second World War came from the Nobel laureate Ivo Andrić, perhaps the first in Tito's Yugoslavia to describe the Bosnian Moslems as part of the Croatian nation. 'Having fallen to Islam,' he claimed, Croatian Bosnia 'lost the possibility of fulfilling its natural role of participating in the cultural development of Christian Europe. Instead, Bosnia became a mighty fortress against the Christian West.'[27] This theme of the fallen Croat nation was to re-emerge with Tudjman's regime in Croatia.

Earlier writers, such as Abdulaf Dizdarević, had also asserted this claim, employing a mixture of racial and linguistic criteria to dismiss Moslem nationalism: 'The uniformity of the physical features of our Croatian nation which, along with its language is one of the dominant characteristics of the same racial group ... They preserved [the Croatian] language in its purest form and as a dialect of clear and undeniable Croatian origin.'[28] The presence of these national traits constituted proof, as it did for the Serbs, that the Moslems were co-nationals. Dizdarević's dramatic description of the Fall of the Croats to Islam is worth reviewing:

> The religious wars that broke out when foreign religions mixed in with our common ancestral Slavic paganism, raged in the midst of our nation for centuries, destroying its most powerful forces, erased that unique national image which reflected the uniformity of national traditions ... The historical moment of converting to Islam was without a doubt the most decisive moment in the history of the Croatian nation ... Thus began the long era in the history of Bosnia, cut off from its mother country ... Never in history was there such a case of injustice as this one. It oppressed a handful of people who, it seems, were condemned by God himself to bathe in the blood of their own children.[29]

Thus Moslems were long-suffering Croats, desperately in need of 'rediscovering' their true ethnicity. Paul Tvrtković, who claims linear descent from the medieval King Tvrtko, similarly saw Bosnian Moslems as 'Islamicised Croats'. Like Andrić and Dizdarević, he asserted that Moslems had no choice in the matter: they were 'by ethnic origin, predominantly Croatian, whether one likes it or not'.[30] Tvrtković also argued that 'Croat Catholics and Moslems' were ethnically identical, and thus of the same nation, while the Serbs were ethnically different.[31]

Mirroring Serbian views, Tvrtković charted the renewal of Croatian consciousness among the Moslems after the occupation of Bosnia-Hercegovina by the Austro-Hungarians in 1878. It was during this time, he claimed, that Moslems once again became proud of their Croatian origin. It was also during 'apocalyptic moments', presumably times when both nations feared the onslaught of 'Greater Serbia', that a common 'Croat–Moslem consciousness' was expressed.[32] In this way, a seemingly natural and lengthy history of Croatian–Moslem alliances was drawn out. Paradoxically, this argument did not imply that the Bosnian Moslems should be treated with respect. Rather, it proved that, since Moslems had historically sided with Croats, they had an obligation to do so during the 1990s, whether or not it was in their own best interest.

Using a mixture of historical facts, Croatian writers used history in very much the same way as their Serbian counterparts, drawing out racial and linguistic similarities between Moslems and Croats. Because of their conversion to Islam, Moslems were forced to fight against their ethnic brothers, a situation that could now be reversed once Croatia was able to 'liberate' Bosnia-Hercegovina. Again, the same theme of 'watershed' was reiterated. In what could almost be a paraphrase of Karadzić's views, Tudjman claimed with pride, after his troops took control of the Hercegovina in September 1995: 'Croatia accepts the task of Europeanisation of Bosnian Moslems at the behest of the Western European powers.'[33]

Bosnia-Hercegovina as a Croatian land

Like the Serbs, Croatian politicians and intellectuals employed historic arguments to buttress their claims to Bosnian territory. Since Moslems were ethnic Croats, it was uncontroversial to suggest that Bosnia-Hercegovina was Croatian. Tudjman included the Moslems in his 1991 affirmation of Croatian sovereignty, hinting that 'territorial adjustments' to existing borders might eventually be required, since 'Croatia and Bosnia constitute a geographical and political unity and have always formed a joint state in history.'[34] Defence Minister Šušak was similarly lucid on the status of Bosnia-Hercegovina in one 1996 interview: '[F]or me Bosnia-Hercegovina is also the state of Croatian people and for me it is Croatia. For a Bosniak it can be Bosnia, and for a Serb whatever, but according to its constitution it is also the state of Croatian people and as such I consider it to be my homeland.'[35] Father Bataković, vice president of the Bosnian HDZ, also described Bosnia as 'an old Croat land', as opposed to 'an old Serb land'.[36] Unsurprisingly, none of these political leaders saw Bosnia as an autonomous region that deserved to be left on its own.

Annexing Bosnia was also a popular theme in academic circles. Even before the breakdown of Yugoslavia, Ante Beljo had described Bosnia-Hercegovina as an integral part of 'Croatian ethnic territory', with both republics constituting 'an entity historically, culturally, linguistically, and economically'.[37] Tvrtković also contrasted the 'artificial' borders between the two countries with the 'natural' linkages between Hercegovina and Dalmatia and south-western Bosnia with Croatia.[38] Other academics contributed to the war effort by inventing spurious statistics to buttress these irredentist claims. Sime Dodan's unambiguously titled book, *Bosnia and Hercegovina: A Croatian Land*, claimed that 95 per cent of Moslems and 30 per cent of Serbians were ethnically Croat, using the somewhat speculative argument that all surnames ending in '-an' were of Iranian origin, and were therefore Croatian.[39]

Even glossy Croatian travel books printed by the government included photographs of Sarajevo and other Bosnian cities. Ante Čuvalo's *Croatia and the Croatians* described Croatia's eastern border as being Serbia, Kosovo and Montenegro. As was stated in the introduction: 'further reference to the Croatians and Croatia in this book encompasses the territory of today's Republic of Croatia and the Republic of Bosnia-Hercegovina'. To this end, the territory of this 'joint' state was added together, as was the population.[40] Such tourist books aimed at attracting foreign visitors were meant to familiarise travellers with the idea of Bosnia-Hercegovina and Croatia being the same state, and expressed clear designs on the region well before the war had even begun. Before a single shot had been fired, libraries throughout the world received free copies of Čuvalo's book, attesting to the indivisibility of these two separate countries.[41]

Analysing Serbian and Croatian arguments

Conflicting national claims are often difficult to deconstruct. Historical revisionism is always a mixture of fact and interpretation, relying on a highly biased interpretation of historical reality. At various times in history, parts of Bosnia-Hercegovina's territory were under Serbian and Croatian rule, thus making it impossible to assert that Bosnia was either Croatian or Serbian. Bosnia proper was under Serbian rule from the mid-tenth century to the end of the eleventh, although while the 'Serbs' ruled Bosnia they controlled very little of what today is considered Serbia. However, their control over Hercegovina, today a Croatian stronghold, was more extensive. Bosnia proper was more closely linked to Croatia for much of its history, notably during the medieval period.[42]

The first time the region was united was under King Stephen II Kotromanić in 1326. His national identity was perhaps 'ambiguous' by the standards of the nineteenth and twentieth centuries, as he was born Orthodox, but converted to Catholicism in 1340.[43] King Tvrtko, the heir and nephew of Stephen II (crowned in 1367), was, according to Noel Malcolm, both a Catholic and a descendant of the Serbian Nemanjić dynasty, leading to claims that he was both a historic Serbian *and* Croatian leader. Steven Runciman, by contrast, argued that Trvtko was 'Orthodox by conviction and a friend of the Patarenes [the heretical church of Bosnia] from policy'.[44] There was a similar confusion over later figures. The ethnic identity of one sixteenth century vizier in the Sultan's court, Mehmed Paša Sokolović, was hotly contested. Paul Tvrtković claimed him for the Croats, while Radovan Simardzić asserted his Serbian origin.[45] These are but three of many examples of how different aspects of history – religious affiliation versus lineage – were used to assert competing claims.

While it is true that much of Bosnia-Hercegovina had once been ruled by 'Serbian' rulers and 'Croatian' rulers, these rulers had little sense of nationalism or ethnic identity. It seems, from a reading of Runciman at least, that from the mid-twelfth century until the Ottoman conquest in the fifteenth century many of the local Slavonic rulers of Bosnia and Hercegovina attempted to maintain some form of independence by playing off the West (Hungary, Austria-Hungary) against the East (Byzantium for a short while, followed by Serbia). The only real constant in this pattern of shifting alliances between the Catholic West and the Orthodox East appears to have been a steady alliance with the dualist 'Bosnian Church', a distinct religious organisation, which existed until the fifteenth century. Thus, making exclusive claims to such figures as Tvrtko or Sokolović for one's own national history is deliberately misleading. Such attempts to impose a twentieth-century re-interpretation of mediaeval history were obviously at variance with the facts, as was the rather futile project of insisting that Bosnia-Hercegovina's early populations could themselves be neatly divided into Serb and Croat.[46] Bosnia-Hercegovina had been subject to Turkish, French, German, Austrian, Italian, and Hungarian administration. Historic rule, even if provable, in no way constituted a justification for invasion in the late twentieth century.

Another aspect of Bosnian history that Serbs, Croats, and Moslems co-opted was the rise and fall of the 'Bosnian Church'. Moslems were the first to identify themselves as the descendants of Bosnian Church members, claiming that they converted *en masse* to Islam, and had therefore never been Orthodox or Catholic (and by extension, neither Serb nor Croat).[47] Some historians, like Runciman, have also insisted that such conversions were often the result of a distinct hatred of 'the arrogant Hungarians and the greedy Dalmatians and their Latin church and culture'. In this sense, those who converted did so as a means of asserting their own religious and cultural autonomy – they were not the hapless pawns that later Serb and Croat ideologues would make them out to be. Rather, such people may well have made a positive pro-active choice in order to bring a better future for themselves, taking up, as Runciman further describes it, 'a new faith that was sufficiently sympathetic and that brought great material advantages'. Predictably, both Serbs and Croats proclaimed the Bosnian Church as merely an offshoot of their own faith. Croatian writers, such as Leo Petrović and Jaroslav Šidak, argued that the Bosnian Church was a heretical Catholic monastic order. Serbian writers, such as Božidar Petranović, argued that the Bosnian Church was an offshoot of the Orthodox Church.[48] Needless to say, there was little convincing evidence given for such assertions, which seem to fly in the face of historical reality.

Problematically for nationalists, there was simply no standardised 'national' consciousness before the nineteenth century, and therefore no means of accurately identifying an authentic Serbian or Croatian 'ethnic' consciousness. In many ways, Tito's Moslem nationality was no more artificial than the arbitrary division of the Slavs into Serb and Croat. John Fine has suggested that, owing to the weakness of Church authority, there were many cases of multiple conversions, to Islam from either Orthodoxy or Catholicism, Catholicism to Orthodoxy, and Orthodoxy to Catholicism.[49] Tone Bringa has described numerous families who tried to 'cover all bases' – where one brother would be Orthodox or Catholic, the other Moslem.[50]

It is clear from historical accounts that the Islamic faith espoused in Bosnia-Hercegovina was rather liberal, what the historian Peter Sugar has described as a 'variety of European or rather Balkan folk-Islam', which included baptism, icons to prevent mental illness and other non-Moslem characteristics. As he explained: 'There were mountaineers who called themselves Constantin in front of Christians and Sulayman in front of Moslems. The dead would be given a service by the Orthodox Church and a subsequent burial in a Moslem cemetery. The religious boundaries were easily and frequently transgressed.'[51] That one-third of the contemporary Sarajevo population were in 'mixed' marriages cements the fact that, even in the twentieth century, religion was not seen as an exclusive category.[52] Clearly, the notion that Bosnian Moslems were simply ethnic Croats or ethnic Serbs was untenable. There was no proof that any of Bosnia's three national groups had any strong sense of exclusive national identity before the nineteenth century, nor, more importantly, that these groups were static and unchanging. Moreover, Moslems would not have been the only ones with a loose interpretation of 'national' labels. Many 'Serbs' and 'Croats' may well have changed their own labels as different political masters dominated the region. Becoming

Catholic (and therefore 'Croat') would certainly have had its advantages during the four decades when Austria-Hungary controlled Bosnia, while classifying oneself as Orthodox (and therefore 'Serb') would have been a useful means of self-preservation during the earlier Ottoman era. Orthodoxy at this time was interpreted as a far weaker and less threatening force than Catholicism – the religion of the Ottomans' Western enemies. Thus, national identity in Bosnia, as elsewhere, can also be interpreted as a political choice, not one derived from any ethnic absolutes or a sense of primordial identity.

The Moslems as 'traitors': the Islamic conspiracy theory

Contrary to Serbian and Croatian desires, Bosnian Moslems had their own sense of identity, their own political parties, and their own military forces to back up their autonomy. It became apparent throughout the conflict that another form of propaganda would be needed to legitimate military intervention in the region. Another soon emerged. If the Moslems rejected their 'true' ethnicity, and continued to promote their own form of identity, it followed logically that they had betrayed their Croatian or Serbian brothers. They had betrayed the nation because of their adherence to Islam. The theme of the Bosnian Moslems as traitors became influential in nationalist circles early on in the conflict. Islam was caricatured as a fundamentalist, exclusivist and thoroughly dangerous religion, bent on the destruction of ethnic nations in the Balkans.

Serbs and Croats would portray themselves as victims of an Islamic conspiracy. Rather than attacking a relatively defenceless minority group, they were defending Europe against the onslaught of an Islamic invasion, comparable only to the Ottoman invasion some five centuries before. Here, Kečmanović's 'plot' theme was often cited, as Serbs and Croats argued that outside powers were going to use the Bosnian Moslems as an 'Islamic Springboard', to penetrate into the heart of Europe. Serbs and Croats were saving their own nations from assimilation and potential genocide, while reliving their historic role – defending the *Antemurale Christianitatis* against a renewed Ottoman invasion.

Serbs and the 'Moslem traitors' in Bosnia-Hercegovina

The theory of Moslems as 'fallen Serbs' was often mixed with a view of the Moslems as traitors to the Serbian nation. Kosovo, as indicated earlier, had elevated the Serbs to the status of a divine and chosen nation, while reducing the Moslems or 'Turks' to the status of 'Christ killers'. Serbs who converted to Islam were seen to have renounced their chosen status, embracing the religion and culture of the invader. Converts were likened to Vuk Branković, and were seen to constitute the worst of Serbia's enemies. While certain propaganda focused on the need to 'save' the Moslems, another more virulent strain called for the Serbs to 'save' themselves and the Western world from Islamic invasion. Of course, anti-Moslem rhetoric had been popular in Serbia for many centuries. Karadzić's popularisation of the Kosovo myth, Cvijić's 'Dinaric Man', and Njegoš's 'Mountain Wreath' were but three early examples of anti-Moslem, anti-Turkish writings that were popular in nineteenth-century Serbia.

Anti-Moslem rhetoric was extensively used in Serbian literature during the 1990s. Miroljub Jevtić, an Islamic specialist at Belgrade University, argued unequivocally that:

> Those who accepted Islam accepted the conquerors *de facto* as their brothers, and the crimes of the latter are their own. That means that their own hands are also covered with the blood of their own ancestors, the former Bosnian non-Muslim population. By converting to Islam, they destroyed Christian Bosnia and caused the Ottomans to rule over Christian Bosnia for a long time.[53]

Jevtić was in many ways typical of the Serbian establishment. For him, as for many of his colleagues, the antipathy between Serbs and Moslems was centuries-old, 'Serbophobia [being] highly developed among fundamentalist Muslims.'[54] Thus, while Serbs may have been the aggressors in Bosnia, they were simply responding to centuries of Moslem aggression. Novelists also picked up on similar themes. Drasković's *Noz* (discussed in Chapter 5) featured a number of Moslem characters, who appeared primarily as treacherous, cold-blooded murderers – ethnic Serbs who had abandoned the 'lessons of Kosovo'.[55] This novel revolves around a massacre of Orthodox Serbs by Moslems on Christmas Day, 1942. The only survivor, a Serbian baby, is raised by Moslems, and taught to hate the Serbs. By some twist of fate, he later discovers his own Serbian identity, and further discovers that his 'Moslem' family is also ethnically Serbian.[56] With its depictions of Moslem violence and wanton acts of cruelty, Moslems were presented in it as misguided traitors, who need to be carefully controlled.

Another novel of this stripe was Vojislav Lubarda's *The Ascension* (1990) with its negative descriptions of Serbian–Moslem relations in Bosnia. Set after the assassination of the Austrian Archduke Franz Ferdinand in 1914, the central action in the story once again consists of a massacre of Serbs by Moslems. Lubarda's work was a typical expression of Serbian 'counteridentification'. The Serbs were presented as noble and heroic, always willing to fight for others, and always willing to forgive and forget. These positive qualities were contrasted with those of the Moslems, who continuously hated the Serbs and massacred them whenever possible.[57] Lubarda thus drew out stereotypical characterisations of the Moslems – their supposedly treacherous and

warlike dispositions, making them little different from their mythical ances-
tor, Vuk Branković.

Novelists reinforced this anti-Moslem paranoia. So did politicians. In one
collection of essays, Dobrica Ćosić warned of a 'pan-Islamic internationaliza-
tion of war in Bosnia', seeing this as 'the greatest danger looming over both
the Balkans and south east Europe'.[58] While Croatian writers almost always
spoke of Serbs as part of the East, Ćosić placed the Serbs solidly in the West,
with the Moslems as little better than the Asian hordes and Vandals to whom
Croats compared the Serbs. Serbs had to continue their historic role, to defend
the West against the evils of Islam. According to Ćosić: '[It was] the Serbian
people who consented, from the 14th century, to the greatest sacrifices for the
defense of Europe and its civilization.'[59]

Other Serbian politicians, including Slobodan Milošević, continued to
hammer out the theme of Serbia standing alone against the forces of Islam,
Serbia as the plucky 'David' against an Islamic 'Goliath'. While he did not fear
Islam, he saw the necessity of controlling it. This 'plot' was extremely popular
among Serbian leaders, who enjoyed the symbolism of fighting against a
powerful Islamic menace.[60] Radovan Karadzić also saw his role in world-
historic proportions. He claimed that his mission as leader of the Bosnian
Serbs was to insure that Islamic fundamentalism did not 'infect Europe from
the south'. For Karadzić and many of his colleagues, Middle Eastern countries,
such as Saudi Arabia, Iran, and Turkey were trying to use Bosnia as a 'springboard for Islamic penetration of Europe'.[61] Serbian leaders enjoyed portraying
themselves as self-sacrificing warriors, waging war in Bosnia in order to
defend the West against a new Ottoman invasion.

Imagining the Islamic state: Serbian perspectives

While general ideas of Moslem treachery and cruelty were important, many
Serbian academics amused themselves by imagining how horrible an Islamic
state could be, what it would look like, how it would operate, and what
features would distinguish it from other state forms. Certainly, a great deal of
creative licence was allowed, as long as this dystopian state was sufficiently
horrific to deter the Serbian public from siding with the Moslems in Bosnia.
Serbian views on what the Moslems were trying to create would have been
laughable, had the authors not been serious.

For Serbian writers, the key to understanding Moslem objectives in
Bosnia was Alija Izetbegović's now infamous tract, *Islamic Declaration* (1972).
This publication, which earned him a prison sentence under the Communist
regime, was touted by Serbs and Croats alike as a blueprint for an expansionist Islamic empire. One quote in particular always caught the eye of Serbian
propagandists. Izetbegović supposedly affirmed in his *Declaration* that 'there

can be no coexistence between the Islamic religion and non-Muslim social and political institutions' in countries where Muslims represent the majority of the population.[62] This passage became an obvious favourite of both Serb and Croat writers, being one of the few that alluded to Izetbegović's plans for a utopian Islamic state.

However, contrary to Serbian and Croatian claims, Izetbegović had never called for an Islamic state in Bosnia. In fact, he had concluded that such a state was impossible, owing to the multiconfessional nature of the republic. Nevertheless, interpretations of the *Declaration* gave a clear indication of Serbian paranoia about a resurgent Islam in the Balkans. Izetbegović's writing was often portrayed as a blueprint for an 'Islamic renaissance', followed by a 'holy war (jihad)' against non-Moslems. Serbs also feared that Izetbegović was trying to create an expanded state, a 'great Islamic federation from Morocco to Indonesia in which the Koran would be the supreme law'.[63] One 1993 Serbian Ministry of Information pamphlet, intended for English-speaking audiences abroad, used a strong form of Orientalism laced with Islamic conspiracy theories. One of the contributors, an Orthodox priest and member of the Bosnian Serb Parliament, stressed the immorality and perfidy of the Moslems and their religion, predicting that:

> They want for the second time to create a Turkish Bosnia or a Bosnia in Turkey ... with the Shariatic law and other life norms unacceptable in the twenty-first century. Behind this century-old dream of a primitive man to live off the backs of a subjugated people, to have his own harem, dreaming of Istanbul, where according to him there was a paradise of earth, where 'fairies are bathing in sherbet' ... They [the Moslems] invited to this bloody feast all other worldy bums, murderers and dogs of war, Mujahadins and jihad fanatics from the Islamic countries came to *fulfil their sacred duty and to exterminate us*. This unscrupulousness completely fits their religion and tradition and culture.[64]

For this particular writer, the Moslem utopia would be a reversion to some species of oriental despotism, where loose morals and low standards of behaviour would prevail. Sexual depravity and the subjugation of women were also common themes, as if to arouse in Serbian males the fear that their wives, mothers, or sisters could be defiled by a Moslem. Thus Serbs objected to the possibility of an alternative society, where 'Eastern' customs and manners would prevail. For them, the fear of another Ottoman empire was too horrible to contemplate. Another article in a similar vein, entitled 'Lying [*sic*] Hands on The Serbian Women', written by a Bosnian Serb official, once more defined the conflict in terms of a Moslem holy war against Serbs. This document described a sort of 'race crime' being committed against Serbs living in and around Sarajevo. Here the image of rape as a weapon of war was stressed:

> By order of the Islamic fundamentalists from Sarajevo, healthy Serbian women

Balkan holocausts?

from 17 to 40 years of age are being separated out and subjected to special treatment. According to their sick plans going back many years, these women have to be impregnated by orthodox Islamic seed in order to raise a generation of janissaries on the territories they surely consider to be theirs, the Islamic republic.[65]

Again, the threat of Serbian women being raped was articulated. While some Serbian women were being raped, and perhaps not only by non-Serbs, rape was not described as an individual act, but as a weapon of war. This document was first brought to light by Roy Gutman in 1993, during his journalistic forays in Bosnia. It was at this time that the world first became exposed to the so-called 'Serbian rape camps', and the Bosnian Serbs were accused of systematically raping some 20,000 Moslem women. While such statistics were later proved to be unrealistically high, Serbian propagandists had a vested interest in deflecting criticism of any Serbian-inspired rape policy. Thus it made perfect sense to accuse the Bosnian Moslems of religiously inspired mass rape, which in many ways was seen to be much worse than any Serbian rapes, since women would have been impregnated in order to raise 'janissaries'.

While such anecdotal evidence was extremely interesting, so too were the many compilations put out by the Serbian government. These featured testimony from Serbian women who claimed to have been raped by Bosnian Moslems. No doubt many of the stories were true, although they were nearly impossible to verify. Nikola Marinović's evocatively titled *Stories from Hell* continued the popular Serbian theme of stereotyping Moslems as sexually depraved Ottomans:

> The greatest humiliation suffered by Serbian women happens whenever a Moslem commander proclaims himself 'bey', 'agha' or 'vizier' (a frequent occurrence) and decides to have a harem. The 'right to sleep' with the 'master' is then brutally applied. Young Serbian women are thus brought to the bottom of human dignity. Such atrocities have particularly been registered in central Bosnia, in the towns of Zenica, Gornji Vakuf, Travnik, Jajce ... In these same zones, Serbian boys have undergone circumcision (the 'sunnett'), and have been forcibly Islamicised.[66]

Once again, the fear of Serbian women being forced into harems was promoted, as well as the fear that Serbian boys would be forcibly converted to Islam, if the Serbs did not act quickly to take over strategic areas. After more than four decades of living side by side with Bosnia's largely secularised Moslem populations, Bosnian Serbs surely knew that such dystopian visions were pure nonsense. The most interesting aspect of this quotation was Marinović's listing of the towns and cities where these harems and forced conversions supposedly took place. Most of these places were those where a form of defensive ethnic cleansing had either taken place, or would take place shortly.

236

The Moslems as genocidal killers

Another general theme in propaganda circles was to compare an exaggerated view of an Islamic conspiracy with the horrors of Nazi Germany. As with the Croats, Serbs could confidently claim to be defending themselves against a Moslem-inspired genocide. Such a view was clearly stated by the Bosnian Serb leader Milorad Ekmečić's oft-quoted speech to the last Congress of Serbian Intellectuals, in Sarajevo:

> In the history of the world only the Jews have paid a higher price for their freedom than the Serbs. Because of their losses in the war, and because of massacres, the most numerous people in Yugoslavia, the Serbs, have, in Bosnia Hercegovina, fallen to second place, and today our policy and our general behaviour carry within themselves the invisible stamp of a struggle for biological survival.[67]

Ekmečić's writings and public statements generally focused on Bosnia-Hercegovina as the target of Eastern and Western expansionism. Sandwiched between two opposing and equally dangerous forces, Serbs were portrayed as Jewish like victims of an attempted genocide. This link figured prominently in many Serbian accounts.

Similarly, the fear of a Moslem-inspired genocide was linked to the Bosnian youth magazine, *Novi Vox*, which supposedly encouraged its readers to participate in an anti-Serbian game – to collect as many Serbian heads as possible.[68] Another recent Bosnian Serb publication drew out similar themes. Here, the authors claimed to have uncovered a Moslem plan to kill 100 Serbs for every Moslem killed, and between 10 and 15 for every wounded. These figures echoed the ratio of Serb to German deaths during the Nazi occupation of Serbia during the Second World War. Mixed with this imagery were reports of Moslem plans to establish an Islamic state, in which all women would be forced to wear veils, while all men would be forced to attend the mosque.[69] Clearly, such imagery was important in creating the impression that Serbs were merely reacting in self-defence to a planned genocide on the part of the Moslems. More recently, Milošević would regale judges and prosecutors alike at the Hague with stories of 'Mujahideen' coming from Saudi Arabia with sabres in hand, solely for the purpose of cutting off Serbian heads in order to 'help Alija Izetbegović'.[70]

Another aspect of this self-defensive posture was the theory that the Moslems had shelled their own people to court sympathy from the West. The most publicised examples were two instances of shelling in Sarajevo, the first in February 1994, where a marketplace was shelled on its busiest day. The second shelling occurred in August 1995, when another marketplace was bombed, killing 37 civilians and wounding another 85.[71] For Serbian writers, Izetbegović, the skilful 'dictator-impostor', was guilty of having staged the shellings himself, in order to falsely portray the Moslems as victims of Serbian aggression.[72] Another theory held that the Moslems shelled their own people in order to deflect Western attention from their extermination campaign against Serbian civilians. Risto Tubić dismissed the marketplace bombings as a cover for a Moslem 'Holocaust' against the Serbs in the 1990s, a 'third genocide', which was to be 'the culmination of all historically known forms of physical and psychological persecution'.[73] Turning the truth completely upside down, Tubić compared the Bosnian Moslems to Nazis, victimising themselves in order to exterminate Serbs. Thus by denying that the Serbs had shelled Sarajevo, he was able to make overt parallels between Serbs and Jews:

> Ever since Hitler organised the Crystal Night, this most cynical and filthiest weapon also became an instrument of modern warfare. Among many, suffice it to mention the massacres in Vasa Miskin Street and at the Markdale market-place. The aim was twofold: first to publicise reports on atrocities in order to arouse the desire for revenge among the public and draw world public support for one side against the other, and secondly, to alarm the world with such reports that would force governments to take action, to intervene militarily.[74]

References such as these were all the more ludicrous in light of the fact that Serbs had been shelling Sarajevo from their mountain positions continually during this time. The Sarajevo Olympic Stadium became a huge cemetery for Moslem casualties, while most Sarajevans were terrified to stray from their homes, lest they be gunned down by Serbian snipers. Even in such an atmosphere, while Moslems were dodging bullets down 'sniper alley' in Sarajevo, the Serbs maintained that Bosnian Moslems were playing the victim to cover up their own genocide against the Serbs.

From a practical standpoint, it was clear that the image of warlike, fanatical Moslems was a key ingredient in activating Serbian violence in many regions of Bosnia. Images of Moslems as traitors and 'Christ-killers' were repeated time and time again in the Serbian media, in an attempt to encourage and justify Serbian aggression. Constantly repeated in the Serbian press, such imagery was often used as a pretext for ethnic cleansing.[75] Serbian writers seem to have used reports of atrocities as a precursor to attacks on strategically important towns and cities. Thus Serbs were reported tortured and killed in Livno, Jajce, Slavonski Brod, Konjic, Travnik, Vitez, Mostar, and even Sarajevo.[76] Such patterns occurred throughout the conflict, suggesting that anti-Moslem propaganda had very practical and negative consequences.

Croatian views of the Bosnian Moslems

While there were many historical instances of co-operation between Croats and Bosnian Moslems, Croatian attitudes were strikingly similar to those of the Serbs. Persecution imagery performed an important role, as did the argument that Moslems were fallen nationals who had to be brought back to the fold. Again like the Serbs, Croatian politicians and academics saw the merits of casting themselves as the victims of a Moslem onslaught as part of their mission to liberate former Croatian territory. An emphasis on victimhood prevented domestic criticism of Croatian actions, in particular by the opposition media. Both Serbian and Croatian government media were issued strict instructions not to report on the negative activities of their own side in the conflict, thus rendering a skewed representation of Moslems as the sole aggressors. The Serbian media were keen to portray the conflict as a 'civil war', and media references to the Moslems described them constantly as 'attackers'.[77]

Similar views were promoted on the Croatian side, even during periods of Croatian–Moslem alliances. This was due to the fact that such alliances were often brokered by the Croatian government, with little regard for the views of Bosnian Croats (Mate Boban was removed by Tudjman during one such alliance). Thus, it was common for the Croatian media to promote messages of goodwill and friendship with the Moslems, while newsrooms in Herceg-Bosna were condemning Moslems as 'enemies' and genocidal killers.[78] As with the Serbs, Croatian propagandists accused the Moslems of trying to take over the Balkans and Europe. Such imagery began in the official media by late 1992. At this stage, it focused primarily on Moslem collaboration with KOS, the Yugoslav military intelligence, and by extension, the Serbs. This soon changed to specific attacks on Islam, with regular news reports decrying the dangers of fundamentalist extremism. By early November 1992, Gojko Šušak, in a bid for Israeli military support, tried to drum up fears of an Islamic conspiracy, alleging that there were 11,000 Bosnian Muslims studying in Cairo alone. He appealed to one Israeli audience by asking: 'Can you imagine a fundamentalist state in the heart of Europe?'[79]

Tudjman likewise referred often to a threat of Islamic Fundamentalism and to an Islamic holy war. He justified intervention in Bosnia by maintaining that Izetbegović's government aimed to 'set up an Islamic state in Europe, which was part of a conflict between the Islamic and Catholic worlds, and of a confrontation between the Islamic world and the West'.[80] For Tudjman, the Islamic threat was real. In a 1992 meeting with ambassador Warren Zimmermann, he outlined the dimensions of the Islamic conspiracy:

> The Muslims want to establish an Islamic fundamentalist state. They plan to do this by flooding Bosnia with 500,000 Turks. Izetbegović has also launched a demographic threat. He has a secret policy to reward large families so that in a few years the Muslims will be a majority in Bosnia (at the time they were 44 per cent). The influence of an Islamic Bosnia will then spread through the Sandzak and Kosovo to Turkey and to Libya. Izetbegović is just a fundamentalist frontman for Turkey; together they're conspiring to create a Greater Bosnia. Catholics and Orthodox alike will be eradicated.[81]

Tudjman's unsubstantiated theories typified official Croatian views: the Moslems could not be trusted, and were plotting to create an Islamic state in Europe. Croatian writers used such fears to legitimise the establishment of Bosnian Croatian autonomous units, such Herceg-Bosna. As with the Serbian side, Izetbegović's *Islamic Declaration* was frequently cited as proof of the Moslems' plan to overrun the region. Croatian journalists, like their Serbian counterparts, often quoted Izetbegović's claim that there could be 'no peace and coexistence between the Islamic faith and non-Islamic social and political institutions.'[82] The *Declaration* was also linked to specific genocidal crimes perpetrated by Moslems against Croats. Like the Serbs, Croatian writers portrayed Izetbegović's work as a blueprint for genocide.

One journalist described how the Bosnian Moslems in 1993, through a certain Operation 'Tito', had begun attacking Croatian settlements in central Bosnia, laying the foundations for a Moslem-instigated genocide against Bosnia's Croatian population. Izetbegović supposedly had plans to make Sarajevo a European Islamic capital, housing some 15 million European Moslems. As for the Bosnian Croats, they were nothing more than an obstacle for Izetbegović, who wanted to construct an Islamic empire from 'Teheran to Slavonski Brod'.[83] One must ask ironically if this would fit inside the Islamic empire that the Serbs envisaged for Izetbegović, destined to stretch from Indonesia to Morocco. Needless to say, there was no documentary evidence of an 'Operation Tito'. The theory that Sarajevo was to become a world Islamic capital was also pure conjecture. More important were the overt accusations of genocide levelled against the Moslems. As in the Serbian case, such writings were useful in obscuring the reality of Croatian ethnic cleansing operations, which were ongoing in Bosnia at that time.

Even when Croats and Moslems formed Tudjman-brokered alliances, the local press continued to condemn the Moslems for trying to destroy their national distinctiveness with multinational federalism. One recent article, written well after the Dayton Accords, accused the Bosnian Moslems of trying to turn the Croats into 'Bosnian Croats', which they interpreted as an attempt to 'eradicate from their life and consciousness national symbols, tradition and language, to destroy their identity'.[84] For many Croatian nationalists, even the prefix 'Bosnian' implied a Moslem identity rather than the former regional appellation it used to signify. When forced into an alliance with the Moslems in 1995, the Bosnian Croats had an extremely difficult time abandoning their hopes for an internationally recognised Greater Croatia.

Assigning blame in Bosnia-Hercegovina

Both Serbian and Croatian academics, journalists, military leaders and politicians consistently used the fear of Islamic expansion and violence to legitimate their own nationalist expansion and violence. Both Serbs and Croats ran 'detention centres' and 'collection camps' where prisoners were housed, fed little to no food, frequently beaten and terrorised, sometimes sexually violated, and often killed. While one should note clearly that the majority of camps were Serb-controlled (13 major camps), the Croats maintained 4 main camps as well. These, however, were only the largest. The International Red Cross, by August, 1994, had documented a total of 51, many small and impromptu – located in camp grounds, schools, even movie theatres. Serbian camps were exposed during 1992, and figured prominently in the famous ITN-Channel 4 series on Bosnia. Roy Gutman's prize-winning dispatches also exposed Serbian crimes, while notably omitting references to Croatian violence.[85] Tudjman publicly admitted to the existence of Croatian 'collection centres', which housed, by 1993, an estimated 20,000 inmates in the territory of Herceg-Bosna. That 'others had them too' was enough of an excuse for Tudjman, who did not seem to deny, nor regret, that such camps existed.[86]

While organised militia groups instigated much of the ethnic cleansing in Bosnia-Hercegovina, the Serbian Orthodox and Croatian Catholic Churches also proved their complicity in many of the violent activities of their supporters. The Serbian warlord Vojislav Šešelj and his militia were blessed by an Orthodox priest after having cleansed several Moslem towns near Sarajevo. In Trebinje, one Orthodox priest led a group of Serbs in expelling several Moslem families from their homes. The town's 500-year-old mosque was later destroyed during celebrations for the feast day of St Sava. Even outside the region, Metropolitan Christopher in the United States described Bosnia's Moslems as slavish followers of the Ayatollah Khomeini, while the Orthodox bishop of Zvornik described how Moslems killed 'unbelievers' as a way of getting closer to heaven.[87] The Church's involvement often lent crucial moral and spiritual support to Serbian nationalists. Rather than speaking out against war, the Church sometimes became a willing collaborator.

The Croatian Catholic Church also proved instrumental in encouraging many of the more violent aspects of Croatian nationalism. While the Cardinal of Zagreb and the Archbishop of Sarajevo bravely condemned the escalation of violence, local branches of the Church were often supporters, particularly in Hercegovina. In Mostar, the local clergy and 250 Franciscan friars lent their support to the HVO, arguing that 'Islamic states don't have free speech, democracy or freedom of religion.' Priests often compared the Bosnian government to 'Turkish occupiers', while portraits of Ustaša leaders such as Ante Pavelić and Ranko Boban were frequent adornments on the walls of Hercegovinian priests, according to Michael Sells.[88]

In the Serbian and Croatian cases, both sides used the myths of assimilation and Islamic conspiracy to sanction the ethnic cleansing and mass destruction that so characterised the Bosnian war. Myths were employed as part of a political agenda, in order to legitimate violence, and in some cases, to instigate it. While the Churches could have prevented the escalation of violence, they did little to discourage it. Unfortunately, their complicity in mass murder and the forced expulsion of populations will remain one of the most enduring and disheartening aspects of the conflict.

The Bosnian Moslem perspective

Serbian and Croatian designs and overall strategies for Bosnia-Hercegovina were often starkly similar, as were the themes and attitudes expressed in their national writings. Unsurprisingly, the Moslem leadership also used images of victimisation and persecution. The fact that the Moslems were the chief victims obviously had much to do with this. Gow and Tisley put it well when they rightly noted: 'If Croatia was weak, but played the victim to emphasise its position, Bosnia was generally a victim.'[89] The Bosnian Moslems, like the Serbs and Croats, found victim-centred imagery useful in articulating their case. The Bosnian conflict was perhaps the only one that saw Moslem leaders comparing themselves to Jews, in order to court Western European support against a Christian-instigated genocide. Clerics such as Mustafa Spahlić were quick to claim that Bosnian Moslems were 'the new Jews of Europe'.[90]

Bosnian Prime Minister Haris Siladzić, amid fears that violence would escalate if the arms embargo was lifted by the United States, used Second World War imagery to advance his case, compared lifting the arms embargo to bombing the railway lines leading to Auschwitz. As far as he was concerned, this alone would save tens of thousands of lives. During the Geneva negotiations, Izetbegović used the same imagery, likening the agreements to those reached between Germany and Czechoslovakia in 1938, except that 'Instead of Munich this is Geneva. Instead of little Czechoslovakia, this is little Bosnia. Instead of Beneš, it is me.'[91]

The purpose of using this imagery for the Moslems was similar, yet different to its use by the Serbs and Croats. The Moslem side was largely fighting a war of self-defence; theirs was clearly the weakest position, and the use of such imagery was not meant to mask their own atrocities, but figured as a public relations tactic, to encourage Western support for a united Bosnia. In the Moslem case, the imagery of persecution and genocide was used in the same manner as it was by the Armenians, the Romani, the Ukrainians, and other groups seeking national rights and international recognition in the face of overwhelming oppression.

Nevertheless, this should not be taken to imply that the Bosnian Moslems were entirely blameless. True to Serbian and Croatian accounts, the Bosnian Moslems had indeed received military support from the Middle East – although as a last resort, and long after war had broken out. Furthermore, the token support offered by Middle Eastern countries was more symbolic and political than practical. Algerian and Saudi veterans of the Afghan wars came to participate in 'Jihad' against the Serbs and Croats, but were alarmed by the 'liberal' or folk-Islam practices in Bosnia, particularly the fact that men and women were fighting side by side. Bosnian Moslems, by contrast, were often angered by the hardline stance of their newfound allies.[92] There was little financial support from the oil-rich countries of the Middle East, except for some government funding from Saudi Arabia and a variety of private contributions.[93] What was given, and primarily from Iran, were offers of fuel, arms, and at one stage 10,000 'peace-keepers' (these were refused by the UN).

Rather than trying to help the Bosnian Moslems, the Iranians seem to have been motivated by a desire to provoke the United States, while antagonising their Saudi rivals. Shiite Iranian relief aid was primarily targeted at areas that were being helped by similar Sunni Saudi agencies, suggesting that Middle Eastern politics was being played out in Bosnia, at the expense of the local population.[94] Saudi and Iranian aid was simply too little too late, and had little effect on the outcome of the war. Contrary to Serbian and Croatian claims, Bosnia was never a springboard for Islamic penetration into Europe, and Islamic countries hardly seemed to care at all what happened in Bosnia. While author Salman Rushdie was hiding for his life from an Iranian *fatwah* after the publication of his *Satanic Verses*, no Islamic regime incited aggression against Serbian or Croatian leaders.[95]

By 1994, some 80 per cent of non-Serbs had been expelled from Serbian-controlled territory. After most of the brutal ethnic cleansing took place, there were signs that the Bosnian government, feeling that it now had nothing to lose, began imposing a distinctly Islamic morality on the territory it still controlled. Several officials in the Bosnian government spoke out against mixed marriages, arguing that they were doomed to failure and should be opposed. Mustafa Ceric, the Grand Mufti of Bosnia, opined that while the policy of systematic rape was 'horrible and incomprehensible', it was 'less painful and easier to accept than all those mixed marriages and all those children born of mixed marriages'.[96] The Culture and Education minister Enes Karić initiated new reforms to make what remained of Moslem Bosnia more Islamic, throwing away 'European trash' – such as drugs, alcohol, and prostitution, while banning Croatian and Serbian music from radio stations in favour of more Arab-sounding music. He also encouraged changes in the 'Bosnian' language (including the addition of Turkish words) to reflect an Islamic heritage.[97]

Curiously, there was a backlash against these reforms, largely from Moslems themselves, including members of the SDA government. Events came to a head in early 1995, when Izetbegović met with members of the Seventh Muslim Brigade, whose banner bore Arabic writings. His official endorsement of Islamic over multiconfessional forces was highly criticised. His reference to one dead Moslem soldier as a *shehid* (martyr), brought open criticism from the boy's family, angered by the fact that their son was described using Arabic words, while being the focus of Arabic prayers. This was a language which neither he nor his family understood.[98] What was obvious among Bosnian Moslems was their continued support for a multiconfessional Bosnia, even among those Moslems who were the obvious victims of Serbian and Croatian aggression. For some reason, a strong sense of nationalism, or even religious conviction, failed to take hold among the population, even during the bloodiest periods of the war.[99]

Conclusions

Serbian and Croatian nationalists advanced startlingly similar ideas and images in their understanding of the Bosnian Moslems. Both claimed Bosnian Moslems as their ethnic kin, while similarly claiming the territory of Bosnia-Hercegovina as historically part of their respective countries. At the same time, negative myths were used to attack the Moslems as an expansionist and dangerous religious group – with different cultural practices and sexual mores. Negative myths of identification, such as 'counteridentification', themes of 'plot', 'threat', 'damage', and 'universal culprit', were common, as well as themes of 'redemption and suffering', and 'unjust treatment'. Both sides portrayed the Moslems as the vanguard of a dangerous Islamic conspiracy, resorting to crude stereotypes and rabid orientalist discourse to assert their false claims. These similarities are best explained by the fact that both Serbs and Croats had similar objectives – to legitimate the force necessary to create autonomous regions of their own, even when this included ethnic cleansing against the Moslem population.

While there were assertions of Moslem nationalism by the Bosnian government, these were certainly mild, and largely in reaction to the atrocities Moslems were forced to endure. The same held for foreign support, which seemed to have been motivated by Iranian–Saudi rivalry more than anything else. The Moslem population at large, even by the end of the conflict, still favoured a multiconfessional society. It remains unclear what the future will bring, even though the Dayton Accords (1995) seem to have brought about a type of peaceful co-existence. The legacies of ethnic cleansing, however, still remain. Around 60 per cent of Bosnia's inhabitants were forced from their homes, and more than 1.3 million people (some 30 per cent of the population) were dispersed in 63 countries.[100] There could be no doubt that Serbs and Croats had been the aggressors throughout the conflict. Their use of victim-centred propaganda proved to be the most effective means of legitimating their conduct, which, while not necessarily genocidal, was extremely brutal.

The Moslem question in Bosnia-Hercegovina

While there was never any proof that the Moslems wanted to spread Islam throughout Yugoslavia, or even to make Bosnia an Islamic state, Serbian and Croatian propagandists worked tirelessly to promote the Moslems as genocidal *mujahadeen*. In both the Serbian and Croatian cases, the threat of genocide, from each other or the Bosnian Moslems, was the key to Redemption in an expanded nation-state. Greater Serbian and Greater Croatian ambitions were premised on the need to protect one's fellow co-nationals throughout the region when Yugoslavia was in the final stages of its life.

NOTES

1 Quoted in Tone Bringa, *Being Muslim the Bosnian Way: Identity and Community in a Central Bosnian Village* (Princeton, NJ: Princeton University Press, 1995) p. 12.
2 Holbrooke, *To End a War* (New York: Random House, 1998) p. 36.
3 This surreal situation is described in Slavenka Drakulić, *Cafe Europa: Life After Communism* (London: Little, Brown and Company, 1996) pp. 188–94. For an excellent discussion of the Milošević-Tudjman accord, see Florence Hartmann, *Milosevic: la diagonale du fou* (Paris: Denoel Impacts, 1999) pp. 127–31.
4 Dušan Bilandžić, 'Termination and Aftermath of the War in Croatia', in Branka Magaš and Ivo Žanić (eds), *The War in Croatia and Bosnia-Herzegovina 1991–1995* (London: Frank Cass, 2001) pp. 85–6.
5 Bringa, *Being Muslim the Bosnian Way*, p. 31.
6 Vladimir Mrkoci, 'Historical Guilt of Alain Finkelkraut', *Hrvatski Obzor*, 17 August 1996 (translated on 5 October 2001) http://free.freespeech.org/ex-yupress/hrobzor/hrobzor12.html (accessed 10 January 2001).
7 Richard Holbrooke, for example, saw all three as 'ethnic groups' during the Dayton negotiations in 1995. However, it is open to dispute whether any of them constitute a stable 'ethnic' given, as Holbrooke suggests: Holbrooke, *To End a War*, p. 97.
8 Bringa, *Being Muslim the Bosnian Way*, p. 26.
9 Rusmir Mahmutćehanjić, 'The Road to War', in Magaš and Žanić (eds), *The War in Croatia and Bosnia-Herzegovina*, p. 144.
10 Dušan Kečmanović, *The Mass Psychology of Ethnonationalism* (New York: Plenum Press, 1996) p. 62.
11 Noel Malcolm, *Bosnia: A Short History* (London: New York University Press/Macmillan, 1994) p. 218.
12 Ivo Banac, *The National Question in Yugoslavia: Orgins, History, Politics* (Ithaca, NY: Cornell University Press, 1992) p. 147.
13 Laura Silber and Alan Little, *The Death of Yugoslavia* (London: BBC Books, 1993) pp. 230–1.
14 David Campbell, *National Deconstruction: Violence, Identity, and Justice in Bosnia* (Minneapolis, MN: University of Minnesota Press, 1998) pp. 58–9.
15 *Ibid.* p. 59.
16 Jovan Ilić, 'Possible Borders of New Yugoslavia', in Stanoje Ivanović (ed.), *The Creation and Changes of the Internal Borders of Yugoslavia* (Belgrade: Ministry of Information of the Republic of Serbia, 1992) p. 100.
17 Serbian Ministry of Information, 'Facts About The Republic of Serbia' (Helsinki: Embassy of the Federal Republic of Yugoslavia, February 1996) p. 24.
18 Melina Spasovski, Dragica Živković, and Milomir Stepić, 'The Ethnic Structure of the Population in Bosnia Hercegovina', in Dušanka Hadži-Jovančić (ed.), *The Serbian*

245

Question in the Balkans: Geographical and Historical Aspects (Belgrade: University of Belgrade Faculty of Geography, 1995) p. 264.

19 Serbian Ministry of Information, 'Facts About The Republic of Serbia', p. 22.

20 See Dušan T. Bataković, 'The Serbs of Bosnia & Herzegovina: History and Politics' (Belgrade: Dušan T. Bataković Web site, 1997) http://www.bglink.com/personal/batakovic/k-serbih.html (accessed 18 June 1998).

21 See Aleksa Djilas, 'A House Divided', in Nader Mousavizadeh (ed.), *The Black Book of Bosnia: The Consequences of Appeasement* (New York: New Republic Books, 1996) p. 20. See also Ilić, 'The Serbs in the Former SR of Croatia', in Hadzi Jovančić (ed.), *The Serbian in the Balkans*, p. 232; and Vera Vratusa-Zunjić, 'The Intrinsic Connection Between Endogenous and Exogenous Factors of Social (Dis)integration: a Sketch of the Yugoslav Case', *Dialogue*, 22–23 (June/September 1997) http://www.bglink.com/business/dialogue/vratusa.html (accessed 18 June 1998).

22 Djordje Janković, 'The Serbs in the Balkans in the Light of Archeological Findings', in Hadži-Jovančić (ed.), *The Serbian Question in the Balkans*, p. 137. The primordialness of Serbian claims was often contrasted with the constructed nature of Moslem identity. Ilić paradoxically claimed that Moslems were Serbs precisely because of their rejection of Serbian ethnicity. He argued that the Moslems possessed the 'psychological and ethical handicap of converts', and that their 'great aversion towards the ethnicity they come from' constituted further proof that they were in fact Serbian. Ilić's psychobabble revealed that the Moslems were merely engaging in a species of psychological projection. Like those suffering from addiction or disease, they were in denial, perhaps needing Serbian 'liberation' as a cure. See Jovan Ilić, 'The Balkan Geopolitical Knot and the Serbian Question', (pp. 3–37) in Hadži-Jovančić (ed.), *The Serbian Question in the Balkans*, p. 16.

23 Quoted in Norman Cigar, *Genocide in Bosnia: The Policy of 'Ethnic Cleansing'* (College Station, TX: Texas A & M University Press, 1995) p. 81.

24 Malcolm, *Bosnia: A Short History*, pp. 226–7.

25 Cigar, *Genocide in Bosnia*, p. 59. Summarily rejecting Moslem claims to national identity, he described how Arabs viewed the Bosnian Moslems with disgust, since they were not really 'Islamic'. See Radovan Karadžić, 'Beginnings of a Secular Battle', in Patrick Barriot and Eve Crépin (eds), *On assassine un peuple: Les serbes de Krajina* (Lausanne: L'Age D'Homme, 1995) pp. 111; 117.

26 Karadzić, 'Beginnings of a Secular Battle', p. 117.

27 Zaljka Corak, 'Croatian Monuments: Wounds Suffered From Other People's Illnesses' in Zvonimir-Separović (ed.), *Documenta Croatica* (Zagreb: VIGRAM-Zagrebi VIDEM Krsko, 1992) p. 38.

28 Quoted in Ante Beljo (ed.), *War Pictures 1991–1993* (Zagreb: Croatian Information Center/Hrvatska Matica Iseljenika, 1993) p. 115.

29 *Ibid.* pp. 115–16.

30 Paul Tvrtković, *Bosnia Hercegovina: Back to the Future* (London: Paul Tvrtković, 1993) p. 36.

31 *Ibid.* p. 17.

32 Tvrtković cited four examples: 1910–14 (Bosnian Parliament); 1914–18 (First World War); 1941–45 (Second World War); and 1991–93, the 'present aggression by Serbia': *ibid.* p. 24.

33 Michael A. Sells, *The Bridge Betrayed: Religion and Genocide in Bosnia* (London: Routledge, 1996) p. 95.

34 Lenard Cohen, *Broken Bonds: Yugoslavia's Disintegration and Balkan Politics in Transition* (Boulder, CO: Westview Press) p. 97.

35 Dubravko Horvatić and Stjepan Šešelj, 'Croatian Culture and Croatian Army: Interview with Croatian Defense Minister Gojko Šušak', *Hrvatsko Slovo* (27 December 1996) www.cdsp.neu.edu/info/students/marko/hrslovo/hrslovo7.html (accessed 18 June 1998).

36 Mark Thompson, *Forging War: The Media in Serbia, Croatia and Bosnia-Hercegovina* (London: Article 19/International Center Against Censorship, 1994) pp. 97–8. Croatian nationalists denied Serbs any right to be considered an indigenous people of Bosnia-Hercegovina. According to most accounts, Serbian presence was the result of immigration, which came after the Ottoman conquest: Ante Čuvalo (ed.), *Croatia and the Croatians* (Zagreb: Northern Tribune Publishing, 1991) p. 75.

37 Ante Beljo, *Genocide in Yugoslavia: A Documentary Analysis* (Sudbury, ON: Northern Tribune Publishing, 1985) p. 12.

38 Tvrtković, *Bosnia Hercegovina*, p. 6.

39 'Review of Sime Dodan, *Bosnia and Hercegovina, a Croatian Land* (Zagreb: Meditor, 1994)', *Feral Tribune* (29 December 1997).

40 Čuvalo, *Croatia and the Croatians*, pp. 19–20.

41 The first time I encountered this book, for example, was in the Regina Public Library in Saskatchewan, Canada.

42 Malcolm, *Bosnia: A Short History*, pp. 11–12.

43 *Ibid.* p. 17.

44 *Ibid.* p. 17. According to Steven Runciman, *The Medieval Manichee* (Cambridge: Cambridge University Press, 1947) p. 110, Kotromanić appears to have converted for political reasons, in an effort to secure an alliance with Hungary in order to protect Bosnia's independence against the threat of annexation by Serbia's Stephen Dušan. I am indebted to David Phelps for his advice and suggestions here. See Runciman, *ibid.*, and Malcolm: *Bosnia: A Short History*, pp. 18–19.

45 Bringa, *Being Muslim the Bosnian Way*, p. 13; see also Tvrtković, *Bosnia Hercegovina*, p. 8.

46 See Runciman, *The Medieval Manichee*, pp. 100–15 *passim*.

47 For a discussion, see Francine Friedman, *The Bosnian Muslims: Denial of a Nation* (Boulder, CO: Westview Press, 1996) p. 21. Malcolm (*Bosnia: A Short History*, pp. 53–5) has controverted the Moslem claim, arguing that conversion took several centuries. Further, he argues that a direct link between the Bosnian Church and the Moslems cannot be proved. Runciman's arguments however contradict those of Malcolm. He posits that mass conversions were common, particularly amongst the Bosnian nobility, since the Sultan had decreed that only those who converted could retain possession of their estates. Furthermore, Runciman writes that, 'The people followed their nobles' lead. By the end of the fifteenth century Bosnia was a predominantly Mohammedan province.' See Runciman, *The Medieval Manichee*, pp. 114–15.

48 Malcolm, *ibid.*, pp. 28–9.

49 Bringa, *Being Muslim the Bosnian Way*, p. 16.

50 *Ibid.* p. 18.

51 Quoted in Fouad Ajami, 'In Europe's Shadows', in Nader Mousavizadeh (ed.), *The Black Book of Bosnia: The Consequences of Appeasement* (New York: Basic Books, 1995) p. 41.

52 Adam Lebor, *A Heart Turned East: Among The Muslims of Europe and America* (London: Little, Brown, 1997) p. 20.

53 His theories are discussed in Cigar, *Genocide in Bosnia*, p. 29.

54 *Ibid.* p. 29.

55 *Ibid.* p. 25.

56 See Andrew Baruch: Wachtel, *Making a Nation Breaking a Nation: Literature and Cultural Politics in Yogoslavia* (Stanford, CA: Stanford University Press, 1998) pp. 203–8.
57 Discussed in Sells, *The Bridge Betrayed*, pp. 223–5.
58 Dobrica Ćosić, *L'éffondrement de la Yougoslavie: positions d'un résistant* (Paris: L'Age D'Homme, 1994) p. 76.
59 *Ibid.* p. 76.
60 Kečmanović, *The Mass Psychology of Ethnonationalism*, pp. 63–4.
61 Quoted in: Cigar, *Genocide in Bosnia*, pp. 99–100.
62 Vratusa-Zunjić, 'The Intrinsic Connection Between Endogenous and Exogenous Factors of Social (Dis)integration', p. 15.
63 *Ibid.* p. 15.
64 Quoted in Cigar, *Genocide in Bosnia*, p. 99.
65 Major Milovan Milutinović was responsible for this document, which also boasted lurid accounts of Moslem atrocities, such as, 'necklaces have been strung of human eyes and ears, skulls have been halved, brains have been split, bowels have been torn out, human spits and children's bodies have been pierced by bayonets ...': quoted in Roy Gutman, *A Witness to Genocide* (New York: Macmillan, 1993) pp. ix–x.
66 Nikola Marinović, *Stories from Hell: Confessions of Serbs, Tortured in the Concentration Camps in Croatia and Bosnia and Herzegovina in 1991 and 1992* (Belgrade: Serbian Ministry of Information, 1993) p. 60.
67 Quoted in Christopher Hitchens, 'Appointment in Sarajevo: Why Bosnia Matters', in Rabia Ali and Lawrence Lifschutz (eds), *Why Bosnia? Writings on the Balkan Wars* (Stoney Creek, CT: Pamphleteer's Press, 1993) p. 9.
68 Drago Jovanović, Gordana Bundalo, and Miloš Govedarica (eds), *The Eradication of Serbs in Bosnia and Hercegovina 1992–1993* (Belgrade: RAD, 1994) p. 14.
69 Lebor, *A Heart Turned East*, p. 18.
70 See page 270 of Milošević's testimony at the Hague Tribunal or ICTY. Full transcripts are available at www.un.org/icty.
71 For a description of the February 1994 bombing, see David Gompert, 'The United States and Yugoslavia's Wars', p. 138; for August 1995, see Richard Ullman, 'Introduction', p. 4; both in Richard Ullman (ed.), *The World and Yugoslavia's Wars* (New York: The Council on Foreign Relations, 1996).
72 Boris Delić, 'Power Without Political Legitimacy or Moral Credibility', *Serbia: News, Comments, Documents, Facts, Analysis*, 41 (1995) p. 51. Much of the ammunition against Izetbegović in Serbian discourse stems from a reading of Alija Izetbegović's book, *Islam Between East and West*, published in 1980, which was supposedly a fundamentalist tract and a political programme for on Islamic expansionism into Western Europe. However, as Ajami counters: 'Izetbegović's book should have been a defense lawyer's dream. An amateurish work, an intellectual hodge-podge, it is the product of an anxious *assimilé*, a child of the Western tradition reassuring himself that all the sources of his mind add up to a coherent whole, a man of our messy world born at the crossroads of cultures. The index alone is sufficient proof of the man's ecleticism. This must be the only book on Islam with nine references to Dostoevski, seven to Albert Camus, eleven to Engels, nine to Hegel, three to Malraux, two to Rembrandt, ten to Bertrand Russell, eight to Kenneth Clark and so on. This is not the work of a Moslem fundamentalist or a traditional apologist': Ajami, 'In Europe's Shadows', p. 51.
73 See Risto Tubić, 'Encyclopaedia of Evil and Crime' (pp. 6–13). in Jovanović, Bundalo, and Govedarica (eds), *The Eradication of Serbs in Bosnia and Hercegovina*, p. 7.
74 *Ibid.* p. 9. (Italics his.)
75 As Michael Sells described the process: 'A massacre would follow local media broad-

casting Croat and Moslem plans to exterminate the Serbs. Once such broadcasts were out, then the inevitable occurred as various Serb groups hurried to "defend" themselves against attack': Michael A. Sells, 'Religion, History and Genocide in Bosnia-Hercegovina', in G. Scott Davis (ed.), *Religion and Justice in the War Over Bosnia* (London: University of California Press, 1996) pp. 36–7.

76 Marinović, *Stories from Hell*, pp. 56–65. The need to shell Sarajevo was further promoted through long 'testimonials' published by the Commissariat for Refugees in Belgrade, describing the horrors of life under Moslem rule. See the Commissariat's volume of testimonies, *Suffering of the Serbs in Sarajevo* (Belgrade: Commissariat for Refugees, 1995).

77 Zdenka Milivojević, 'Serbia', in James Gow, Richard Paterson, and Alison Preston (eds), *Bosnia By Television* (London: BFI, 1996). See p. 152.

78 Sandra Bašić-Hrvatin, 'Television and National/Public Memory', in Gow, Paterson, and Preston (eds), *Bosnia By Television*, pp. 62–3.

79 Cigar, *Genocide in Bosnia*, p. 124.

80 *Ibid.*

81 Warren Zimmermann, *Origins of a Catastrophe: Yugoslavia and its Destroyers – America's Last Ambassador Tells What Happened and Why* (New York: Random House, 1996) pp. 181–2.

82 Dubravko Horvatić, 'Our Existence is a Crime', *Hrvatsko Slovo* (22 March 1996) www.cdsp.neu.edu/info/students/marko/hrslovo/hrslovo5.html (accessed 18 June 1998).

83 *Ibid.*

84 Marko Vidić, 'Croats an Obstacle to the Creation of the New Bosnian Nation', *Slobodna Dalmacija* (28 April 1998) www.cdsp.neu.edu/info/students/marko/slodal/slodal9.html (accessed 18 June 1998).

85 Gutman, *Witness to Genocide*, p. 23.

86 Gordan Malić, 'Herceg Camp', *Feral Tribune* (29 April 1996) www.cdsp.neu.edu/info/students/marko/feral/feral31.html (accessed 18 June 1998).

87 See Sells, *The Bridge Betrayed*, pp. 80–1.

88 *Ibid.* p. 106.

89 James Gow and James Tisley, 'The Strategic Imperative for Media Management', in Gow, Paterson, and Preston (eds), *Bosnia By Television*, p. 108.

90 David Campbell, *National Deconstruction; Violence, Identity, and Justice in Bosnia* (Minneapolis, MN: University of Minnesota Press, 1998) p. 8.

91 Quoted in *ibid.* p. 8.

92 Lebor, *A Heart Turned East*, p. 40.

93 *Ibid.* p. 55.

94 *Ibid.* pp. 56–7.

95 In this regard, one curious example of Serbian hypocrisy deserves mention. One of the accusations against the Moslems was that Siladzić and other Bosnian Moslem notables had visited Libya in the hope of setting up their own *Jamhariyya* (Momar Qadafi's 'People's State') in Bosnia. While there was no evidence to support this claim, Qadafi was actually an enthusiastic supporter of Milošević's Serbia. By December 1994, Tanjug reported that high-level Serbian diplomats were regularly visiting Libya. In this case, it is clear that the Serbs' accusations were a direct screen for their own actions. Throughout this conflict, the idea of accusing someone of various activities while you are in fact engaged in doing them yourself has been a recurring pattern – a theme. As discussed in Sells, *The Bridge Betrayed*, p. 120.

96 Campbell, *National Deconstruction*, pp. 112–13.

97 *Ibid.* p. 113.
98 *Ibid.*
99 A sociological overview to this effect can be found in Brigitte Hiplf, Klaus Hipfl, and Jan Jagodzinski, 'Documentary Films and the Bosnia-Hercegovina Conflict: From Production to Reception', in Gow, Paterson, and Preston (eds), *Bosnia By Television*, p. 45.
100 Campbell, *National Deconstruction*, p. 221.

Conclusions: confronting relativism in Serbia and Croatia

The New Aristocracy will consist exclusively of hermits, bums and permanent invalids. The Rough Diamond, the Consumptive Whore, the bandit who is good to his mother, the epileptic girl who has a way with animals will be the heroes and heroines of the New Tragedy, when the general, the statesman, and the philosopher have become the butt of every farce and joke. (W. H. Auden)

WHEN AUDEN PENNED this cynical projection early in the last century, he reflected on a new state of affairs that was coming to pass, a cultural transformation privileging the victim over the aggressor, the loser over the winner. This extract adequately encapsulates the importance of the Yugoslav conflict as yet another era when the aestheticisation of the victim was paramount, along with the demonisation of the powerful and the proud. In Yugoslavia, Serbs and Croats cast themselves as the natural heirs to much of Yugoslavia's land mass – through the argument that their historic persecution gave them the right to expand their nation states to include all co-nationals.

This concluding section highlights some of the main themes in this study, drawing together many of the theoretical and empirical strands that have been discussed in the preceding eight chapters. As I described throughout, a teleological understanding of history proved to be of central importance for both Serbian and Croatian nationalist writers during the 1990s. Myths of Covenant, Fall, and Redemption were of particular importance, as was the general theme of good against evil. Serbs and Croats were particularly susceptible to these types of myths because of the religious nature of their national identification. Religion seemingly imbued each side with primordial national characteristics – making the self appear more enlightened, democratic, noble, peace-loving, generous, and sacrificial. Religious faith was presented as the most basic form of national differentiation, influencing culture, traditions, language, and openness to the outside world. The clash between positive and progressive religions and backward and racist religions was seen to be at the

251

root of conflict.

In trying to analyse the successes and failures of Serbian and Croatian propaganda, we need to understand clearly whether or not any *actual* genocides took place in the Balkans, either in history, or during the more contemporary period. This includes the general question of whether the manipulation of Holocaust imagery is a useful means for nations to advance their political agendas. I have argued that general Fall imagery and imagery of the Holocaust have played an extremely important role in rallying co-nationals for the defence of the nation. As an instrumental means of gaining power and holding on to it, negative imagery has been very useful. Nevertheless, Holocaust imagery never succeeded in accomplishing its primary objective – courting massive Western sympathy and support. The comparative genocide debate in Serbia and Croatia was very much akin to the tragedy of the commons – as soon as the Serbs invoked it, Croats, Kosovar Albanians, and Bosnian Moslems all joined in, and picked this stock of metaphors and symbols clean.

Religious nationalism and 'ethnic' nations

An obvious aspect of Serbian and Croatian revisionism was the theme of evil. Northrop Frye identified the importance of a continuous negative agency, bringing about Falls and driving history forward. For the early Hebrews, enemies came from a variety of cultural, linguistic, and religious backgrounds. They all worshipped 'false gods', but they were not unified by any mutual similarity in their belief systems. What unified them was their role as different aspects of a negative agency, acting to destroy the Hebrew nation.[1] While the Egyptians, Philistines, Romans, and others were *metaphorically* linked, this was the extent of their connection.

Serbian and Croatian history was boiled down to a series of monumental encounters between these two groups, whereas the Hebrews faced a wide variety of enemies over many centuries. Through the bogeymen of Serbophobia or Greater Serbia, contemporary politicians and military leaders were linked to their counterparts a century before. In these two case studies, true historical enemies were excised from history. In Croatia, the Hungarians, and not the Serbs, were the objects of Croatian hatred in the nineteenth century, and their 'concentration camps' were quietly forgotten. The sword on the famous bronze statue of Ban Jelačić was, after all, pointing at Budapest, not at Belgrade. His rebellion in 1848 was staged against the growing power of Hungary, not Greater Serbia. Furthermore, Croats were not forced into the first Yugoslavia in 1918. Rather, joining with other South Slavs was infinitely preferable to annexation by Italy, which had coveted the Istrian Peninsula for many decades.

Serbia's greatest historical enemy – the Ottoman Empire – seemed largely irrelevant in reinterpretations of Serbian history. While there was a great deal of anti-Moslem, anti-Islamic rhetoric, there were few attacks on Turkey itself for its past occupation of the region. Nor was there much anti-Ottoman propaganda. Other traditional enemies – such as Bulgaria, a constant threat during the first half of the twentieth century and a key mover and shaker during the Balkan Wars – were consigned to obscurity. When history was reinterpreted in the 1990s, these other countries were conveniently disregarded. Even German and Italian invasion was seen as a facilitator of Serbian or Croatian genocide, with collaboration often seen to be worse than the crimes either of these invading countries had perpetrated in the region. Manufacturing a history of Serbian–Croatian rivalry was much more important, and so elements of a useable past were grafted together with pure fiction, to render a completely new vision of the past.

An important reason for this exclusion of historical enemies had to do with a teleological view of history maintained by both Serbs and Croats. History was reinterpreted, not simply as a contest between nations, or countries, but more importantly as one between religious entities, entities that seemed more important than race, language, or tradition. At no time did it appear that nationalism was competing with religion. The nation was never elevated to be, as William Pfaff put it, 'a simulacrum of the Deity'.[2] Rather, the Croatian Catholic Church and the Serbian Orthodox Church appear to have remained exceedingly loyal to their respective regimes, which in turn promoted religion as a central aspect of national identity. While Kečmanović was correct that there were many 'pseudo-religious qualities' in Serbian and Croatian 'ethnic identification', nationalism did not replace religion: it collaborated with, and manipulated it.[3]

Catholicism and Orthodoxy, long submerged through decades of Communism, now had the chance to re-emerge. Because Serbs and Croats largely defined their sense of national identity by their religious beliefs and their membership in a religious community, it was natural that their emerging nationalisms would rely on the moral and spiritual legitimacy conferred by the Church. Religion and nationalism were one in Communist Yugoslavia. It was impossible for nationalism to replace religion, because without religion these nations would, in any practical sense, cease to exist. While the self would be defined by religious criteria, imparting certain primordial characteristics to the nation, so too would the others come to be defined by their beliefs.

Samuel Huntington's 'clash of civilisations' thesis was invoked time and again, to explain why peoples of other faiths were dangerous and threatening. Both the Serbs and the Croats followed Huntington's hierarchy of religions, also described by Milica Bakić-Hayden as 'nesting orientalisms'. In this hierarchy, Protestantism was seemingly the most enlightened and the most

'Western', followed by Catholicism, then Orthodoxy, then Islam, presented as the most violent, barbaric and backward of all religions. Huntington claimed that Islam was the religion responsible for most of the world's conflicts. These categorisations seem to have been assimilated into Serbian and Croatian propaganda.

While Milošević could happily share a weekend at Karadjordjevo with Tudjman, carving up Bosnia, there was no friendliness between Milošević and the Kosovar leader Ibrahim Rugova or the Bosnian President Alija Izetbegović. While these men were seemingly in favour of peace, not war, Milošević preferred the company of a fellow warmonger and opportunist. The Battle of Kosovo had seemingly sealed the fate of the Moslems. There could be no reconciliation between these two groups.

A similar dynamic was evident in Croatia. While there were many myths about the Bosnian Moslems as 'Brother Slavs' and 'the flower of the Croatian nation', a strong anti-Islamic current informed many Croatian arguments and government policies. Tudjman's hatred of the Moslems seemed both personal and emotional – this was well known among Western diplomats who met with him. While one might be tempted to believe that the Croato-Moslem Federation in Bosnia today testifies to the closeness of Croats and Bosnian Moslems, historically this was decidedly not the case. As we saw in Chapter 8, Tudjman betrayed the beliefs of his nationalist supporters in Hercegovina in an attempt to cast himself as a peacemaker.

For Croatian writers, Serbian Orthodoxy was closer to Islam than it was to Catholicism, making the Serbs more Eastern – seemingly part of an inferior civilisation. Because of this Easternness, the Serbian civilisation was portrayed as less tolerant, less democratic, and less enlightened than that in Croatia. From the Great Schism of 1054 onwards, the Serbs were presented as the enemies of the Croats. Like those who converted to Islam, the Serbs had seemingly chosen to be part of an inferior, more bloodthirsty, more barbaric, and more backward civilisation.

For the Serbs, Croatian Catholicism was replete with negative traits – intolerance, xenophobia, and the desire to convert non-Catholics by force. Catholics were expansionist and genocidal; and because of this, the Croats were seen to be only indirectly evil. It was their Catholicism that made them want to kill Serbs, and their expansionism was motivated by Vatican plans to enslave the Balkans. Milan Bulajić's insistence that most of the Ustaša death camp-officials were members of the Catholic clergy reinforced the idea that the Catholic faith inspired violent aggression, as well as hatred of Serbs. Additionally, Serbian national identity, like that of Croats and Moslems, appeared to hang by a thread. The idea that Serbs could be transformed into Croats in one generation by a Catholic education indicated that national identity was far less primordial than many propagandists claimed.

Religion was all-important because it created the conditions for a series of covenants with the divine. Throughout this study, we have seen many examples of covenantal relationships, as described by Northrop Frye, Conor Cruise O'Brien,[4] Donald Harman Akenson,[5] Martin Buber,[6] Hans Kohn,[7] and others. Some good examples included the Serbian myth of Kosovo. Lazar's choice created a heavenly people of the Serbs – a nation of martyrs. This covenantal relationship was often likened to that made between God and the Hebrew people. Both Serbs and Jews had to suffer in order to undergo Redemption. Nevertheless, each group was seen to have special divine favour.

For the Croats, the *Pacta Conventa* could be interpreted as a type of covenant, although this was not a Covenant with the divine, but more with History – with a big 'H'. Certainly, the *Pacta* myth indicated that the Croatian nation had been chosen by History, they were allowed to preserve aspects of their statehood for a thousand years. Several myths, like 'state right' tradition and that of the *Antemurale Christianitatis*, proved the existence of a civilised, peace-loving and enlightened Croatia. Similarly, the myth of the *Antemurale Christianitatis* was seen to be a form of covenantal relationship. Their adoption of Roman Catholicism made them more peace-loving, more honest and fairer in their dealings with others. Their conversion also conferred God's blessing and the promise of protection in case of attack. The Croats, through Medjugorje, maintained a more obvious Covenant with the Virgin Mary, through her many apparitions during the 1980s. This implied, as Meštrović and his colleagues maintained, that the Croats had been chosen as more Western, more civilised, more democratic, better educated and more European than the Serbs, who were relegated to the East. While myths like that of Medjugorje might at some levels have confirmed, at least in Protestant eyes, that the Croats were somehow backward, superstitious 'southern' Europeans, such myths were high successful domestically. In some respects, what constituted proof of 'Westerness' within Croatia may well have had different implications outside the country, where Catholicism was not necessarily the be-all and end-all of European culture and tradition.

The Serbs also used Schöpflin's 'myths of divine election', arguing that they, and not the Croats, were the most enlightened and civilised. Dušan Bataković, for example, privileged the nineteenth-century Ottoman *millet* tradition as an authentic expression of Serbian democratic and European values, seemingly a better method of rule than the xenophobic and clerical system found in Croatia. Both Serbs and Croats adhered to Frye's view of a 'covenential cycle', where every negative event in history was followed by an equally positive reward, or Redemption.[8] However, neither nation had much interest in exploring a truly teleological view of history. History was for both nations a series of Falls, some large, and some small, through which nations were forced to labour. There was little emphasis on Redemption in these highly revised historical accounts, nor on the promise of future deliverance.

A lack of interest in the great positive heroes of the past was a notable phenomenon in both nationalisms. Heroes such as Prince Lazar, Ban Jelačić, Draža Mihailović, and Alojzije Stepinac were tragic figures. They saw their nations through times of valiant defeat, rather than dazzling victories. It was as if nationalists were scared to promote other periods of Redemption, as if it were necessary to save up every historic Fall – and then cash them in for statehood.

Contrary to Smith's assumptions about the Golden Age, neither Serbs nor Croats tried to recapture historic high points in the life of the nation, but rather focused most of their attention on proving, and then overcoming, their many Falls. No one really wanted to, 'unfold a glorious past', or 'a golden age of saints and heroes'.[9] Smith's 'myth of the historical renovation' – where the nation was to return to its basic national 'essence' – was not a top priority.[10] The closest example of this type of imagery was the myth of the separate Croatian language, which was somehow seen to contain their national essence.

However, the six hundredth anniversary of Kosovo did, as Smith described, vividly re-create the 'glorious past' of the Serbian nation.[11] The marketing of Kosovo products and the ubiquitous use of the symbols and images of the Battle did suggest an obsession with a past moment of glory in Serbian history. Perhaps the willingness to sacrifice for an ideal was a captivating theme for Serbian nationalists; but this was not a time of high culture, or the spreading of Serbian civilisation around the world. While history was to a certain extent a usable past, nationalists selected myth of Fall, which were deemed more necessary for rallying people together to reclaim national greatness.[12]

Holocaust imagery and the comparative genocide debate

Certainly Serbian and Croatian revisionist historians wove a rich tapestry of myths and images. Myths of persecution and Fall were 'discovered' in almost every period of history. Certainly, we saw many examples of Kečmanović's myths of 'counteridentification', myths of 'plot', 'damage', 'threat', and 'universal culprit', all of which were used with reference to perceived enemies. We saw many examples of Claude Lefort's myth of the 'people as one', standing against a series of dangerous and united external enemies. We also saw many examples of Schöpflin's myths of 'redemption and suffering', 'powerlessness and compensation for powerlessness', and 'unjust treatment'. All of these types of myth proved to be extremely useful in articulating Serbian and Croatian victimisation. So why invoke Nazism and the Holocaust?

As I argued in Chapter 2, Holocaust imagery has become a more and more acceptable way of advancing national, social, and political projects. With the universalisation of the Holocaust, the symbols and metaphors that have made the Jewish people 'the gold standard of oppression', to quote Finkielkraut, have become readily available to other groups. Our tendency to see the Nazis as the ultimate manifestation of secular evil, and the Jews as the paradigm of the victim, has given nations a template within which to structure and understand their national histories.

The frequent use of the terms 'Holocaust', 'death camps', 'death marches', 'exoduses', and 'pogroms' highlighted the victimised qualities of Serbs and Croats. These were combined with distinctly Christian images – 'Calvary', 'way of the cross', and 'crucifixion'. Such imagery deflected attention from continuous media reports about Serbs and Croats 'attacking' each other, 'rounding up' Bosnian Moslems, 'invading' territory, and 'looting' property, while committing 'ethnic cleansing'. In this way, the use of Holocaust imagery was designed to deflect criticism of the many disreputable acts of statecraft deemed necessary by Serbian and Croatian leaders to expand their respective states and consolidate their bases of power.

By the mid-1990s, Serbian and Croatian troops occupied more than two-thirds of Bosnia-Hercegovina. They were 'liberating' territory that had never been theirs before, while Serbian and Croatian regions were dotted with various 'autonomous republics', each with their own parliaments, radio stations, and currencies. But if the 'liberation' of territory was part of a historic mission, there was little rejoicing in the media whenever a town was conquered. There was little jingoism expressing the awesome power of the Serbian or Croatian military machines. War was not seen as a means of punishing enemies – it was portrayed as necessary to protect co-nationals from the threat of genocide. Military victory was most often portrayed as the proper state of affairs, the correction of historic injustices. News reports from liberated towns did not exude a sense of victory, but dwelled instead on the devastation caused by the aggressor, and the tremendous amount of work yet to be undertaken. There were few books detailing Serbian or Croatian victories. What abounded were glossy publications depicting lurid atrocities and bombed-out buildings. Indeed, it seemed that the only point in 'liberating' towns at all was so that the victors could then take pictures of the devastation, to buttress their claims of victimisation still further.

In the end, invoking the Holocaust filled in many blanks. Historically, Serbs and Croats had not been enemies, they had been fellow Slavs, trapped in neighbouring states controlled by rival empires. By contrast with their common hatred of Islam, there was little about the other side as such that could provoke the same revulsion as references to a jihad or to janissaries and harems. Thus a form of hatred had to be created. Claiming that the enemy was a genocidal power in the present and in the past allowed each side to reconstruct its own history, but also, more importantly, the history of the other. This was the stage at which narratives were inscripted and performative dramas were enacted. Fears of a nineteenth-century 'Greater Serbia' confronted the 'Civitas Dei', and Yugoslavism and Illyrianism were quietly forgotten. While those promoting South Slavic unity were condemned as misguided or naïve, Juraj Strossmayer, Ljudevit Gaj and other well-meaning 'Yugoslavs' had in fact merely reflected the reality of their age – that Serbs and Croats were not yet enemies, nor had they any reason to be.

Unfortunately, historical accuracy gave way to revisionism and demonisation. Rather than interacting with members of the other side as colleagues, Serbian and Croatian academics and journalists chose to reinterpret their relationships with their new enemies through their newly-minted historical propaganda. Bodgan Denitch described this phenomenon very well, when he wrote:

> Each side consistently presented itself as victims, or potential victims, the Other as a threat or potential threat, so that neither party responded to the Other directly, but only to its own projections of the Other. Each reacts to the Other as a threat, and in its own reactions, reinforced the behaviour that appears threatening. Nor were these perceptions questioned by those who had increasingly identified with their own 'people'. Victimisation appeared to be an all-powerful mobiliser of ethnic solidarity.[13]

A sense of persecution appealed to Serbian and Croatian historians; but this sense was somewhat different from that cherished by the Jews. For example, there was a constant emphasis on sacrifice for an ideal, which was more a Christian than a Jewish concept. Serbs sacrificed themselves at Kosovo to become a chosen and holy nation; they sacrificed themselves at the *Antemurale Christianitatis*, to defend the West against the East. They sacrificed themselves in the First World War, during the first Yugoslavia, and then during the Second World War, through their contributions to Partisan victory. In the contemporary period, they were defending the West against Kosovar- and Bosnian Moslem-led Islamic expansionism. They were also sacrificing themselves to defend the East against the dangers of Roman Catholic expansionism.

The Croatian ideal of sacrifice was not as pronounced, but it existed nonetheless. Croats also sacrificed themselves at the *Antemurale Christianitatis*, to defend the West against the East. Croats also sacrificed themselves during the Second World War, first of all, to create an independent state, and then, in order to redeem that state in history, by their massacre at Bleiburg. They also sacrificed themselves in defending the West against Islamic expansionism in Bosnia-Hercegovina. These themes of sacrifice are important, because they draw their strength from the crucifixion, not the loss of Israel two thousand years ago, the Jewish pogroms, or the Holocaust. There is no strong sense of sacrifice in Zionism, no sense of voluntarism, no decision on the part of Jews to martyr themselves for some larger ideal. Jews suffered because negative forces were persecuting them. Masada was the exception, rather than the rule.

However, while this myth of sacrifice played an important role in re-evaluating Serbian and Croatian history, Schöpflin's 'myths of powerlessness and compensation for powerlessness' were not commonly used during the 1990s. Such myths were typically Christian, as Schöpflin explained, 'mak[ing] a virtue of fatalism and passivity' while allowing the nation to claim, 'a special moral superiority for having suffered'.[14] While the Serbs articulated this theme with regard to their many sacrifices for Yugoslavia during the first Yugoslavia and the Second World War, this was often seen to be a failing on the part of the Serbian nation, not a strength. The maxim: 'winners in war, losers in peace' underscored Serbian magnanimity, drawing out a sharp contrast between Serbian generosity and Croatian duplicity. However, during the contemporary wars, there was little interest in turning the other cheek, or passively accepting the collapse of the Federation. Both sides fought, and then used myths to legitimate their 'self-defensive' activities. They had little interest in passivity or what it implied.

Instrumentalising the Fall

From an instrumental perspective, negative imagery and myths of Fall were crucial to the rise of Tudjman and Milošević. By portraying national histories as long periods of Fall, they argued that their own regimes were historical turning-points, palingenetic moments when all the Falls of the past would be reversed, and new utopian nations would be forged, bigger, richer, prouder, and more authentic. In coming to power, both Tudjman and Milošević seemed to have faith in a national renaissance. They understood Henry Tudor's description of historical teleology, that 'mythical time is reversible', and that 'what was done is not forever lost'.[15] The promise of re-creating the past, of reversing the years of hardship and Fall, was integral to the appeal of nationalism. Kečmanović's myths of 'watershed' and 'the right moment' were often used to justify Tudjman and Milošević's attempts to make 'a new order emerge.'[16] The use of Schöpflin's 'myths of rebirth and renewal' were equally apparent.[17]

Curiously, both Tudjman and Milošević seemed to have embraced a Modernist view of nationalism's practical uses for gaining power. Ernest Gellner's purely instrumental explanation for the nation made sense in describing Milošević's rise to power.[18] John Breuilly's observations also reflected the reality of Milošević and Tudjman's rise to power, since they both saw nationalism as 'institutional' instrument for gaining control.[19] Tom

Nairn's view of nationalist legitimacy as a 'popular revolution' or 'national liberation struggle' was certainly true. Whether it was 'Tudjmanism' or the 'Happening of the people', the promise of revolutionary change legitimated the rise of nationalism.[20] That nationalist leaders manipulated history to suit their own ends comes as no surprise. What was surprising about the conflict was the extent to which ordinary historians, political scientists, geographers, and even artists, psychiatrists, dentists and architects were willing to submerge themselves fully in these nationalist experiments.

Had more people questioned the established truths of what they were seeing and hearing, war might have been prevented, or stopped much earlier. Early in the conflict, British journalist Cvijeto Job rightly criticised intellectuals in Serbia and Croatia for contributing to the 'collective madness' that was going on around them.[21] He made the following damning quote in 1993, which expressed, I believe, the fundamental importance of propaganda and myth-makers during the war:

> All nations have self-serving myths, which play havoc with historical truths. But the public life in many countries permits the challenge of these myths. Stabler and more tolerant cultures leave room for the puncturing of their own egos, but in Yugoslavia, the pervasive culture of ethnocentric myths unchallenged even by their intellectuals weighs down the lives of the people. Yugoslav peoples have indeed been betrayed by their intelligentsias.[22]

Job's statement could apply equally well to Croatia. Nationalist intellectuals in both countries appeared to have taken leave of their senses – or at least their capacity for critical reasoning. By 1993, many Serbs and Croats who disagreed with their respective regimes had already left. Few objective voices remained, and most of these people were purged from government institutions, or faced harassment if they spoke against the regime. A strong Manichaean morality did not allow for any ambiguity. One was either a supporter of the nation and its objectives or a traitor. While there were often attacks on the governments of Milošević and Tudjman, including demonstrations, few people questioned the rise of nationalism, or the themes expressed in nationalist writings.

While it was perhaps permissible to argue that Tudjman or Milošević were not doing enough to promote nationalism, it was unacceptable to question whether the rise of nationalism was a positive phenomenon. It would have been impossible to go back to the 'good old days' of Communism. As Slavenka Drakulić lamented during the war, Croatian nationalism was like an 'ill fitting shirt', with sleeves that were too long, and a collar that was too high. But she noted with disdain that 'You might not like the colour and the cloth might itch. But there is no escape; there is nothing else to wear.'[23] Eventually both Croats and Serbs would rid themselves of their respective shirts – there was an escape, and it surprisingly came through the democratic processes. The rise of Stipe Mesić and Ivica Racan in Croatia, and Vojislav Kostunica in Serbia, all through the democratic process, was indeed a miracle.

Was there ever genocide in Serbia or Croatia?

Serbs and Croats both cast themselves as victims of 'holocausts' during the Second World War and genocide in the 1990s, and this issue remains highly contentious. While both nations suffered from atrocious massacres, did either really suffer from genocide? The Croats were certainly in no danger of being exterminated at Bleiburg, where Partisans aimed to kill collaborators – not all Croats. Even though there is clear indisputable evidence of Četnik massacres of Croats and Moslems throughout the NDH, there was no concrete proof that the Četniks aimed to exterminate the entire Croatian nation – nor would they have had the means to do so. The only letter to this effect, describing a plan to create an 'ethnically pure Greater Serbia', was dismissed by impartial historians as a forgery, according to Tim Judah and others.[24]

Were the Ustaša-run concentration camps geared towards annihilating all Serbs? This is not an easy question to answer. That one-third of Serbs in the NDH were targeted for extermination might constitute genocide, in that the Genocide Convention argues that any attempt to destroy a group 'in part' is constitutive of genocide. While I am not persuaded of a Serbian genocide in the 1940s, this argument was made recently by Damir Mirković in the *Journal of Genocide Research*, wherein he cites a variety of historians and sociologists, including Helen Fein, Sava Bosnitch, and others. Bosnitch for one, argues: 'The genocide, a joint enterprise of the Roman Catholic and Muslim Ustashas, was to Serbs what the Holocaust was to Jews across Europe.'[25]

Problematically, however, Mirković fails to convince us of the past when he applies his research to the present, citing the 1941 'genocide' as an 'important contributory factor' in the uprising of Serbs in Croatia, coupled with 'the new [Croatian] government's drastic practices of discrimination and mass violations of civil rights'.[26] While he alludes to the exploitation of genocide by both Serbian and Croatian leaders during the conflict, Mirković fails to engage with Milošević's manipulation of the Croatian Serbs, the use of warlords to terrorise populations, and the role of moderates, such as Jovan Rasković, who were trying to prevent an escalation of violence. Referring to Croatian 'scorched earth policies' and 'blitzkriegs', he has linked past atrocities with the 1990s, tracing a continuous theme of 'Croatian ultra-nationalism and Serbophobia as a driving force that rationalizes destruction, killing, expulsion, and even forced conversion to Roman Catholicism'.[27] While some historians may contend that the NDH regime was indeed genocidal, Mirković's use of stock Serbian genocide propaganda (and I have reviewed much of it) raises questions about his motivations, particularly since he has no interest in discussing Serbian crimes from the Second World War or the more recent past.

What interests me particularly about Mirković's research is his operationalisation of denialism. He argues that 'As with other genocides, the Ustasha genocide has its own deniers', a phenomenon that he links to political correctness movements in North America, and their demonisation of the Serbs during the 1990s. [28] The labelling of anyone who questions the Serbian 'genocide' as a denier certainly echoes Katz, Goldhagen and others who have used similar imagery in the case of the Holocaust, demonstrating clearly that even peer-reviewed professional journals in Western countries can be co-opted into new and ambiguous comparative genocide debates.

My personal opinion, which may well be refuted in future years, is that genocide (of Serbs or Croats) in the occupied and divided Yugoslavia during the Second World War is very difficult to prove, although it seems clear that here, as elsewhere, the Jews were targeted for mass extermination. I say this for the following reasons: Raphael Lemkin's *Axis Rule in Occupied Europe* (1944) clearly laid out that genocide was '*a coordinated plan of different actions aiming at the destruction of essential foundations of the life of national groups, with the aim of annihilating the groups themselves*'. While the Genocide Convention does use the term 'in part', the purpose of genocide traditionally has been to eliminate a group in its entirety. Alain Destexhe has also claimed recently in *Rwanda and Genocide in the 20th Century*, that: 'Genocide is a crime on a different scale to all other crimes against humanity and implies an intention to completely exterminate the chosen group.' [29] Claiming that eliminating one-third in a given territory, while ignoring the target population in neighbouring areas, constitutes a genocide is a contentious proposition.

A related problem is the propagandisation of the numbers of dead, which I have tried to review in Chapters 5 and 6. Mirković's research, as well as that of Bataković (whom Mirković seems to esteem greatly) and others, is rife with anti-Croatian vocabulary, not only from the past but also in the present. It seems impossible to separate their present-day political motivations from their analysis of past events, and this throws their research into question. In evaluating historic genocides in Yugoslavia, some distance and objectivity is required, and I hope that more impartial historians in the years ahead will critically examine the past here, once the legacies of Communist corruption and bloody ethnic conflict have dissipated.

I would similarly argue that there is little evidence that in the 1990s either Serbs or Croats were targeted with an outright policy of genocide. While in 1991 the Croats were clearly the victims of Serbian and JNA aggression, I have argued that this aggression was not unprovoked. Tudjman's insensitive and often xenophobic reactions to Croatia's Serbian population, and his overt support of former Ustaša leaders, raised justifiable concerns that Serbian national rights were under threat. Of course, the Serbian reaction was not an appropriate reflection of the level of persecution to which they were being exposed. Milošević and his allies needed little pretext to launch a full-scale invasion of Croatia. Tudjman's xenophobia gave the Serbs the excuse they needed, but the invasion would probably have happened anyway. While it was true that Tudjman brought back elements of an Ustaša past, and remained ambiguous about the NDH throughout his life, Milošević's actions also demonstrated his interest in the Nazi ideal of *Lebensraum*. But let us be clear – neither nation can be realistically compared to Nazi Germany. Ethnic cleansing (at least in Croatia) was not genocide, and it was not a continuation of the Holocaust.

The attempt to form greater national states, to invade and conquer territory while violently expelling populations from it, does not constitute genocide. Genocide refers to people – specifically defined national or ethnic groups – not strategic parcels of land in neighbouring countries, although perhaps it may in the future. Had either Serbs or Croats favoured genocide over irredentism, many more people would have been killed – millions as opposed to hundreds of thousands. Both sides – lest we forget – had the capacity to inflict far greater casualties than they did. While I mean no offence to the victims of Yugoslavia's wars, compared with the Nazis, Serbian and Croatian propaganda was relatively mild. Nothing Serbs or Croats ever wrote or filmed could ever compare with the chilling Nazi classic *Der Ewige Jüde*, or the proliferation of Nazi textbooks (such as *The Poisoned Toadstool*), wall charts, and phrenological heads, detailing the subhuman and parasitic nature of the enemy.

The Bosnian Moslem case was obviously more complex, since we do have proven cases of genocide here. On 2 August 2001, the International Criminal Tribunal for the former Yugoslavia found the Bosnian Serb General Radislav Krstić guilty of genocide for his role in the execution of some 7,000 Bosnian Muslim men and boys near Srebrenica in July 1995.[30] More recently, Milošević himself was handed over to the Tribunal, to stand charges of genocide in Bosnia, evidence having been finally handed over on 27 May 1999, during the NATO bombing of Yugoslavia.[31] Croatian leaders may in turn face trials for genocide in Bosnia, although Tudjman's death will at least spare *him* from sharing the humiliating fate of his former rival. As for Kosovo, the locus of NATO's 'humanitarian' initiative, a UN court recently ruled that while the Serbian regime did commit crimes against humanity and war crimes: 'the exactions committed by Milosevic's regime cannot be qualified as criminal acts of genocide, since their purpose was not the destruction of the Albanian ethnic group ... but its forceful departure from Kosovo.'[32]

of both nations, how does one explain the gratuitous cruelty and vandalism that so characterised the war? Did two nations in search of land really have to create collection centres? Did they really have to destroy half of Mostar, which even today is a burned-out shell run by the Hercegovinian mafia? Was it really necessary to destroy well over one thousand mosques and churches? In coming to terms with the level of destruction, it is unclear why so much of the region had to be reduced to rubble in order to construct a better future. These are obviously questions that are far beyond the scope of this study; but they do bring to mind the obvious contradictions between what Serbs and Croats did to the Bosnian Moslems, and what they claimed the Moslems were going to do to them.

In the end, fears of Greater Serbia, and the invention of Serbophobia, played much the same role for Serbs and Croats as did anti-Semitism for nineteenth- and twentieth-century Zionists. As Hannah Arendt maintained, such generalised fears were 'an excellent means for keeping the people together ... an eternal guarantee of ... existence'.[35] For both Serbs and Croats, the concept of Diaspora was also important. Theodor Herzl's theory of a Diaspora in danger as the guiding principle for a homeland was constantly invoked. External threats to the nation unified disparate co-nationals into 'one people'. For Tudjman and Milošević, as for Herzl, a nation-state that included all co-nationals was the only adequate solution to the threat of victimisation and persecution, or even worse – genocide.[36]

Certainly, we face the possibility of the Holocaust being manipulated over and over again in the service of nationalism. Curiously, however, few Serbs or Croats adopted the tone of Stannard, Dadrian, or Hancock (Tudjman of course being the exception). While they participated in the comparative genocide debate, they were not looking for Jewish enemies, partly because each side was looking to Israel as a potential military ally and source of arms, but also because Holocaust imagery was crucial to the success of both propaganda campaigns. Unlike serious comparative genocide scholars whose nations had experienced real genocides, and therefore wanted to promote their histories within an academic context, neither Serbs nor Croats seemed interested in the merits of intellectual debate with fellow victims, especially outside the Balkans.

David Stannard attacked the idea that the Jews were 'chosen', and that other groups were by definition '*un*-chosen'.[37] This was not a strategy favoured by Serbs or Croats. Both were happy for the Jews to maintain their pre-eminent role as an archetypal victim, as long as they could continue to expropriate Jewish symbols. For Serbs and Croats, the comparative genocide debate was not an end in itself, it was a means to another end. Neither side had much interest in having Bleiburg or Jasenovac become a major part of school curriculums in North America or Israel. However, no one can say with any he earned the unfortunate nickname 'Finkiel-croate'. His *chef d'oeuvre* on the Balkans, *Comment peut-on être croate?*, appeared in 1992, at a time when many of Croatia's excesses in Bosnia were not well known. Nevertheless, Tudjman had been roundly criticised for his autocratic style, his revisionist writings, and his purges of government institutions and the police force. While Croatia was the victim of Serbian aggression at that time, Tudjman was no saint, making Finkielkraut's musings all the more bizarre. Words such as 'emancipation' and 'democracy' were bandied about, and Croatian nationalism was paralleled with the rise of Czech democracy: Tudjman was even favourably compared with Vaclav Havel.[39] Finkielkraut, it appears, was completely swayed by Croatian fears that Eastern Serbs were attacking a part of the Western world. He stressed the *européanéité*, or 'Europeanness' of the Croats, arguing that Croatia deserved to be saved, because of its 'Roman churches, its baroque churches and its Venetian palaces'.[40]

As others had done with the Serbs, Finkielkraut's text compared the plight of the Croats with the Jews, and he intimated that each had suffered in a similar fashion. For him, the Croats were the victims of a 'double suffering', first, suffering under Serbian attacks, and then having the 'truth of their suffering' denied or downplayed.[41] He even managed to excuse Tudjman's historical revisionism as being an attempt to show up the victimological pretensions of the Serbs. He went so far as to warn that the Serbs were inherently evil because 'the Nazis of this history wanted to pass themselves as Jewish'.[42] Their strategy, as Finkielkraut posited, was to make Slavonia *Croatenrein*, an obvious reminiscence of the *Judenrein* policies of the Nazis in the Second World War.[43]

Why Finkielkraut completely reversed his arguments only eight years after his *Future of a Negation* remains a mystery. While first denouncing groups who manipulated Holocaust imagery, he now used such arguments to support a nation whose leader was a Holocaust revisionist, at the helm of an authoritarian government. While it is tempting to call Finkielkraut a hypocrite, it is possible that he truly believed the propaganda stories coming out of Croatia at that time. Much of this information was very persuasive. Perhaps he truly thought that the Croats were suffering from genocide, and saw the practical implications of using Holocaust imagery to highlight their suffering to the world. It is more likely, however, that Finkielkraut became opportunistic, and thought the dissolution of Yugoslavia a good time for him to write a *J'accuse* type of essay, in the style of Emile Zola, to ensure his place in French intellectual history. Unfortunately, Tudjman's past and present were far more sullied than the life of Alfred Dreyfus.

By far the most common reaction to Serbian and Croatian propaganda was to discount all of it. A form of myopia often informed Western policymaking, particularly that of the United States. It became far easier for former

US Ambassador Lawrence Eagleberger to proclaim: 'Until the Bosnians, Serbs and Croats decide to stop killing each other, there is nothing the outside world can do about it.'[44] While the CIA estimated by 1992 that some 90 per cent of atrocities in Croatia and Bosnia-Hercegovina had been carried out by the Serbs, it was far easier for the American government to present all parties as moral equals, and therefore to abdicate any responsibility. By believing both all and none of the propaganda coming out of the Balkans, US policy-makers were able to avoid plunging headlong into a conflict that held no geostrategic appeal. One can therefore argue that Serbian and Croatian propaganda succeeded in spite of itself.

In reviewing Serbian and Croatian nationalist propaganda from the collapse of Yugoslavia until the beginning of 1999, the presence of Fall and persecution imagery was an obvious corollary to the horrific ground wars that began after 1991. Myth-makers performed a crucial role in legitimating the rise of Serbian and Croatian nationalism, as well as in excusing the many violent acts of statecraft that flowed from the expansionist designs of Franjo Tudjman and Slobodan Milošević. Clearly, we live in an age when history can be revised to suit any contingency. The conflict in Yugoslavia demonstrated how dangerous the manipulation of Biblical and Holocaust imagery could be in the hands of skilled propagandists.

This conflict also highlighted the dangers of authoritarianism and of a lack of critical reflection. Academics, journalists, and politicians bear a heavy responsibility for the nationalist fever that so dominated these countries in the 1990s. George Santayana's banal and over-quoted observation that 'those who neglect the past are condemned to repeat it' was thoroughly debunked in both the Serbian and Croatian cases. It was precisely this obsession with past mistakes and past injustices that led to the tragedies of war – with the helping hand of nationalist elites, of course. Future generations will now inherit even more painful legacies than did their grandfathers and grandmothers in the 1940s. However, with the recent ratification of the Rome Statute finally establishing a permanent International Court, and the international community forging ahead with a new role and new responsibilities, they will hopefully not have the chance to make the same mistakes all over again.

NOTES

1 Northrop Frye, *The Great Code: The Bible and Literature* (Toronto: Academic Press, 1982) p. 169.
2 William Pfaff, *The Wrath of Nations: Civilisation and the Furies of Nationalism* (New York: Simon & Schuster, 1993) p. 53.
3 Dušan Kečmanović, *The Mass Psychology of Ethnonationalism* (New York: Plenum Press, 1996) pp. 68–9.
4 Conor Cruise O'Brien, *God Land: Reflections on Religion and Nationalism* (Cambridge, MA: Harvard University Press, 1988) pp. 1–4; 7; 26.

5 Bruce Cauthen, 'The Myth of Divine Election and Afrikaner Ethnogenesis' in Geoffrey Hosking and George Schöpflin (eds), *Myths and Nationhood* (London: C. Hurst & Company, 1997) p. 113.

6 Harold Fisch, *The Zionist Revolution* (London: Weidenfeld & Nicolson, 1978) p. 17.

7 Hans Kohn, *The Idea of Nationalism: A Study in its Origins and Background* (New York: Macmillan, 1945) p. 36.

8 Frye, *The Great Code*, p. 24.

9 Anthony Smith, *Theories of Nationalism* (New York: Holmes & Meier, 1983) pp. 153–4.

10 *Ibid.* p. 22.

11 Anthony Smith, *National Identity* (London: Penguin Books, 1990) pp. 65–6.

12 *Ibid.* p. 37.

13 Bogdan Denitch, *Ethnic Nationalism: The Tragic Death of Yugoslavia* (Minneapolis, MN: University of Minnesota Press, 1994) p. 56.

14 George Schöpflin, 'The Functions of Myth and a Taxonomy of Myth' in Geoffrey Hosking and George Schöpflin (eds), *Myths and Nationhood*, p. 29.

15 Henry Tudor, *Political Myth* (London: Pall Mall Press, 1972) pp. 138–9.

16 Kečmanović, *The Mass Psychology of Ethnonationalism*, p. 62.

17 Schöpflin, 'The Functions of Myth and a Taxonomy of Myth', pp. 32–3.

18 Ernest Gellner, *Nations and Nationalism: New Perspectives on the Past* (Oxford: Blackwell, 1983) p. 56.

19 *Ibid.* p. 381.

20 Tony Nairn, *The Break-up of Britain, New Edition* (London: Verso, 1981) p. 41.

21 Cvijeto Job, 'Yugoslavia's Ethnic Furies', *Foreign Policy* (Fall, 1993) p. 64.

22 *Ibid.* p. 74.

23 Slavenka Drakulić, *The Balkan Express: Fragments from the Other Side of the War* (London: W.W. Norton & Company, 1993) p. 52.

24 This issue is discussed in Tim Judah, *The Serbs: History, Myth and the Destruction of Yugoslavia* (New Haven, CT: Yale University Press, 1997) p. 120.

25 Damir Mirković, 'The Historical Link between the Ustasha Genocide and the Croato-Serb Civil War: 1991–1995', *Journal of Genocide Research*, 2:3 (2000) p. 363.

26 *Ibid.* pp. 366–7.

27 *Ibid.* pp. 369–70.

28 *Ibid.* p. 364.

29 'Analysis: Defining Genocide', *BBC News* (10 December 2001).

30 TOL, 'Guilty of Genocide', *Transitions Online* (7 August, 2001) http://balkanreport.tol.cz/look/BRR/article (accessed June 2001).

31 William Shawcross has concluded that the timing, if not the charges themselves, has a political dimension, since the Western powers seemed happy enough to 'play ball' with Milošević before the bombing, only delivering him to the Tribunal for crimes in Bosnia when he escalated his persecution of Kosovar Albanians: see William Shawcross, *Deliver Us From Evil: Warlords and Peacekeepers in a World of Endless Conflict* (London: Bloomsbury, 2001), p. 347.

32 'Kosovo assault "was not genocide"', *BBC News* (7 September 2001).

33 For a discussion, see Jonathan Glover, *Humanity: A Moral History of the Twentieth Century* (London: Cape, 1999) pp. 127–9. Two excellent accounts of the Srebrenica massacre are Jan Willem Honig and Norbert Both's *Srebrenica: Record of a War Crime* (London: Penguin, 1996) and David Rohde's Pulitzer Prize-winning classic, *Endgame: The Betrayal and Fall of Srebrenica* (New York: Farrar, Straus and Giroux, 1997).

34 Jovan Divjak, 'The First Phase, 1992–1993', in Branka Magaš and Ivo Žanić (eds), *The War in Croatia and Bosnia-Herzegovina 1991–1995* (London: Frank Cass, 2001) pp. 136–7.

35 Glover, *Humanity*, pp. 7–8.
36 Quoted in Howard M. Sachar, *A History of Israel: From the Rise of Zionism to Our Time* (Oxford: Basil Blackwell, 1977) p. 40.
37 *Ibid.* p. 194.
38 See Barry Lituchy, 'The War Against the Serbs and the New American Fascism', *The College Voice* (October 1995).
39 Alain Finkielkraut, *Comment peut-on être croate?* (Paris: Éditions Gallimard, 1992) p. 35.
40 *Ibid.* p. 30.
41 *Ibid.* pp. 26–7.
42 *Ibid.* p. 50.
43 *Ibid.* p. 112.
44 Quoted and discussed in Richard Holbrooke, *To End a War* (New York: Random House, 1998) p. 23.

BIBLIOGRAPHY

Books and articles

Aarons, Mark and John Loftus, *Ratlines: How the Vatican's Nazi Networks Betrayed Western Intelligence to the Soviets* (London: Heinemann, 1991).

Adamović, Bojana, 'Expulsion of Serbs and Montenegrins From Kosovo and Metohija – The Most Sweeping Ethnic Cleansing in Europe', in Nebojša Jerković (ed.), *Kosovo and Metohija, An Integral Part of the Republic of Serbia and FR of Yugoslavia: Documents and Facts* (Belgrade: Review of International Affairs, 1995).

Adamović, Louis, *My Native Land* (New York: Harper & Brothers, 1943).

Ajami, Fouad, 'In Europe's Shadows', in Nader Mousavizadeh (ed.), *The Black Book of Bosnia: The Consequences of Appeasement* (New York: Basic Books, 1995).

Ali, Rabia and Lawrence Lifschutz (eds), *Why Bosnia? Writings on the Balkan Wars* (Stoney Creek, CT: The Pamphleteer's Press, 1993).

Alter, Peter, *Nationalism* (London: Edward Arnold, 1992).

Anderson, Benedict, *The Spectre of Comparisons: Nationalism, Southeast Asia, And The World* (London: Verso, 1998).

——, *Imagined Communities: Reflections on the Origin and Spread of Nationalism* (London: Verso, 1987).

Anzulović, Branimir, *Heavenly Serbia: From Myth to Genocide* (London: C. Hurst & Company, 1999).

Arendt, Hannah, *Eichmann in Jersulsam: A Report on the Banality of Evil* (London: Faber & Faber, 1963).

——, *The Origins of Totalitarianism* (London: Harcourt Brace Jovanovich, 1975).

Association of Architects of Mostar, *Mostar 92 Urbicide* (Mostar: Croatian Defence Council, 1992).

Association of Serbs from Croatia, *The Persecution of the Serbs in Croatia 1990/91 Documents* (Belgrade: Association of Serbs from Croatia, 1991).

Association of University Teachers and Scholars of Serbia, *Information on the New Crime of Genocide Against the Serbian People Within the Administrative Borders of Croatia* (Belgrade: The Association of University Teachers and Scholars of Serbia, 1991).

Auty, Phyllis, *Yugoslavia* (London: Thames and Hudson, 1965).

Avramov, Smilja, *Genocide Against the Serbs* (Belgrade: Museum of Modern Art, 1992).

271

Bakić-Hayden, Milica, 'Nesting Orientalisms: The Case of Former Yugoslavia', *Slavic Review* (Winter 1995).

Balas, Sven, 'The Opposition in Croatia', in Jasminka Udovički and James Ridgeway (eds), *Burn This House: The Making and Unmaking of Yugoslavia* (London: Duke University Press, 1997).

Baletić, Milovan (ed.), *Croatia 1994* (Zagreb: INA-Konzalting, 1994).

Banac, Ivo, *The National Question in Yugoslavia: Origins, History, Politics* (Cornell: Cornell University Press, 1992).

——, 'Preface/Introduction', in Zvonimir Separović (ed.), *Documenta Croatica* (Zagreb: VIGRAM-Zagreb i VIDEM Krsko, 1992).

—— (ed.), *Eastern Europe in Revolution* (Ithaca, NY: Cornell University Press, 1992).

Barkan, Elazar, *The Guilt of Nations: Restriction and Negotiating Historical Injustices* (New York: W. W. Norton & Company, 2000).

Barriot, Patrick, and Eve Crépin, *On assassine un peuple: Les serbes de Krajina* (Lausanne: L'Age D'Homme, 1995).

Bašić-Hrvatin, Sandra, 'Television and National/Public Memory', in James Gow, Richard Paterson and Alison Preston (eds), *Bosnia By Television* (London: British Film Institute, 1996).

Bebler, Anton, 'Yugoslavia's Variety of Communism and Her Demise', *Communist and Post Communist Studies* (March 1993).

Beljo, Ante (ed.), *War Pictures 1991–1993* (Zagreb: Croatian Information Center/Matica Hrvatska Iseljenika, 1993).

—— (ed.), *Greater Serbia: From Ideology to Aggression* (Zagreb: Croatian Information Center, 1993).

——, *Genocide in Yugoslavia: A Documentary Analysis* (Sudbury, ON: Northern Tribune Publishing, 1985).

Bellamy, Elizabeth, *Affective Genealogies: Psychoanalysis, Postmodernism, and the 'Jewish Question' After Auschwitz* (Lincoln, NB: University of Nebraska Press, 1997).

Bennett, Christopher, *Yugoslavia's Bloody Collapse: Causes, Course and Consequence* (London: C. Hurst & Company, 1995).

Bojić, Dusica (ed.), *Stradanja Srba U Sarajevuknjiga Dokumenatadokumentacionu Gradu Sakupila I Priredila/Suffering of the Serbs in Sarajevo: Document Book* (Belgrade: Komeserijat za izbeglice SR Srbije, 1995).

Bojić, Vesna, and David Dyker, *Sanctions on Serbia* (Brighton: Sussex European Institute, 1993).

Bonifaćić, Antun F. and Clement S. Mihanovich (eds), *The Croatian Nation in its Struggle for Freedom and Independence: A Symposium by Seventeen Croatian Writers* (Chicago: 'Croatia' Cultural Publication Center, 1955).

Bowman, Glenn, 'Xenophobia, Phantasy and the Nation: The Logic of Ethnic Violence in Former Yugoslavia', in Michael Freeman, Dragomir Pantić, and

Dušan Janjić (eds), *Nationalism and Minorities* (Belgrade: Institute of Social Sciences, 1995).

Brandt, Miroslav, 'Antimemorandum', and 'Maps of Greater Serbia Launched into the World', in Bože Ćović (ed.), *Roots of Serbian Aggression: Debates/Documents/ Cartographic Reviews* (Zagreb: Centar za Strane Jezike/AGM, 1993).

Brčin, Dragutin (ed.), *Genocide Once Again: The Ustasha Terror Over Serbs in 1991* (Belgrade: Serbian Ministry of Information, 1991).

Breuilly, John, *Nationalism and the State* (Manchester: Manchester University Press, 1985).

Bringa, Tone, *Being Muslim the Bosnian Way: Identity and Community in a Central Bosnian Village* (Princeton, NJ: Princeton University Press, 1995).

Browning, Christopher, *Fateful Months: Essays on the Emergence of the Final Solution* (London: Holmes & Meier, 1991).

Buckley, William F., *In Search of Anti-Semitism* (New York: Continuum, 1992).

Buittenhuis, Peter, *The Great War of Words: British, American and Canadian Propaganda and Fiction, 1914–1933* (Vancouver, BC: University of British Columbia Press, 1987).

Bulajić, Milan, *Tudjman's 'Jasenovac Myth': Genocide Against, Serbs, Jews and Gypsies* (Belgrade: Stručna Kniga, 1994).

——, *The Role of the Vatican in the Break-up of Yugoslavia* (Belgrade: Serbian Ministry of Information, 1993).

——, Antun Miletić, and Dragoje Lukić (eds), *Never Again: Ustashi Genocide in the Independent State of Croatia (NDH) from 1941–1945* (Belgrade: The Ministry of Information of the Republic of Serbia, 1991).

Burdett, Anita L. P. (ed.), *The Historical Boundaries Between Bosnia, Croatia, Serbia: Documents and Maps, 1815–1945* (London: Archive Editions, 1995).

Burleigh, Michael, *Death and Deliverance: Euthanasia in Germany 1900–1945* (Cambridge: Cambridge University Press, 1994).

Campbell, David, *National Deconstruction: Violence, Identity, and Justice In Bosnia* (Minneapolis, MN: University of Minnesota Press, 1998).

——, *Politics Without Principle: Sovereignty, Ethics and the Narratives of the Gulf War* (Boulder, CO: Lynne Rienner, 1993).

Cauthen, Bruce, 'The Myth of Divine Election and Afrikaner Ethnogenesis', in Geoffrey Hosking and George Schöpflin (eds), *Myths and Nationhood* (London: C. Hurst & Company, 1997).

Čavoški, Kosta, 'The Formation of Borders and the Serbian Question', in Stanoje Ivanovic (ed.), *The Creation and Changes of the Internal Borders of Yugoslavia* (Belgrade: Ministry of Information of the Republic of Yugoslavia, 1992).

Charny, Israel, 'Toward a Generic Definition of Genocide', in George

Andreopoulos (ed.) *Genocide: Conceptual and Historical Dimensions* (Philadelphia, PA: University of Pennsylvania Press,1994).

Cigar, Norman, *Genocide in Bosnia: The Policy of 'Ethnic Cleansing'* (College Station, TX: Texas A & M University Press, 1995).

Cohen, Lenard J., *Broken Bonds: Yugoslavia's Disintegration and Balkan Politics in Transition* (Boulder, CO: Westview Press, 1995).

Cohen, Philip J., *The World War II and Contemporary Chetniks: Their historic-political continuity and implications for stability in the Balkans* (Zagreb: Ceres, 1997).

——, *Serbia's Secret War: Propaganda and the Deceit of History* (College Station, TX: Texas A & M University Press, 1996).

Cohn, Norman, *The Pursuit of the Millennium* (London: Mercury Books, 1962).

Colter, Irwin, 'International Antisemitism', in Menachem Z. Rosensaft and Yehuda Bauer (eds), *Antisemitism: Threat to Western Civilization: Selected Papers Based on a Conference Held at the New York University School of Law 27 October 1985* (Jerusalem: Vidal Sassoon Center for the Study of Antisemitism/Hebrew University of Jerusalem, 1989).

Commissariat for Refugees, Belgrade, *Suffering of the Serbs in Sarajevo* (Belgrade: The Commissariat, 1995).

Corak, Zaljka, 'Croatian Monuments: Wounds Suffered From Other People's Illnesses', in Zvonimir Separović (ed.), *Documenta Croatica* (Zagreb: VIGRAM-Zagreb i VIDEM Krsko, 1992).

Ćosić, Dobrica, *L'éffondrement de la Yougoslavie: positions d'un résistant* (Paris: Age D'Homme, 1994).

Ćović, Bože (ed.), *Roots of Serbian Aggression: Debates, Documents, Cartographic Reviews* (Zagreb: Centar za Strane Jezike/AGM, 1993).

—— (ed.), *Croatia Between War and Independence* (Zagreb: University of Zagreb/OKC – Zagreb, 1991).

Crkvenčić, Ivan and Mladen Klemenžić, *Aggression Against Croatia: Geopolitical and Demographic Facts* (Zagreb: Republic of Croatia Central Bureau of Statistics, 1993).

Crnobrnja, Mihailo, *The Yugoslav Drama* (Toronto: McGill-Queens University Press, 1993).

Čuvalo, Ante (ed.), *Croatia and the Croatians* (Zagreb: Northern Tribune Publishing, 1991).

Cviić, Christopher, 'Who's to Blame for the War in Ex-Yugoslavia?', *World Affairs* (Fall 1993).

Dadrian, Vahakn N., 'The Comparative Aspects of the Armenian and Jewish Cases of Genocide: A Sociohistorical Perspective', in Alan S. Rosenbaum (ed.), *Is the Holocaust Unique? Perspectives on Comparative Genocide* (Boulder, CO: Westview Press, 1996).

Dakić, Mile, *The Serbian Krayina: Historical Roots and Its Rebirth* (Knin:

Information Agency of the Republic of Serbian Krayina, 1994).

Damjanov, Petar, 'Yugoslavia in the World War Two', *Review of International Affairs*, 46 (15 May 1995).

Davidowicz, Lucy, *The War Against the Jews, 1933–1945* (London: Weidenfeld and Nicolson, 1975).

Davis, Mike, *Late Victorian Holocausts: El Niño Famines and the Making of the Third World* (London: Verso, 2001).

Dedijer, Vladimir, Ivan Božić, Sima Ćirković, and Milorad Ekmečić, *History of Yugoslavia* (New York: McGraw-Hill, 1974).

de Hoyos, Ladislas, *Klaus Barbie: The Untold Story* (London: W. H. Allen, 1985).

Deichmann, Thomas, '"I Accuse": Radovan Karadzic Interview', *Living Marxism*, 102 (July/August, 1997).

Delić, Boris, 'Power Without Political Legitimacy or Moral Credibility', *Serbia: News, Comments, Documents, Facts, Analysis*, 41 (1995).

Denitch, Bogdan, *Ethnic Nationalism: The Tragic Death of Yugoslavia* (Minneapolis, MN: University of Minnesota Press, 1994).

Dinko, David, *War Damage Sustained by Orthodox Churches in Serbian Areas of Croatia in 1991* (Belgrade: Ministry of Information of the Republic of Serbia, 1992).

Djilas, Aleksa, 'A House Divided', in Nadar Mousavizadeh (ed.), *The Black Book of Bosnia: The Consequences of Appeasement* (New York: New Republic Books, 1996).

——, 'A Profile of Slobodan Milosevic', *Foreign Affairs*, 72:3 (Summer, 1993).

Djilas, Milovan, *The New Class: An Analyis of the Communist System* (New York: Praeger Publishing, 1957).

——*Wartime* (London: Harcourt, Brace, Jovanovich, 1977).

——, *The Contested Country: Yugoslav Unity and Communist Revolution 1919–1953* (Cambridge, MA: Harvard University Press, 1991).

Doder, Dusko 'Yugoslavia: New War, Old Hatreds', *Foreign Policy* (Summer 1993).

Doder, Dusko and Louise Branson, *Milosevic: Portrait of a Tyrant* (New York: Simon & Schuster, 1999).

Draginović, Krunoslav, 'The Biological Extermination of the Croats in Tito's Yugoslavia', in Antun Bonifačić and Clement Mihanovich (eds), *The Croatian Nation: Its Struggle for Freedom and Independence* (Chicago, IL: 'Croatia' Cultural Publishing Center, 1955).

Dragnitch, Alex, *Serbs and Croats: The Struggle in Yugoslavia* (New York: Harcourt Brace Jovanovich, 1992).

Drakulić, Slavenka, *Cafe Europa: Life After Communism* (London: Abacus, 1996).

——, *The Balkan Express: Fragments from the Other Side of the War* (London: W.

W. Norton & Company, 1993).

Drasković, Vuk, *Le Couteau* (Paris: J. C. Lattes, 1993).

Drescher, Seymour, 'The Atlantic Slave Trade and the Holocaust: A Comparative Analysis', in Alan S. Rosenbaum (ed.), *Is the Holocaust Unique? Perspectives on Comparative Genocide* (Boulder, CO: Westview Press, 1996).

Đurđević, Svetozar, *The Continuity of a Crime: The Final Settlement of the Serbian Question in Croatia* (Belgrade: IDEA Publishing House, 1995).

Emmert, Thomas A., *Serbian Golgotha, Kosovo, 1389* (New York: Columbia University Press, 1990).

Esler, Gavin, *The United States of Anger* (London: Michael Joseph, 1997).

Finkelstein, Norman, *The Holocaust Industry: Reflections on the Exploitation of Jewish Suffering* (New York: Verso, 2000).

Finkielkraut, Alain, *The Future of a Negation: Reflections on the Question of Genocide* translated by Mary Byrd Kelly (Lincoln, NB: University of Nebraska Press, 1998).

——, *Comment peut-on etre croate?* (Paris: Gallimard, 1992).

——, *Le juif imaginaire* (Paris: Gallimard, 1982).

Fisch, Harold, *The Zionist Revolution* (London: Weidenfeld & Nicolson, 1978).

Foley, Richard, *The Drama of Medjugorje* (Dublin: Veritas, 1992).

Freeman, Michael, Dragomir Pantić and Dusan Janjić (eds), *Nationalism and Minorities* (Belgrade: Institute of Social Sciences, 1995).

Friedman, Francine, *The Bosnian Moslems: Denial of a Nation* (Boulder, CO: Westview Press, 1996).

Frye, Northrop, *Words With Power: Being a Second Study of The Bible and Literature* (London: Harcourt, Brace, Jovanovich, 1990).

——, *The Great Code: The Bible and Literature* (Toronto: Academic Press Canada, 1982).

Furnemont, Jean François, *Le Vatican et l'ex Yougoslavie* (Paris: L'Harmattan, 1996).

Galić, Mirka, *Croatia Land and People* (Zagreb: Motovun Publishing House/Committee for Information of the Socialist Republic of Croatia, 1988).

Gellner, Ernest, *Nations and Nationalism: New Perspectives on the Past* (Oxford: Blackwell, 1983).

——, *Thought and Change* (London: Weidenfeld and Nicolson, 1964).

Glenny, Misha, *The Fall of Yugoslavia: The Third Balkan War* (London: Penguin Books, 1993).

Gligorov, Vladimir, *Why do Countries Break Up? The Case of Yugoslavia* (Uppsala, Sweden: Uppsala University Press, 1994).

Glover, Jonathan, *Humanity: A Moral History of the Twentieth Century* (London: Cape, 1999).

Goldhagen, Daniel Jonah, *Hitler's Willing Executioners: Ordinary Germans and the Holocaust* (New York: Alfred A. Knopf, 1996).

Gompert, David, 'The United States and Yugoslavia's Wars', in Richard Ullman (ed.), *The World and Yugoslavia's Wars* (New York: The Council on Foreign Relations, 1996).

Gothelf, Yehuda (ed.), *Zionism: The Permanent Representative of the Jewish People* (Israel: World Labour Zionist Congress, no date given).

Gow, James, and James Tisley, 'The Strategic Imperative for Media Management', in James Gow, Richard Paterson and Alison Preston (eds), *Bosnia By Television* (London: BFI, 1996).

Greenfeld, Liah, *Nationalism: Five Roads to Modernity* (Cambridge, MA: Harvard University Press, 1992).

Grmek, Mirko, Marc Gjidara and Neven Simac, *Le nettoyage ethnique: Documents historiques sur une idéologie serbe* (Paris: Fayard, 1993).

Gruden, Viktor, 'Psychological Sources of the Serbian Aggression Against Croatia', *Croatian Medical Journal*, War Supplement 2:21 (1991).

Gutman, Roy, *A Witness to Genocide* (New York: Macmillan, 1993).

Guzina, Dejan, 'Yugoslavia's Disintegration: An Interpretation', MA Thesis (Ottawa, ON: Carleton University, 1995).

Hadži-Jovančić, Dušanka (ed.), *The Serbian Question in the Balkans: Geographical and Historical Aspects* (Belgrade: University of Belgrade Faculty of Geography, 1995).

Hall, Brian, *The Impossible Country: A Journey Through the Last Days of Yugoslavia* (Boston: David Godine Publishers, 1994).

Hancock, Ian, 'Responses to the Porrajmos: The Romani Holocaust', in Alan S. Rosenbaum (ed.), *Is the Holocaust Unique? Perspectives on Comparative Genocide* (Boulder, CO: Westview Press, 1996).

Hartmann, Florence, *Milosevic: la diagonale du fou* (Paris: Denoël Impacts, 1999).

Hastings, Adrian, *The Construction of Nationhood: Ethnicity, Religion and Nationalism* (Cambridge: Cambridge University Press, 1997).

Hawksworth, Celia, *Colloquial Serbo-Croat* (London: Routledge 1993).

Hayden, Robert M. and Milica Bakić-Hayden, 'Orientalist Variations on the Theme Balkan: Symbolic Geography in Recent Yugoslav Politics', *Slavic Review* (Spring 1992).

Hedges, Chris, 'Words Replacing Bullets in Latest Balkans Battle', *The Globe and Mail* (16 May 1996).

Hefer, Stjepan, *Croatian Struggle for Freedom and Statehood* (Argentina: Croatian Information Service/Croatian Liberation Movement, 1979).

Henkin, Louis, 'Human Rights: Idealogy and Aspiration, Reality and Prospect', in Samantha Power and Graham Allison (eds), *Realizing Human Rights: Moving from Inspiration to Impact* (New York: St Martin's Press, 2000).

Herzog, Yaakov, *A People That Dwells Alone* (London: Weidenfeld and

Nicolson, 1975)

Hipfl, Brigitte, Klaus Hipfl and Jan Jagodzinski, 'Documentary Films and the Bosnia-Hercegovina Conflict: From Production to Reception', in James Gow, Richard Paterson and Alison Preston (eds), *Bosnia By Television* (London: British Film Institute, 1996).

Hitchens, Christopher, 'Appointment in Sarajevo: Why Bosnia Matters', in Rabia Ali and Lawrence Lifschutz (eds), *Why Bosnia? Writings on the Balkan Wars* (Stoney Creek, CT: Pamphleteer's Press, 1993).

Hobsbawm, Eric J. *Age of Extremes: The Short Twentieth Century 1914–1991* (London: Penguin Group, 1994).

——, *Nations and Nationalism Since 1780: Programme, Myth, Reality* (Cambridge: Cambridge University Press, 1995).

Holbrooke, Richard, *To End a War* (New York: Random House, 1998).

Honig, Jan Willem and Norbert Both, *Srebrenica: Record of a War Crime* (London: Penguin, 1996).

Hughes, Robert, *The Culture of Complaint* (Oxford: Oxford University Press, 1993).

Huntington, Samuel P., *The Clash of Civilizations and the Remaking of World Order* (New York: Simon and Schuster, 1996).

Igić, Zivorad, 'Kosovo – Metohija – A Demographic Time Bomb in Southern Serbia', in Nebojša Jerković (ed.), *Kosovo and Metohija, An Integral Part of the Republic of Serbia and FR of Yugoslavia: Documents and Facts* (Belgrade: Review of International Affairs, 1995).

Ignatieff, Michael, *Virtual War: Kosovo and Beyond* (London: Penguin, 2001).

——, *The Warrior's Honour* (London: Chatto and Windus, 1998).

——, *Blood and Belonging: Journeys into the New Nationalism* (Toronto: Viking Books, 1993).

Ilić, Jovan, 'The Balkan Geopolitical Knot and the Serbian Question', in Dušanka Hadži-Jovančić (ed.), *The Serbian Question in the Balkans: Geographical and Historical Aspects* (Belgrade: University of Belgrade Faculty of Geography, 1995).

——, 'The Serbs in the Former SR of Croatia', in Dušanka Hadži-Jovančić (ed.), *The Serbian Question in the Balkans: Geographical and Historical Aspects* (Belgrade: University of Belgrade Faculty of Geography, 1995).

——, 'Characteristics and Importance of Some Ethno-National and Political-Geographic Factors Relevant for the Possible Political-Legal Disintegration of Yugoslavia', in Stanoje Ivanović (ed.), *The Creation and Changes of the Internal Borders of Yugoslavia* (Belgrade: Ministry of Information of the Republic of Serbia, 1992).

——, 'Possible Borders of New Yugoslavia' in Stanoje Ivanović (ed.), *The Creation and Changes of the Internal Borders of Yugoslavia* (Belgrade: Ministry of Information of the Republic of Serbia, 1992).

Ivančević, Radovan (ed.), *Cultural Heritage of Croatia in the War 1991–1992* (Zagreb: Hrvatska Sveučilišna Naklada, 1993).

Ivanović, Stanoje (ed.), *The Creation and Changes of the Internal Borders of Yugoslavia* (Belgrade: Ministry of Information of the Republic of Serbia, 1992).

Iveković, Rada (ed.), *La Croatie depuis d'effondrement de la Yougoslavie* (Paris: L'Harmattan, 1994).

Jacobsen, Carl G., *The New World Order's Defining Crises: The Clash of Promise and Essence* (Aldershot: Dartmouth Publishing, 1996).

Jakovljević, M., 'Psychiatric Perspective of the War against Croatia, *Croatian Medical Journal*, 33 (1992) (War Supplement 2).

Janičijević, Jovan (ed.), *Serbian Culture Through Centuries: Selected List of Recommended Reading* (Belgrade: Yugoslav Authors' Agency, 1990).

Janjić, Dušan, 'Serbia Religion and War' Conference: Summer School of Interconfessional Dialogue and Understanding: 1st 1993 Novi Pazar, Serbia and Sjenica (Belgrade: IKV European Movement in Serbia, 1994).

Janković, Djordje, 'The Serbs in the Balkans in the Light of Archeological Findings', in Dušanka Hadži-Jovančić (ed.), *The Serbian Question in the Balkans: Geographical and Historical Aspects* (Belgrade: University of Belgrade Faculty of Geography, 1995).

Jelavich, Barbara, *History of the Balkans Volume II* (London: Cambridge University Press, 1993).

Jerković, Nebojša (ed.), *Kosovo and Metohija, An Integral Part of the Republic of Serbia and FR of Yugoslavia: Documents and Facts* (Belgrade: Review of International Affairs, 1995).

Job, Cvijeto, 'Yugoslavia's Ethnic Furies', *Foreign Policy* (Fall, 1993).

Jovanović, Drago, Gordana Bundalo, and Miloš Govedarica (eds) *The Eradication of Serbs in Bosnia and Hercegovina 1992–1993* (Belgrade: RAD, 1994).

Jovičić, Zoran, *Croatia Bosnia-Hercegovina: War Crimes Committed by the Yugoslav Army 1991–1992* (Zagreb: Croatian Information Center, 1993).

Judah, Tim, *The Serbs: History, Myth and the Destruction of Yugoslavia* (New Haven, CT: Yale University Press, 1997).

Kaličanin, Predrag, *Stresses of War* (Belgrade: Institute for Mental Health, 1993).

Kaplan, Harold, *Conscience and Memory: Meditations in a Museum of the Holocaust* (Chicago: University of Chicago Press, 1994).

Kaplan, Robert D., *Balkan Ghosts: A Journey Through History* (New York: St Martin's Press, 1993).

Karadzić, Radovan, 'Beginnings of a Secular Battle', in Patrick Barriot and Eve Crépin (eds), *On assassine un peuple: Les Serbes de Krajina* (Lausanne: L'Age D'Homme, 1995).

279

Katz, Steven T., 'The Uniqueness of the Holocaust: The Historical Dimension', in Alan S. Rosenbaum (ed.), *Is the Holocaust Unique? Perspectives on Comparative Genocide* (Boulder, CO: Westview Press, 1996).

Kečmanović, Dušan, *The Mass Psychology of Ethnonationalism* (New York: Plenum Press, 1996).

Klain, Eduard, 'Yugoslavia as a Group', *Croatian Medical Journal*, 33 (1992) (War Supplement 1).

Klier, John, 'The Myth of Zion Amongst East European Jewry', in Geoffrey Hosking and George Schöpflin (eds), *Myths and Nationhood* (London: C. Hurst & Company, 1997).

Kljakić, Slobodan, *A Conspiracy of Silence: Genocide in the Independent State of Croatia and Concentration Camp Jasenovac* (Belgrade: The Ministry of Information of the Republic of Serbia, 1991).

Knezević, Anto, *An Analysis of Serbian Propaganda: The Misrepresentation of the Writings of Historian Franjo Tudjman in Light of the Serbian Croatian War* (Zagreb: Croatian Information Center/Hrvatska Matica Iseljenika, 1992).

Kohn, Hans, *The Idea of Nationalism: A Study in Its Origins and Background* (New York: The Macmillan Company, 1945).

Kontić, Radoje, 'Great Jubilee of World and Our Own History: Victory Over Fascism the Most Important Event of the XX Century', *Review of International Affairs*, 46 (15 May 1995).

Kostović, Ivica and Miloš Judaš (eds), *Mass Killing and Genocide in Croatia 1991/92: A Book Of Evidence (Based upon the evidence of the Division of Information, the Ministry of Health of the Republic of Croatia)* (Zagreb: Hrvatska Sveučilišna Naklada, 1992).

Kovačević, Radovan, 'How Could the Serbs Forgive Vatican', *Serbia: News, Comments, Documents, Facts, Analysis*, 41 (February 1995).

Kresović, Tomislav, *UN Embargo: Serbia and Sanctions – Chronicle of A Punishment* (Belgrade: BINA, 1994)

Krestić, Vasilije, *History of the Serbs in Croatia and Slavonia, 1848–1992* (Belgrade: Beogradski izdavacko-graficki zavod, 1997).

——, 'First Phase: Until 1918', in Božidar Zečević (ed.), *The Uprooting: A Dossier of the Croatian Genocide Policy Against the Serbs* (Belgrade: Velauto International, 1992).

——, *The Same Old Story: Serbs in Croatia* (Belgrade, 1991).

Krsmanović, Momir, *The Blood-Stained Hands of Islam* (Belgrade: BIGZ, 1994).

Kumar, Radha, *Divide and Fall? Bosnia in the Annals of Partition* (London: Verso, 1997).

Lagerwey, Mary D., *Reading Auschwitz* (London: Sage, 1998).

Lajtman, Ivo (ed.) *War Crimes Against Croatia* (Zagreb: Verčenji list, 1991).

Lampe, John R., *Yugoslavia as History: Twice There Was a Country* (Cambridge: Cambridge University Press, 1996).

Landau, Ronnie S., *Studying the Holocaust: Issues, Readings and Documents* (London: Routledge, 1998).

Langer, Lawrence L., *Preempting the Holocaust* (New Haven, CT: Yale University Press, 1998).

Laplace, Yves, *L'Âge d'homme en Bosnie: petit guide d'une nausée suisse* (Lausanne: En bas, 1997).

Lebor, Adam, *A Heart Turned East: Among The Muslims of Europe and America* (London: Little, Brown, 1997).

Letica, Slaven, 'Introduction', in Zvonimir Separović (ed.), *Documenta Croatica* (Zagreb: VIGRAM-Zagreb i VIDEM Krsko, 1992).

Levinsohn, Florence Hamish, *Belgrade: Among the Serbs* (Chicago: Ivan R. Dee, 1994).

Lewis, Florag, 'Israel on the Eve of Eichman's Trial', in Bill Adler (ed.), *Israel: A Reader* (Philadelphia, PA: Chilton Books, 1968).

Lituchy, Barry, 'The War Against the Serbs and the New American Fascism', *The College Voice* (October 1995).

Lučić, Milan, *Teror Nad Srbima '91/The Extermination of Serbs '91* (Novi Sad: Pokrajinski sekretarijat za informacije AP Vojvodine, 1991).

Lukić, Nikola, 'Education Problems of the Albanian National Minority in Kosovo and Metohija', in Nebojša Jerković (ed.), *Kosovo and Metohija, An Integral Part of the Republic of Serbia and FR of Yugoslavia: Documents and Facts* (Belgrade: Review of International Affairs, 1995).

Macan, Trpimir, 'The History of the Croatian People' (Zagreb: University of Zagreb/Matica Hrvatska Iseljenika, 1994).

Macartney, C. A., *Hungary: A Short History* (Edinburgh: Edinburgh University Press, 1961).

MacDonald, David B., 'La Croatie: un exemple d'« épuration langagière »?', *Raisons Politiques*, 2 (May, 2001).

——, 'The Myth of "Europe" in Croatian Politics and Economics', *Slovo: An Interdisciplinary Journal of Russian, East European and Eurasian Affairs*, Special Issue (March 2000).

——, 'Political Zionism and the "Nebeski Narodniks": Towards an Understanding of the Serbian National Self', *Slovo: An Interdisciplinary Journal of Russian, East European and Eurasian Affairs*, 10:1–2 (1998).

Magaš, Branka, and Ivo Žanić (eds), *The War in Croatia and Bosnia-Herzegovina 1991–1995* (London: Frank Cass, 2001).

Magaš, Branka, *The Destruction of Yugoslavia: Tracing the Breakup 1980–92* (London: Verso, 1993).

Malcolm, Noel, *Kosovo: A Short History* (London: Macmillan, 1998).

——, *Bosnia: A Short History* (London: New York University Press/Macmillan, 1994).

Malesić Marjan, *The Role of the Mass Media in the Serbian–Croatian Conflict*

(Stockholm: Stryelsen for Psykologist Forsvar, 1993).

Maliqi, Shkelzen, 'The Albanian Movement in Kosova', in David A. Dyker and Ivan Vejdoda (eds), *Yugoslavia and After: A Study in Fragmentation, Despair and Rebirth* (London: Longman, 1996).

Marinović, Nikola, *Stories from Hell: Confessions of Serbs, Tortured in the Concentration Camps in Croatia and Bosnia and Herzegovina in 1991 and 1992* (Belgrade: Serbian Ministry of Information, 1993).

'Marking the 52nd anniversary of Bleiburg and the Croatian Calvary,' *Croatia Weekly* (5 March 1998).

Markotich, Stan, 'Milosević's Renewed Attacks on the Independent Media', *Transition*, 1:3 (March 1995).

Marković, Mira, *Answer* (London: Minerva Press, 1996).

——, *Night and Day: A Diary* (London: Minerva Press, 1996).

Marković, Ratko, 'What are Yugoslavia's Internal Borders?', in Stanoje Ivanović (ed.), *The Creation and Changes of the Internal Borders of Yugoslavia* (Belgrade: Ministry of Information of the Republic of Serbia, 1992).

Marriott, J. A. R., *The Eastern Question: An Historical Study in European Diplomacy* (Oxford: Clarendon Press, 1925).

Marshland, David, 'Caught Red-Handed: The Black Hand and War in Europe', *Croatian Times*, 2 (February 1996).

McAdams, C. Michael, 'Croatia's Ancient Borders', *American Croatian Review* (November 1995).

——, 'The Truth is ... (about those "Bosnian Serbs")', *American Croatian Review* (June 1995).

——, *Croatia: Myth & Reality* (New York: Croatian Information Center, 1994).

McCrone, David, *The Sociology of Nationalism* (London: Routledge, 1998).

Messinger, Gary S., *British Propaganda in the First World War* (Manchester: Manchester University Press, 1992).

Mesić, Stjepan, 'The Road to War', in Branka Magaš and Ivo Žanić (eds), *The War in Croatia and Bosnia-Herzegovina 1991–1995* (London: Frank Cass, 2001).

Meštrović, Stjepan (ed.), *The Conceit of Innocence: Losing the Conscience of the West in the War Against Bosnia* (College Station, TX: Texas A & M University Press, 1997).

——, Miroslav Goreta and Slaven Letica, *The Road from Paradise: Prospects for Democracy in Eastern Europe* (Lexington, KY: The University Press of Kentucky, 1993).

——, Slaven Letica and Miroslav Goreta, *Habits of the Balkan Heart: Social Character and the Fall of Communism* (College Station, TX: Texas A & M University Press, 1993).

Milenković, Milutin, 'Kosovo in Serbia or ...?', in Nebojša Jerković (ed.),

Bibliography

Kosovo and Metohija, An Integral Part of the Republic of Serbia and FR of Yugoslavia: Documents and Facts (Belgrade: Review of International Affairs, 1995).

Mileusnić, Slobodan, *Duhovni Genocid pregled Porusenih, Ostecenih I Obesvecenih Crkava, Manastira I Drugih Crkvenih Objekata U Ratu 1991–1993 / Spiritual Genocide: A Survey of Destroyed, Damaged and Desecrated Churches, Monasteries and Other Church Building(s) During the War 1991–1993* (Belgrade: Beograd Muzej srpske prvoslavne crkve [Belgrade Museum of the Serbian Orthodox Church], 1995).

Milivojević, Zdenka, 'Serbia', in James Gow, Richard Paterson and Alison Preston (eds), *Bosnia By Television* (London: British Film Institute, 1996).

Miljus, Branko, *Assassins au nom de Dieu* (Lausanne: L'Age D'Homme, 1991).

Milosević, Milan, 'The Media Wars', in Jasminka Udovicki and James Ridgeway (eds), *Yugoslavia's Ethnic Nightmare: The Inside Story of Europe's Unfolding Ordeal* (New York: Lawrence Hill Books, 1995).

Minogue, Kenneth R., *Nationalism* (London: B. T. Batsford, 1967).

Mirković, Damir, 'The Historical Link between the Ustasha Genocide and the Croato-Serb Civil War: 1991–1995', *Journal of Genocide Research*, 2:3 (2000).

Mirković, Mirko, 'Fourth Phase: 1945–1990', Božidar Zečević (ed.), *The Uprooting: A Dossier of the Croatian Genocide Policy Against the Serbs* (Belgrade: Velauto International, 1992).

Mojzes, Paul, *Yugoslavian Inferno: Ethnoreligious Warfare in the Balkans* (New York: Continuum, 1994).

Myrvar, Vatro, 'The Croatian Statehood and its Continuity', in Antun F. Bonifačić and Clement S. Mihanovich (eds), *The Croatian Nation in its Struggle for Freedom and Independence: A Symposium by Seventeen Croatian Writers* (Chicago: 'Croatia' Cultural Pub. Center, 1955).

Nairn, Tom, *Faces of Nationalism: Janus Revisited* (London: Verso, 1997).

——, *The Break-up of Britain New Edition* (London: Verso, 1981).

Nakrada, Radmila, *The Disintegration of Yugoslavia and the New World Order* (Belgrade: Institute for European Studies, 1994–5).

Nedeljković, Mile, *The Serbs of the March – Guardians of the Border/Les Serbes defenseurs des frontiers* (Belgrade: The Ministry of Information of the Republic of Serbia, 1992).

Neumann, Iver B., *Uses of the Other: 'The East' in European Identity Formation* (Minneapolis, MN: University of Minnesota Press, 1999).

Nouvel Observateur et Raporteurs sans Frontières, *Le Livre Noir de L'ex-Yougoslavie: Purification Ethnique et Crimes de Guerre* (Paris: Publications Arléa, 1993).

Novick, Peter, *The Holocaust and Collective Memory: The American Experience* (New York: Bloomsbury, 1999).

Obradović Đorđe, *Suffering of Dubrovnik* (Dubrovnik: Dubrovački Vjesnik, 1993).

O'Brien, Conor Cruise, *God Land: Reflections on Religion and Nationalism* (Cambridge, MA: Harvard University Press, 1988).

Omerčanin, Ivo, *Sacred Crown of the Kingdom of Croatia* (Philadelphia, PA: Dorrance, 1973).

——, *The Pro-Allied Putsch in Croatia in 1944 and the Massacre of Croatians by Tito's Communists in 1945* (Philidelphia, PA: Dorrance & Company, 1975).

Ozkirimli, Umut, *Theories of Nationalism: A Critical Introduction* (London: Macmillan, 2000).

Pavič, Radovan, 'Greater Serbia from 1844 to 1990/91', in Bože Ćović (ed.), *Roots of Serbian Aggression: Debates, Documents, Cartographic Reviews* (Zagreb: Centar za Strane Jezike/AGM, 1993).

Pavković, Aleksander, 'From Yugoslavism to Serbism: The Serb National Idea 1986–1996', *Nations and Nationalism*, 4:4 (October 1998).

——, *The Fragmentation of Yugoslavia: Nationalism in a Multi-Ethnic State* (Basingstoke: Macmillan, 1996).

Pavlović, Marko, 'Yugoslavia and Serbian Lands', in Stanoje Ivanović (ed.), *The Creation and Changes of the Internal Borders of Yugoslavia* (Belgrade: Serbian Ministry of Information, 1992).

Pavlovich, Paul, *The Serbians* (Toronto: Serbian Heritage Books, 1988).

Pavlowitch, Stefan K., *The Improbable Survivor: Yugoslavia and Her Problems, 1918–1988* (London: C. Hurst & Company, 1988).

Péroche, Gregory, *Histoire de la Croatie et des nations slaves du Sud 395–1992* (Paris: F. X. de Guibert, 1992).

Penkower, Monty Noam, *The Holocaust and Israel Reborn: From Catastrophe to Sovereignty* (Urbana, IL.: University of Illinois Press, 1994).

Peroche, Gregory *Histoire de la Croatie et des nations slaves du Sud 395–1991* (Paris: F.-X. De Guibert, 1992).

Petković, Ranko, 'Will Yugoslavia Survive?', *Review of International Affairs* (20 February 1991).

Petrović, Radislav, *The Extermination of Serbs on the Territory of the Independent State of Croatia* (Belgrade: Serbian Ministry of Information, 1991).

Pfaff, William, *The Wrath of Nations: Civilization and the Furies of Nationalism* (New York: Simon & Schuster, 1993).

Pifat-Mrzljak, Greta (ed.), *Scientists Against the War in Croatia: World Responses to the Ruđer Bošković Institute's Endeavour for Peace in Croatia* (Zagreb: Hrvatska Sveučilišna Naklada, 1992).

Pokrajac, Jovan, 'Religious Instruction for New Croats', *Serbia: News, Comments, Documents, Facts, Analysis*, 41 (February 1995).

Popov, Nebojša, 'La populisme serbe' (suite), *Les Temps Modernes* (May 1994).

Popović, Velimir (ed.), *Events in the Sap of Kosovo: The Causes and Consequences of Irredentist and Counter-revolutionary Subversion* (Belgrade: Review of International Affairs, 1981).

Poulton, Hugh, *Balkans: Minorities and States in Conflict* (London: Minority Rights Group, 1991).

Pozzi, Henry, *Black Hand Over Europe* (Zagreb: Croatian Information Center, 1994; first published 1935).

Pusić, Vesna, 'A Country by Any Other Name: Transition and Stability in Croatia and Yugoslavia', *East European Politics and Society*, 6:3.

Radovanović, Svetlana, 'Demographic Growth and Ethnodemographic Changes in the Republic of Serbia', in Dušanka Hadži-Jovančić (ed.), *The Serbian Question in the Balkans: Geographical and Historical Aspects* (Belgrade: University of Belgrade Faculty of Geography, 1995).

Radulović, Marjorie, *Rage of the Serbs* (Lewes, E. Sussex: The Book Guild, 1998).

Ramet, Sabrina Petra, *Balkan Babel* (Boulder, CO: Westview Press, 1996).

——, *Nationalism and Federalism in Yugoslavia: 1962–1992* (Boulder, CO: Westview Press, 1993).

Read, James Morgan, *Atrocity Propaganda 1914–1919* (New Haven, CT: Yale University Press, 1941).

'Review of Sîme Dodan, *Bosnia and Hercegovina, a Croatian Land* (Zagreb: Meditor, 1994)', *Feral Tribune* (29 December 1997).

Ridley, Jasper, *Tito* (London: Constable, 1994).

Roberts, Adam, 'Sins of the Secular Missionaries', *The Economist* (29 January 2000).

Robertson, Geoffrey, *Crimes Against Humanity: The Struggle for Global Justice* (London: Penguin, 2000).

Robin, Mireille, and Danka Sosić-Vijatović, *La Croatie depuis l'effondrement de la Yougoslavie: l'opposition non-nationaliste: textes traduits du croate et du Serbo-croate* (Paris: L'Harmattan, 1994).

Rohde, David, *Endgame: The Betrayal and Fall of Srebrenica* (New York: Farrar, Straus and Giroux, 1997).

Rosensaft, Menachem Z. and Yehuda Bauer (eds), *Antisemitism: Threat to Western Civilization: Selected Papers Based on a Conference Held at the New York University School of Law 27 October 1985* (Jerusalem: Vidal Sassoon Center for the Study of Antisemitism, Hebrew University of Jerusalem, 1989).

Ross, Marc Howard, 'Psychocultural Interpretation Theory and Peacemaking in Ethnic Conflicts', *Political Psychology*, 16:3 (1995).

Roth, Hugo, *Kosovski Iskonipozadina Aktuelnih Zbivanja Na Kosovu I Metohiji: Kosovo Origins: the Background to the Present-day Situation in Kosovo and Metohia* (Belgrade: Nikola Pasić, 1996).

Roux, Michel, *Les Albanais en Yougoslavie: minorité nationale, territoire et développement* (Paris: Editions de la Maison des sciences de l'homme, 1992).

Rubenstein, Richard L., 'Religion and the Uniqueness of the Holocaust', in Alan S. Rosenbaum (ed.), *Is the Holocaust Unique? Perspectives on Comparative Genocide* (Boulder, CO: Westview Press, 1996).

Runciman, Steven, *The Medieval Manichee* (Cambridge: Cambridge Univesity Press, 1947).

Sachar, Howard M., *A History of Israel: From the Rise of Zionism to Our Time* (Oxford: Basil Blackwell, 1977).

SANU, 'Memorandum on the Ethnic Cleansing of and Genocide Against the Serb People of Croatia and Krajina', *Review of International Affairs*, 41 (15 November, 1995).

——, (A group of members of the Serbian Academy of Science and Arts on current questions in Yugoslav society), *Memorandum*, in Bože Ćović (ed.), *Roots of Serbian Aggression: Debates/Documents/Cartographic Reviews* (Zagreb: Centar za Strane Jezike/AGM, 1993).

Schöpflin, George, 'The Functions of Myth and a Taxonomy of Myth', in Geoffrey Hosking and George Schöpflin (eds), *Myths and Nationhood* (London: C. Hurst & Company, 1997).

Segedin, Petar, 'Genocidal Nature of a Nation', in Zvonimir Separović (ed.), *Documenta Croatica* (Zagreb: VIGRAM-Zagreb i VIDEM Krsko, 1992).

Sekelj, Laslo, 'Antisemitism and Jewish Identity in Serbia After the 1991 Collapse of the Yugoslav State', *Analysis of Current Trends in Antisemitism, 1997 acta no. 12* (Jerusalem: The Vidal Sassoon International Center for the Study of Antisemitism/The Hebrew University of Jerusalem, 1997).

Sells, Michael A., 'Religion, History and Genocide in Bosnia-Hercegovina', in G. Scott Davis (ed.), *Religion and Justice in the War Over Bosnia* (London: Routledge, 1996).

——, *The Bridge Betrayed: Religion And Genocide In Bosnia* (London: University of California Press, 1996).

Šentija, Josip, 'Croatia from 1941 to 1991' (Zagreb: University of Zagreb/Matica Hrvatska Iseljenika, 1994).

Serbian Ministry of Information, 'Facts About The Republic of Serbia' (Helsinki: Embassy of the Federal Republic of Yugoslavia, February 1996).

Serbian National Defense Council of America, *Genocide in Croatia 1941–1945* (Chicago, IL: Serbian National Defense Council of America, 1993).

Seroka, Jim and Vukasin Pavlović, *The Tragedy of Yugoslavia* (London: M. E. Sharpe, 1992).

Shawcross, William, *Deliver Us From Evil: Warlords and Peacekeepers in a World of Endless Conflict* (London: Bloomsbury, 2001).

Sherman, Arnold, *Perfidy in the Balkans: The Rape of Yugoslavia* (Athens: Psichogios Publications, 1993).

Silber, Laura and Alan Little, *The Death of Yugoslavia* (London: BBC Books, 1995).

Singleton, Fred, *A Short History of the Yugoslav Peoples* (London: Cambridge University Press, 1985).

Skrabelo, Ivo, 'They Shoot Monuments, Don't They?', in Zvonimir Separović (ed.), *Documenta Croatica* (Zagreb: VIGRAM-Zagreb i VIDEM Krsko, 1992).

Smith, Anthony, *Nationalism and Modernism* (London: Routledge, 1998).

——, 'The "Golden Age" and National Revival', in Geoffrey Hosking and George Schöpflin (eds), *Myths and Nationhood* (London: C. Hurst & Company, 1997).

——, *The Ethnic Origins of Nations* (Oxford: Blackwell, 1986).

——, *National Identity* (London: Penguin Books, 1990).

——, *Theories of Nationalism* (New York: Holmes & Meier, 1983).

——, *The Ethnic Revival* (Cambridge: Cambridge University Press, 1981).

——, *Nationalism in the Twentieth Century* (New York: New York University Press, 1979).

Soldo, Ivan, Bozica Ercegovac Jambrović and Jadranka Radloff, *Croatia, Hospitals on Target: Deliberate Military Destruction of the Hospitals in Croatia* (Zagreb: Croatia Information Centre, 1992).

Spajić-Vrkaš, Vedrana, *Croatia Discovers Janus* (Zagreb: Croatian University Press, 1992).

Spasovski, Melina, Dragica Živković and Milomir Stepić, 'The Ethnic Structure of the Population in Bosnia Hercegovina', in Dušanka Hadži-Jovančić (ed.), *The Serbian Question in the Balkans: Geographical and Historical Aspects* (Belgrade: University of Belgrade Faculty of Geography, 1995).

Stannard, David E., *American Holocaust: Columbus and the Conquest of the New World* (Oxford: Oxford Univesity Press, 1992).

——, 'Uniqueness as Denial: The Politics of Genocide Scholarship', in Alan S. Rosenbaum (ed.), *Is the Holocaust Unique? Perspectives on Comparative Genocide* (Boulder, CO: Westview Press, 1996).

Stefan, Lubrica, *From Fairy Tale to Holocaust: Serbia: Quisling Collaboration with the Occupier During the Period of the Third Reich with Reference to Genocide Against the Jewish People* (Zagreb: Hrvatska Matica Iseljenika, 1993).

Steiner, George, *The Portage to San Cristobal of A. H.* (London: Faber & Faber, 1981).

——, *In Blue Beard's Castle: Some Notes on the Redefinition of Culture* (New Haven, CT: Yale University Press, 1972).

Stern, Paul C., 'Why Do People Sacrifice for their Nations?', *Political Psychology*, 16:2 (1995).

Štitkovac, Ejub, 'Croatia: The First War', in Jasminka Udovicki and James Ridgeway (eds), *Burn This House: The Making and Unmaking of Yugoslavia* (London: Duke University Press, 1997).

Stojanović, Nikola, 'To Extermination: Ours or Yours?', in Aute Beljo (ed.), *Greater Serbia: From Ideology to Aggression* (Zagreb: Croatian Information Center, 1993).

Suljak, Dinko N., *Croatia's Struggle for Independence: A Documentary History* (Arcadia, CA: Croatian Information Service, 1977).

Tanner, Marcus, *Croatia: A Nation Forged in War* (New Haven, CT: Yale University Press, 1997).

Thomas, Robert, *Serbia Under Milošević: Politics in the 1990s* (London: C. Hurst & Company, 1999).

Thompson, Mark, *Forging War: The Media in Serbia, Croatia and Bosnia-Hercegovina* (London: Article 19/International Center Against Censorship, 1994).

Thomson, Oliver, *Mass Persuasion in History: An Historical Analysis of the Development of Propaganda Techniques* (New York: Crane, Russak & Company, 1977).

Tishkov, Valery, *Ethnicity, Nationalism and Conflict In and After the Soviet Union: The Mind Aflame* (London: Sage Publications, 1997).

Todorov, Tsvetan, *The Conquest of America: The Quest for the Other* (New York: Harper & Row, 1984).

Tonković, Vladimir, 'In Memoriam to Innocent Victions', in Ante Beljo and Bozica Erčegova-Jambrović (eds), *Genocide: Ethnic Cleansing in Northerwestern Bosnia* (Zagreb: Croatian Information Center, 1993).

Topalovič, Dusko, 'The Territorialization of the "Greater Serbian" Idea', in Ante Beljo and Bozica Erčegovac-Jambrovič (eds), *Genocide: Ethnic Cleansing in Northwestern Bosnia* (Zagreb: Croatian Information Center, 1993).

Trevor-Roper, Hugh, *Jewish and Other Nationalism* (London: Weidenfeld and Nicolson, 1962).

Tubić, Risto, 'Encyclopaedia of Evil and Crime', in Drago Jovanović, Gordana Bundalo and Miloš Govedarica (eds), *The Eradication of Serbs in Bosnia and Hercegovina 1992-1993* (Belgrade: RAD, 1994).

Tudjman, Franjo, *Horrors of War: Historical Reality and Philosophy – Revised Edition*, translated by Katarina Mijatović (New York: M. Evans and Company, 1996).

——, *Croatia on Trial: The Case of the Croatian Historian Dr F. Tudjman* (London: United Publishers, 1981).

Tudor, Henry, *Political Myth* (London: Pall Mall Press, 1972).

Tus, Anton, 'The War up to the Sarajevo Ceasefire', in Branka Magaš and ivo Žanić (eds), *The War in Croatia and Bosnia-Herzegovina 1991–1995* (London: Frank Cass, 2001).

Tvrtković, Paul, *Bosnia Hercegovina: Back to the Future* (London: Paul Tvrtković, 1993).

Ugrešić, Dubravka, *The Culture of Lies* (London: Phoenix House, 1998).

Ullman, Richard (ed.), *The World and Yugoslavia's Wars* (New York: The Council on Foreign Relations, 1996).

United States Holocaust Memorial Museum, *Genocide in Yugoslavia During the Holocaust* (Washington DC: United States Holocaust Memorial Museum, 1995).

Vankovska, Biljana, 'Civil–Military Relations in the Third Yugoslavia', *COPRI Working Papers* (Copenhagen: Copenhagen Peace Research Institute, 2000).

Vilić, Dušan, and Boško Todorović, *Breaking of Yugoslavia and Armed Secession of Croatia* (Beli Manastir: Cultura Centre 'Vuk Karadzić', 1996).

Vučelić, Milorad, *Kosovo and Albanian Separatism: The Defense of Kosovo* (Belgrade: Secretariat for Information of the Socialist Republic of Serbia, 1990).

Vulliamy, Ed, *Seasons in Hell: Understanding Bosnia's War* (London: St Martin's Press, 1994).

Wachtel, Andrew Baruch, *Making a Nation Breaking a Nation: Literature and Cultural Politics in Yugoslavia* (Stanford, CA: Stanford University Press, 1998).

Weber, Cynthia, 'Performative States', *Millennium: Journal of International Studies*, 27:1 (1998).

White, Hayden, *The Content of the Form: Narrative Discourse and Historical Representation* (Baltimore, MD: Johns Hopkins University Press, 1987).

Williams, Paul, 'The International Community', in Branka Magaš and Ivo Žanić (eds), *The War in Croatia and Bosnia-Herzegovina 1991–1995* (London: Frank Cass, 2001).

Yelen, Anne, *Kossovo 1389–1989: bataille pour les droits de l'âme* (Lausanne: Editions L'Age D'Homme, 1989).

Zečević, Božidar (ed.), *The Uprooting: A Dossier of the Croatian Genocide Policy Against the Serbs* (Belgrade: Velauto International, 1992).

Zečević, Momčilo, 'Second Phase: 1918–1941', in Božidar Zečević (ed.), *The Uprooting: A Dossier of the Croatian Genocide Policy Against the Serbs* (Belgrade: Velauto International, 1992).

Zemetica, John, *The Yugoslav Conflict: Adelphi Paper #270* (London: International Institute for Strategic Studies, 1992).

Zimmermann, Warren, *Origins of a Catastrophe: Yugoslavia and its Destroyers – America's Last Ambassador Tells What Happened and Why* (New York: Random House, 1996).

Žunec, Ozren, 'Operations Flash and Storm', in Branka Magas and Ivo Žanić (eds), *The War in Croatia and Bosnia-Herzegovina 1991–1995* (London: Frank Cass, 2001).

Internet documents

Abramović, Antun, 'Excerpts from: "Bihac, a Bulwark of Croatian Glory and Suffering"', *Hrvatsko Slovo* (9 August 1995) www.cdsp.neu.edu/info/students/marko/hrslovo/hrslovo3.html (accessed 18 June 1998).

Barisić, Marko, 'Soros' Network of Information Agencies for the Rebuilding of Former Yugoslavia', *Vjesnik* (8 May 1997) (slightly edited translation by Danijela Nadj, Croatian Information Center) www.cdsp.neu.edu/info/students/marko/vjesnik/vjesnik15.html (accessed 18 June 1998).

Bataković, Dušan T., 'Bosnia & Herzegovina From Berlin to Dayton: The System of Alliances', Paper delivered at the 29th National Convention of the American Association for the Advancement of Slavic Studies (Seattle: 23 November 1997) www.bglink.com/personal/batakovic/seattle.html (accessed 18 June 1998).

——, 'Frustrated Nationalism in Yugoslavia: From Liberal to Communist Solution', *Serbian Studies*, 11:2 (1997) www.bglink.com/personal/batakovic/boston.html (accessed 18 June 1998).

——, 'The Serbs of Bosnia & Herzegovina: History and Politics' (Belgrade: Dušan T. Bataković Web site, 1997) www.bglink.com/personal/batakovic/k-serbih.html (accessed 18 June 1998).

——, 'Serbia in the 21st Century: the Problem of Kosovo-Metohija' (Belgrade: Serbian Unity Congress Sixth Annual Convention, 1996) www.yugoslavia.com/Society_and_Law/Kosovo/ GLAVA13.HTM (accessed 18 June 1998).

——, 'The Balkan Piedmont: Serbia and the Yugoslav Question', *Dialogue*, 1. (1994) www.bglink.com/personal/batakovic/piedmont.html (accessed 18 June 1998).

——, 'The National Integration of the Serbs and Croats: A Comparative Analysis', *Dialogue*, 7–8 (September–December 1994) www.bglink.com/personal/batakovic/national.html (accessed 18 June 1998).

——, 'Le Génocide dans l'état indépendant croate 1941–1945', *Hérodote*, 67 (1992) www.bglink.com/personal/batakovic/ustasefr.html (accessed 18 June 1998).

Beljo, Ante, 'The Ideology of Greater Serbia', from: Aleksander Ravlić (ed.), *Southeastern Europe 1918–1995* (Zagreb: Croatian Heritage Foundation/ Croatian Information Center, 1998) http://www.hic.hr/books/seeurope/index-e.htm#top (accessed 5 February 2000).

—— 'Excerpts from: *YU-Genocide: Bleiburg – Death Marches – UDBA (Yugoslav Secret Police)* (Toronto and Zagreb: Northern Tribune Publishing / Croatian Information Center, 1998)'
zagreb.matis.hr/books/yu-genocide/foreword.htm (accessed 18 June 1998).

Bobanović, Marinko, 'Interview with Philip J. Cohen: The International Community is Meddling in Croatia's Internal Affairs', *Vjesnik* (27 April 1998)
www.cdsp.neu.edu/info/students/marko/vjesnik/vjesnik27.html (accessed 18 June 1998).

Buden, Boris, 'Mission: Impossible', *ARKzin*, 83 (31 January 1997)
www.cdsp.neu.edu/info/students/marko/ARKzin/arkzin5.html (accessed 18 June 1998).

Bujanec, Velimir, 'Reply to Partisan Ivan Fumić', reprinted from *Vjesnik* in *Nezavisna Drzava Hrvatska* (March 1996)
www.cdsp.neu.edu/info/students/marko/ndh/ndh1.html (accessed 18 June 1998).

Bulajić, Milan, 'Never Again: Genocide in the NDH: Ustashi Genocide the Independent State of Croatia (NDH) From 1941–1945' (Belgrade: Serbian Ministry of Information)
www.yugoslavia.com/Society_and_Law/Jasenovac/ndh.htm (accessed 18 June 1998).

Cohen, Philip J., 'Holocaust History Misappropriated', *MIDSTREAM: A Monthly Jewish Review*, 39:8 (November 1992)
http://teletubbie.het.net.je/~sjaak/domovina/domovina/archive/1992/english/holocaust.html (accessed 10 June 2000).

'Commemorating the Bleiburg Tragedy', *Vjesnik* (12 May 1997)
www.cdsp.neu.edu/info/students/marko (accessed 18 June 1998).

Croatian Information Center, 'The Bleiburg Tragedy' (Zagreb: Croatian Information Center)
www.hrnet.org/BLEIBURG/The Bleiburg Tragedy (accessed 5 July 1999).

D.O., 'June 22 1941 – Defeat of the Croat People by Serbo-Communist Partisans', *NDH* (December 1997)
www.cdsp.neu.edu/info/students/marko/ndh/ndh3.html (accessed 18 June 1998).

Dabić, Vojin, and Ksenija Lukić, 'Crimes Without Punishment: War Crimes Committed by Croatian Armed Forces During Armed Clashes in Vukovar and Vicinity' (Serbian Unity Congress, 1997)
www.suc.org/politics/war_crimes/vukovar/index.html (accessed 6 June 2000).

Dezulović, Boris, 'Industry of Death: Death Squads Go on a Rampage Through Krajina', *Feral Tribune* (16 October 1995) www.cdsp.neu.edu/info/students/marko/feral/feral24.html (accessed 18 June, 1998).

——,'Population Census: The Inventory of an Exodus: The Great Mover', *Feral Tribune* (11 September 1995) www.cdsp.neu.edu/info/students/marko/feral/feral24.html (accessed 18 June 1998).

Dizdar, Zdravko, 'Chetnik Genocidal Crimes Against Croatians and Muslims in Bosnia and Herzegovina and Against Croatians in Croatia During World War II (1941–1945)', from: Aleksander Ravlić (ed.), *Southeastern Europe 1918–1995* (Zagreb: Croatian Heritage Foundation/Croatian Information Center, 1998) www.hic.hr/books/seeurope/index-e.htm#top (accessed 5 February 2000).

Djurich, Ksenija, 'On Political Manipulations with the Albanian National Minority in the FRY in the Abuse of the Provisions of International Law by Albanian Secessionists in Kosovo and Metohija' (Belgrade: Serbian Ministry of Information, 1997) www.yugoslavia.com/Society_and_Law/Kosovo/GLAVA5.HTM (accessed 18 June 1998).

Duretak, Darko, and Mladenka Sarić, 'HDZ Will Regain Support of Voters with Clear Policies, not Cheap Tricks: Dr. Franjo Tudman's Speech: We Must Not Allow Sheep and Geese to Lead Us into Fog!', *Vecernji List* (8 December 1998) www.cdsp.neu.edu/info/students/marko/vecernji/vecernji12.html (accessed 18 June 1998).

Erceg, Heni, 'Goebbels From Our Neighborhood: Interview with Edo Murtić', *Feral Tribune* (2 June 1995) www.cdsp.neu.edu/info/students/marko/feral/feral2.html (accessed 18 June 1998).

Freundlich, Maja, 'Bull's Eye: Trials on the Way to the Promised Land', *Vjesnik* (20 December 1998) www.cdsp.neu.edu/info/students/marko/vjesnik/vjesnik29.html (accessed 18 June 1998).

Goldstein, Slavko, 'Slaughter in Peace', *Feral Tribune* (13 January 1997) www.cdsp.neu.edu/info/students/marko/feral/feral42.html (accessed 18 June 1998).

Grkovski, Trajko, 'Plitvice Waters are Clean', *Vjesnik* (13 September 1995) www.cdsp.neu.edu/info/students/marko/vjesnik/vjesnik1.html#plitvice (accessed 18 June 1998).

Gruden, Živko, Toni Gabrić, and Ivica Buljan, 'Black Chronicle of Croatian History: Methods Used to Rehabilitate Ustashe and Stigmatize Antifascists: Depravity and Now', *Feral Tribune* (29 December 1997) www.cdsp.neu.edu/info/students/marko/feral/feral53.html (accessed 5 July 1999).

Hauswitschka, A., 'Croatia Cannot Be a Part of the Balkans', *Vjesnik* (24 May 1996)
www.cdsp.neu.edu/info/students/marko/vjesnik/vjesnik7.html (accessed 18 June 1998).

Horvatić, Dubravko, 'Our Existence is a Crime', *Hrvatsko Slovo* (22 March 1996)
www.cdsp.neu.edu/info/students/marko/hrslovo/hrslovo5.html (accessed 18 June 1998).

——, 'Victory Over Fascism', *Hrvatsko Slovo* (5 May 1995)
www.cdsp.neu.edu/info/students/marko/hrslovo/hrslovo1.html (accessed 18 June 1998).

—— and Stjepan Šešelj, 'Croatian Culture and Croatian Army: Interview with Croatian Defense Minister Gojko Šušak', *Hrvatsko Slovo* (27 December 1996)
http://www.cdsp.neu.edu/info/students/marko/hrslovo/hrslovo7.html (accessed 18 June 1998).

Hrenovica, Muhamed Zlatan, 'Structural Aspects of Greater Serbian Crimes in Bosnia and Herzegovina from 1991 to 1995', from: Aleksander Ravlić (ed.), *Southeastern Europe 1918–1995* (Zagreb: Croatian Heritage Foundation/Croatian Information Center, 1998)
www.hic.hr/books/seeurope/index-e.htm#top (accessed 5 February 2000).

Ivancić, Viktor, 'Dossier: Pakracka Poljana, Part l', *Feral Tribune* (21 August, 1995)
www.cdsp.neu.edu/info/students/marko/feral/feral13.html (accessed 18 June 1998).

Ivetić, Velimir, 'The Serbs in the Anti-fascist Struggle in the Territory of the Independent State of Croatia' (Belgrade: Serbian Ministry of Information)
http://cypress.mcsr.olemiss.edu/~eesrdan/ndh/ndh-sastav_partizana_u_ndh.html (accessed 18 June 1998).

Jezić, Mislav, 'Problems of Understanding XXth Century History of Croatia' (Zagreb: University of Zagreb)
www.dalmatia.net/croatia/history/jezic.htm (accessed 18 June 1998).

Jurčević, Josip, 'The Serbian Armed Aggression Against Croatia From 1990 to 1995', in Aleksander Ravlić (ed.), *Southeastern Europe 1918–1995* (Zagreb: Croatian Heritage Foundation & Croatian Information Centre, 1998)
www.hic.hr/books/seeurope/index-e.htm#top (accessed 5 July 1999).

Klemenčić, Mladen, 'Creation of a Greater Serbia', *Croatia Monitor* (21 June 1992)
gopher://zagreb.matis.hr:70/00/eng/hic/knjige/encirclement/Part%201 (accessed 18 June 1998).

Kostich, Lazo M., 'Synopsis of: *The Holocaust in the Independent State of Croatia:*

An Account Based on German, Italian and the Other Sources (Chicago: Liberty Press, 1981)'
http://suc.Suc.Org/~kosta/tar/knjige/book-holocaust-lazoKostic.html (accessed 18 June 1998).

Kovačević, Radovan, 'Idea of Big Albania in the Service of the "New World Order"', *Politika* (29 January 1999)
www.serbia-info.com/news/1999–02/01/8607.html (accessed 18 June 1998).

——, 'The Collapse of Delusions and Illusions of a Unitary Bosnia' (Belgrade: Serbian Ministry of Information, February 1995)
www.yugoslavia.com/Bulletin/95/95feb/95feb7.htm (accessed 18 June 1998).

Krestić, Vasilije, 'Genocide in the Service of the Idea of a Greater Croatia Through Genocide to a Greater Croatia' (Belgrade: Bigz – Izdavacko preduzece d.o.o./Serbian Unity Congress, 1997)
http://suc.suc.org/culture/library/genocide/k7.htm (accessed 5 February 2000).

Krmpotić, Marijan, 'Why is Croatian Language Still Suppressed in Croatia?', *NDH* (December 1997)
http://www.cdsp.neu.edu/info/students/marko/ndh/ndh2.html (accessed 18 June 1998).

Latković, Roman, 'Tudjman has Definitely Shown That He Is a Brutal Dictator', *Novi List* (8 January 1996)
http://www.cdsp.neu.edu/info/students/marko/novi/novi3.html (accessed 18 June 1998).

Levak, Nevenka, 'Were Croatian Serbs Expelled from Croatia?', *Glas Slavonije* (28 February 1998)
www.cdsp.neu.edu/info/students/marko/glasslav/glasslav5.html (accessed 18 June 1998).

Lucić, Predrag, 'Dr. Tudjman and Mr. George', *Feral Tribune* (3 August 1997)
www.cdsp.neu.edu/info/students/marko/feral/feral49.html (accessed 18 June 1998).

Lupić, Zeljko Jack, 'History of Croatia: Povijest Hrvatske (200 BC – 1998 AD)' (Zagreb: Croatian Information Center, 21 February 1999)
www.dalmatia.net/croatia/history/index.htm (accessed 18 June 1998).

Makarov, Petar, 'Croatian Cardinal Stepinac Was Pavelić's Head Military Chaplain',
http://cypress.mcsr.olemiss.edu/~eesrdan/ndh/ndh-kojeko.html (accessed 18 June 1998).

——, 'The Embodied Devils: Who Was Who in NDH?',
http://cypress.mcsr.olemiss.edu/~eesrdan/ndh/ndh-kojeko.html (accessed 18 June 1998).

Malić, Gordan, 'Herceg Camp', *Feral Tribune* (29 April 1996) www.cdsp.neu.edu/info/students/marko/feral/feral31.html (accessed 18 June 1998).

McAdams, C. Michael, 'The Demise of "Serbo-Croatian"' (Zagreb: Croatian Information Center Web Page, 1998) www.algonet.se/~bevanda/mceng.htm (accessed 18 June 1998).

——, 'Yalta and The Bleiburg Tragedy', Presented at the International Symposium for Investigation of the Bleiburg Tragedy (Zagreb, Croatia and Bleiburg, Austria: 17 and 18 May 1994) www.dalmatia.net/croatia/mcadams/bleiburg_and_yalta1.htm (accessed 18 June 1998).

Miletić, Branko, 'History: Causes of Serbian Aggression' (Zagreb: Croatian Information Center Web Page, 1998) http://www.algonet.se/~bevanda/aggression.htm (accessed 18 June 1998).

Mrkoci, Vladimir, 'Historical Guilt of Alain Finkelkraut', *Hrvatski Obzor*, (17 August 1996 (translated on 5 October 2001) http://free.freespeech.org/ex-yupress/hrobzor/hrobzor12.html (accessed 10 January 2002).

Odović, Pavle, 'Serbian Reaction to Separatism in Kosovo' (Belgrade: Serbian Ministry of Information, 1997) www.yugoslavia.com/Bulletin/95/9505/950507.htm (accessed 18 June 1998).

Pavličević, Dragutin, 'Persecution and Liquidation of Croats on Croatian Territory From 1903 To 1941', and, 'South-Eastern Europa and Balkan Peninsula on the Margin of the Worlds: Foreword', in Aleksander Ravlić (ed.), *Southeastern Europe 1918–1995* (Zagreb: Croatian Heritage Foundation/Croatian Information Center, 1998) www.hic.hr/books/seeurope/index-e.htm#top (accessed 5 February 2000).

Pečarić, Josip, 'Author's summary of *Serbian Myth about Jasenovac* (Zagreb: Naklada Stih, 2001)' www.hr/darko/etf/pec.html (accessed 12 December 2001).

Perić, Stjepan, 'Anti-Croatian Activities of International Non-Governmental Organizations', *Vjesnik* (17 May 1996) www.cdsp.neu.edu/info/students/marko/vjesnik/vjesnik8.html (accessed 18 June 1998).

Petrovich, Borivoje, 'Declaration on Human Rights and the Rights of the National Minorities' (Knin: National Parliament of the Republic of Serbia, 27 November 1992) www.yugoslavia.com/Society_and_Law/Kosovo/GLAVA3.HTM (accessed 18 June 1998).

Potezica, Oliver, 'The Balkans – Constant Geopolitical Enigma (Critical Review of the Book "The Secrets of the Balkans")' (Belgrade: Serbian Ministry of Information, 1998) www.yugoslavia.com/Bulletin/95/9512/951218.htm (accessed 18 June 1998).

Primoratz, Igor, 'Israel and the War in the Balkans', http://www.hr/darko/etf/isr2.html (accessed 23 November 2000).

Raseta, Boris, 'Home and Hell: Six Months After the Adoption of the Plan for Return, Only About One Hundred Ethnic Serb Refugees Managed to Return to Their Houses', *Feral Tribune* (9 November 1998) http://www.cdsp.neu.edu/info/students/marko/feral/feral64.html (accessed 18 June 1998).

Sabol, Zeljko, 'Democracy According to Banac', *Hrvatsko Slovo* (14 February 1997) www.cdsp.neu.edu/info/students/marko/hrslovo/hrslovo9.html (accessed 18 June 1998).

Samardzić, Slobodan, 'Yugoslav Federalism – Unsuccessful Model of a Multinational Community' (Belgrade: Institute of European Studies, Belgrade, 1994) www.suc.org/politics/papers/history/samard.html (accessed 5 July 1999).

Semiz, Dzenana Efendia, 'Serbian Land Reform and Colonization in 1918', in Aleksander Ravlić (ed.), *Southeastern Europe 1918–1995* (Zagreb: Croatian Heritage Foundation/Croatian Information Center, 1998) www.hic.hr/books/seeurope/index-e.htm#top (accessed 5 February 2000).

Serbian Ministry of Information, 'The History of Serbia' (Belgrade: Serbian Ministry of Information, 1998) www.bglink.com/personal/batakovic/ustasefr.html (accessed 18 June 1998).

——, 'Update on Kosovo' (Belgrade: Serbian Ministry of Information, 1997) www.yugoslavia.com/Society_and_Law/Kosovo/GLAVA12.HTM (accessed 18 June 1998).

——, 'Declaration of Scientific Conference Working Group' (Belgrade: Serbian Ministry of Information, June 1997) www.yugoslavia.com/Society_and_Law/Kosovo/GLAVA4.HTM (accessed 18 June 1998).

——, 'On Political Manipulations with the Albanian National Minority in the FRY in the Abuse of the Provisions of International Law by Albanian Secessionists in Kosovo and Metohija' (Belgrade, Serbian Ministry of Information, 1997) www.yugoslavia.com/Society_and_Law/Kosovo/GLAVA5.HTM (accessed 18 June 1998).

——, '"Blitz-Krieg" Aggression as a Method of "Ethnic Cleansing" of the Serbs: The Road of Crime "Final Solution to the Serbian Question in Croatia"' (Belgrade: Serbian Ministry of Information, 1995) http://www.yugoslavia.com/Bulletin/95/9509/950901.htm (accessed 18 June 1998).

——,'Washington's Janissaries' (Belgrade: Serbian Ministry of Information, 1995) www.yugoslavia.com/Bulletin/95/9509/950923.htm (accessed 18 June 1998).

Serbian Unity Congress, 'Jasenovac' (21 April 1996) http://suc.Suc.Org/~kosta/tar/jasenovac/intro.html (accessed 18 June 1998).

——, 'Yugoslav Crisis – One Hundred Irrefutable Facts' (Serbian Unity Congress, 1996) www.suc.org/politics/100facts/index.html (accessed 16 February 2000).

Silber, Laura, 'Milosevic Family Values: The Dysfunctional Couple that Destroyed the Balkans', *The New Republic* (1999). Available at: www.abc.net.au/rn/talks/lnl/stories/s55079.htm (accessed 5 February 2000).

Slobodna Dalmacija, 'A Chronology of Operation "Storm": 84 Hours of War', *Slobodna Dalmacija* (5 August 1996) www.cdsp.neu.edu/info/students/marko/slodal/slodal7.html (accessed 18 June 1998).

Stefan, Lubica, 'Anti-Semitism in Serbia During World War II' (Zagreb: Hrvatski Iseljenicki Zbornik, 1996) www.hr/darko/etf/jews.html (accessed 28 May 1999).

Stojanović, Dubravka, 'Construction of Historical Consciousness', *Association for Social History Journal* (1999) www.udi.org.yu/Founders/Stojanovic/conscious.htm (accessed 5 February 2002).

TOL, 'Guilty of Genocide', *Transitions Online* (7 August 2001) http://balkanreport.tol.cz/look/BRR/article (accessed June 2001).

Velimirovich, Nikolai, and Justin Popovich, 'The Mystery and Meaning of the Battle of Kosovo' (Grayslake, IL: The Serbian Orthodox New Gracanica Metropolitanate Diocese of America and Canada, 1996) http://members.aol.com/ gracanica/index.html (accessed 18 June 1998).

Vidić, Marko, 'Croats an Obstacle to the Creation of the New Bosnian Nation', *Slobodna Dalmacija* (28 April 1998) www.cdsp.neu.edu/info/students/marko/slodal/slodal9.html (accessed 18 June 1998).

Vratusa-Zunjić, Vera, 'The Intrinsic Connection Between Endogenous and Exogenous Factors of Social (Dis)integration: A Sketch of the Yugoslav

Case', *Dialogue*, 22–23 (June–September 1997)
www.bglink.com/business/dialogue/vratusa.html (accessed 18 June 1998).

Vujačić, Veljko, 'Serbian Nationalism, Slobodan Milosevic and the Origins of the Yugoslav War', *The Harriman Review*, 8:4 (December 1995) www.suc.org/politics/papers/history/vujacic.html (accessed 5 July 1999).

Vurusić, Vlado, 'After 35 Years, We Have Moved Our Ustashe Newspaper "Independent State Croatia" from Toronto to Zagreb', *Globus* (1 December, 1995)
www.cdsp.neu.edu/info/students/marko/globus2.html (accessed 18 June 1998).

Žerjavić, Vladimir, *Yugoslavia – Manipulations with the Number of Second World War Victims* (Zagreb: Croatian Information Center, 1998) http://hrvati.cronet.com/cic/manip/sadrzaj.ht (accessed 18 June 1998).

——, 'The Inventions And Lies of Dr. Bulajić on Internet' (Zagreb: Croatian Institute of History, 30 July 1997)
http://misp.isp.hr/dokumenti/bulajic.htm (accessed 18 June 1998).

Zivko Gruden, Toni Gabrić, and Ivica Buljan, 'Black Chronicle of Croatian History: Methods Used to Rehabilitate Ustashe and Stigmatize Antifascists: Depravity and Now', *Feral Tribune* (29 December 1997) www.cdsp.neu.edu/info/students/marko/feral/feral53.html (accessed 18 June 1998).

Zubrinić, Darko, 'Cardinal Alojzije Stepinac and Saving the Jews in Croatia During the WW 2' (Zagreb: Croatian Information Center, 1996) www.hr/darko/etf/jews.html (accessed 18 June 1998).

Unattributed book reviews

'A Review of Antun Bauer, Franjo Sanjek, and Nedjeljko Kujundzić (eds), *Who Are Croats and Where Did They Come From: A Revision of an Ethnogenesis* (Zagreb: Collection of Works, Scientific Society for the Study of the Ethnogenesis of Croats)', *Feral Tribune* (29 December 1997) www.cdsp.neu.edu/info/students/marko/feral/feral53.html (accessed 12 March 1998).

'A Review of: Dominik Mandić, *Croats and Serbs – Two Ancient Different Nations* (Zagreb: Nakladni Zavod Matice Hrvatske, 1990)', *Feral Tribune* (29 December 1997) Available at:
www.cdsp.neu.edu/info/students/marko/feral/feral53.html (accessed 12 March 1998).

'Review of Eugen Dido Kvaternik, Memories and Observations 1925–1945 (Zagreb: Nakladnico Drustvo Starcevic, 1995)', *Feral Tribune* (29 December 1997) www.cdsp.neu.edu/info/students/marko/feral/feral53.html (accessed 12 March 1978).

'Review of Ivo Rojnica, *Meetings and Experiences* (Zagreb: Do Ne Ha, 1994)', *Feral Tribune* (29 December 1997)
www.cdsp.neu.edu/info/students/marko/feral/feral53.html (accessed 12 March 1998).

'A Chronology of Operation "Storm": 84 Hours of War', *Slobodna Dalmacija* (5 August, 1996)
www.cdsp.neu.edu/info/students/marko/slodal/slodal7.html (accessed 5 July 1999).

'Suzanne Brooks-Pinčević, *Britain And The Bleiburg Tragedy*, *The Zajednicar* (11 November 1998)
www.dalmatia.net/croatia/history/bleiburg.htm (accessed 18 June 1998).

INDEX

Note: 'n.' after a page reference indicates a note number on that page.